I0885179

Sustainable Consumption Experience and Business Models in the Modern World

Maria Amélia Machado Carvalho
Business School, Polytechnic Institute of Porto, Portugal

Maria Antónia Rodrigues
CEOS, Business School, Polytechnic Institute of Porto, Portugal

A volume in the Advances in Business Strategy and Competitive Advantage (ABSCA) Book Series

IGI Global
PUBLISHER of TIMELY KNOWLEDGE

Published in the United States of America by
IGI Global
Business Science Reference (an imprint of IGI Global)
701 E. Chocolate Avenue
Hershey PA, USA 17033
Tel: 717-533-8845
Fax: 717-533-8661
E-mail: cust@igi-global.com
Web site: http://www.igi-global.com

Library of Congress Cataloging-in-Publication Data

Names: Machado Carvalho, Maria Amélia, 1989- editor. | Rodrigues, Maria Antónia, 1977- editor.
Title: Sustainable consumption experience and business models in the modern world / edited by Maria Amélia Machado Carvalho, Maria Rodrigues.
Description: Hershey, PA : Business Science Reference, [2024] | Includes bibliographical references and index. | Summary: "The purpose of this book is to contribute to the literature on sustainable marketing and develop the topics of sustainable business models and customer experience to highlight changes in business, customers' attitudes, motivations, and experiences with sustainable consumption"-- Provided by publisher.
Identifiers: LCCN 2023034580 (print) | LCCN 2023034581 (ebook) | ISBN 9781668492772 (hardcover) | ISBN 9781668492789 (paperback) | ISBN 9781668492796 (ebook)
Subjects: LCSH: Consumption (Economics)--Environmental aspects. | Green marketing. | Consumer satisfaction.
Classification: LCC HB801 .S887 2024 (print) | LCC HB801 (ebook) | DDC 339.4/7--dc23/eng/20230811
LC record available at https://lccn.loc.gov/2023034580
LC ebook record available at https://lccn.loc.gov/2023034581

This book is published in the IGI Global book series Advances in Business Strategy and Competitive Advantage (ABSCA) (ISSN: 2327-3429; eISSN: 2327-3437)

British Cataloguing in Publication Data
A Cataloguing in Publication record for this book is available from the British Library.

All work contributed to this book is new, previously-unpublished material.
The views expressed in this book are those of the authors, but not necessarily of the publisher.

For electronic access to this publication, please contact: eresources@igi-global.com.

Advances in Business Strategy and Competitive Advantage (ABSCA) Book Series

ISSN:2327-3429
EISSN:2327-3437

Editor-in-Chief: Patricia Ordóñez de Pablos, Universidad de Oviedo, Spain

MISSION

Business entities are constantly seeking new ways through which to gain advantage over their competitors and strengthen their position within the business environment. With competition at an all-time high due to technological advancements allowing for competition on a global scale, firms continue to seek new ways through which to improve and strengthen their business processes, procedures, and profitability.

The **Advances in Business Strategy and Competitive Advantage (ABSCA) Book Series** is a timely series responding to the high demand for state-of-the-art research on how business strategies are created, implemented and re-designed to meet the demands of globalized competitive markets. With a focus on local and global challenges, business opportunities and the needs of society, the **ABSCA** encourages scientific discourse on doing business and managing information technologies for the creation of sustainable competitive advantage.

COVERAGE

- Globalization
- Business models
- Resource-Based Competition
- Value Chain
- Core Competencies
- Tacit Knowledge
- Strategic Alliances
- Small and Medium Enterprises
- Ethics and Business Strategy
- Strategy Performance Management

The Advances in Business Strategy and Competitive Advantage (ABSCA) Book Series (ISSN 2327-3429) is published by IGI Global, 701 E. Chocolate Avenue, Hershey, PA 17033-1240, USA, www.igi-global.com. This series is composed of titles available for purchase individually; each title is edited to be contextually exclusive from any other title within the series. For pricing and ordering information please visit http://www.igi-global.com/book-series/advances-business-strategy-competitive-advantage/73672. Postmaster: Send all address changes to above address.

Titles in this Series

For a list of additional titles in this series, please visit:
http://www.igi-global.com/book-series/advances-business-strategy-competitive-advantage/73672

Ecosystem Dynamics and Strategies for Startups Scalability
Neeta Baporikar (Namibia University of Science and Technology, Namibia & SP Pune University, India)
Business Science Reference • © 2024 • 360pp • H/C (ISBN: 9798369305270) • US $275.00

Smart Strategies and Societal Solutions for Sustainable International Business
Abdelkader Mohamed Sghaier Derbali (Taibah University, Saudi Arabia)
Business Science Reference • © 2024 • 228pp • H/C (ISBN: 9798369305324) • US $275.00

Applying Interdisciplinarity to Globalization, Management, Marketing, and Accountancy Science
Vladislav Pavlát (The University of Finance and Administration, Czech Republic) Ladislava Knihová (The University of Finance and Administration, Czech Republic) Lubomír Civín (AMBIS, Czech Republic) Jaroslav Halík (Metropolitan University, Prague, Czech Republic) and Radka MacGregor Pelikánová (Metropolitan University, Prague, Czech Republic & Anglo-American University, Czech Republic & Czech University of Life Sciences, Prague, Czech Republic)
Business Science Reference • © 2023 • 310pp • H/C (ISBN: 9781799886693) • US $240.00

Transformational Interventions for Business, Technology, and Healthcare
Darrell Norman Burrell (Marymount University, USA)
Business Science Reference • © 2023 • 584pp • H/C (ISBN: 9798369316344) • US $295.00

Innovation, Strategy, and Transformation Frameworks for the Modern Enterprise
Anacleto Correia (Portuguese Naval Academy, Portugal) and Pedro B. Agua (Portuguese Naval Academy, Portugal)
Business Science Reference • © 2023 • 431pp • H/C (ISBN: 9798369304587) • US $275.00

For an entire list of titles in this series, please visit:
http://www.igi-global.com/book-series/advances-business-strategy-competitive-advantage/73672

IGI Global
PUBLISHER of TIMELY KNOWLEDGE

701 East Chocolate Avenue, Hershey, PA 17033, USA
Tel: 717-533-8845 x100 • Fax: 717-533-8661
E-Mail: cust@igi-global.com • www.igi-global.com

Table of Contents

Detailed Table of Contents

Trade integration is a mechanism for fostering prosperity. African countries have created several regional economic integration arrangements. The African Continental Free Trade Area (AfCFTA) is the most ambitious initiative in this vein. The AfCFTA also seeks to build on the integration already achieved by existing REAs. The AfCFTA has the potential to increase income and welfare significantly; however, these benefits are unequally distributed for member countries. Maximizing potential welfare and income gains by member countries requires substantial and strategic reduction of non-tariff barriers. Also, improved quality of trade logistics and the provision of infrastructural deficits are critical. Net impact of the AfCFTA on tax revenues depends on the combined effect of four channels; direct tax revenue reduction, trade diversion, higher GDP, and increased consumption. Thus, ensuring a strong governance framework of the AfCFTA, is germane to reduce trade policy uncertainty.

This chapter proposes a corporate sustainability evaluation framework by creating a composite index, the Perceived Sustainability Index, which integrates the company's environmental, social, and corporate governance (ESG) score and the consumer perception of corporate sustainability. This index uses MSCI ESG ratings and X data. The framework conceptually aligns with the multidimensional nature of sustainability, the stakeholder theory, and the customer-centric nature of companies. The index enables researchers to examine corporate sustainability from a dual perspective: the consumers and the rating agencies. It also provides companies with an indicator to progress on their sustainability journey while meeting the consumers' societal needs, which, if not met, might adversely impact the corporate reputation and, eventually, the business performance. The authors illustrate their argument by analyzing the Perceived Sustainability Index for 100 companies and then discuss three case studies – a high performer, a low performer, and a potential greenwashing.

China has a major impact on global sustainability, and this chapter examines the nexus of sustainable consumerism, corporate innovation, and customer experience in this influential country. The story develops as it examines how growing environmental awareness and a more environmentally conscious middle class are altering traditional patterns of purchasing. The focus then moves to creative sustainable business models across sectors, providing concrete examples of how corporations are rethinking their strategy and value chains to become more environmentally friendly. This chapter delves deeper into the topic of how well constructed customer experiences are shaping customer satisfaction and loyalty on the part of enterprises. It highlights the importance of sustainable marketing for contemporary Chinese enterprises.

Museums have left behind their history as mere warehouses, curators, and art exhibitors. Its cultural and educational functions, intrinsically linked to heritage, have expanded. Theoretically, they have become transmedia communication spaces open to everyone and committed to society and, therefore, to sustainability. The commitment now regarding education delves into the issue of learning, a more participatory process than classic education that is unidirectional and with paternalistic nuances. After renewing their concept, where joint work with the community is emphasized, the museums are assuming their new challenge: sustainability, where governance, the environment, and human capital are the axes of work to achieve a better coexistence

Preface

The growing degradation of the environment and natural resources has motivated companies and consumers to make their production and consumption more sustainable to guarantee a better future. In the same way, in recent decades, sustainability has been at the top of the international political agenda and has been a key driver of innovation. Consequently, the number of companies developing green products has increased rapidly along with consumers who demonstrate increasing interest in this type of product. However, these concerns about environmental sustainability and climate change are posing several challenges to companies, namely how to integrate environmental issues into business strategy and activities (Dangelico and Vocalelli, 2017).

Sustainable consumption and production are related to the use of goods and services that seek to reduce negative impacts on the environment (Paavola, 2001). The reduction of negative impacts can occur by reducing the use of natural resources, toxic materials, and polluting emissions without jeopardizing the satisfaction of the needs of future generations. In this sense, sustainability can be linked to companies and consumers.

From a business perspective, concern for sustainability issues leads to the development of new sustainable products and services and the development of new business models (Gopalakrishnan and Matthews, 2018; Katarzyna, 2022, Turoń, 2022). According to Ottman et al. (2006, p. 24), "although no consumer product has a zero impact on the environment, in business, the terms 'green products' or 'environmental product' are used commonly to describe those that strive to protect or enhance the natural environment by conserving energy and/or resources and reducing or eliminating use of toxic agents, pollution, and waste". In addition to helping to sustain the environment, green products must satisfy society's needs and desires. Therefore, sustainability must address three pillars: economic, environmental, and social (Taghvaee et al., 2023).

From the consumer's perspective, consumers with sustainability concerns tend to seek more and more sustainable alternatives, resorting to the purchase of green products and services, the exchange of goods, the do-it-yourself, the purchase of second-hand products or sharing of goods and services (Akehurst et al., 2012; Chaudhuri, et al., 2022; Harris et al., 2016; Machado et al., 2019). Moreover, in recent years, some alternative lifestyles have gained popularity. For example, minimalism and voluntary simplicity lifestyles appeal to a simpler life with less negative impact on the environment (Fu et al., 2023). These types of lifestyles are also characterized by reduced consumption, reduced accumulation of material goods and wealth, and increased focus on personal growth and values, particularly environmental and social responsibility (Hook et al., 2023). Despite the potential benefits of these lifestyles for sustainable development, the existing literature on this topic is limited (Fu et al., 2023).

Sustainability is a current topic, both for academics and marketing professionals. Particularly the link between sustainability and the new business models or the consumer experience are two research topics of great interest, but the investigation of these topics is still scarce in the field of marketing (Almeida et al., 2021; Fu et al., 2023 Wibowo et al., 2022).

This book, entitled *Sustainable Consumption Experience and Business Models in the Modern World*, provides a broad range of themes within sustainable management. As such, it is designed to offer some explanation, contextualization, and discussion of each theme, supported by applied case studies and international examples, as well as, a detailed dissertation regarding some of the current contemporary debates in sustainable management.

The book provides relevant theoretical and empirical implications for the field of sustainable marketing, providing critical insight into business management and consumer perception and behavior. This information is a valuable marketing tool for professionals, students, and researchers in the field of sustainable marketing.

ORGANIZATION OF THE BOOK

The book is organized into eight chapters. The book begins with the chapters that address issues relating to sustainability and sustainable management in a more general way, followed by chapters relating to consumer perception and behavior. A brief description of each of the chapters follows.

Chapter 1, entitled "Intra-Regional Economic Integration-The African Continental Free Trade Area Initiative", was written by Godfrey C. Onuwa and Oludare Adedire from the Federal College of Forestry, Jos (Nigeria). The chapter focuses on the African Continental Free Trade Area (AfCFTA), the implementation of which aims to boost intra-African trade. The chapter analyzes issues related to the African trade context and highlights potential challenges arising from the expected growth of the economy. In this sense, the authors raised several concerns, particularly about the welfare effects and the sustainable management of new businesses, which are discussed in detail in this chapter.

Chapter 2, entitled "Perceived Sustainability Index: A Composite Index of ESG Ratings and Consumer Perception", was written by Amandine Bavent and Elisabeth Paulet from ICN Business School, Nancy (France). The chapter reviews the literature on corporate sustainability measurement and concludes that a more comprehensive measurement system is needed. Thus, the authors introduce and develop the Perceived Sustainability Index that assesses a company's sustainability performance and offers a dual-perspective analysis of corporate sustainability. This approach, by leveraging social media data, allows for the analysis of long-term trends spanning several years, is applicable across all consumer-oriented sectors, and serves as a tool to identify potential cases of greenwashing and SDG-washing.

Chapter 3, entitled "Navigating the Green Path: A Perspective on Sustainable Consumption, Business Innovation, and Customer Experience in China", was written by Dr. Mohamad Zreik from the School of International Studies, Sun Yat-sen University (China). Based on the Chinese context, the chapter investigates the nexus of sustainable consumerism, corporate innovation, and customer experience. The authors argue that growing environmental awareness and consciousness are altering traditional purchasing patterns, thus sustainability is key to a company's success in the future. In this vein, the author presents and examines some examples from different industries (from technological giants to startups) that illustrate China's progress toward sustainable development and discover how to implement similar practices that help achieve sustainable development.

Chapter 4, entitled "Sustainability in Fashion: A Mandatory Approach from Museums", was written by Julio Alexander Gonzalez Liendo from Universitat Politècnica de València (Spain). The chapter addresses how museums can be a way of promoting actions related to achieving the SDGs (Sustainable Development Goals) and the other challenges of the 2030 Agenda. The author also examines some challenges in the ethical management of information, namely transmedia communication, shops as a hub of communication, and greenwashing in museums and institutions dedicated to fashion.

Chapter 5, entitled "Is oil price hike a new threat to consumers' buying pattern?", was written by Sarika Faisal, Syed Far Abid Hossain, Rayisa Rayhana, and Shawnila Nawshin from BBS, BRAC University, Dhaka (Bangladesh). The chapter presents the existing problem of the continuous increase in the prices of daily fundamental commodities, namely the increase in the price of oil, and discusses how this can impact the consumer decision-making process. The chapter presents and examines three propositions (increase in the price of soyabean oil, positive effect on consumer's health, and availability of alternative oil), and how they influence consumers' intentions to switch to alternative oils (vegetable oils). The results reveal that the increase in the price of soybean oil encourages consumers to opt for alternatives, changes their purchasing habits, and makes them more aware of the health benefits.

Chapter 6, entitled "Minimalism: A Game Changer for Industries", was written by Dr. Amritesh and Arjinder Kaur, both from the Indian Institute of Technology, Ropar (India). The chapter introduces the concept of "Minimalism", which has become a lifestyle for many consumers who deliberately reject the consumerist narrative. Based on a bibliographic review, the authors contribute to broadening the idea of minimalism and highlight its critical implications in different industries. The authors, after identifying possible links between minimalism, health and well-being, and environmental sustainability, identify the disruptive capacity of minimalism in various sectors and the emerging demand for a minimalism-driven lifestyle and products.

Chapter 7, entitled "Exploring Consumer Behavior in the Context of Voluntary Simplicity", was written by Dr. Nesenur Altinigne from Istanbul Bilgi University, Istanbul (Turkey). This chapter reviews and discusses the concept of voluntary simplicity about the motivations, types, and consequences of this behavior. By presenting a categorization of voluntary simplicity, the chapter contributes to the understanding of the concept, its antecedents and impacts, and to the assessment of research gaps and future research directions.

Chapter 8, entitled "The Attitude of Portuguese Consumers of Green Cosmetics: The Influence of Environmental Concerns and Health Concerns", was written by Prof. Zaila Oliveira from the University of Maia – ISMAI, CEOS.PP (Portugal), Prof. Sara Teixeira from CEOS.PP, ISCAP, Polytechnic of Porto (Portugal), Sara Teixeira from ISCAP, Polytechnic of Porto (Portugal), and Prof. Sandrina Teixeira from CEOS.PP, ISCAP, Polytechnic of Porto (Portugal). Following a quantitative methodology, the authors examine how environmental and health concerns influence consumers' attitudes toward green cosmetics. The conclusions, resulting from the analysis of responses from 141 Portuguese consumers, made it possible to disclose several insights into consumers' attitudes and behaviors in relation to green cosmetics.

Maria Amélia Carvalho
Business School, Polytechnic Institute of Porto, Portugal

Maria Antónia Rodrigues
CEOS, Business School, Polytechnic Institute of Porto, Portugal

REFERENCES

Akehurst, G., Afonso, C., & Gonçalves, H. M. (2012). Re-examining green purchase behaviour and the green consumer profile: New evidences. *Management Decision*, *50*(5), 972–988. doi:10.1108/00251741211227726

Alaei, S., Aslani, S., & Talebian, M. (2022). The relative importance of the business model motive for customer participation in the sharing economy. *Sustainable Production and Consumption*, *34*, 190–201. doi:10.1016/j.spc.2022.09.012

Almeida, R. P., Proença, J. F., & Ferreira, F. N. H. (2021). Value Co-Creation and Sustainability: A systematic literature review. *International Journal of Marketing, Communication and New Media*, (9).

Chaudhuri, R., Chatterjee, S., Ghosh, A., Vrontis, D., & Thrassou, A. (2022). Sustainable innovation for shared mobility: contextual and consumer factors of an Indian car subscription business model. *International Journal of Entrepreneurial Behavior & Research*.

Dangelico, R. M., & Vocalelli, D. (2017). "Green Marketing": An analysis of definitions, strategy steps, and tools through a systematic review of the literature. *Journal of Cleaner Production*, *165*, 1263–1279. doi:10.1016/j.jclepro.2017.07.184

Fu, L., Zhang, Z., & Nagai, Y. (2023). Minimalism and personal well-being: A study of current trends in China. *Journal of Human Behavior in the Social Environment*, 1–21. doi:10.1080/10911359.2023.2231987

Gopalakrishnan, S., & Matthews, D. (2018). Collaborative consumption: A business model analysis of second-hand fashion. *Journal of Fashion Marketing and Management*, *22*(3), 354–368. doi:10.1108/JFMM-05-2017-0049

Harris, F., Roby, H., & Dibb, S. (2016). Sustainable clothing: Challenges, barriers and interventions for encouraging more sustainable consumer behaviour. *International Journal of Consumer Studies*, *40*(3), 309–318. doi:10.1111/ijcs.12257

Hook, J. N., Hodge, A. S., Zhang, H., Van Tongeren, D. R., & Davis, D. E. (2023). Minimalism, voluntary simplicity, and well-being: A systematic review of the empirical literature. *The Journal of Positive Psychology*, *18*(1), 130–141. doi:10.1080/17439760.2021.1991450

Machado, M. A. D., de Almeida, S. O., Bollick, L. C., & Bragagnolo, G. (2019). Second-hand fashion market: Consumer role in circular economy. *Journal of Fashion Marketing and Management*, *23*(3), 382–395. doi:10.1108/JFMM-07-2018-0099

Paavola, J. (2001). Towards Sustainable Consumption: Economics and Ethical Concerns for theEnvironment in Consumer Choices. *Review of Social Economy*, *59*(2), 227–248. doi:10.1080/00346760110036175

Taghvaee, V. M., Arani, A. A., Soretz, S., & Agheli, L. (2023). Diesel demand elasticities and sustainable development pillars of economy, environment and social (health): Comparing two strategies of subsidy removal and energy efficiency. *Environment, Development and Sustainability*, *25*(3), 2285–2315. doi:10.100710668-021-02092-7

Turoń, K. (2022). From the classic business model to open innovation and data sharing—The concept of an open car-sharing business model. *Journal of Open Innovation*, *8*(1), 36. doi:10.3390/joitmc8010036

Wibowo, A. J. I., Sumarwan, U., Suharjo, B., & Simanjuntak, M. (2022). Car Sharing in Marketing. *Jurnal Manajemen Indonesia*, *22*(2), 226–244. doi:10.25124/jmi.v22i2.4291

Acknowledgment

The editors would like to acknowledge the IGI Global editorial team and all the researchers involved in this project for their support. Between editors, authors, and reviewers, the book had the participation and commitment of twenty-three researchers.

Sixteen authors from diverse countries, namely Bangladesh, China, France, India, Nigeria, Portugal, Spain, Turkey, and the United States of America contributed to the creation of this book. The editors would like to thank each one of the authors for their contributions.

All chapters were reviewed by two or more reviewers, whose valuable work contributed to enriching and improving the final result of the book. Therefore, we would like to thank the support of all researchers who contributed to this book in the process of reviewing each chapter, which included the collaboration of Amandine Bavent (ICN Business School), Anabela Ribeiro (ISCAP/ Polytechnic of Porto), Arjinder Kaur (Indian Institute of Technology), Elisabeth Paulet (ICN Business School), Fábia Esteves (University of Porto), Godfrey Onuwa (Federal College of Forestry), Inês Pereira (ISCAP/ Polytechnic of Porto), Joaquim Pratas (ISCAP/ Polytechnic of Porto), Jorge Remondes (ISCAP/ Polytechnic of Porto), José Santos (ISCAP/ Polytechnic of Porto), Mohamad Zreik (Sun Yat-sen University), Nesenur Altinigne (Istanbul Bilgi University), Rayisa Rayhana (BRAC University), Sara Teixeira (ISCAP/ Polytechnic of Porto, CEOS.PP), Sarika Faisal (BRAC University), and Zaila Oliveira (University of Maia – ISMAI, CEOS.PP).

The editors also appreciate IGI Global's support throughout the process.

Chapter 1
Intra-Regional Economic Integration:
The African Continental Free Trade Area Initiative

Godfrey C. Onuwa
https://orcid.org/0000-0001-5657-9427
Federal College of Forestry, Jos, Nigeria

Oludare Adedire
Federal College of Forestry, Jos, Nigeria

ABSTRACT

Trade integration is a mechanism for fostering prosperity. African countries have created several regional economic integration arrangements. The African Continental Free Trade Area (AfCFTA) is the most ambitious initiative in this vein. The AfCFTA also seeks to build on the integration already achieved by existing REAs. The AfCFTA has the potential to increase income and welfare significantly; however, these benefits are unequally distributed for member countries. Maximizing potential welfare and income gains by member countries requires substantial and strategic reduction of non-tariff barriers. Also, improved quality of trade logistics and the provision of infrastructural deficits are critical. Net impact of the AfCFTA on tax revenues depends on the combined effect of four channels; direct tax revenue reduction, trade diversion, higher GDP, and increased consumption. Thus, ensuring a strong governance framework of the AfCFTA, is germane to reduce trade policy uncertainty.

DOI: 10.4018/978-1-6684-9277-2.ch001

INTRODUCTION

Over the past century, African countries have created several regional economic integration arrangements. The overriding objective of these arrangements is the promotion of intraregional trade to achieve faster economic growth and reduce poverty (UNCTAD, 2020). The African Continental Free Trade Area (AfCFTA) is the most ambitious initiative in this vein (Figure 1). Past regional integration arrangements have delivered less than was originally envisaged, but they have contributed to a significant expansion of intra-African trade. Despite these integration arrangements, African intraregional trade trails that of other regions, and Africa's insertion into global value chains (GVCs) is still dominated by its exports of raw materials. As a result, past integration efforts have been considered as underperforming (De Melo and Tsikata 2015; Hailu, 2014). Several reasons have been advanced for this underperformance, including lack of complementary domestic reforms to improve domestic supply responses and a low level of implementation of the arrangements, owing partly to the absence of strong institutional frameworks supporting them (WTO, 2020). Still, these arrangements have facilitated a large expansion of intra-African trade in the last couple of decades. The AfCFTA could affect income distribution, unemployment, and fiscal revenue, especially in the short term; however, the benefits of the AfCFTA would outweigh the costs. To mitigate these potential adjustment costs, policymakers would need to implement a complementary set of measures to strengthen the social protection framework, increase labor market flexibility, and mobilize domestic revenues. Africa lacks a continent-wide trading hub (AfDB, 2019; Vanzetti *et al.*, 2018). Given the shift in international trade from goods to services, for the AfCFTA to have a transformative effect on member countries, it would need to spur the development of the nascent supply chain on the continent (AfDB, 2019).

Thus, the African Continental Free Trade Area (AfCFTA) is a trade agreement among African Union (AU) member states aimed at creating a single market for goods and services in Africa. The African Continental Free Trade Area (AfCFTA) is a major initiative of the African Union (AU) to create an integrated African market with the potential to increase economic growth and reduce poverty in Africa (UNCTAD, 2021). It is the largest free trade agreement ever concluded on the continent. The AfCFTA was launched in 2018 and is expected to enter into force in 2021. The agreement has the potential to create the largest free-trade area in the world, with more than 1.2 billion people and a combined GDP of over US$3 trillion (Abrego *et al.*, 2020).The AfCFTA is a result of decades of regional integration efforts on the continent, which began in the 1960s. The early efforts focused on creating regional economic communities, such as the Economic Community of West African States (ECOWAS), the East African Community (EAC), and the Southern African Development Community (SADC) (TRALAC, 2019). These regional economic communities helped to create a framework for regional trade and investment, and many of them have grown to become powerful economic blocs (Albert, 2019).However, these regional economic blocs remained largely isolated from each other, and intra-African trade remained low. This was due to a number of factors, including tariffs and non-tariff barriers, lack of infrastructure, and lack of access to finance (TRALAC, 2018). The AfCFTA seeks to address these issues by creating a single market for goods, services, and investments in Africa, with the aim of increasing intra-African trade by up to 50 percent (PWC, 2023).

The AfCFTA builds upon existing regional economic communities and trade agreements in Africa, and was established with the goal of promoting economic integration, boosting intra-African trade, and driving sustainable growth and development across the continent (AU, 2019; UNCTAD, 2018). In addition to the liberalization of trade, the AfCFTA also seeks to promote economic integration, enhance the competitiveness of African businesses, and create jobs (TRALAC, 2021). To do this, the agreement establishes a number of measures, such as the elimination of tariffs on the majority of traded goods, the elimination of non-tariff barriers, and the establishment of an investment protection framework. It also seeks to strengthen economic and trade linkages among African countries, as well as with the rest of the world (UNCTAD, 2019). The AfCFTA presents a major opportunity for African countries to reduce poverty and increase economic growth (TRALAC, 2020). However, its successful implementation will depend on several factors, such as improved infrastructure, access to finance, and an effective legal and regulatory framework. In addition, it will require the cooperation of all African countries in order to ensure that the benefits of the agreement are equally shared (Abrego *et al.*, 2020).Overall, the AfCFTA is a major step forward for regional integration in Africa and has the potential to create a single, integrated market for African countries. While the successful implementation of the agreement will require an effective legal and regulatory framework, improved infrastructure, and access to finance, it could have a tremendous impact on economic growth and poverty reduction in Africa (Albert, 2019). The successful implementation of the AfCFTA is expected to have significant benefits for Africa. However, challenges remain, including the need for infrastructure development, addressing non-tariff barriers, and ensuring that the benefits of the agreement are inclusive and reach all segments of society (AfDB, 2018).

Figure 1. Infographic summary of the AfCFTA
Source: UNCTAD, 2020

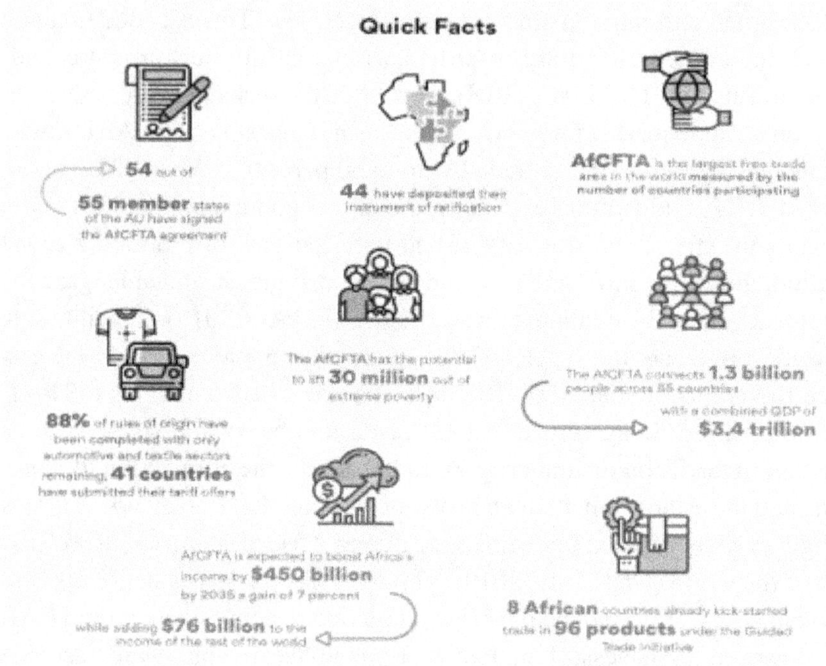

FORMATION OF THE AFCFTA

The African Continental Free Trade Area (AfCFTA) is a historic agreement that was signed by African Union (AU) member states in March 2018 (Albert, 2019). The idea of a continental free trade area in Africa was first proposed in 2012, and negotiations for the agreement began in 2015. The AfCFTA was officially launched on January, 2021, at the 12th Extraordinary Session of the AU Assembly in Niamey, Niger, after it received the required number of ratifications from AU member states (Figure 2). As at September, 2021; 54 out of the 55 AU member states had signed the agreement, after the ratification of the agreement by 44 AU member states (AU, 2018). Going forward, the African Union will continue to monitor and update the progress of the agreement, in order to ensure that its objectives are met and the benefits of the agreement are shared equitably among African countries (Abrego *et al.*, 2020). The agreement is the first of its kind, as it seeks to create a single market for goods and services across the African continent (TIPS, 2018). The goal of the agreement is to reduce tariffs on goods and services, promote intra-

African trade, and create a unified African market (WTO, 2020).The AfCFTA is an ambitious project that seeks to create a continental market with a population of over 1.2 billion people and a combined GDP of more than $3 trillion (PWC, 2023). The AfCFTA was created to reduce, eliminate, or harmonize tariffs on goods, services, and investments; promote intra-African trade; and create a unified market for African countries (Onuwa *et al*., 2021). The agreement also seeks to increase access to markets across the continent, develop regional value chains, and create a conducive environment for trade and investment (WEF, 2018). Additionally, the AfCFTA aims to facilitate the movement of people, and promote the development of small and medium-sized enterprises (Abrego *et al*., 2020).In order to achieve these objectives, the AfCFTA has established a number of rules and regulations. These include rules on market access, trade in services, investments, intellectual property rights, and dispute settlement (PWC, 2023). The agreement also includes provisions to ensure that the benefits of the agreement are shared equitably among African countries (Albert, 2019). Highlights of the formation of the AfCFTA are enumerated below:

1. **Background:** The idea of establishing a continental free trade area in Africa has been discussed for many years. The African Union (AU) has long recognized the potential benefits of regional integration and trade liberalization for the continent's development.
2. **Negotiations:** The negotiation process for the AfCFTA began in 2015. African leaders and policy makers engaged in extensive discussions and consultations to develop a framework for the agreement. The negotiations covered various aspects, including tariff reductions, trade facilitation, intellectual property rights, and dispute settlement mechanisms.
3. **Agreement signing:** On March 21, 2018, the African Union member states gathered in Kigali, Rwanda, to sign the AfCFTA agreement. Initially, 44 out of the 55 AU member states signed the agreement, demonstrating a strong commitment to regional economic integration.
4. **Ratification process:** After the signing, the agreement went through a ratification process in each participating country. To come into force, at least 22 countries needed to ratify the agreement. This process involved domestic legislative procedures and consultations with key stakeholders.
5. **Entry in to force:** The AfCFTA officially entered into force on May 30, 2019, after the required 22 ratifications were achieved. This milestone marked the operationalization of the agreement and the beginning of its implementation.
6. **Phase- wise implementation:** The AfCFTA implementation is being carried out in several phases to allow for a gradual transition and adjustment. The first

phase focuses on trade in goods and services, while subsequent phases will address investment, intellectual property rights, and competition policy.

7. **African Union Commission:** The African Union Commission (AUC) plays a central role in facilitating the implementation of the AfCFTA. The AUC provides technical support, coordination, and monitoring of the agreement's progress, working closely with various stakeholders, including member states, regional economic communities, and the private sector.

Figure 2. Graphic details of the AfCFTA
Source: WEF, 2018

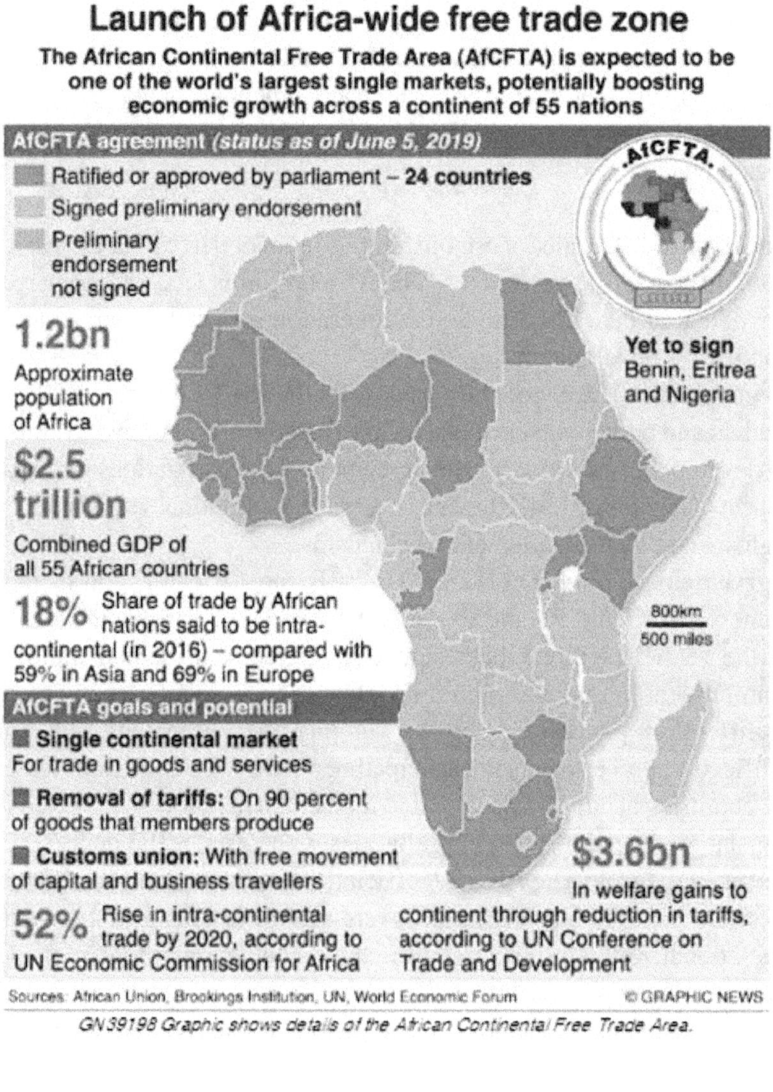

BROAD OUTLINE OF THE AFCFTA AGREEMENT

By the end of January 2020, 54 (of 55) member countries of the African Union (AU) had signed the AfCFTA agreement (Figure 3). Once fully implemented, the AfCFTA is expected to cover all 55 African countries, with an estimated combined GDP of US$2.5 trillion and a population of over 1.2 billion. In terms of population, it will be the largest free trade area in the world. The AfCFTA can support the realization of the continent's economic promise. It has the potential to raise Africa's low productivity and promote higher investment, thereby helping increase income levels and reduce poverty. The AfCFTA builds on negotiations of the Tripartite Free Trade Area (TFTA). The TFTA is composed of the Southern African Development Community (SADC), the Common Market for Eastern and Southern Africa (COMESA), and the EAC. The AfCFTA has eight strategic objectives: The AfCFTA is an overall framework agreement of which various protocols, annexes, and appendices form an integral part. Most of the details still need to be negotiated. Thus far, agreement has been reached on the objectives, principles, and institutions and on a work plan for completing the negotiations, which includes; (1) Creating a single market for goods and services, facilitated by the movement of people; (2) Contributing to the movement of capital and people and facilitating investment; (3) creating a continental customs union; (4) expanding intra-African trade; (5) resolving the challenges of overlapping memberships in REAs; (6) promoting sustainable and inclusive economic development; (7) boosting industrial development; and (8) enhancing competitiveness.

The AfCFTA also seeks to build on the integration already achieved by existing REAs, which are expected to contribute to its institutional structure. In the long run, the REAs' trade functions are expected to be consolidated at the continental level (Vanzetti *et al.*, 2018). The AfCFTA envisages the gradual elimination of tariff and non-tariff barriers to trade on the continent. The agreement sets the path for the elimination of tariffs on 90% of tariff lines (Dix-Carneiro and Kovak, 2017). For services, member countries have also agreed to propose liberalization through a request- and-offer approach, based on seven identified priority sectors: logistics and transport, financial services, tourism, professional services, energy services, construction, and communications. A protocol on free movement of people and an action plan for boosting intra-African trade (BIAT) have also been proffered alongside the AfCFTA. Adoption of this protocol and plan will help advance the cause of the AfCFTA. The protocol on the free movement of people seeks to extend visa-free entry to all African countries, a feature already in place in some REAs. At the same time, the BIAT plan contains elements of the AfCFTA agenda, including trade facilitation and customs harmonization. The agreement will be implemented in two phases. Phase 1, which went into effect at the end of May 2019, provides a framework for the liberalization of trade in goods and services and a mechanism for dispute settlement. Phase 2 will cover competition policy, investment, and intellectual property rights. Negotiations for Phase 2 are scheduled to begin soon. The next milestone will be the creation of a continental customs union and then the ultimate transition to a continental single market. The dates for these milestones are undefined.

Figure 3. Agreement establishing the AfCFTA
Source: UNCTAD, 2021

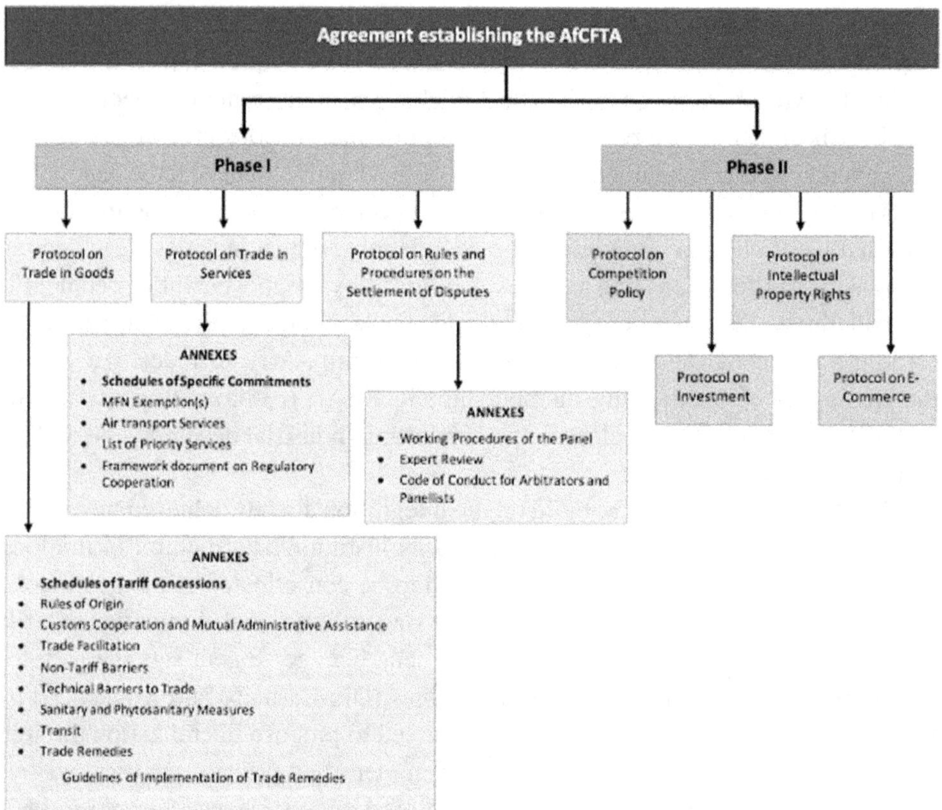

The main objectives of the AfCFTA agreement are to:

1. **Establish a single market:** The AfCFTA aims to create a single African market by liberalizing trade in goods and services, facilitating the movement of capital and people, and promoting investment among member states; and as such promote the free movement of goods and services across borders.

2. **Boost intra-African trade:** The AfCFTA seeks to enhance trade among African countries by removing trade barriers, promoting economic diversification, and facilitating the expansion of regional value chains.
3. **Economic diversification and industrialization:** The AfCFTA aims to promote economic diversification and industrial development by encouraging value addition, intra-African supply chains, and the development of regional value chains. Also, the agreement aims to promote the growth of manufacturing and industrial sectors in Africa, encouraging countries to move away from dependence on raw material exports and towards value-added production.
4. **Enhance competitiveness:** The AfCFTA seeks to improve Africa's competitiveness in the global market by creating a larger market size, attracting foreign direct investment, and promoting innovation and technology transfer.
5. **Job creation and poverty reduction:** The AfCFTA aims to stimulate economic growth, create employment opportunities, and reduce poverty by expanding trade and promoting inclusive economic development.

Since the agreement's signing in March, 2018, significant progress has been made in advancing the AfCFTA and some key developments have been outlined as follows:

1. **Operationalization:** The AfCFTA Secretariat was established in Accra, Ghana, to oversee the implementation and administration of the agreement.
2. **Tariff reductions:** Member states have been engaged in negotiations to determine specific tariff reduction schedules. The agreement aims to eliminate tariffs on 90% of goods, with the remaining 10% designated as sensitive products with longer tariff phase-out periods. By September, 2021, most countries had submitted their tariff offers, and negotiations are ongoing.
3. **Rules of origin:** Rules of origin have been developed to determine the eligibility of goods for preferential treatment within the AfCFTA. These rules help prevent non-African goods from entering member states through preferential trade arrangements/routes and ensure that only products originating from member countries receive the benefits of reduced tariffs.
4. **Trade in services and intellectual property:** Negotiations have been ongoing to establish a liberalized and regulated services market, with the aim of developing frameworks to promote services trade and protect intellectual property, particularly in sectors such as telecommunications, finance, and tourism.
5. **Trade facilitation:** The AfCFTA seeks to simplify and harmonize trade procedures and customs documentation to facilitate smoother and more efficient cross-border trade. This includes initiatives to improve border management, customs cooperation, and the implementation of trade facilitation measures.

6. **Pan-African payments and digital platforms:** Efforts are underway to establish pan-African payment systems and digital platforms to facilitate trade transactions and enhance connectivity among member states.

CHALLENGES AND OPPORTUNITIES OF THE AFCFTA

Challenges of the AfCFTA

By addressing the challenges effectively, African countries can unlock the full potential of these initiatives and promote sustainable economic growth, job creation, and development across the continent (AfDB, 2018; AU, 2018).

1. **Clarifying the process of absorbing existing REAs into the AfCFTA and their subsequent role:** The agreement (Article 19) states that REAs would be permitted to maintain their integration arrangements where such arrangements are deeper than those of the AfCFTA. However, there is no specific protocol on relations between the AfCFTA and existing REAs. An additional issue is the status of the relationship between the AfCFTA and other regional trade agreements in Africa that have not been recognized as building blocks of the AFCFTA.
2. **Implementing a rules-based system for trade under the AfCFTA would depend on a strong secretariat:** This is required to reap the potential rewards of the AfCFTA. The scope and legal entity of the secretariat needs to be clarified (Erasmus, 2019). The secretariat should have the legal authority to conduct monitoring and oversight, along with the capacity to provide technical assistance and practical guidance.
3. **Implementation and Compliance:** One of the major challenges is ensuring effective implementation and compliance across all participating countries. This requires harmonizing trade policies, customs procedures, and regulatory frameworks. Some countries may face difficulties in aligning their domestic laws with the AfCFTA's regulations, which could impede the smooth functioning of the agreement. Challenges may arise due to differences in regulations, infrastructure gaps, and bureaucratic bottlenecks, which can impede the smooth functioning of trade under these agreements.
4. **Infrastructure Deficits:** Africa faces significant challenges in terms of inadequate infrastructure, including transportation networks, logistics, energy supply, and digital connectivity; which hampers trade facilitation within Africa. Insufficient infrastructure can limit the movement of goods and services, increase costs, and cause delays at borders, affecting the full potential of the

AfCFTA. Addressing these infrastructure deficits poses a significant challenge to the success of the AfCFTA.

5. **Non-Tariff Barriers:** Non-tariff barriers, such as import quotas, customs procedures, technical standards, and licensing requirements, can hinder trade flows. Eliminating these barriers requires coordination among participating countries and regulatory harmonization. Overcoming protectionist tendencies and addressing non-tariff barriers is crucial for the AfCFTA to realize its full potential.
6. **Economic Disparities:** African countries have diverse economic structures and levels of development. Some countries rely heavily on commodity exports, while others have more diversified economies. Regional trade initiatives can exacerbate existing economic disparities among participating countries. Developed economies may have a competitive advantage over less developed economies, leading to trade imbalances and potential challenges for smaller or less industrialized nations to compete effectively. Harmonizing trade policies and ensuring equitable benefits across countries with different economic capacities is a complex task.
7. **Managing the political economy aspects of the AfCFTA without compromising its economic benefits:** The appropriate handling of the agreement's political economy will buttress the success of negotiations, smooth ratification processes, and keep the momentum of implementation of the various planned phases of the AfCFTA (Moser and Rose, 2012). While this may involve some trade-offs in terms of efficiency, it would be crucial to ensure that the economic benefits of the AfCFTA are not compromised in the process.
8. **Adjustment Costs:** Opening up markets under regional trade agreements may require industries to adjust to increased competition. Certain sectors or industries may face short-term challenges, such as job losses or declining competitiveness, which can create social and economic disruptions.
9. **Informal Trade:** Informal trade, which often occurs outside formal channels, represents a significant portion of trade in Africa. Integrating informal traders into the formal economy and addressing regulatory challenges they face is critical for the success of the AfCFTA.
10. **Resisting the temptation of making the AfCFTA an obstacle to trade liberalization with countries outside Africa:** It would be a mistake to use the AfCFTA to shield domestic markets from global markets and competition, preferring an inward-looking approach to trade and development. Instead, the creation of the AfCFTA provides an opportunity for Africa to negotiate trade agreements with overseas REAs from a position of strength. Such trade

connections could also help set up reforms required to ensure that the AfCFTA becomes a success.

11. **Capacity and Implementation:** Building the necessary capacity at the institutional, legal, and regulatory levels to implement the AfCFTA effectively is a challenge. This includes training customs officials, enhancing trade facilitation mechanisms, and establishing dispute resolution mechanisms.

Opportunities of the AfCFTA

While the AfCFTA and other similar trade initiatives encounter challenges, the opportunities they present are significant (AU, 2019).

1. **Expanded Market Access:** Regional trade initiatives create larger integrated markets by eliminating or reducing trade barriers among participating countries. The AfCFTA creates a massive market of over 1.3 billion people and a combined GDP of more than $3.4 trillion. It offers businesses the opportunity to access new markets and a larger consumer base, leading to increased trade volumes and economic growth. Increased market access can lead to economies of scale, greater specialization, and enhanced competitiveness for African businesses.
2. **Boost to Intra-African Trade:** Intra-African trade currently accounts for a relatively small share of total African trade. The AfCFTA aims to boost intra-regional trade by reducing tariffs and removing trade barriers. Increased trade among African countries can foster economic diversification, stimulate industrialization, and promote intra-regional investment and cooperation.
3. **Economic Integration and Development:** The AfCFTA supports economic integration and fosters collaboration among African countries. It encourages the development of industries and sectors that can drive economic growth and job creation. Enhanced economic integration can contribute to poverty reduction, improve living standards, and create a more resilient African economy.
4. **Economic Diversification:** Trade integration can foster economic diversification by encouraging countries to specialize in industries where they have a comparative advantage. This diversification can lead to increased productivity, innovation, and competitiveness, ultimately driving sustained economic growth.
5. **Foreign Direct Investment (FDI):** The AfCFTA has the potential to attract increased foreign direct investment into Africa. Regional trade agreements can attract greater FDI inflows by offering a larger market, reduced trade barriers, and improved business environment. A larger, more integrated market with streamlined trade procedures can make the continent more attractive to foreign investors. FDI inflows can bring technology transfer, knowledge sharing, and

capital infusion, supporting the growth of industries and promoting sustainable economic development.

6. **Pan-African Cooperation:** The AfCFTA provides a platform for increased cooperation and dialogue among African countries. It fosters a sense of unity and collective decision-making, allowing countries to address shared challenges and collaborate on regional issues beyond trade. This cooperation can extend to areas such as infrastructure development, energy connectivity, and political stability, enhancing overall regional integration.
7. **Regional Value Chains:** Regional trade initiatives promote the development of regional value chains, where countries specialize in different stages of the production process. This can lead to increased intra-regional trade, job creation, and improved competitiveness of regional industries on the global stage.
8. **Infrastructure Development:** Regional trade agreements often involve infrastructure development projects, such as transportation networks, logistics hubs, and energy facilities. These projects can enhance connectivity, reduce trade costs, and improve overall regional competitiveness.
9. **Fiscal Revenue Impact:** The reduction in trade barriers stemming from the AfCFTA would affect tax revenues through four channels. First, a direct reduction in tax revenue is to be expected from the removal of tariffs on intra-continental imports. Second, trade diversion owing to lower tariffs would also reduce revenues. Third, higher GDP, owing to increased efficiency, would lead to more revenue. Fourth, higher consumption, because of increased imports and income, would also raise revenue. Importantly, the last three channels would reflect the impact not only of tariff removal but also of NTB removal. In sum, the net impact of the AfCFTA on tax revenues would depend on the combined effect of the four channels (Erasmus, 2019).

Figure 4. Infographic summary of the expected derivatives of the AfCFTA
Source: UNCTAD, 2021

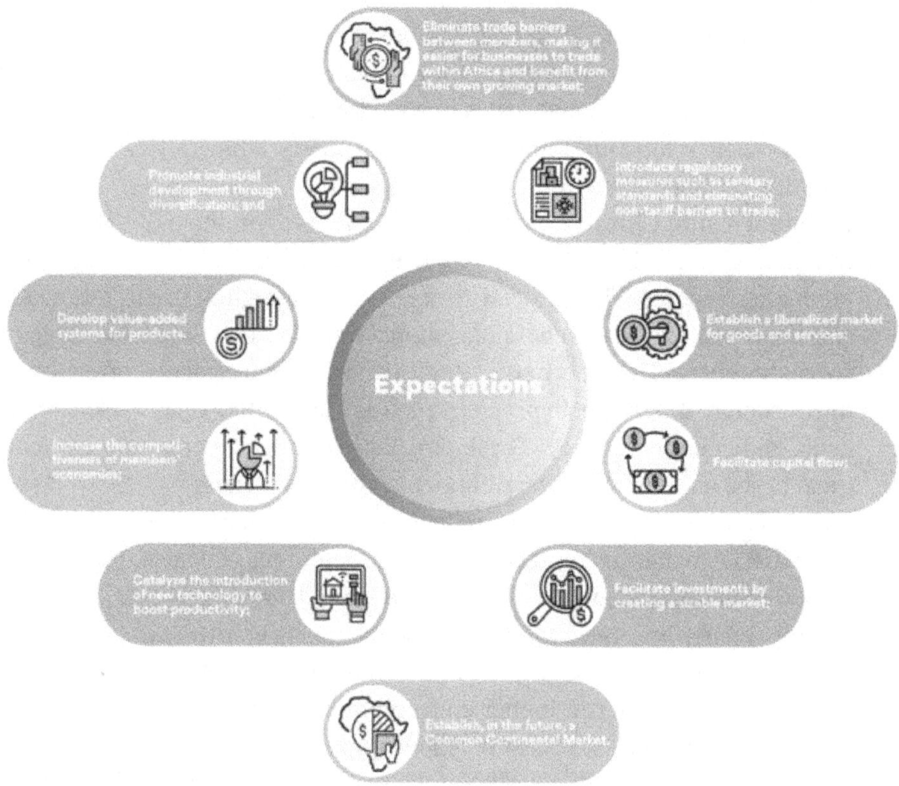

SYSTEMATIC REVIEW OF SELECTED STUDIES ON THE IMPACT OF THE AFCFTA

These studies provide insights into the potential effects of the AfCFTA on specific sectors and can help policy makers and stakeholders understand the opportunities and challenges associated with the agreement. It's important to note that the reviews of studies on the effects of the AfCFTA are ongoing, and the full impact of the trade agreement may take time to materialize (AfDB, 2018). Additionally, the actual outcomes of the AfCFTA will depend on various factors such as effective implementation, infrastructure development, institutional reforms, and addressing potential challenges related to non-tariff barriers, customs procedures, and regulatory harmonization (UNECA, 2019). General overviews of the systematic reviews of studies on the effects of the AfCFTA are outlined below:

1. **Economic Modeling Studies:** Several economic modeling studies have been conducted to assess the potential impact of the AfCFTA. These studies use quantitative models to estimate the effects of the trade agreement on various economic indicators such as GDP, trade flows, employment, and welfare. While the specific findings may vary across studies, the general consensus is that the AfCFTA has the potential to significantly boost intra-African trade and economic growth (CFR, 2019).
2. **Case Studies:** Some studies have taken a qualitative approach by conducting case studies of specific countries or regions to understand the potential impact of the AfCFTA at a more granular level. These studies examine factors such as tariff reductions, non-tariff barriers, infrastructure development, and institutional reforms. By analyzing specific cases, researchers aim to provide context-specific insights into the potential benefits and challenges of the AfCFTA (France 24, 2019).
3. **Impact Assessment Reports:** Various organizations, including the African Union Commission and the United Nations Economic Commission for Africa (UNECA), have published impact assessment reports on the AfCFTA (UNECA, 2019; AU, 2018). These reports provide comprehensive analyses of the potential economic, social, and environmental impacts of the trade agreement (AU, 2019; UNECA, 2019). They often include recommendations for policymakers and highlight areas that require attention to maximize the benefits of the AfCFTA.
4. **Trade Creation and Diversion Effects:** Several empirical studies have analyzed the potential trade creation and trade diversion effects of the AfCFTA. Trade creation refers to an increase in trade between member countries due to the removal of trade barriers, while trade diversion occurs when trade shifts from more efficient non-member countries to less efficient member countries (TRALAC, 2019). Studies have generally found that the AfCFTA is expected to generate trade creation effects, leading to increased intra-African trade.
5. **Macro-economic Effects:** Several researches have also examined the potential macroeconomic effects of the AfCFTA. By promoting trade and economic integration, the agreement is expected to contribute to economic growth, job creation, and poverty reduction in participating countries (ICTSD, 2019). However, the magnitude of these effects can vary depending on factors such as the level of trade facilitation measures, infrastructure development, and the diversification of economies.
6. **Regional Integration and Value Chains:** The AfCFTA aims to enhance regional integration and promote the development of regional value chains. Empirical analyses have explored the potential effects on regional value chains, industrialization, and the distribution of value-added activities across

participating countries; these studies consider factors such as regional production networks, investment flows, and technology transfer (IMF, 2019).

7. **Non-Tariff Barriers and Trade Facilitation:** Non-tariff barriers (NTBs) and trade facilitation measures such as cumbersome customs procedures, technical barriers to trade, and regulatory differences, can impede trade flows. Studies have examined the potential impact of the AfCFTA in addressing these barriers and enhancing trade facilitation, which can contribute to increased efficiency and competitiveness (ITC, 2018).
8. **Sector-Specific Studies:** Researchers have also examined the potential effects of the AfCFTA on specific sectors of the economy. For example, studies have focused on sectors such as manufacturing, agriculture, services, and small and medium-sized enterprises (SMEs). These studies provide insights into how the trade agreement may affect different industries and highlight potential opportunities and challenges.

Examples of Sector-Specific Studies on the Impact of the AfCFTA

These sector specific studies provide valuable insights into the potential impact of the AfCFTA on agriculture, manufacturing, trade services, the digital economy and energy; as well as to evaluate the opportunities and challenges that may arise. These studies consider factors such as sector-specific competitiveness, productivity, and market access.

1. **Agriculture:** Assessing the Implications of the African Continental Free Trade Area (AfCFTA) on Agriculture and Food Security in Africa, by the United Nations Economic Commission for Africa (UNECA). This study analyzes the potential benefits and challenges of the AfCFTA on agricultural trade, food security, and rural livelihoods in Africa. It examines how the agreement can promote agricultural trade, enhance food production, and improve food security across the continent. The study explores the opportunities and challenges related to tariff reductions, non-tariff barriers, and trade facilitation in the agricultural sector. It also emphasizes the need for policy coherence, investment in infrastructure, and support for small-scale farmers to maximize the benefits of the AfCFTA (UNECA, 2019).
2. **Manufacturing:** An IMF study analyzed the economic and distributional effects of the African Continental Free Trade Area (AfCFTA), with a specific focus on manufacturing sectors in Africa. It uses quantitative modeling techniques to estimate changes in output, employment, and trade flows resulting from the agreement. It also assesses the distributional effects across countries and

income groups. It emphasizes the importance of complementary policies, such as investment in human capital, regulatory reforms, and infrastructure development, to unlock the full potential of the AfCFTA in the manufacturing sector (IMF, 2019).

3. **Trade services:** The World Trade Organization (WTO) conducted this study to assess the economic impact of the AfCFTA on services sectors. It examines the potential benefits of services trade liberalization under the agreement, particularly in areas such as tourism, finance, telecommunications, and professional services. It assesses the opportunities and challenges for services trade liberalization under the AfCFTA. The study explores the opportunities for increased foreign direct investment (FDI), job creation, and productivity growth in the services sector. It also highlights the importance of regulatory reforms, harmonization of standards, and improved connectivity to foster services trade within Africa (WTO, 2020).
4. **Digital Economy:** This study by the United Nations Conference on Trade and Development (UNCTAD) focuses on the potential of the AfCFTA to boost the digital economy in Africa. It examines the opportunities for e-commerce, digital services, and digital innovation under the agreement. The study highlights the opportunities for small and medium-sized enterprises (SMEs) to engage in global digital value chains and expand their market reach. It also addresses the challenges related to digital infrastructure, data protection, and regulatory frameworks that need to be addressed to fully leverage the potential of the digital economy under the AfCFTA (UNCTAD, 2019).
5. **Energy:** This study conducted by the African Development Bank (AfDB) assesses the potential impact of the AfCFTA on energy trade and investment in Africa. It examines how the agreement can promote cross-border energy infrastructure development, regional power markets, and renewable energy integration. The study highlights the opportunities for increased energy trade, investment, and access to affordable and sustainable energy across the continent. It also addresses the challenges related to regulatory frameworks, policy coordination, and financing mechanisms for energy projects under the AfCFTA (AfDB, 2018).

Socio-Economic Implications of the AfCFTA

The socio economic implications of the African Continental Free Trade Area (AfCFTA) are significant and can have both positive and negative effects on various aspects of society. Here are some key implications to consider:

1. **Increased intra-African trade:** The AfCFTA aims to boost trade among African countries, by creating a large market of over 1.3billion people with a combined GDP of over $3.4trillion; it can encourage greater trade and economic integration within Africa. The agreement aims to facilitate the movement of goods and services across the continent. This increased trade has the potential to stimulate higher productivity, economies of scale, stimulate economic growth, enhance market access for businesses; promote specialization and efficiency (ONU-CNUCED, 2019).
2. **Diversification of African economies:** Historically, many African countries have relied heavily on the export of primary commodities (natural resources/ raw materials). The AfCFTA provides an opportunity for countries to diversify their economies by promoting trade in manufactured goods, services, and value-added products; and as such, make African economies more resilient and sustainable. This diversification can lead to the development of manufacturing, services, and other value-added industries, which can contribute to sustainable economic growth and job creation. By promoting intra-African trade, countries can tap into new markets and expand their export base (Onuwa *et al.*, 2020).
3. **Job creation and industrialization:** The AfCFTA has the potential to stimulate industrialization, business expansion and create employment opportunities across different sectors. With reduced trade barriers, businesses can expand their market access, leading to increased production and investment, trade and economic growth. This, in turn, can generate new jobs across various sectors, including manufacturing, agriculture, services, and logistics; and reduced unemployment rates in participating countries (Onuwa *et al.*, 2021).
4. **Infrastructure development:** The successful implementation of the AfCFTA requires addressing infrastructure and logistical challenges that hinder trade within Africa; it relies on efficient transportation, logistics, and digital infrastructure to facilitate the movement of goods and services across borders. The agreement can serve as a catalyst for infrastructure development. Improving transportation networks, ports and customs procedures, digital connectivity and reducing non-tariff barriers will be crucial to realizing the full potential of the agreement. Investments in infrastructure development can enhance connectivity, reduce trade costs, and improve the overall competitiveness of African economies (UNCTAD, 2018).
5. **Enhanced competitiveness:** The AfCFTA can spur competition among African businesses, which can drive innovation, improve product quality, and lower prices for consumers. Increased competition can also incentivize businesses to become more efficient and productive, leading to economic growth (Reuters, 2019).

6. **Poverty Reduction:** The agreement has the potential to uplift millions of people out of poverty. Increased trade and economic integration can boost productivity and competitiveness, leading to higher incomes and improved living standards for individuals and communities.
7. **Agricultural Sector:** The AfCFTA could have a significant impact on the agricultural sector, which is a crucial source of livelihood for many Africans. Increased competition from imports may pose challenges for small-scale farmers who may struggle to compete with larger, more efficient agricultural producers. Adequate support and investment in the agricultural sector are necessary to mitigate potential negative effects (TIPS, 2018).
8. **Gender Equality:** The AfCFTA provides an opportunity to address gender disparities and promote gender equality. By supporting women's economic empowerment and removing barriers to their participation in trade, the agreement can help create a more inclusive and equitable society.
9. **Cultural Exchange:** Increased trade and economic integration facilitated by the AfCFTA can also lead to greater cultural exchange among African countries. This exchange can foster a deeper sense of African identity, promote understanding, and strengthen social ties across borders (TRALAC, 2020).
10. **Health and Safety Standards:** The AfCFTA includes provisions for harmonizing standards and regulations, including health and safety standards. This can help improve the quality of goods and services traded within the continent, ensuring consumer protection and public health.
11. **Migration and Mobility:** The AfCFTA may influence patterns of migration and mobility within Africa. With increased economic opportunities and trade, there may be shifts in population movement as individuals seek better livelihoods in countries with stronger economies. Managing migration and ensuring the protection of migrants' rights will be important considerations (TRALAC, 2019).
12. **Market expansion and economies of scale:** The AfCFTA creates a larger market of over 1.3 billion people and a combined GDP of more than $3 trillion. This expanded market size can attract foreign direct investment (FDI) and encourage economies of scale for African businesses. With a larger consumer base, businesses can potentially achieve cost efficiencies, increase production capacities, and attract more investment.
13. **Displacement of certain industries:** While the AfCFTA presents opportunities, it may also lead to the displacement of certain industries that cannot compete effectively in the liberalized market. Industries that rely on protectionist measures, subsidies, or inefficient production methods might face increased competition from more efficient and competitive firms. Governments must

consider strategies to support affected industries and ensure a smooth transition to a more open and competitive market (TRALAC, 2018).

14. **Unequal distribution of benefits:** The benefits of the AfCFTA might not be evenly distributed across all countries and sectors. Countries with larger economies and more developed industries might initially benefit more from increased market access, while smaller and less developed countries could face challenges in competing. It will be essential to implement supportive policies and mechanisms that promote inclusivity and address potential inequalities to ensure that all countries and segments of society can benefit from the agreement.
15. **Challenges and disparities:** While the AfCFTA holds great promise, there are challenges that need to be addressed. These include ensuring harmonization of trade rules and regulations, addressing non-tariff barriers, building capacity for small and medium-sized enterprises (SMEs) to participate effectively, and addressing infrastructure gaps. Additionally, there may be concerns about the potential impact of the agreement on vulnerable sectors and countries that may face difficulties in adjusting to increased competition (WTO, 2020).
16. **Economic Disparities:** While the AfCFTA aims to promote inclusive growth, there is a risk that economic disparities between countries and regions may widen. Countries with more advanced economies and infrastructure could benefit more from the agreement, leaving behind those with less developed economies. Ensuring that the benefits of trade are distributed equitably is a crucial challenge.

It is important to note that the socio-economic implications of the AfCFTA will depend on how the agreement is implemented, the level of commitment from participating countries, and the policies put in place to address potential challenges. Monitoring and addressing any negative social-economic impacts will be crucial to maximizing the benefits of the AfCFTA for all Africans. Overall, the AfCFTA has the potential to significantly impact Africa's socioeconomic landscape by promoting trade, diversification, job creation, and industrialization. However, realizing these benefits will require concerted efforts from African governments, businesses, and other stakeholders to address implementation challenges and ensure inclusive and sustainable growth (WEF, 2018).

CASE STUDIES OF REGIONAL TRADE INITIATIVE SIMILAR TO THE AFCFTA

While the AfCFTA is unique in its scope and scale, there have been other regional trade initiatives around the world that share similar objectives. Regional trade initiatives are agreements or arrangements between countries or territories within a specific geographic region that aim to promote and facilitate economic integration, increase intra-regional trade, fosters economic development and economic cooperation. These initiatives typically involve the reduction or elimination of trade barriers such as tariffs, quotas, and regulatory barriers to create a more integrated and seamless trading environment within the region (TRALAC, 2020). Highlighted below is an overview of some few case studies of regional trade initiatives comparable to the AfCFTA:

1. **European Union (EU):** The EU is a regional economic integration organization comprised of 27 member countries in Europe. It established a single market with the free movement of goods, services, capital, and labor among its member states. The EU's aim is to promote economic integration, reduce trade barriers, and facilitate cross-border trade. The EU also has a common external trade policy, allowing it to negotiate trade agreements on behalf of its member states. The EU is often cited as a successful example of regional economic integration, with the Eurozone representing a monetary union within the EU.
2. **Association of South-East Asian Nations (ASEAN):** ASEAN is a regional intergovernmental organization consisting often South-east Asian countries. ASEAN aims to promote economic integration and cooperation in the region. It has established the ASEAN Free Trade Area (AFTA) to reduce tariffs and trade barriers among member countries and create a more open and competitive market. ASEAN has also signed free trade agreements with several external partners. ASEAN also has plans to establish the ASEAN Economic Community (AEC), which seeks to deepen economic integration by harmonizing policies and facilitating the free flow of goods, services, investment, and skilled labor.
3. **Mercosur:** Mercosur, formally known as the Southern Common Market, is a regional trade bloc in South-America, consisting of Argentina, Brazil, Paraguay, and Uruguay, with several associate and observer countries. Mercosur aims to promote free trade, economic integration and cooperation among its member countries. It has implemented a common external tariff, allowing for the free movement of goods within the bloc. Mercosur has also pursued trade agreements with other countries and regional blocs to expand its trade relations.
4. **Gulf Cooperation Council (GCC):** The GCC is a political and economic alliance of six Arab countries in the Persian Gulf region: Bahrain, Kuwait, Oman, Qatar, Saudi Arabia, and the United Arab Emirates. The GCC aims to promote economic integration and cooperation among its member states, including the establishment of a customs union. The customs union aims to eliminate customs duties on goods traded between member countries and establish a common external tariff.

5. **North American Free Trade Agreement (NAFTA):** NAFTA was an agreement between the United States, Canada, and Mexico, which came into effect in 1994. It aimed to eliminate trade barriers and promote economic integration among the three countries. In 2020, NAFTA was replaced by the United States-Mexico-Canada Agreement (USMCA), which introduced updated provisions to address modern trade challenges.
6. **Comprehensive and Progressive Agreement for Trans-Pacific Partnership (CPTPP):** The CPTPP is a trade agreement among eleven countries in the Asia-Pacific region, including Australia, Canada, Japan, and Singapore, among others. It aims to lower trade barriers and establish common rules and standards for trade and investment among member countries.
7. **East African Community (EAC):** The EAC is a regional intergovernmental organization comprising six member states: Burundi, Kenya, Rwanda, South Sudan, Tanzania, and Uganda. The EAC promotes economic integration in East Africa through the establishment of a common market, monetary union, and customs union. It facilitates the free movement of goods, services, capital, and people within the region.
8. **Economic Community of West African States (ECOWAS):** ECOWAS is a regional economic bloc consisting of 15 member states in West Africa. It aims to promote economic integration, stability, and development in the region. ECOWAS has made progress in implementing a common external tariff, facilitating the free movement of people and goods, and harmonizing economic policies.
9. **Southern African Development Community (SADC):** SADC is a regional organization comprising 16 member states in Southern Africa. It aims to promote sustainable economic development, enhance regional integration, and deepen cooperation among member states. SADC has pursued initiatives such as the SADC Free Trade Area and the SADC Customs Union to facilitate trade and economic integration in the region.
10. **Common Market for Eastern and Southern Africa (COMESA):** COMESA is a regional economic community made up of 21 member states in Eastern and Southern Africa. It aims to promote economic integration, trade facilitation, and industrial development in the region. COMESA has implemented initiatives such as the COMESA Free Trade Area, which eliminates tariffs on goods traded among member states.
11. **Arab Maghreb Union (AMU):** The AMU is a regional organization that comprises five North African countries: Algeria, Libya, Mauritania, Morocco, and Tunisia. It aims to promote economic cooperation, trade liberalization, and integration among member states. However, progress toward economic

integration within the AMU has been limited due to political and security challenges in the region.

These are just a few examples of regional trade initiatives that exist around the world that share similarities with the AfCFTA in terms of promoting regional economic integration and reducing trade barriers. Each initiative has its own specific objectives, membership, and rules, unique characteristics and challenges (UNCTAD, 2019). These initiatives, among others, reflect regional commitment to promote regional trade and economic cooperation within their respective regions; as well as foster economic integration, growth and development (TRALAC, 2021).

Figure 5. Existing African regional economic communities
Source: TRALAC, 2021

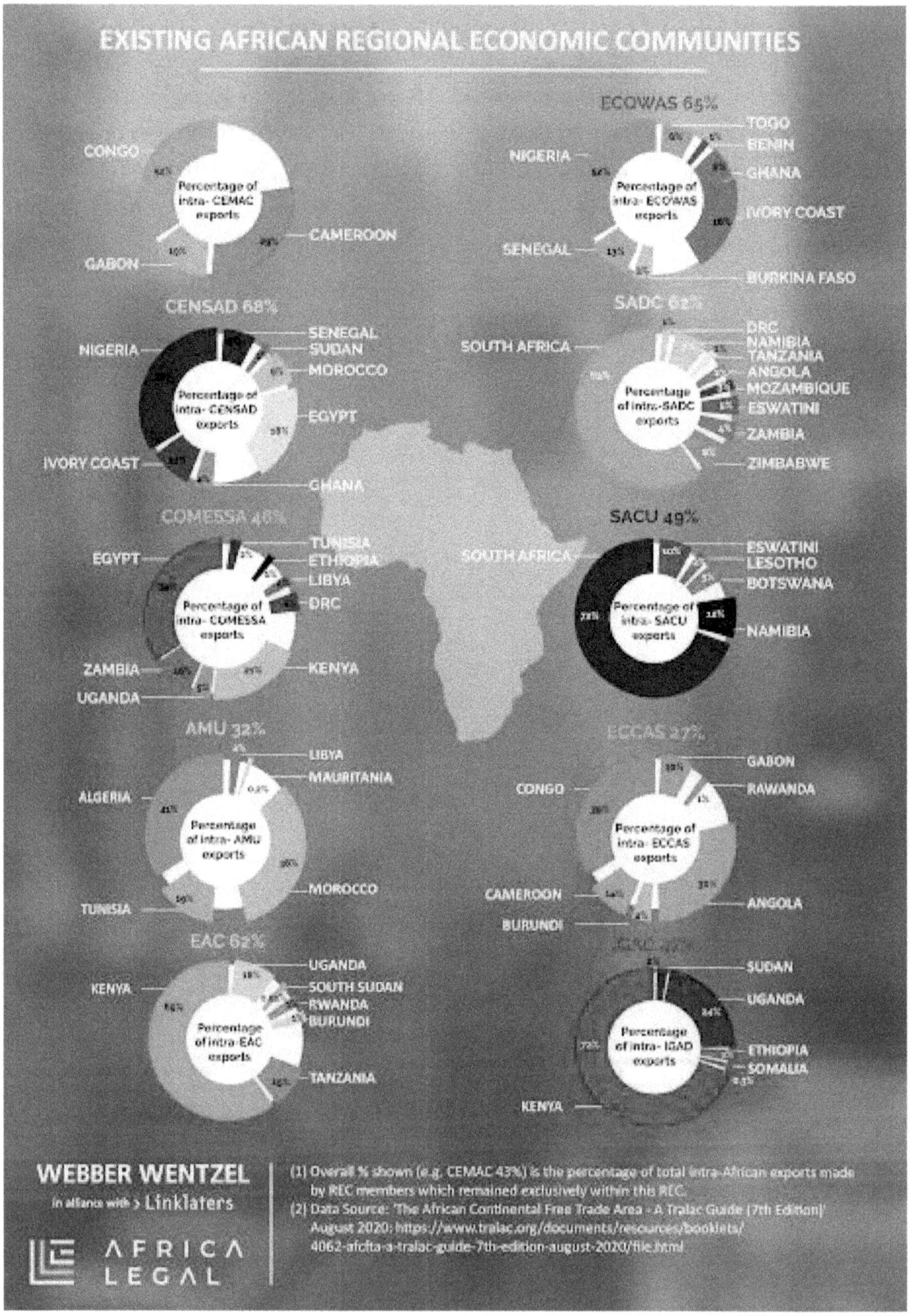

EFFECTS OF THE AFCFTA ON WELFARE, INCOME, AND ECONOMIC DEVELOPMENT

To maximize the positive effects of the African Continental Free Trade Area (AfCFTA), it is essential to integrate sustainable development goals into the implementation process, including policies and regulations that promote environmental protection, social inclusion, and responsible business practices (IMF, 2019). It's worth noting that the effects of AfCFTA on sustainable practices and economic development will depend on various factors, including the commitment and actions of member states, the implementation of supportive policies, and the engagement of stakeholders across sectors (Onuwa *et al.*, 2020). Monitoring and evaluating the impacts of the agreement on sustainability will be important to ensure that it aligns with the broader goals of sustainable development in Africa.

Welfare and Income Effects

The welfare effects of preferential trade arrangements are theoretically ambiguous (Limao, 2016). Lower trade barriers allow countries to expand trade within membership (trade creation), which increases welfare. At the same time, the removal of trade barriers among members may reduce trade with more efficient countries outside the membership (trade diversion), thus reducing welfare. The impact of reducing trade barriers on efficiency and welfare depends on whether trade diversion or trade creation dominates. Whether preferential trade arrangements increase or decrease welfare is therefore an empirical question. General-equilibrium-based empirical studies typically find that preferential trade arrangements have a positive effect on welfare, with the size of the gains depending largely on initial conditions (for example, level of trade barriers and the extent of trade liberalization) (Onuwa *et al.*, 2020).

Empirical studies find that the AfCFTA would increase overall income and welfare for the majority of African countries. These studies are based on ex ante simulations using multi- sector, multi-country computable general equilibrium (CGE) trade models. They consider both import-tariff elimination and NTB reduction. The size of income and welfare gains varies, depending on the specific features of the model: some studies (OECD, 2019) find income gains of up to 5%. Recent work at the IMF has used newer, quantitative trade models to estimate the AfCFTA's potential welfare effects. Abrego *et al.* (2019) find very small welfare gains from import tariff elimination and much larger gains from a moderate reduction in NTBs. In their baseline simulations (perfect competition, with a 35% reduction in NTBs), there is an overall welfare gain of 2.6% for sub-Saharan Africa (SSA) and 2.1% for the continent as a whole (PWC, 2023). As is standard in general equilibrium trade models, the reduction in tariffs and NTBs affects welfare both through consumption and output (by reducing distortions) and thereby improves efficiency. A notable feature of the model used by Abrego *et al.* (2019) is that international prices are endogenous, allowing for changes in the terms of trade. Therefore, in addition to changes in efficiency, terms-of-trade movements also affect welfare outcomes, and this has a material impact on the distribution of welfare gains across countries.

However, while all African countries experience increased welfare from a reduction in NTBs, these benefits are unequally distributed (OECD, 2019). By far, the largest proportional gains go to countries with the most open economies, which also tend to be the smallest economies. In contrast, the larger economies are less open and tend to benefit less, because of adverse terms-of-trade movements, which offset efficiency gains, among other reasons (Saygili *et al.*, 2018). The AfCFTA would have a strong impact on intra-African trade volumes, but its effects on overall trade would be limited. Abrego *et al.* (2019) estimated intra-African trade growth of 8% per annum owing to the AfCFTA, which represents an increase of about US$60 billion in African exports. Econometric analysis at the firm level for African countries also shows that the reduction in trade barriers has a positive effect on firms' decisions to export (OECD, 2019).

Effects on Sustainable Economic Development

The African Continental Free Trade Area (AfCFTA) has the potential to significantly impact sustainable economic development in Africa. By promoting intra-African trade, it can diversify economies, reduce dependence on resource extraction, and foster regional value chains. This can facilitate the growth of sustainable industries, generate employment opportunities, and enhance economic resilience (UNCTAD, 2019). However, it is important to ensure that the benefits of increased trade are distributed equitably. The AfCFTA can contribute to sustainable economic development in several ways including:

1. **Trade Facilitation:** AfCFTA aims to create a single market for goods and services in Africa, eliminating trade barriers such as tariffs and non-tariff barriers. By reducing trade costs and improving market access, it can stimulate intra-African trade and attract foreign direct investment. Increased trade can lead to economies of scale, enhanced productivity, and greater competitiveness, which are all essential for sustainable economic development.
2. **Diversification and Industrialization:** AfCFTA provides an opportunity for African countries to diversify their economies and reduce their reliance on commodity exports. By promoting regional value chains and intra-African trade in manufactured goods, it can encourage industrialization and the

development of higher value-added industries. This can contribute to job creation, technology transfer, and the development of skills, which are crucial for sustainable economic growth.

3. **Small and Medium Enterprises (SMEs) Development:** AfCFTA can benefit small and medium-sized enterprises (SMEs), which form the backbone of many African economies. By simplifying trade procedures, reducing trade costs, and providing access to a larger market, AfCFTA can enable SMEs to expand their businesses, participate in regional supply chains, and access new opportunities. This can foster entrepreneurship, innovation, and inclusive economic growth, particularly for women and youth-led enterprises.
4. **Infrastructure Development:** The successful implementation of AfCFTA requires adequate infrastructure, including transportation, logistics, energy, and digital connectivity. Investments in infrastructure development can improve trade facilitation, reduce transaction costs, and enhance regional connectivity. Moreover, infrastructure development can have broader developmental benefits, such as increased access to basic services, improved livelihoods, and reduced poverty.
5. **Policy Coordination and Harmonization:** AfCFTA encourages African countries to harmonize their policies, regulations, and standards to facilitate trade and promote regional integration. This coordination can lead to greater policy coherence, efficiency, and transparency, which are essential for attracting investments, fostering business confidence, and promoting sustainable economic development (Onuwa *et al.*, 2021).
6. **Sustainable Development Goals (SDGs):** AfCFTA aligns with the United Nations' Sustainable Development Goals (SDGs), which provide a global framework for addressing poverty, inequality, and environmental sustainability. By promoting economic growth, job creation, and poverty reduction, AfCFTA can contribute to several SDGs, including SDG1 (No Poverty), SDG8 (Decent Work and Economic Growth), and SDG9 (Industry, Innovation, and Infrastructure).

While AfCFTA holds significant potential for sustainable economic development in Africa, its successful implementation requires addressing several challenges (TRALAC, 2018). Additionally, it is essential to ensure that the benefits of AfCFTA are equitably distributed and that environmental and social sustainability considerations are integrated into trade and investment policies (France 24, 2019). Overall, AfCFTA represents a significant opportunity for Africa to unlock its economic potential, stimulate sustainable development, and improve livelihoods (Reuters, 2019). However, its long-term impact will depend on effective implementation, robust institutions, and supportive policies at the national, regional, and continental levels.

POTENTIAL MEASURES TO BOLSTER INTRA-REGIONAL TRADE INITIATIVES

To bolster intra-regional trade initiatives, several measures have been considered. Some recommended potential strategies include:

1. **Free Trade Agreements (FTAs):** Encourage the negotiation and implementation of comprehensive FTAs among regional countries. FTAs eliminate or reduce trade barriers such as tariffs, quotas, and regulatory barriers, fostering increased trade flows (TRALAC, 2019).
2. **Customs Cooperation and Simplification:** Enhance customs procedures and promote cooperation among regional countries to simplify and expedite trade processes. Streamlining customs procedures and reducing administrative burdens can significantly reduce trade costs and facilitate intra-regional trade (WTO, 2020).
3. **Trade Facilitation:** Implementing measures to improve trade facilitation, including harmonizing trade documentation, simplifying customs procedures, and enhancing border infrastructure; to reduce trade costs, improve efficiency, and promote smoother trade flows (ONU-CNUCED, 2019).
4. **Infrastructure Development:** Invest in the development of transportation, logistics, and digital infrastructure within the region. Efficient and well-connected infrastructure networks can lower transportation costs, facilitate trade, and enhance the competitiveness of regional businesses (WEF, 2018).
5. **Regional Supply Chain Integration:** Encourage deeper integration of regional supply chains by promoting collaboration among businesses across the region. This can lead to increased specialization, economies of scale, and enhanced competitiveness, benefiting all participating countries (TRALAC, 2019).
6. **Market Access and Non-Tariff Measures:** Address non-tariff barriers to trade, such as technical standards, licensing requirements, and sanitary and phyto-sanitary measures. Harmonizing standards and regulations can facilitate market access and reduce trade costs (UNCTAD, 2018).
7. **Trade Promotion and Capacity Building:** Strengthen trade promotion activities and provide capacity-building support to businesses, particularly small and medium-sized enterprises (SMEs). This can help SMEs overcome trade-related barriers, enhance their competitiveness, and facilitate their participation in intra-regional trade.
8. **Financial Integration:** Promote financial integration within the region, including the development of regional payment systems and the facilitation of cross-border investments. Improved financial infrastructure can enhance

trade financing options and support investment flows, further facilitating intra-regional trade (Onuwa *et al.*, 2021).

9. **Information Sharing and Collaboration:** Foster greater information sharing, data exchange, and collaboration among regional countries. This can help businesses identify trade opportunities, access market information, and forge partnerships, thereby promoting intra-regional trade.
10. **Public-Private Partnerships:** Encourage public-private partnerships to drive intra-regional trade initiatives. Collaboration between governments and businesses can lead to more effective policy formulation, targeted interventions, and the alignment of interests to promote trade within the region (TRALAC, 2018).

It is important to note that the effectiveness of these measures may vary depending on the specific characteristics and challenges of each region. Tailoring these strategies to the unique circumstances of the region and ensuring strong commitment and coordination among participating countries are key factors for successful implementation (ICTSD, 2019).

CONCLUSION

The AfCFTA is a crucial initiative that could have a transformative impact on African economies. Building on progress already made by the existing REAs, the AfCFTA aims at deepening economic integration on the continent. Various potential income and welfare gains from the AfCFTA are significant, most would derive from NTB reductions. Lowering NTBs beyond the levels typically assumed in the literature can significantly increase the size of gains. In addition, the economic restructuring that the implementation of the AfCFTA could unleash would offer African economies new opportunities for a deeper backward (as opposed to the current forward) integration in global value chains. This process would also expand trade, as well as employment and income for the African work force. To get there, African countries need to reduce the high costs of trading within the continent. The highest costs stem from NTBs, which must be substantially and strategically reduced. Among those that ought to be tackled first are inefficient customs and entry requirement procedures and technical barriers to trade. The reduction in the infrastructure deficit and the improvement of the low quality of trade logistics are also crucial to deepening continental free trade and integration. Member countries must also overcome political economy issues in the distribution of the gains from the AfCFTA, the setting up of the AfCFTA secretariat, and the management of special interest groups within and across countries. Addressing potential AfCFTA costs would require a complementary set of reforms. African governments would need to adopt policy reforms to mitigate these costs, while supporting sustainable and inclusive growth, which is fundamental to the success of the AfCFTA.

REFERENCES

Abrego, M. L., Amado, M. A., Gursoy, T., Nicholls, G. P., & Perez-Saiz, H. (2019). *The African Continental Free Trade Agreement: welfare gains estimates from a general equilibrium model*. International Monetary Fund. doi:10.5089/9781498314398.001

Abrego, M. L., de Zamaroczy, M. M., Gursoy, T., Nicholls, G. P., Perez-Saiz, H., & Rosas, J. N. (2020). *The African Continental Free Trade Area: Potential Economic Impact and Challenges*. International Monetary Fund. doi:10.5089/9781513542379.006

AfDB - African Development Bank. (2018). African Economic Outlook. AfDB. https://www.AfDB.org/fileadmin/uploads/AfDB/Documents/Publications/African_Economic_Outlook_2018_-_EN.pdf

AfDB - African Development Bank. (2019). *Integration for Africa's Economic Prosperity*. AfDB. https://www.afdb.org/fileadmin/uploads/afdb/Documents/Publications/2019AEO/AEO_2019-EN-CHAP3.pdf

Albert, T. (2019). *The African Continental Free Trade Agreement: Opportunities and Challenges*. CUTS International, Geneva.

AU - African Union. (2018). Template for Goods and Services. *7th African Union Ministers of Trade Meeting*. AU.

AU - African Union. (2019). Agreement Establishing the African Continental Free Trade Area. *African Union Trade Meeting*. AU.

CFR - Council on Foreign Relations. (2019). *African Continental Free Trade Area: A New Horizon for Trade in Africa*. CFR. https://www.cfr.org/blog/african-continental-free-trade-area-new-horizon-trade-africa

De Melo, J., & Tsikata, Y. (2015). Regional Integration in Africa: Challenges and Prospects. In C. Monga & J. Y. Lin (Eds.), *The Oxford Handbook of Africa and Economics* (Vol. 2). Oxford University Press.

Dix-Carneiro, R., & Kovak, B. K. (2017). Trade Liberalization and Regional Dynamics. *The American Economic Review*, *107*(10), 29–46. doi:10.1257/aer.20161214

Erasmus, G. (2019). *The AfCFTA Institutions: Could the Secretariat Hold the Key to Implementation?* Working Paper No. U S19WP01/2019.

France 24. (2019). *Leaders launch landmark trade deal at African Union Summit.* France24. https://www.france24.com/en/20190707-africa-au-leaders-sign-landmark-afcfta-trade-deal-african- union-summit-Niamey

Hailu, M. B. (2014). Regional Economic Integration in Africa: Challenges and Prospects. *Mizan Law Review*, *8*(2), 299–332. doi:10.4314/mlr.v8i2.2

ICTSD - International Center for Trade and Sustainable Development. (2019). *Towards Africa's own mega-regional: The CFTA*. ICTSD. https://etradeforall.org/fr/ictsd-african-leaders-launch-continental-free-trade-area/ICTSD

IMF - International Monetary Fund. (2018). *Sub-Saharan Africa Regional Economic Outlook: Recovery Amid Elevated Uncertainty*. IMF.

IMF - International Monetary Fund. (2019). *The African Continental Free Trade Agreement: Welfare Gains Estimates from a General Equilibrium Model.* IMF. https://www.imf.org/en/Publications/WP/Issues/2019/06/07/The-African-Continental-Free-Trade- Agreement-Welfare-Gains-Estimates-from-a-General-46881

ITC - International Trade Center. (2018). *A business Guide to the African Free Trade Agreement.* ITC. https://www.intracen.org/uploadedFiles/intracenorg/Content/Publications/AfCFTA%20Business%20Guide_final_Low-res.pdf

Limao, N. (2016). Preferential Trade Arrangements. In Handbook of Commercial Policy (vol. 1B, pp. 279–367), edited by K. Bagwell and Robert W. Staiger. Amsterdam: Elsevier.

Moser, C., & Rose, A. K. (2012). Why Do Trade Negotiations Take So Long? *Journal of Economic Integration*, *2*, 80–90.

OECD - Organisation for Economic Co-operation and Development. (2010). *Seizing the Benefits of Trade for Employment and Growth.* OECD, International Labour Organization, World Bank, and World Trade Organization final report. Presented at the G20 Summit meeting, Seoul.

Onuwa, G. C., Mailumo, S. S., Okeke-Agulu, K. I., & Chizea, C. I. (2020). Globalization and Economic Growth in Nigeria: An Econometric Approach. *International Research Journal of Modernization in Engineering Technology and Science (IRJMETS)*, *2*(9), 1685-1694. https://irjmets.com/rootaccess/forms/uploads/IRJMETS999913.pdf

Onuwa, G. C., Yitnoe, G., & Wuyep, G. (2021). Meta-Analysis of Illicit Financial Flows from Nigeria. *Proceedings of the 1st International Economic Conference, Department of Economics, Gombe State University..*

PWC. (2023). *The African Continental Free Trade Agreement: The much-needed shapeshifter for the African trade community*. PWC. www.pwc.co.za/tax-alert

Reuters (2019). *Economic 'game changer'? African leaders launch free-trade zone.* Reuters. https://www.reuters.com/article/us-africa-trade/economic-game-changer-african-leaders-launch-free-trade- zone-idUSKCN1U20BX

Saygili, M., Peters, R., & Knebel, C. (2018). *African continental free trade area: challenges and opportunities of tariff reductions.* (UNCTAD Blue Series Papers, 82). TRALAC. https://www.tralac.org/resources/by- region/cfta.html

TIPS - Trade and Industrial Policy Strategies. (2018, December). Advancing the Continental Free Trade Area in the Context of Changing Architecture of Global Trade. *Agenda (Durban, South Africa)*, 2063.

TRALAC - Trade Law Centre. (2018). *Where does the AfCFTA fit in Africa's development Agenda?* E-Newsletter.

TRALAC - Trade Law Centre. (2019). *The African Continental Free Trade Area (AfCFTA).* TRALAC - Trade Law Centre. https://www.tralac.org/resources/by-region/cfta.html

TRALAC - Trade Law Centre. (2021). *Regional Integration as a building block for the Multilateral Trading System*. TRALAC. https://www.tralac.org/blog/article/13683-regional-integration-as-a-building-block-for-the-multilateral- trading-system.html

UNCTAD - United Nations Conference on Trade and Development. (2018). *African Continental Free Trade Area, Policy and Negotiation Options for Trade in Goods.* New York and Geneva. https://unctad.org/en/PublicationsLibrary/webditc2018d7_en.pdf

UNCTAD - United Nations Conference on Trade and Development. (2019). *African Continental Free Trade Area: Developing and strengthening Regional Value Chains in Agricultural Commodities and Processed Food Products.* New York and Geneva. https://unctad.org/en/PublicationsLibrary/webditc2019d4_en.pdf

UNCTAD - United Nations Conference on Trade and Development. (2020). *AfCFTA: Challenges and opportunities of Tariff Reductions*. UNCTAD. https://unctad.org/en/PublicationsLibrary/ser-rp-2020d15_en.pdf

UNCTAD - United Nations Conference on Trade and Development. (2021). *Rules of Origin Key to Success of African Continental Free Trade Area*. UNCTAD. https://unctad.org/en/pages/newsdetails.aspx?OriginalVersionID=2128

UNECA - United Nations Economic Commission for Africa. (2019). *Assessing Regional Integration in Africa IX*. UNECA. https://www.uneca.org/sites/default/files/PublicationFiles/aria9_en_fin_web.pdf

Vanzetti, D., Peters, R., & Knebel, C. (2017). *Non-Tariff Measures: Lifting CFTA and ACP trade to the next level* (No. 78). *United Nations Conference on Trade and Development*.

WEF - World Economic Forum. (2018). Who are the winners and the losers Africa's Continental Free Trade area? WEF.

WTO - World Trade Organization. (2020). *African nations to seize opportunities for trade facilitation assistance*. WTO. https://www.wto.org/english/news_e/news17_e/ddgra_08may20_e.html

KEY TERMS AND DEFINITIONS

African Continental Free Trade Area (AfCFTA): A group of countries that have agreed to remove tariffs on most goods and services over a period of time, depending on the country's level of development or the nature of the products.

Global value chains (GVC): Full range of activities that economic actors engage in to bring a product to market.

Non-Tariff Barriers (NTB): Trade barriers that restrict imports or exports of goods or services through mechanisms other than the simple imposition of tariffs. For example, market-specific prohibitions or requirements that make product transactions difficult and/or expensive.

Regional Economic Agreements (REA): Agreements signed by two or more countries to improve the free movement of goods and services.

Resource Efficiency: Maximizing supply with minimum waste of (natural) resources.

Sustainable Development: Development capable of meeting the needs of the existing generation, without compromising the ability of future generations to meet their own needs.

Tripartite Free Trade Area (TFTA): An African free trade zone that aims to establish a common market.

Welfare: The efficient allocation of goods and resources within an economy and the distribution of income associated with it to promote social well-being.

Chapter 2
Perceived Sustainability Index: A Composite Index of ESG Ratings and Consumer Perception

Amandine Bavent
ICN Business School, France

Elisabeth Paulet
https://orcid.org/0000-0001-6898-071X
ICN Business School, France

ABSTRACT

This chapter proposes a corporate sustainability evaluation framework by creating a composite index, the Perceived Sustainability Index, which integrates the company's environmental, social, and corporate governance (ESG) score and the consumer perception of corporate sustainability. This index uses MSCI ESG ratings and X data. The framework conceptually aligns with the multidimensional nature of sustainability, the stakeholder theory, and the customer-centric nature of companies. The index enables researchers to examine corporate sustainability from a dual perspective: the consumers and the rating agencies. It also provides companies with an indicator to progress on their sustainability journey while meeting the consumers' societal needs, which, if not met, might adversely impact the corporate reputation and, eventually, the business performance. The authors illustrate their argument by analyzing the Perceived Sustainability Index for 100 companies and then discuss three case studies – a high performer, a low performer, and a potential greenwashing.

DOI: 10.4018/978-1-6684-9277-2.ch002

INTRODUCTION

The common objective of today's world is to achieve sustainable development. The United Nations (UN) defines the concept of sustainable development as meeting the needs of the present without compromising the ability of future generations to meet their own needs. Sustainable development is an integrative concept aiming to balance environmental, social, and economic issues in a mutually beneficial way (Steurer et al., 2005). In 2015, the United Nations introduced a 'shared blueprint' named the Sustainable Development Goals (SDGs) to achieve a more sustainable world. It is an agreement between governments, citizens, civil society, and businesses on sustainability-related priorities. The UN's resolution on the SDGs specifically urges businesses to channel their creativity and innovation toward addressing sustainable development challenges (United Nations, 2015). Moreover, the 2030 Agenda designates the private sector as a key development agent (Scheyvens et al., 2016). Sustainable development can hardly be achieved without the support of businesses (Bansal, 2002; García-Sánchez et al., 2020; Mio et al., 2020; Sullivan et al., 2018; van Zanten & van Tulder, 2021). A recent report in 2023, the Sustainable Development Goals Report, underscores the slow progress made in several target areas and reiterates the indispensable role of the private sector in forging a more sustainable future (United Nations Department of Economic and Social Affairs, 2023). This critical role of companies has fostered the emergence of corporate sustainability (Hahn et al., 2015). Corporate sustainability serves as a model that seeks to balance corporations' short-term and long-term economic, societal, and environmental performance (Montiel & Delgado-Ceballos, 2014; Nikolaou et al., 2018; Steurer et al., 2005). Concurrently, Environmental, Social, and Governance (ESG) investing has witnessed remarkable growth (Meira et al., 2023), and asset managers have prioritized the integration of ESG factors into investment solutions (Cardillo et al., 2023). Driven by heightened investor expectations and burgeoning interest, most companies track and communicate their ESG performance in sustainability reports. ESG ratings have also gained significant popularity. Corporate sustainability demands simultaneous economic growth while addressing societal and environmental challenges (Elkington, 1997; Hahn et al., 2015). According to the managerial literature, stakeholder interests are critical for the company's success (Freeman, 1984), and how those stakeholders perceive the company's actions is essential to see economic benefits from responsible behaviors (Costa & Menichini, 2013).

Over the past few years, the literature regarding corporate sustainability measurement has grown very fast (Searcy, 2012; Maas et al., 2016; Mura et al., 2018a). Following calls for a more comprehensive measurement system (Bititci et al., 2012; Harik et al., 2015; Moldavska & Welo, 2019), composite scores, like

ESG ratings, have been created. However, those ratings only reflect one perspective: the external assessment of the rating agency. With companies becoming more and more customer-centric (Drucker, 1974) and consumers becoming more responsible over the years, what about considering the consumers' perception along with ESG score? Some prominent brands have experienced declines in sales due to consumer backlashes, stemming from suspicions of greenwashing or, more recently, because brands may have pushed boundaries too aggressively, catching consumers off guard. The existing literature has demonstrated that corporate sustainability presents managers with inherent tensions(Carmine & De Marchi, 2022; Hahn et al., 2015; Joseph et al., 2020). Yet, further research is needed to comprehensively understand these tensions and provide effective tools for their identification. This chapter seeks to address the following research questions: How can companies uncover tensions and opportunities within the nexus of their corporate sustainability performance and consumer perception? How can the integration of consumer perception and ESG performance be utilized to enhance corporate sustainability measurement and detect potential greenwashing/SDG-washing risks? Within these pages, we introduce a novel tool designed specifically to expose these dynamics. It operates by creating two distinct scores, then aligning and merging them to form a comprehensive composite index called the Perceived Sustainability Index (PSI). The PSI empowers managers and external stakeholders to adopt a multi-perspective approach to measuring corporate sustainability. Moreover, as we use social media data to measure consumers' perceptions, this indicator enables the identification of potential risks associated with greenwashing or SDG-washing (Nieuwenkamp, 2017).

The chapter is structured as follows: In the first section, we present a literature review of corporate sustainability and the existing frameworks to measure firms' sustainability performance. After establishing the importance of considering the consumers' viewpoint for the company's future success, the second section introduces the Perceived Sustainability Index (PSI) and the associated proposed framework. In Section 3, we calculate the Perceived Sustainability Index for 100 companies and discuss our results, illustrated afterward by specific case studies (Section 4). Finally, we present our conclusions, the academic and managerial implications, as well as suggestions for future research.

LITERATURE REVIEW

Corporate Sustainability: Multidimensional Nature and Stakeholder Theory

While there is no agreed definition of corporate sustainability, a broad definition of the concept is 'company activities—voluntary by definition—demonstrating the inclusion of social and environmental concerns in business operations and in interactions with stakeholders' (van Marrewijk, 2003). Different authors established similar definitions (Dyllick & Hockerts, 2002; Steurer et al., 2005). Social, Environmental, and, through business operations, Economic represent the tripartite core of corporate sustainability called pillars (Boussemart et al., 2020; Carmine & De Marchi, 2022; Hahn et al., 2015; J. Kim et al., 2015). From a theoretical perspective, the stakeholder theory is commonly used to substantiate a corporate sustainability framework (Fatima et al., 2022). According to this theory (Freeman, 1984), an organization can become more sustainable by engaging with its stakeholders to understand their needs and expectations (Freudenreich et al., 2020). Stakeholders are any groups or individuals who can affect (strategic stakeholders) or are affected (moral stakeholders) by the achievement of the firm's objective (Clarkson, 1995; Freeman, 1984; Frooman, 1999; Goodpaster, 1991). Corporations are not self-contained or self-sufficient (Pfeffer & Salancik, 1978); they must rely on external stakeholders (including Natural Capital like land or water) for their future prosperity (Deng et al., 2023; Frooman, 1999; Steurer et al., 2005; Shin et al., 2023) and to achieve sustainability. Our management tool considers the tripartite core of corporate sustainability. Recognizing the critical role of stakeholders in shaping corporate sustainability and business performance, we advocate for juxtaposing stakeholders' perceptions and ESG performance and consolidating both aspects into a unified corporate sustainability measurement approach. In this chapter, our focus is directed toward a particular subset of stakeholders: consumers.

Corporate Sustainability Measurement Methods: Assessment and Perceptions

Sustainability may be measured by single indicators and composite indices (Searcy, 2016). Several measurement frameworks have been developed according to different perspectives, processes, and contributions to practices (Mura et al., 2018).

Those measurement methods can be categorized according to two objectives: internal assessment (assessment done by the company and then communicated internally and externally) and external assessment (perceptions of an external entity based on publicly available information). Considering the surge in ESG investing and the pivotal role designated to the private sector by the United Nations, it is imperative for companies to convey their ESG advancements.

Companies need to be able to measure their sustainability performance and communicate this performance with internal and external stakeholders. Those internal assessment frameworks include, for example, the Triple Bottom Line. In 1999, John Elkington developed it to help companies measure their sustainability performance and communicate their results with the world in business terms. A few years later, in 2011, the Sustainability Accounting Standard Board (SASB) was founded to help businesses and investors develop a common framework for disclosure of the financial impact of sustainability and a common language. Concurrently, some companies opted for alternative tools and frameworks, such as Kering's Environmental Profit and Loss or the Sustainability Balanced Scorecard (Figge et al., 2002; Hahn & Figge, 2018; Hansen & Schaltegger, 2016; Hristov & Chirico, 2019). This internal assessment usually leads to the production of sustainability-related reports often directed towards regulatory bodies and investors (Aksoy et al., 2022). Those reports then trigger an assessment of the corporate sustainability made by internal and external stakeholders. We refer to it as external assessment or perceived corporate sustainability.

The most known framework for external assessment is Environmental, Social, and Governance (ESG). ESG transforms a complex, multidimensional, and intangible asset into a tangible score that is easy to understand and use for their key audiences of investors and financial markets.

Based on disclosed information, individuals like customers or employees can also have their perceptions of the company's behavior. The literature is also rich in measurement methods related to stakeholders' perceptions of corporate sustainability, especially employees (Asante Boadi et al., 2020; Farid et al., 2019; Wang et al., 2020), suppliers (Lund-Thomsen, 2020; Yang & Jiang, 2023), and customers (Kim et al., 2015; Koh et al., 2022; Swaen et al., 2021).

The Role of ESG

In 2005, the Freshfields report established that Environmental, Social, and Governance (ESG) considerations could be integrated into investment analyses to predict financial performance more reliably. Because it was created mainly for investors, the ESG framework uses a financial lens to assess corporate sustainability and evaluate the company's management of financially relevant ESG-related risks and opportunities. As corporate sustainability is an unobservable quality, rating agencies play the role of intermediaries (Drempetic et al., 2020) and reduce the information asymmetry between the company and the investors (Cui et al., 2018; Drempetic et al., 2020; S. Y. Cho et al., 2013). Each agency uses its methodology to translate its perception of corporate sustainability. They produce composite indicators that may diverge from one agency to another (Berg et al., 2022), but they all synthesize a complex situation into one score. Investors increasingly use ESG scores to obtain information about risks rather than competitive positioning (Amel-Zadeh & Serafeim, 2017). Understanding how current and prospective consumers perceive corporate sustainability would be a valuable indicator for investors to supplement ESG scores.

The Significant Role of Customers

Companies have become more customer-centric (Bettencourt et al., 2013; Drucker, 1974; Keiningham et al., 2020), and businesses have focused on driving economic performance through customer satisfaction and loyalty. In parallel, consumers now pay more attention to corporate sustainability. According to PwC, 83% of consumers think companies should be actively shaping ESG best practices (PricewaterhouseCoopers, 2021). Not responding adequately to societal pressures could adversely impact the corporate reputation, increase costs, cause customers to choose not to purchase associated products and services, and ultimately decrease shareholder value (Fatima & Elbanna, 2023; Steurer et al., 2005). The firm's ESG efforts greatly depend on the support of its customers. (Aksoy et al., 2022). There is significant literature analyzing consumers' perceptions of CSR activity (Huang et al., 2019; Öberseder et al., 2013; Shukla et al., 2019; Y. Lee & Lin, 2021) and its impact on consumer attitude and purchase behavior (Becker-Olsen et al., 2006; Joo et al., 2019; Kim, 2019; Lee et al., 2012;). So, we can see how business returns on corporate sustainability practices depend on how customers perceive the company's commitments to ESG (Costa & Menichini, 2013).

Corporate Sustainability and Greenwashing

There is an aspect of corporate sustainability that lacks external evaluation: greenwashing or SDG-washing. The term 'greenwashing' was coined by Jay Westervelt in 1986. According to the Oxford English Dictionary, greenwashing means misleading the public by falsely representing a person, a company, or a product as being environmentally responsible. By extension, SDG-washing means misleading the public by falsely representing the company's contribution to Sustainable Development Goals, including environmental and social aspects. Greenwashing and SDG-washing can take many forms, like selective disclosure, decoupling, deceptive manipulation, or dubious labels. (Siano et al., 2017; Yang et al., 2020;). While companies can feel pressured to 'greenwash' because of societal pressure, it is dangerous for their reputation (de Jong et al., 2020) and the world. As of today, progress is being made to improve the transparency of sustainability disclosure (e.g., SASB), but there has yet to be any control over what the companies disclose on social media. Gathering corporate sustainability communication on social media, customer perception, and ESG scores in one place or one score would allow stakeholders to flag risks of greenwashing or SDG-washing.

PERCEIVED SUSTAINABILITY INDEX

Combining Consumer Perception and ESG Scores Into a Composite Index

The previous section demonstrates the importance of consumer perception towards corporate sustainability and how it can complete ESG scores. We propose combining these corporate sustainability perspectives and indicators into a composite index. A decision-maker confronted with a variety of information will use a composite indicator. It is also a tool academics, practitioners, and policymakers use to consolidate various aspects of a topic into a single metric (OECD, 2008). Composite indexes are already used to measure corporate sustainability, like ESG ratings and other metrics developed by scholars (Hahn & Figge, 2011; Kuriakose, 2022; Ortas et al., 2015; Puggioni & Stefanou, 2019; Singh et al., 2007). The Perceived Sustainability Index (PSI) combines the Consumer Perception Index (CPI) and ESG Index (EI) (Figure 1).

Figure 1. Perceived sustainability framework
Source: Authors own creation

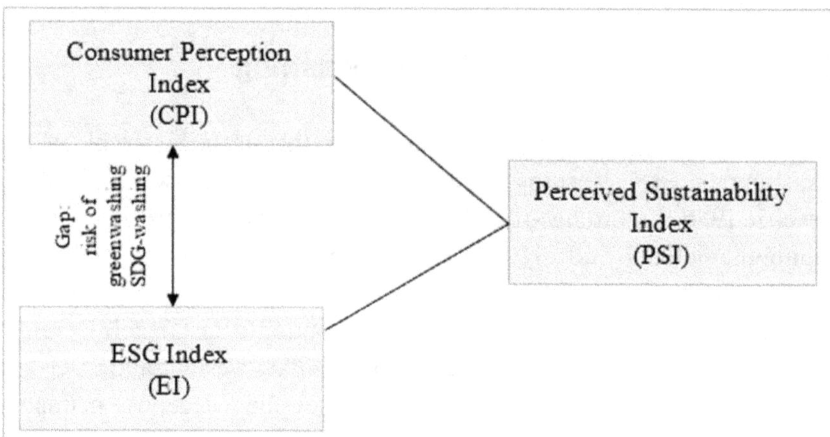

Data

- **MSCI ESG scores:** Different rating agencies provide annual Environmental, Social, and Governance (ESG) scores, e.g., MSCI or Standard and Poor's. In this study, we used MSCI's ESG rating because it is commonly used in articles related to ESG, it has over 40 years of experience in measuring and modeling ESG scores, and the ratings are publicly available. Their database also includes 2,900 companies. It ensures the independence of our study and the possible extension of the analysis to other companies and industries. Finally, their methodology is disclosed in detail on MSCI's website, which allows for a good understanding of what is being measured and a deeper analysis of the results.
- **Social media:** Sustainability is an unobservable quality. The information asymmetry limits the stakeholders' capacity to distinguish between firms that do good from those that do bad. Using the signaling theory (Connelly et al., 2011), transmitting signals can mitigate the problem.

Firms actively use social media to communicate with their consumers and spread their messages, including for corporate sustainability communication (Heggestuen& Danova, 2013). Corporate sustainability communication on social media has received more attention recently (Chu et al., 2020a; Cowan & Guzman, 2020; Kesavan et al., 2013; Saxton et al., 2017). Social media represents a valuable means of communication for corporate sustainability (Sutton, 2016) because it gives consumers a channel to learn about the companies' actions and allows them to share their opinions (H.-H. M. Lee et al., 2013; M. Cho et al., 2017; Morsing & Schultz, 2006). This two-way dialogue has pushed companies to improve the quality and transparency of the information disclosed on their social media (Montgomery, 2013). It also enables us to capture how consumers are engaged with the communicated content (Chu et al., 2020b) and can be used to understand better what matters to them.

- **Measuring consumer engagement on X:** Using the Social Media Tracking Method developed by Rust et al. (2021), we can track consumers' engagement with sustainability-related content published on social media. According to Rust et al. (2021) and Colicev (2018), brand tweet volume can be viewed as how engaged consumers are with a brand or a company. Increasing positive consumer engagement is a key goal for companies on social media (Schaefers et al., 2021). The reason behind fostering consumer engagement is the impact it has on what consumers think about brands and, ultimately, its impact on the firm's financial performance (e.g., Alvarez-Milan et al., 2018; Gensler et al., 2013; Keller & Lehmann, 2006; Kumar et al., 2013; Steinhoff et al., 2019).

This study quantifies consumer engagement using the total number of likes, replies, and retweets per company's tweet. Like Rust et al. (2021), we use X for similar reasons as the authors. Most X accounts are public, i.e., the conversations between consumers and the company are public, ensuring the data's reliability. Many companies maintain an active presence on the platform. Thus, it is possible to separate the conversation about the company into that related to user-generated content and company-produced content.

- **Corporate sustainability dictionaries:** To measure consumers' engagement with sustainability-related tweets, we must use dictionaries. To establish those dictionaries, we primarily used two frameworks, the MSCI framework (*ESG Ratings Methodology*, 2023) and Sustainable Development Goals, augmented by a third one, the impact accounting framework (Cohen & Serafeim, 2020). These frameworks focus on several aspects of sustainability measurement: financial-related risks and opportunities, more humanitarian issues, and the cost of impacts. Using these three frameworks, which are different but complementary, allows for a broad and diverse scope of keywords linked to the definition of sustainability and its core pillars. Ninety-eight keywords were selected and then grouped into five categories named after the three pillars (environment, social, economic), governance, and sustainability. (See the complete list in Appendix A)

Consumer Perception Index (CPI)

- **Consumer Engagement Index (CEI):** Consumer engagement significantly affects the relationship between corporate social responsibility and purchase intention (Al-Haddad et al., 2022). There is no consensus on measuring consumer engagement on social media (Al-Yazidi et al., 2020). In 2022, Muñoz developed a composite index to measure engagement on X by combining two approaches: a follower approach (an engagement measure by follower) and a tweet approach (an engagement measure by tweet). The follower approach involves tracking the number of followers over time. If the number of followers has not been tracked over the past years, months, or weeks, it is impossible to calculate a historical index. Longitudinal trends are usually helpful in making sense of the current index. Because of this limitation, the model uses an approach similar to the tweet approach, i.e., engagement per tweet.

The below paragraph describes the step-by-step process used to calculate the Consumer Engagement Index:

(1) Calculate the Total Consumer Engagement. Total Consumer Engagement = Sum of all likes, replies, and retweets.
(2) Calculate the Total Sustainability Consumer Engagement. Total Sustainability Consumer Engagement = Sum of all likes, replies, and retweets for sustainability-related tweets.
(3) Calculate the Average Consumer Engagement. Average Consumer Engagement = Total Consumer Engagement/Total number of tweets.
(4) Calculate the Average Sustainability Consumer Engagement. Average Sustainability Consumer Engagement = Total Sustainability Consumer Engagement/Total number of sustainability-related tweets.
(5) Calculate the Consumer Engagement Index (CEI). Consumer Engagement Index = Average Sustainability Consumer Engagement/Average Consumer Engagement *100.

The CEI compares the average engagement towards sustainability-related tweets, or Average Sustainability Consumer Engagement, versus the average engagement towards all tweets during the year, also called Average Consumer Engagement. An Average Sustainability Consumer Engagement inferior to the Average Consumer Engagement results in an index below 100. It means that sustainability-related topics are less engaging than other communications published by the company on X and less likely to influence consumers' behavior. An Average Sustainability Consumer Engagement higher than the Average Consumer Engagement results in an index above 100. This situation means that sustainability-related topics are more engaging and will likely influence consumers' behaviors.

- **The proportion of sustainability-related tweets:** The average engagement does not reflect how much the company communicates about sustainability topics. The companies could have high engagement on only a few tweets, resulting in less meaningful insights. To calculate the CPI, we factor in the portion of sustainability-related tweets to the company's communication during the year. This proportion is calculated as follows: Total number of sustainability-related tweets/total number of tweets during the measurement period.
- **Consumer Perception Index (CPI):** We multiply the CEI by the proportion of sustainability-related tweets to calculate the CPI. For example, if a company's CEI is 130 and 40% of its communication includes at least one sustainability-related keyword, CPI is calculated as follows: 130x40% = 52.

ESG Index (EI)

MSCI ESG's assessment provides an industry-relative rating using a seven-point AAA-CCC scale. As shown in Table 1, we converted the Letter rating into a number between 0 and 100.

Table 1. MSCI letter rating converted into a number from 0 to 100

Letter Rating	ESG Index
AAA	100
AA	83
A	67
BBB	50
BB	33
B	17
CCC	0

Source: MSCI's website and own conversion.

Weighting CPI and EI

The weighting of indicators is one of the main obstacles when constructing a composite index (Paredes-Gazquez et al., 2016). A common practice is using equal weights (Gaganis et al., 2021). As we did not want to prioritize one element over the other, we followed this practice to calculate the Perceived Sustainability Index, i.e., the ESG Index and Consumer Perception Index are equally weighted in the composite measure.

Perceived Sustainability Index (PSI)

Finally, we average the ESG Index and Consumer Perceived Index to get the Perceived Sustainability Index.

PERCEIVED SUSTAINABILITY INDEX FOR AMERICAN AND EUROPEAN COMPANIES

We calculated PSI using the methodology described in Section 2 of this chapter, selecting companies from the US and Europe based on their market capitalization as of November 2021.

Selection of Companies

We selected companies from two continents to avoid bias towards a specific region. Fifty-one companies are from Europe, and forty-nine are from the US. They are consumer-facing companies, as these will generate social media interactions that can be used in our study. They were selected through four industries: communication services, consumer discretionary, consumer staples, and information technology.

This classification comes from the Global Industry Classification Standard (GICS), a common global classification standard used by thousands of market participants (*Global Industry Classification Sector (GICS®)*, 2023). The communication services sector includes companies that provide communications services. The consumer discretionary sector encompasses those businesses that tend to be the most sensitive to economic cycles (e.g., automotive, household durable goods, apparel, hotels, and restaurants). The consumer staples sector comprises companies whose businesses are less sensitive to economic cycles (e.g., food, beverages, tobacco, personal products, and food retailers). The information technology sector includes companies that offer software and information technology services and manufacturers and distributors of technology hardware and equipment. Table 2 presents the distribution of companies by sector.

Table 2. Number of companies by sector

Sector	Number of companies
Communication Services	19
Consumer Discretionary	40
Consumer Staples	37
Information Technology	4
Total	100

Source: Authors own creation

Selection of X Accounts

For each company, we identify the X username associated with the company. If no corporate brand was found, we checked the consumer-facing brand name to see if there was a valid username or the name of the CEO who published sustainability-related communication. We found three cases where we could not use the corporate account: Inditex (we used Zara), Apple (we used Tim Cook), and Compagnie Financière Richemont (we used Cartier). The complete list of X usernames is presented in Appendix B.

Collection of Tweets

To collect the tweets, we used Python and a social networking service scraper in Python named Snscrape. We gathered usernames, dates, tweets (i.e., the tweet's text), number of replies, retweets, and likes for all companies included in this analysis. We collected about 128,000 tweets (excluding retweets) between January 2019 and May 2022.

Using the dictionaries described previously, we selected all tweets generated by the company that included at least one of ninety-eight keywords and obtained 34,789 tweets in total.

Collection of ESG Scores

We used the MSCI website to retrieve ESG ratings for all selected companies in 2019, 2020, and 2021 (https://www.msci.com/our-solutions/indexes/esg-indexes). For future analyses, we also collected the contribution of each pillar, Social, Environmental, and Governance, to the final ratings.

Calculation of PSI

We calculated the PSI according to the methodology prescribed in Section 2 of this chapter. In the following section, we further analyze the scores.

RESULTS AND DISCUSSIONS

In total, we have calculated 291 PSI between 2019 and 2021. Nine companies do not have a PSI for each of the three years due to the absence of an ESG score or historical social media activity. For the studied sample of companies, PSI ranges from 0 to 100. Figure 2 presents the frequency distribution of PSI among our sample, i.e., the possible value of PSI and the count of occurrences per group of indices.

Figure 2. Frequency distribution of Perceived Sustainability Index
Source: Authors own creation

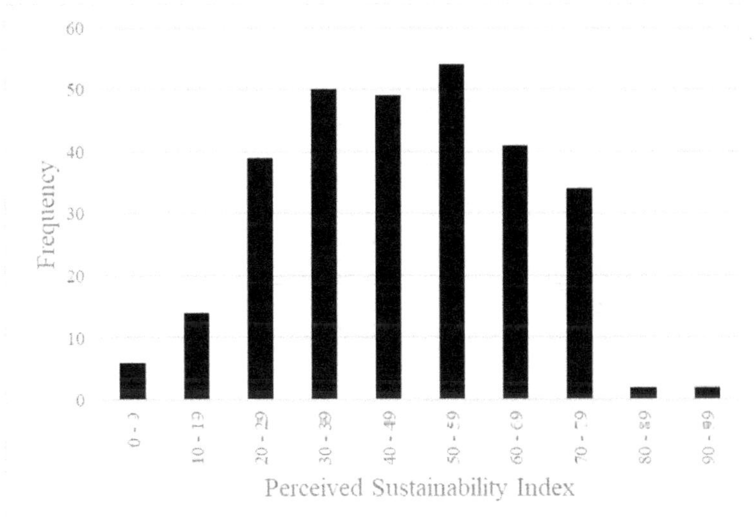

In all sectors, we observe leaders (high index) and laggards (low index) on the PSI while noting that the information technology sector must be carefully interpreted due to the relatively low sample size. Table 3 shows that the average PSI for the consumer staples sector is higher than for the other three sectors. ESG scores and consumer perception of sustainability differ from sector to sector. These disparities suggest there may not be a 'one-size-fits-all approach' related to corporate sustainability communication, consumers' expectations, the companies' actions, and ESG priorities. Instead, it highlights the necessity for industry-specific approaches. These findings have the potential to influence the strategic decisions made by the companies.

Table 3. Perceived Sustainability Index by sector

Sectors	Average PSI	Lowest PSI	Highest PSI
Communication Services	43	13	87
Consumer Discretionary	39	4	77
Consumer Staples	57	2	95
Information Technology	53	37	71

Source: Authors own creation

To continue this sectorial analysis, we also observe differences in the number of sustainability-related tweets as a proportion of the total tweets published by the company. As presented in Table 4, on average, companies communicate more about sustainability in the consumer staples sector than in the other sectors. Forty-four percent of their total tweets are linked to a sustainability-related topic.

Table 4. Proportion of total tweets with a sustainability-related message

Sector	Average	Lowest	Highest
Communication Services	24%	3%	55%
Consumer Discretionary	24%	0%	59%
Consumer Staples	44%	2%	73%
Information Technology	33%	21%	49%

Source: Authors own creation

This observation is not only limited to the number of tweets. Table 5 demonstrates that the Consumer Engagement Index is also higher in the consumer staples sector. This result is similar to the one obtained by ElAlfy et al. (2020). For goods whose consumption is immediate, ESG claims seem to be vital. Therefore, companies have incentives to include these claims in their communication strategies to influence consumers' purchasing decisions.

Table 5. Average consumer engagement index (CEI) by sector

Sectors	Average CEI
Communication Services	98
Consumer Discretionary	93
Consumer Staples	100
Information Technology	82

Source: Authors own creation

Then, aiming to identify the potential relationship between ESG Index, communication, and consumer engagement, we split the Perceived Sustainability Indices into quintiles. The number 1 represents the group with a lower PSI, and the number 5 represents the group with a higher PSI. Figure 3 visually illustrates the frequency distribution of PSI Quintiles, which resembles a normal distribution.

Figure 3. Frequency distribution of PSI quintiles
Source: Authors own creation

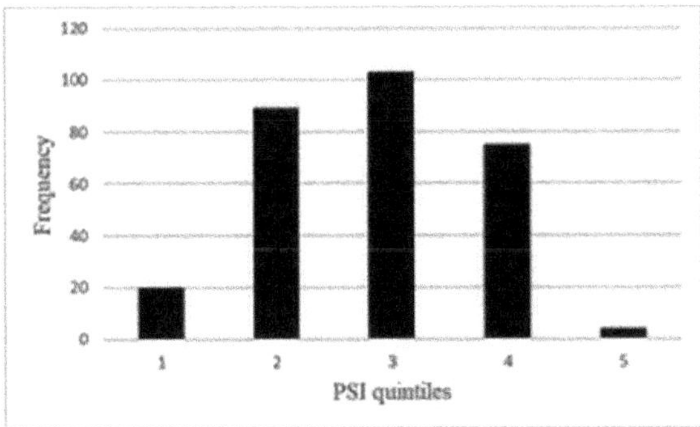

We obtained five groups and looked at the average Consumer Engagement Index, the proportion of sustainability-related tweets, and the ESG index for each group. We observe higher levels of communication, consumer engagement, and ESG performance for group 5 and lower numbers for group 1. Those results suggest a potential relationship between ESG performance, content of communication, and consumer engagement (See Table 6).

Table 6. Average CEI, ESG index, and proportion of sustainability-related tweets by group of PSI

Group	Average CEI	Average proportion of sustainability-related tweets	Average ESG Index
1	72	11%	17
2	94	20%	46
3	89	31%	72
4	114	51%	85
5	131	64%	100

Source: Authors own creation

So, progressing further in this analysis and using the average Consumer Perception Index (which combines the Consumer Engagement Index and the proportion of tweets related to sustainability), we observe higher CPI for the highest ESG indices (see Table 7). Those results complete the study by Albitar et al. (2022), concluding that firms with higher ESG disclosure scores have a more positive CSR narrative tone.

So, not only is the message more positive, but it is also more frequently shared on social media, and the message resonates among consumers.

Table 7. Average consumer perception index (CPI) by ESG index

ESG Index	Average CPI
0	17
17	18
33	27
50	24
67	29
83	39
100	35

Source: Authors own creation

Then, we used those findings to help us understand the ranges of PSI within sectors (see Table 3). In the consumer staples sector, the scores suggest the premise of a positive relationship between CPI (combination of the Consumer Engagement Index and proportion of tweets related to sustainability) and ESG Index (see Table 8): the higher the ESG Index, the higher the Consumer Perception Index.

Table 8. Average CPI by ESG index in the consumer staples sector

ESG Index	Average CPI
0	4
17	2
33	28
50	37
67	42
83	50
100	53

Source: Authors own creation

As we can see in Table 9, the results are mixed in the consumer discretionary sector. This sector includes diverse sub-sectors like apparel, retail, restaurants, and hotels. The literature shows that ESG claims are more difficult to make in some sub-sectors. For example, in the apparel industry, consumers are confused about the meaning of sustainable consumption (White et al., 2017). In the restaurant industry, consumers are more skeptical of corporate sustainability communication, and the perceived authenticity of the message is essential for the consumers to behave favorably towards the firm (Kim & Stepchenkova, 2020).

Table 9. Average CPI by ESG index in the consumer discretionary sector

ESG Index	Average CPI
0	23
17	14
33	28
50	17
67	24
83	25
100	19

Source: Authors own creation

We have found similar findings in the communication services sector, which could further support the fact that ESG performance, companies' priorities, and consumers' expectations are different from one sector to another. Those results suggest that companies need to understand the consumers' societal needs in the specific context of their industry. This understanding can significantly influence companies' strategies concerning ESG communication and priorities.

We also analyzed the evolution of those scores over time. Table 10 below shows an improvement in PSI between 2019 and 2021. While the Consumer Perception Index has slightly increased, the main driver behind this positive trend is ESG performance. Under societal pressure, companies introduced green production practices (Baah et al., 2021). Customers were more focused on how companies responded to the COVID-19 crisis during the pandemic (Farmaki et al., 2022), which could explain why engagement toward more general ESG-related topics did not spike during this period.

Table 10. Average PSI, CPI, and ESG index between 2019 and 2021

Years	Average PSI	Average CPI	Average EI
2019	46	30	62
2020	46	30	62
2021	49	31	66

Source: Authors own creation

This study is the first one analyzing both ESG ratings and engagement on social media across four different sectors and over time. The results show that the pandemic has pushed companies to invest more in sustainability, improving ESG scores over time. With strong ESG scores, companies communicate more with consumers. Maximizing business results from good behavior is likely driving those publications. However, consumers' perceptions of corporate sustainability differ from one sector to another and sometimes from one company to another. Companies may have to understand what matters to consumers in their industry. In addition, they must address the key issues that make consumers skeptical of corporate sustainability. Consumer perception is critical for business return on ESG investment in the short, medium, and long terms (Aksoy et al., 2022). Finally, we will end this section by analyzing three outliers: the top performer in the discretionary sector, one of the lowest performers in the consumer staples sector, and one case of potential greenwashing.

In the consumer discretionary sector, in 2021, the average PSI score is 40, the average ESG Index is 60, the average CEI is 72, and the average proportion of sustainability-related tweets is 25%. The top performer in this category is Michelin. According to MSCI, the company has an ESG score of AAA (ESG Index:100). Its CEI is 105, meaning sustainability communication resonates among consumers. Over the past three years, the company has improved its ESG score, communicated more about sustainability on X, and progressively increased CEI. In 2021, about 50% of its tweets were related to sustainability topics. The company aims to make all its tires from recycled and bio-sourced materials by 2050. To achieve this goal, the company will invest in its R&D teams and partner with other companies to accelerate innovations. Those actions will have a cost. In 2021, the company announced its strategic plan for 2030. This plan includes a sustained growth in sales and a ROCE of 10% (Return on Capital Employed: ratio which assesses the company's profitability and capital efficiency). To sustain commercial and economic growth while investing in a greener future, Michelin needs its consumers to understand and adhere to greener products to buy or pay more for them. Consumers' perceptions of product quality and corporate sustainability are critical for its future financial success. Monitoring

ESG performance and consumer perception will help the company hit its goals. As of 2021, the data shows that the company is working on both aspects.

On the other side of the scale, in the consumer staples sector, Walmart is among the worst performers on PSI. According to MSCI, the company has an average ESG rating of BBB (ESG Index: 50) with serious issues related to corporate governance and supply chain labor standards. The company does not communicate much about sustainability as, in 2021, only 8% of the tweets are related to this topic. The messages also resonate less among consumers than its other communications on X. It could be explained by the fact that the company was reportedly involved in several scandals like dumping hazardous waste, social media backlashes over Juneteenth-related products, or labor relations. As consumers pay more attention to sustainability and could go to another retailer for their grocery shopping, this could be a risk for Walmart's business. To sustain value creation, the company must work first on its ESG performance and then improve how consumers perceive its corporate sustainability. Paula Maria Bogel (2019) did a study that suggested companies with prior negative reputations do not need to stay silent, and corporate sustainability communication could help improve consumers' trust in the company. Once it has improved its corporate sustainability, there could be a path for Walmart to communicate and engage with consumers on this topic. However, it is important to mention that positive development is short-lived. It might be a long road for Walmart.

Finally, the Perceived Sustainability Index can be used to detect some risks of greenwashing. The fast-food company Yum! Brands is an interesting example to explore for this topic. Within the consumer discretionary sector, its proportion of sustainability-related tweets is among the highest (59%), but MSCI rates the company with an average score of BBB in 2021. According to the rating agency, the company has issues with corporate behavior and product safety & quality, and it is not a leader in any key ESG-related issues identified for the restaurant industry. Additionally, MSCI indicates the company is involved in severe to moderate-level controversies in the following categories: customer relations, product safety & quality, health & safety, labor-management relations, bribery & fraud. So, the elevated level of tweets related to sustainability could bring suspicions and raise red flags regarding potential greenwashing or SDG-washing, primarily when a substantial number of the tweets is related to the social pillar.

CONCLUSION

ESG ratings offer insights into a company's progress along its ESG journey. Typically, this information is tailored for investors and regulatory bodies. However, it is important to note that customers often do not refer to these reports. Instead, they engage with a company's corporate messaging via social media platforms. Given customers' pivotal role in determining the success of a firm's ESG initiatives, monitoring their perceptions of corporate sustainability has emerged as a critical imperative. This chapter presents a method for tracking and assessing consumer perception of corporate sustainability on social media platforms. Furthermore, it introduces a management tool designed to assist both internal managers and external stakeholders in identifying and understanding the disparities, tensions, and opportunities that arise between consumer perception and the company's ESG objectives.

The Perceived Sustainability Index introduces a unique approach to assessing a firm's sustainability performance, offering a dual-perspective analysis of corporate sustainability. By amalgamating ESG scores and consumer perceptions of corporate sustainability—two pivotal factors in enhancing ESG performance and achieving a superior return on investment—it furnishes a singular metric that can be analyzed in granular detail. By leveraging social media data, this index enables the examination of long-term trends spanning several years, in contrast to surveys, which only provide insights from their initiation. This indicator is applicable across all consumer-oriented sectors and serves as a tool for identifying potential instances of greenwashing and SDG-washing. Authenticity in corporate sustainability communication is essential for consumers and the United Nations. Our analysis has the following implications.

THEORETICAL AND PRACTICAL IMPLICATIONS

First, this chapter contributes to the existing body of knowledge on performance measurement systems. It introduces a novel approach rooted in multiple perspectives for gauging corporate sustainability performance. Drawing inspiration from the integrated view of corporate sustainability outlined by Hahn et al. (2015) and recognizing the imperative for firms to address diverse sustainability facets, this research offers a valuable tool for organizational leaders and external stakeholders. This tool juxtaposes the perceptions of consumers with the ESG (Environmental, Social, and Governance) performance of companies. Given the pivotal role of customers in deriving economic benefits from ESG endeavors (Aksoy et al., 2022), it provides businesses with a means to advance across the three crucial pillars of corporate sustainability: Economic, Social, and Environmental.

Furthermore, it facilitates the identification of potential conflicts and opportunities. Indeed, consumers' expectations concerning a company's sustainability journey may not always align harmoniously with the firm's stated objectives and targets. These discrepancies can give rise to tensions that, in turn, have the potential to impact the company's economic performance.

Thirdly, this study broadens the scope of research in the realm of Greenwashing/SDG-washing. It introduces the concept of the Perceived Sustainability Index as a tool for detecting the risks associated with Greenwashing/SDG-washing. Beyond its academic contribution, this tool also holds practical utility for organizations dedicated to combating deceptive sustainability practices.

Finally, this research offers a comprehensive cross-sector analysis encompassing ESG indices, corporate sustainability communication, and consumer engagement. It underscores the critical role of the sector in both corporate sustainability communication and the assessment of consumer perception. The study reveals that the efficacy of sustainability-related communication varies depending on the industry, and it sheds light on the challenges faced by companies in certain sectors in making ESG claims. By doing so, it contributes to the existing body of literature on corporate sustainability communication and consumer engagement within the context of corporate sustainability.

LIMITATIONS AND SUGGESTIONS FOR FUTURE RESEARCH

This study presents some limits that could be overcome by future research. Our sustainability index uses X data and MSCI ESG Ratings. Both could disappear or run out of business, and research would have to migrate to another social media platform or rating agency. Although we have collected thousands of tweets, the analysis of the tweets remains a manual process. Our collection is limited to English tweets. Keywords used by the company may also change over time, and the sustainability dictionary may need to be updated periodically. While it offers a more comprehensive view of a company's sustainability performance, we have focused our analysis on the customers. Future research could add the perception of other stakeholders to the indicator.

REFERENCES

Aksoy, L., Buoye, A. J., Fors, M., Keiningham, T. L., & Rosengren, S. (2022). Environmental, Social and Governance (ESG) metrics do not serve services customers: A missing link between sustainability metrics and customer perceptions of social innovation. *Journal of Service Management*, *33*(4/5), 565–577. doi:10.1108/JOSM-11-2021-0428

Al-Haddad, S., Sharabati, A.-A. A., Al-Khasawneh, M., Maraqa, R., & Hashem, R. (2022). The Influence of Corporate Social Responsibility on Consumer Purchase Intention: The Mediating Role of Consumer Engagement via Social Media. *Sustainability (Basel), 14*(11), 11. doi:10.3390u14116771

Al-Yazidi, S., Berri, J., Al-Qurishi, M., & Al-Alrubaian, M. (2020). Measuring Reputation and Influence in Online Social Networks: A Systematic Literature Review. *IEEE Access : Practical Innovations, Open Solutions, 8*, 105824–105851. doi:10.1109/ACCESS.2020.2999033

Albitar, K., Abdoush, T., & Hussainey, K. (n.d.). Do corporate governance mechanisms and ESG disclosure drive CSR narrative tones? *International Journal of Finance & Economics*. doi:10.1002/ijfe.2625

Alvarez-Milan, A., Felix, R., Rauschnabel, P., & Hinsch, C. (2018). Strategic customer engagement marketing: A decision making framework. *Journal of Business Research, 92*, 61–70. doi:10.1016/j.jbusres.2018.07.017

Amel-Zadeh, A., & Serafeim, G. (2017). *Why and How Investors Use ESG Information: Evidence from a Global Survey* (SSRN Scholarly Paper 2925310). doi:10.2139/ssrn.2925310

Asante Boadi, E., He, Z., Bosompem, J., Opata, C. N., & Boadi, E. K. (2020). Employees' perception of corporate social responsibility (CSR) and its effects on internal outcomes. *Service Industries Journal, 40*(9–10), 611–632. doi:10.1080/02642069.2019.1606906

Baah, C., Opoku-Agyeman, D., Acquah, I. S. K., Agyabeng-Mensah, Y., Afum, E., Faibil, D., & Abdoulaye, F. A. M. (2021). Examining the correlations between stakeholder pressures, green production practices, firm reputation, environmental and financial performance: Evidence from manufacturing SMEs. *Sustainable Production and Consumption, 27*, 100–114. doi:10.1016/j.spc.2020.10.015

Bansal, P. (2002). The corporate challenges of sustainable development. *The Academy of Management Perspectives, 16*(2), 122–131. doi:10.5465/ame.2002.7173572

Becker-Olsen, K. L., Cudmore, B. A., & Hill, R. P. (2006). The impact of perceived corporate social responsibility on consumer behavior. *Journal of Business Research, 59*(1), 46–53. doi:10.1016/j.jbusres.2005.01.001

Berg, F., Kölbel, J. F., & Rigobon, R. (2022). Aggregate Confusion: The Divergence of ESG Ratings*. *Review of Finance, 26*(6), 1315–1344. doi:10.1093/rof/rfac033

Bettencourt, L. A., Brown, S. W., & Sirianni, N. J. (2013). The secret to true service innovation. *Business Horizons*, *56*(1), 13–22. doi:10.1016/j.bushor.2012.09.001

Bititci, U., Garengo, P., Dörfler, V., & Nudurupati, S. (2012). Performance Measurement: Challenges for Tomorrow. *International Journal of Management Reviews*, *14*(3), 305–327. doi:10.1111/j.1468-2370.2011.00318.x

Bögel, P. M. (2019). Company reputation and its influence on consumer trust in response to ongoing CSR communication. *Journal of Marketing Communications*, *25*(2), 115–136. doi:10.1080/13527266.2016.1166146

Cardillo, G., Bendinelli, E., & Torluccio, G. (2023). COVID-19, ESG investing, and the resilience of more sustainable stocks: Evidence from European firms. *Business Strategy and the Environment*, *32*(1), 602–623. doi:10.1002/bse.3163 PMID:35942337

Carmine, S., & De Marchi, V. (2022). Reviewing Paradox Theory in Corporate Sustainability Toward a Systems Perspective. *Journal of Business Ethics*, *184*(1), 139–158. doi:10.100710551-022-05112-2

Cho, M., Furey, L. D., & Mohr, T. (2017). Communicating Corporate Social Responsibility on Social Media: Strategies, Stakeholders, and Public Engagement on Corporate Facebook. *Business and Professional Communication Quarterly*, *80*(1), 52–69. doi:10.1177/2329490616663708

Cho, S. Y., Lee, C., & Pfeiffer, R. J. Jr. (2013). Corporate social responsibility performance and information asymmetry. *Journal of Accounting and Public Policy*, *32*(1), 71–83. doi:10.1016/j.jaccpubpol.2012.10.005

Chu, S.-C., Chen, H.-T., & Gan, C. (2020a). Consumers' engagement with corporate social responsibility (CSR) communication in social media: Evidence from China and the United States. *Journal of Business Research*, *110*, 260–271. doi:10.1016/j.jbusres.2020.01.036

Chu, S.-C., Chen, H.-T., & Gan, C. (2020b). Consumers' engagement with corporate social responsibility (CSR) communication in social media: Evidence from China and the United States. *Journal of Business Research*, *110*, 260–271. doi:10.1016/j.jbusres.2020.01.036

Clarkson, M. E. (1995). A Stakeholder Framework for Analyzing and Evaluating Corporate Social Performance. *Academy of Management Review*, *20*(1), 92–117. doi:10.2307/258888

Cohen, R., & Serafeim, G. (2020, September 3). How to Measure a Company's Real Impact. *Harvard Business Review*. https://hbr.org/2020/09/how-to-measure-a-companys-real-impact

Colicev, A., Malshe, A., Pauwels, K., & O'Connor, P. (2018). Improving Consumer Mindset Metrics and Shareholder Value through Social Media: The Different Roles of Owned and Earned Media. *Journal of Marketing*, *82*(1), 37–56. doi:10.1509/jm.16.0055

Connelly, B., Certo, T., Ireland, R., & Reutzel, C. (2011). Signaling Theory: A Review and Assessment. *Journal of Management -. Journal of Management*, *37*(1), 39–67. doi:10.1177/0149206310388419

Costa, R., & Menichini, T. (2013). A multidimensional approach for CSR assessment: The importance of the stakeholder perception. *Expert Systems with Applications*, *40*(1), 150–161. doi:10.1016/j.eswa.2012.07.028

Cowan, K., & Guzman, F. (2020). How CSR reputation, sustainability signals, and country-of-origin sustainability reputation contribute to corporate brand performance: An exploratory study. *Journal of Business Research*, *117*, 683–693. doi:10.1016/j.jbusres.2018.11.017

Cui, J., Jo, H., & Na, H. (2018). Does Corporate Social Responsibility Affect Information Asymmetry? *Journal of Business Ethics*, *148*(3), 549–572. doi:10.100710551-015-3003-8

de Jong, M. D. T., Huluba, G., & Beldad, A. D. (2020). Different Shades of Greenwashing: Consumers' Reactions to Environmental Lies, Half-Lies, and Organizations Taking Credit for Following Legal Obligations. *Journal of Business and Technical Communication*, *34*(1), 38–76. doi:10.1177/1050651919874105

Deng, D., Wu, Y., & Qin, L. (2023). CSR preference, market competition, and corporate financial performance. *MDE. Managerial and Decision Economics*, *44*(3), 1396–1409. doi:10.1002/mde.3754

Drempetic, S., Klein, C., & Zwergel, B. (2020). The Influence of Firm Size on the ESG Score: Corporate Sustainability Ratings Under Review. *Journal of Business Ethics*, *167*(2), 333–360. doi:10.100710551-019-04164-1

Drucker, P. F. (1974). *Management: Tasks, Responsibilities, Practices*. Harper & Row.

Dyllick, T., & Hockerts, K. (2002). Beyond the business case for corporate sustainability. *Business Strategy and the Environment*, *11*(2), 130–141. doi:10.1002/bse.323

Elalfy, A., Darwish, K., & Weber, O. (2020). Corporations and sustainable development goals communication on social media: Corporate social responsibility or just another buzzword? *Sustainable Development (Bradford)*, *28*(5), 1418–1430. doi:10.1002d.2095

Elkington, J. (1997). *Cannibals with forks – Triple bottom line of 21st century business*. New Society Publishers.

ESG Ratings Methodology. (2023). MSCI. https://www.msci.com/esg-and-climate-methodologies

Farmaki, A., Hadjielias, E., Olya, H., Taheri, B., & Hadjielia Drotarova, M. (2022). CSR communication and international marketing: Insights from the COVID-19 pandemic. *International Marketing Review*. doi:10.1108/IMR-12-2021-0375

Fatima, T., & Elbanna, S. (2023). Corporate Social Responsibility (CSR) Implementation: A Review and a Research Agenda Towards an Integrative Framework. *Journal of Business Ethics*, *183*(1), 105–121. doi:10.100710551-022-05047-8 PMID:35125567

Figge, F., Hahn, T., Schaltegger, S., & Wagner, M. (2002). The Sustainability Balanced Scorecard – linking sustainability management to business strategy. *Business Strategy and the Environment*, *11*(5), 269–284. doi:10.1002/bse.339

Freeman, R. E. (1984). *Strategic management: A stakeholder approach*. Pitman.

Freudenreich, B., Lüdeke-Freund, F., & Schaltegger, S. (2020). A Stakeholder Theory Perspective on Business Models: Value Creation for Sustainability. *Journal of Business Ethics*, *166*(1), 3–18. doi:10.100710551-019-04112-z

Frooman, J. (1999). Stakeholder Influence Strategies. *Academy of Management Review*, *24*(2), 191–205. doi:10.2307/259074

Gaganis, C., Pasiouras, F., Tasiou, M., & Zopounidis, C. (2021). CISEF: A composite index of social, environmental and financial performance. *European Journal of Operational Research*, *291*(1), 394–409. doi:10.1016/j.ejor.2020.09.035

García-Sánchez, I.-M., Rodríguez-Ariza, L., Aibar-Guzmán, B., & Aibar-Guzmán, C. (2020). Do institutional investors drive corporate transparency regarding business contribution to the sustainable development goals? *Business Strategy and the Environment*, *29*(5), 2019–2036. doi:10.1002/bse.2485

Gensler, S., Völckner, F., Liu-Thompkins, Y., & Wiertz, C. (2013). Managing brands in the social media environment. *Journal of Interactive Marketing*, *27*(4), 4. doi:10.1016/j.intmar.2013.09.004

Global Industry Classification Sector (GICS®). (2023). MSCI. https://www.msci.com/our-solutions/indexes/gics

Goodpaster, K. E. (1991). Business Ethics and Stakeholder Analysis. *Business Ethics Quarterly*, *1*(1), 53–73. doi:10.2307/3857592

Hahn, T., & Figge, F. (2018). Why architecture does not matter: On the fallacy of sustainability balanced scorecards. *Journal of Business Ethics*, *150*(4), 919–935. doi:10.100710551-016-3135-5

Hahn, T., Pinkse, J., Preuss, L., & Figge, F. (2015). Tensions in Corporate Sustainability: Towards an Integrative Framework. *Journal of Business Ethics*, *127*(2), 297–316. doi:10.100710551-014-2047-5

Hansen, E. G., & Schaltegger, S. (2016). The Sustainability Balanced Scorecard: A Systematic Review of Architectures. *Journal of Business Ethics*, *133*(2), 193–221. doi:10.100710551-014-2340-3

Harik, R. E. L., Hachem, W., Medini, K., & Bernard, A. (2015). Towards a holistic sustainability index for measuring sustainability of manufacturing companies. *International Journal of Production Research*, *53*(13), 4117–4139. doi:10.1080/00207543.2014.993773

Hristov, I., & Chirico, A. (2019). The Role of Sustainability Key Performance Indicators (KPIs) in Implementing Sustainable Strategies. *Sustainability (Basel)*, *11*(20), 20. doi:10.3390u11205742

Huang, Y.-F., Do, M.-H., & Kumar, V. (2019). Consumers' perception on corporate social responsibility: Evidence from Vietnam. *Corporate Social Responsibility and Environmental Management*, *26*(6), 1272–1284. doi:10.1002/csr.1746

Joo, S., Miller, E. G., & Fink, J. S. (2019). Consumer evaluations of CSR authenticity: Development and validation of a multidimensional CSR authenticity scale. *Journal of Business Research*, *98*, 236–249. doi:10.1016/j.jbusres.2019.01.060

Joseph, J., Borland, H., Orlitzky, M., & Lindgreen, A. (2020). Seeing Versus Doing: How Businesses Manage Tensions in Pursuit of Sustainability. *Journal of Business Ethics*, *164*(2), 349–370. doi:10.100710551-018-4065-1

Keiningham, T., Aksoy, L., Bruce, H. L., Cadet, F., Clennell, N., Hodgkinson, I. R., & Kearney, T. (2020). Customer experience driven business model innovation. *Journal of Business Research*, *116*, 431–440. doi:10.1016/j.jbusres.2019.08.003

Keller, K. L., & Lehmann, D. R. (2006). Brands and Branding: Research Findings and Future Priorities. *Marketing Science*, *25*(6), 740–759. doi:10.1287/mksc.1050.0153

Kesavan, R., Bernacchi, M. D., & Mascarenhas, O. A. J. (2013). *Word of Mouse: CSR Communication and the Social Media, 9*(1).

Kim, J., Taylor, C., Kim, K. H., & Lee, K. (2015a). Measures of perceived sustainability. *Journal of Global Scholars of Marketing Science, 25*(2), 182–193. doi:10.1080/21639159.2015.1015473

Kim, J., Taylor, C. R., Kim, K. H., & Lee, K. H. (2015b). Measures of perceived sustainability. *Journal of Global Scholars of Marketing Science, 25*(2), 182–193. doi:10.1080/21639159.2015.1015473

Kim, M., & Stepchenkova, S. (2020). Corporate social responsibility authenticity from the perspective of restaurant consumers. *Service Industries Journal, 40*(15–16), 1140–1166. doi:10.1080/02642069.2020.1760249

Kim, S. (2019). The Process Model of Corporate Social Responsibility (CSR) Communication: CSR Communication and its Relationship with Consumers' CSR Knowledge, Trust, and Corporate Reputation Perception. *Journal of Business Ethics, 154*(4), 1143–1159. doi:10.100710551-017-3433-6

Koh, H.-K., Burnasheva, R., & Suh, Y. G. (2022). Perceived ESG (Environmental, Social, Governance) and Consumers' Responses: The Mediating Role of Brand Credibility, Brand Image, and Perceived Quality. *Sustainability (Basel), 14*(8), 8. doi:10.3390u14084515

Kumar, V., Bhaskaran, V., Mirchandani, R., & Shah, M. (2013). Creating a Measurable Social Media Marketing Strategy: Increasing the Value and ROI of Intangibles and Tangibles for Hokey Pokey. *Marketing Science, 32*(2), 194–212. doi:10.1287/mksc.1120.0768

Kuriakose, F. (2022). Measuring Corporate Social Responsibility in India: A Composite Indicator Model. *Indian Journal of Corporate Governance, 15*(2), 295–320. doi:10.1177/09746862221129334

Lee, E. M., Park, S.-Y., Rapert, M. I., & Newman, C. L. (2012). Does perceived consumer fit matter in corporate social responsibility issues? *Journal of Business Research, 65*(11), 1558–1564. doi:10.1016/j.jbusres.2011.02.040

Lee, H.-H. M., van Dolen, W., & Kolk, A. (2013). *On the Role of Social Media in the 'Responsible' Food Business: Blogger Buzz on Health and Obesity Issues* (*SSRN* Scholarly Paper 2355697). https://papers.ssrn.com/abstract=2355697 doi:10.1007/s10551-013-1955-0

Lee, Y., & Lin, C. A. (2021). The effects of a sustainable vs conventional apparel advertisement on consumer perception of CSR image and attitude toward the brand. *Corporate Communications*, *27*(2), 388–403. doi:10.1108/CCIJ-05-2021-0051

Lund-Thomsen, P. (2020). Corporate social responsibility: A supplier-centered perspective. *Environment and Planning A. Environment & Planning A*, *52*(8), 1700–1709. doi:10.1177/0308518X20948070

Maas, K., Schaltegger, S., & Crutzen, N. (2016). Reprint of Advancing the integration of corporate sustainability measurement, management and reporting. *Journal of Cleaner Production*, *136*, 1–4. doi:10.1016/j.jclepro.2016.08.055

Matters, D. (2017, September 25). *Ever heard of SDG washing? The urgency of SDG Due Diligence*. Development Matters. https://oecd-development-matters.org/2017/09/25/ever-heard-of-sdg-washing-the-urgency-of-sdg-due-diligence/

Meira, E., Cunha, F. A. F. de S., Orsato, R. J., Miralles-Quirós, M. M., & Miralles-Quirós, J. L. (2023). The added value and differentiation among ESG investment strategies in stock markets. *Business Strategy and the Environment*, *32*(4), 1816–1834. doi:10.1002/bse.3221

Mio, C., Panfilo, S., & Blundo, B. (2020). Sustainable development goals and the strategic role of business: A systematic literature review. *Business Strategy and the Environment*, *29*(8), 3220–3245. doi:10.1002/bse.2568

Moldavska, A., & Welo, T. (2019). A Holistic approach to corporate sustainability assessment: Incorporating sustainable development goals into sustainable manufacturing performance evaluation. *Journal of Manufacturing Systems*, *50*, 53–68. doi:10.1016/j.jmsy.2018.11.004

Montiel, I., & Delgado-Ceballos, J. (2014). Defining and Measuring Corporate Sustainability: Are We There Yet? *Organization & Environment*, *27*(2), 113–139. doi:10.1177/1086026614526413

Morsing, M., & Schultz, M. (2006). Corporate social responsibility communication: Stakeholder information, response and involvement strategies. *Business Ethics (Oxford, England)*, *15*(4), 323–338. doi:10.1111/j.1467-8608.2006.00460.x

Muñoz, M. M., Rojas-de-Gracia, M.-M., & Navas-Sarasola, C. (2022). Measuring engagement on twitter using a composite index: An application to social media influencers. *Journal of Informetrics*, *16*(4), 101323. doi:10.1016/j.joi.2022.101323

Mura, M., Longo, M., Micheli, P., & Bolzani, D. (2018a). The Evolution of Sustainability Measurement Research. *International Journal of Management Reviews, 20*(3), 661–695. doi:10.1111/ijmr.12179

Mura, M., Longo, M., Micheli, P., & Bolzani, D. (2018b). The Evolution of Sustainability Measurement Research. *International Journal of Management Reviews, 20*(3), 661–695. doi:10.1111/ijmr.12179

Nikolaou, I., Tsalis, T., & Evangelinos, K. (2018). A framework to measure corporate sustainability performance: A strong sustainability-based view of firm. *Sustainable Production and Consumption, 18*, 1–18. Advance online publication. doi:10.1016/j.spc.2018.10.004

Öberseder, M., Schlegelmilch, B. B., & Murphy, P. E. (2013). CSR practices and consumer perceptions. *Journal of Business Research, 66*(10), 1839–1851. doi:10.1016/j.jbusres.2013.02.005

Ortas, E., Gallego-Alvarez, I., & Etxeberria, I. Á. (2015). Financial Factors Influencing the Quality of Corporate Social Responsibility and Environmental Management Disclosure: A Quantile Regression Approach. *Corporate Social Responsibility and Environmental Management, 22*(6), 362–380. doi:10.1002/csr.1351

Paredes-Gazquez, J. D., Rodriguez-Fernandez, J. M., & de la Cuesta-Gonzalez, M. (2016). Measuring corporate social responsibility using composite indices: Mission impossible? The case of the electricity utility industry. *Revista de Contabilidad, 19*(1), 142–153. doi:10.1016/j.rcsar.2015.10.001

Pfeffer, J., & Salancik, G. R. (1978). *The External Control of Organizations: A Resource Dependence Perspective* (SSRN Scholarly Paper 1496213). https://papers.ssrn.com/abstract=1496213

PricewaterhouseCoopers. (2021). *How much does the public care about ESG?* PwC. https://www.pwc.com/gx/en/services/sustainability/publications/cop26/how-much-does-the-public-care-about-esg-pwc-cop26.html

Puggioni, D., & Stefanou, S. E. (2019). The value of being socially responsible: A primal-dual approach. *European Journal of Operational Research, 276*(3), 1090–1103. doi:10.1016/j.ejor.2019.01.065

Rust, R. T., Rand, W., Huang, M.-H., Stephen, A. T., Brooks, G., & Chabuk, T. (2021). Real-Time Brand Reputation Tracking Using Social Media. *Journal of Marketing, 85*(4), 21–43. doi:10.1177/0022242921995173

Saxton, G. D., Gomez, L. M., Ngoh, Z., Lin, Y., & Dietrich, S. (2017). *Do CSR Messages Resonate? Examining Public Reactions to Firms' CSR Efforts on Social Media.* (SSRN Scholarly Paper 3673584). https://papers.ssrn.com/abstract=3673584

Schaefers, T., Falk, T., Kumar, A., & Schamari, J. (2021). More of the same? Effects of volume and variety of social media brand engagement behavior. *Journal of Business Research, 135*, 282–294. doi:10.1016/j.jbusres.2021.06.033

Scheyvens, R., Banks, G., & Hughes, E. (2016). The Private Sector and the SDGs: The Need to Move Beyond 'Business as Usual.'. *Sustainable Development (Bradford), 24*(6), 371–382. doi:10.1002d.1623

Searcy, C. (2012). Corporate Sustainability Performance Measurement Systems: A Review and Research Agenda. *Journal of Business Ethics, 107*(3), 239–253. doi:10.100710551-011-1038-z

Searcy, C. (2016). Measuring Enterprise Sustainability. *Business Strategy & the Environment (John Wiley & Sons, Inc), 25*(2), 120–133. doi:10.1002/bse.1861

Shin, J., Moon, J. J., & Kang, J. (2023). Where does ESG pay? The role of national culture in moderating the relationship between ESG performance and financial performance. *International Business Review, 32*(3), 102071. doi:10.1016/j.ibusrev.2022.102071

Shukla, A., Goel, G., & Tiwari, N. (2019). Consumer perception of corporate social responsibility and purchase behaviour. *International Journal of Business Excellence, 18*(1), 22–41. doi:10.1504/IJBEX.2019.099448

Siano, A., Vollero, A., Conte, F., & Amabile, S. (2017). "More than words": Expanding the taxonomy of greenwashing after the Volkswagen scandal. *Journal of Business Research, 71*, 27–37. doi:10.1016/j.jbusres.2016.11.002

Singh, R. K., Murty, H. R., Gupta, S. K., & Dikshit, A. K. (2007). Development of composite sustainability performance index for steel industry. *Ecological Indicators, 7*(3), 565–588. doi:10.1016/j.ecolind.2006.06.004

Steinhoff, L., Arli, D., Weaven, S., & Kozlenkova, I. (2019). Online relationship marketing. *Journal of the Academy of Marketing Science, 47*(3), 369–393. doi:10.100711747-018-0621-6

Steurer, R., Langer, M. E., Konrad, A., & Martinuzzi, A. (2005). Corporations, Stakeholders and Sustainable Development I: A Theoretical Exploration of Business-Society Relations. *Journal of Business Ethics, 61*(3), 263–281. doi:10.100710551-005-7054-0

Sullivan, K., Thomas, S., & Rosano, M. (2018). Using industrial ecology and strategic management concepts to pursue the Sustainable Development Goals. *Journal of Cleaner Production*, *174*, 237–246. doi:10.1016/j.jclepro.2017.10.201

Swaen, V., Demoulin, N., & Pauwels-Delassus, V. (2021). Impact of customers' perceptions regarding corporate social responsibility and irresponsibility in the grocery retailing industry: The role of corporate reputation. *Journal of Business Research*, *131*, 709–721. doi:10.1016/j.jbusres.2020.12.016

United Nations. (2015). Transforming our world: the 2030 Agenda for Sustainable Development, Resolution adopted by the General Assembly on 25 September 2015, A/RES/70/1, General Distribution, 21 Oct 2015.

United Nations Department of Economic and Social Affairs. (2023). *The Sustainable Development Goals Report 2023* (Special Edition). United Nations. doi:10.18356/9789210024914

van Marrewijk, M. (2003). Concepts and Definitions of CSR and Corporate Sustainability: Between Agency and Communion. *Journal of Business Ethics*, *44*(2/3), 95–105. doi:10.1023/A:1023331212247

van Zanten, J. A., & van Tulder, R. (2021). Analyzing companies' interactions with the Sustainable Development Goals through network analysis: Four corporate sustainability imperatives. *Business Strategy and the Environment*, *30*(5), 2396–2420. doi:10.1002/bse.2753

Wang, Y., Xu, S., & Wang, Y. (2020). The consequences of employees' perceived corporate social responsibility: A meta-analysis. *Business Ethics (Oxford, England)*, *29*(3), 471–496. doi:10.1111/beer.12273

White, C. L., Nielsen, A. E., & Valentini, C. (2017). CSR research in the apparel industry: A quantitative and qualitative review of existing literature. *Corporate Social Responsibility and Environmental Management*, *24*(5), 382–394. doi:10.1002/csr.1413

Yang, Y., & Jiang, Y. (2023). Buyer-supplier CSR alignment and firm performance: A contingency theory perspective. *Journal of Business Research*, *154*, 113340. doi:10.1016/j.jbusres.2022.113340

Yang, Z., Nguyen, T., Nguyen, N., Nguyen, T., & Cao, T. (2020). Greenwashing behaviours: Causes, taxonomy and consequences based on a systematic literature review. *Journal of Business Economics and Management*, *21*(5), 1486–1507. doi:10.3846/jbem.2020.13225

KEY TERMS AND DEFINITIONS

Average Consumer Engagement: The average consumer engagement represents the total consumer engagement during the measurement period divided by the number of tweets published during the same period.

Consumer Engagement Index: Index measuring the average consumer engagement towards sustainability-related tweets compared to the average engagement towards the overall tweets published by the company during the measurement period.

Consumer Perception Index: Index that combines the company's Consumer Engagement Index with the proportion of sustainability-related tweets.

Corporate Sustainability: The way of doing business that creates value for all company's stakeholders by acting socially and environmentally responsibly.

ESG Index: Index created by converting MSCI's letter rating into numbers from 0 to 100.

Perceived Sustainability Index: A composite index that combines the company's ESG rating with Consumer Perception Index.

Stakeholder: Any group or individual which can affect or be affected by the company's activity.

Total Consumer Engagement: The total consumer engagement on X represents the sum of likes, retweets, and replies during the measurement period.

APPENDIX A

Sustainability pillars and keywords associated

Environment			
Agriculture	Durable	Recyclability	Ocean
Biodiversity	Footprint	Recycle	Packaging
Carbon	Forest	Reduce	Planet
Chemical	Green	Renewable	Sea
Clean	Impact	Resources	Toxic
Climate	Justice	Ecosystem	Waste
Consumption	Marine	Energy	Water
Customer	Pollutant	Environment	
Desertification	Pollution	Natural	
Social			
Access	Empower	Labor	Social
Affordable	Equitable	Liability	Societies
Cities	Food	Nutrition	Society
City	Gender	Peace	Sourcing
Community	Girl	Poverty	Supply
Data	Health	Privacy	Underserved
Decent	Human	Quality	Wage
Demographic	Hunger	Responsible	Well-Being
Education	Inclusion	Safety	Women
Employee	Inclusive	Sanitation	
Employment	Inequality	Security	
Economic			
Development	Global	Innovation	Productive
Economic	Growth	Opportunity	Resilient
Foster	Industrialization	Opportunities	
Governance			
Accountable	Ethics	Pay	
Accounting	Governance	Reliable	
Behavior	Partnership	Tax	
Sustainability			
Sustainability	Sustainable		

APPENDIX B

List of companies included in the study and associated X accounts

	Company Name	X account name
1	Anheuser-Busch InBev SA/NV	abinbev
2	adidas AG	Adidas
3	Koninklijke Ahold Delhaize N.V.	AholdDelhaize
4	Airbnb, Inc.	Airbnb
5	Altria Group, Inc.	AltriaNews
6	Amazon.com, Inc.	Amazon
7	AT&T Inc.	ATT
8	AutoZone, Inc.	autozone
9	British American Tobacco p.l.c.	BATplc
10	Beiersdorf Aktiengesellschaft	Beiersdorf_AG
11	Bayerische Motoren Werke Aktiengesellschaft	BMWGroup
12	Booking Holdings Inc.	BookingHoldings
13	BT Group plc	BTGroup
14	Carlsberg A/S	CarlsbergGroup
15	Compagnie Financière Richemont SA	Cartier
16	Constellation Brands, Inc.	cbrands
17	Charter Communications, Inc.	CharterNewsroom
18	Chipotle Mexican Grill, Inc.	ChipotleTweets
19	The Coca-Cola Company	CocaColaCo
20	Comcast Corporation	Comcast
21	Colgate-Palmolive Company	CP_News
22	Danone S.A.	Danone
23	Delivery Hero SE	deliveryherocom
24	Deutsche Telekom AG	deutschetelekom
25	Diageo plc	Diageo_News
26	Dollar General Corporation	DollarGeneral
27	eBay Inc.	eBaynewsroom
28	The Estée Lauder Companies Inc.	elcompanies
29	EssilorLuxottica Société anonyme	Essilor
30	Essity AB (publ)	Essity
31	Ferrari N.V.	Ferrari
32	Flutter Entertainment plc	FlutterPLC
33	Ford Motor Company	Ford
34	Garmin Ltd.	Garmin
35	General Mills, Inc.	GeneralMills
36	General Motors Company	GM
37	Alphabet Inc.	Google
38	Carrefour SA	GroupeCarrefour
39	Davide Campari-Milano N.V.	GruppoCampari
40	Heineken N.V.	Heineken
41	Henkel AG & Co. KGaA	Henkel
42	Hermès International Société en commandite par actions	Hermes_Paris
43	The Hershey Company	HersheyCompany
44	Hilton Worldwide Holdings Inc.	HiltonNewsroom
45	H & M Hennes & Mauritz AB	hm

	Company Name	X account name
46	The Home Depot, Inc.	Homedepot
47	HP Inc.	HP
48	Imperial Brands PLC	ImperialBrands
49	Philip Morris International Inc.	InsidePMI
50	Kimberly-Clark Corporation	KCCorp
51	Kering SA	KeringGroup
52	The Kroger Co.	Krogernews
53	Koninklijke KPN N.V.	KPN
54	The Kraft Heinz Company	KraftHeinzCo
55	Liberty Global plc	libertyglobal
56	L'Oréal S.A.	LOrealGroupe
57	Lowe's Companies, Inc.	LowesMedia
58	LVMH Moët Hennessy - Louis Vuitton, Société Européenne	lvmh
59	Marriott International, Inc.	MarriottIntl
60	McDonald's Corporation	McDonaldsCorp
61	Mondelez International, Inc.	MDLZ
62	Mercedes-Benz Group AG	MercedesBenz
63	Compagnie Générale des Établissements Michelin SCA	Michelin
64	Microsoft Corporation	Microsoft
65	Moncler S.p.A.	Moncler
66	Monster Beverage Corporation	MonsterEnergy
67	Nestlé S.A.	Nestle
68	Netflix, Inc.	Netflix
69	NIKE, Inc.	Nike
70	Ocado Group plc	OcadoGroup
71	Orange S.A.	Orange
72	PayPal Holdings, Inc.	Paypal
73	PepsiCo, Inc.	Pepsico
74	Pernod Ricard SA	Pernod_Ricard
75	Porsche Automobil Holding SE	PorscheNewsroom
76	The Procter & Gamble Company	ProcterGamble
77	PUMA SE	PUMA
78	Snap Inc.	snap
79	Starbucks Corporation	starbucks
80	Stellantis N.V.	stellantis
81	The Swatch Group AG	Swatch
82	Swisscom AG	Swisscom
83	Target Corporation	TargetNews
84	Telefónica, S.A.	Telefonica
85	Telenor ASA	TelenorGroup
86	Telia Company AB (publ)	TeliaCompany
87	Tesco PLC)	Tesconews
88	Tesla, Inc.	Tesla
89	Reckitt Benckiser Group plc	ThisIsReckitt
90	Apple Inc.	tim_cook
91	T-Mobile US, Inc.	Tmobile
92	Unilever PLC	Unilever
93	Verizon Communications Inc.	Verizon
94	Vodafone Group Public Limited Company	VodafoneGroup
95	Volkswagen AG	volkswagen

	Company Name	X account name
96	Walmart Inc.	Walmart
97	The Walt Disney Company	WaltDisneyCo
98	Walgreens Boots Alliance, Inc.	WBA_Global
99	Industria de Diseño Textil, S.A.	Zara
100	Yum! Brands, Inc	yumbrands

Chapter 3
Navigating the Green Path: A Perspective on Sustainable Consumption, Business Innovation, and Customer Experience in China

Mohamad Zreik
https://orcid.org/0000-0002-6812-6529
Sun Yat-sen University, China

ABSTRACT

China has a major impact on global sustainability, and this chapter examines the nexus of sustainable consumerism, corporate innovation, and customer experience in this influential country. The story develops as it examines how growing environmental awareness and a more environmentally conscious middle class are altering traditional patterns of purchasing. The focus then moves to creative sustainable business models across sectors, providing concrete examples of how corporations are rethinking their strategy and value chains to become more environmentally friendly. This chapter delves deeper into the topic of how well constructed customer experiences are shaping customer satisfaction and loyalty on the part of enterprises. It highlights the importance of sustainable marketing for contemporary Chinese enterprises.

INTRODUCTION

At its heart, sustainable consumption is about maximizing human well-being and reducing negative effects on the environment (Anderson & Anderson, 2022). This entails a change from conventional consumption habits to ones that are better for the environment, such as purchasing goods created from renewable materials, decreasing

DOI: 10.4018/978-1-6684-9277-2.ch003

waste, and reusing or recycling existing items (Neves & Marques, 2022). In recent years, it has become abundantly evident that businesses also have a responsibility to provide environmentally friendly options for consumers.

The goal of sustainable business innovation is to reduce an organization's negative impact on the environment while simultaneously increasing the company's bottom line. Renewable energy, more efficient supply chains, decreased waste, and more durable, recyclable products are all potential routes to this goal (Dyllick & Muff, 2016). Successful firms of the future will be those who strike a good ecological and financial balance. As the demand for eco-friendly products increases, businesses are working to position themselves to take full advantage of the market.

The term "customer experience" (CX) is used to describe the impression made on customers during their interactions with a company (Bascur & Rusu, 2020). Emotional factors, such as the brand's values, which increasingly incorporate sustainability pledges, are becoming increasingly important in creating a favorable consumer experience. That means it's not enough for companies to merely offer environmentally friendly goods and services; they also need to make sure their customers have a positive experience (Gómez-Suárez & Yagüe, 2021). Businesses can gain an edge in today's environmentally sensitive market by incorporating sustainability into their customers' experiences at every stage of the buying cycle.

Sustainable consumption, corporate innovation, and customer experience all work together to push the market in the direction of a greener tomorrow. Together, these factors are essential for solving our most severe environmental problems, expanding the economy, satisfying customers, and achieving corporate goals.

There are a number of important reasons why it is crucial to have a firm grasp of the relationship between sustainable consumption, corporate innovation, and customer experience in China. China's influence on global sustainability trends is substantial duc to the country's status as the world's most populated and second-largest economy (Zreik, 2023a). Increasing numbers of well-off consumers have a domino effect on the environment both at home and abroad. The Chinese government's promotion of an "ecological civilization" is hastening the adoption of environmentally friendly policies and procedures, making the country an intriguing case study.

China is become a major player on the international stage for commercial innovation. Large IT businesses and innovative startups alike may be found across the country, each one a pioneer in sustainable business methods. China's thriving economy and policy climate make it an ideal testing ground for innovative approaches to sustainability on the part of the country's corporate sector (Greeven, Yip, & Wei, 2023). If other markets want to strike a similar balance between economic growth and environmental responsibility, they may learn a lot from studying these developments.

Particularly among China's expanding middle class, the importance of focusing on the customer experience as a key business factor is rising. Consumers in China are becoming more conscious of environmental issues, and as a result, they are giving preference to companies that share their beliefs. Because of this change, companies now have to offer eco-friendly options and integrate sustainability into their service delivery. Understanding how Chinese companies are creating these experiences can teach companies throughout the world important lessons.

CONTEXT OF SUSTAINABLE CONSUMPTION IN CHINA

The Socio-Economic Characteristics Shaping Sustainable Consumption

Sustainable consumption trends in China are heavily impacted by the country's unique socioeconomic profile. China's consumption habits are especially relevant to global sustainability because of the country's large population. The rising purchasing power of the middle class is a direct result of the country's fast economic expansion over the previous few decades. China's huge population and growing middle class together provide for a huge consumer market with varied tastes and preferences (Cui, 2014).

The level of living in China has risen dramatically as the country's economy has developed. As a result of this expansion, consumers' tastes have shifted toward those that are more high-end, specialized, and focused on quality. The rising demand for eco-friendly goods is directly related to the public's heightened awareness of and concern for global warming.

Sustainable consumption is also heavily influenced by the policies of the Chinese government. The government has made protecting the environment and fostering sustainable development a top priority, supporting causes like the "ecological civilization" and pushing for a circular economy in its planning and policymaking (Lo, 2020). These mandates help shift both the business and consumer markets toward more environmentally friendly operations and goods.

There's also the advent of digitalization to consider. China has one of the world's highest internet penetration rates, making Chinese e-commerce platforms important hubs for the spread of news and the sale of goods (Couture et al., 2021). These mediums are crucial for the dissemination of environmental awareness and eco-friendly products to the general public.

But it's important to remember that there are significant economic and social gaps inside China, whether you're comparing urban and rural areas or provinces. Because of these differences, the landscape for sustainable consumption is more complicated than it otherwise would be.

Shift in Consumers' Behavior Towards Greener Products

The growing demand for environmentally friendly goods in China is a major development in this field. Consumers in China have been increasingly environmentally conscious in recent years. The media's increased focus on environmental issues, the government's policies that prioritize sustainable development, and the growing influence of global sustainability trends are all contributors. That's why an increasing number of Chinese shoppers are thinking twice about how their purchases will affect the planet.

The growing purchasing power of China's middle class is driving increased interest in environmentally friendly goods. They have more spare income to spend, so they are preferring products that are good for the environment, ethical, and socially responsible (Li, 2010). There has been a significant movement in consumer values, and this demographic is now prepared to pay more for environmentally friendly goods.

In addition, millennial and Gen Z buyers are driving this change in consumer behavior toward more sustainable practices. Younger generations that have grown up with increased access to the internet and global culture have demonstrated a marked preference for eco-friendly products and labels (Song, Qin, & Qin, 2020).

Chinese businesses are adapting by creating and promoting environmentally friendly goods. Organic foods and cosmetics are just the beginning; there are also eco-friendly cars and home equipment available. To meet the growing demand for eco-friendly goods, companies are investing in waste-free production processes and eco-friendly packaging (Ottman, Stafford, & Hartman, 2006).

The rise of digital tools has contributed to this change in consumer habits. Consumers now have access to a plethora of online resources that allow them to investigate the environmental friendliness of various companies and goods. Green items are being highlighted on e-commerce sites, and sustainability ratings are being incorporated so that buyers can make educated decisions.

The changing preferences of Chinese customers toward environmentally friendly goods is a major trend. It exemplifies the growing influence of environmental concerns on consumer choices and the consequent shift in the market toward more sustainable business methods.

The Impact of the Rising Middle Class and Increased Environmental Awareness

The sustainable consumer landscape in China will be significantly impacted by the country's expanding middle class and growing environmental consciousness. China's rapid economic development over the past three decades has resulted in a burgeoning middle class with greater purchasing power and improved living conditions (Zreik, Iqbal, & Rahman, 2022). This generational change is having far-reaching effects on the consumer market, one of which is a rising interest in eco-friendly goods and services.

The Chinese middle class, which is more educated and well-connected than ever before, is showing a growing preference for eco-friendly and ethically made goods, in addition to those that just perform well. The demand for organic foods, energy-efficient appliances, eco-friendly personal care items, and electric vehicles has increased as a result of this shift in consumer habits. Opportunities arise for companies that can meet the needs of these customers, who are willing to pay a premium for goods that reflect their commitment to environmental sustainability (Wijekoon & Sabri, 2021).

Also, the general populace in China has become much more environmentally conscious. This newfound awareness can be attributed in part to the media's coverage of environmental issues, improved education, and the impact of global sustainability trends. Increased environmental regulation and the Chinese government's advocacy of an "ecological civilization" have also contributed to a heightened sense of environmental consciousness.

As people become more aware of the impact they can have on the planet, they become more vocal about their demands for environmentally friendly items. As a result of this shift, businesses are being more open about their sustainability efforts and implementing concrete plans to lessen their negative impact on the planet.

Sustainable consumption is on the rise in China due to the country's expanding middle class and growing environmental consciousness. They are stimulating demand for environmentally friendly goods and services and driving innovation in the business sector. This change is having a profound effect on China's consumer market and the global sustainability movement as a whole.

INNOVATIVE SUSTAINABLE BUSINESS MODELS IN CHINA

Analysis of Sustainability-Oriented Strategies in Chinese Businesses

Sustainable business strategies have flourished in China as a result of the country's fast-paced economic and environmental development. Chinese businesses across all sectors are implementing sustainability-focused strategies in order to keep up with the increasing demand for environmentally friendly goods, conform to more stringent environmental rules, and gain a competitive edge in the marketplace.

The circular economy concept, which seeks to minimize waste and make the most of resources, is one strategy that many Chinese enterprises are implementing

(Su et al., 2013). In contrast to the classic linear economy (take, make, use, dispose), the design, manufacture, consumption, and recycling phases of a product's lifecycle are all taken into account in this model. It promotes resource efficiency, reduced environmental impact, and possible economic savings by emphasizing material reduction, reuse, and recycling. Some businesses are even finding new things to sell by repurposing old ones.

The use of environmentally friendly technologies is still another option. The manufacturing industry, for instance, is making significant investments in clean energy, pollution prevention, and energy-efficient technology. The rapid growth of China's electric vehicle industry, spearheaded by firms like BYD and NIO, is another instance of how corporations are employing technology to lessen their goods' negative effects on the environment (Li, 2015).

Sustainability is being included into the value chains of a growing number of Chinese firms. Sustainable techniques include using less resources during production, such as water and electricity, and using environmentally friendly materials for packaging. Responsible marketing strategies are also being implemented by businesses to encourage sustainable consumption. One example is the disclosure of product-level environmental impacts.

Furthermore, some companies are employing cutting-edge business models that encourage sharing or renting rather than buying, hence decreasing the desire for new products. One prominent use of this tactic is the rise of bike-sharing services like Ofo and Mobike (Reddick, Zheng, & Liu, 2020).

Examples From Various Industries, Ranging From Tech Giants to Startups

Numerous case studies from a wide range of sectors illustrate China's progress toward sustainable development. This includes both established companies with green divisions and newer, more nimble ones that are making strides in the sustainability field.

When it comes to environmentally responsible business practices, internet giants like Alibaba and Tencent are setting the standard. Alibaba's cloud division, Alibaba Cloud, is leading the charge to make data centers more efficient and cut down on emissions. The Green Data Center can reduce the company's energy consumption by as much as 70% (Gupta, Kumar, & Karam, 2020). Meanwhile, Tencent is emphasizing eco-friendly packaging, energy-efficient data centers, and the promotion of digital solutions to lower paper use (Cenci et al., 2022).

JD.com, the largest online retailer in China, is yet another illustration. It is encouraging sustainable packaging in an effort to cut down on waste, investing extensively in renewable energy sources, and integrating energy-saving technologies throughout its vast logistics network. To meet the growing demand for eco-friendly items, e-commerce giant JD.com has developed a sustainable goods sales platform (Shen & Sun, 2023).

When it comes to electric vehicles (EVs), BYD and NIO are at the forefront of innovation. BYD, one of the leading EV producers in the world, is pioneering cleaner, more powerful battery solutions (Sperling, 2018). But NIO isn't only making EVs; they're also developing battery swapping technology, which could be a long-term answer to the problem of long EV charging sessions.

There has been a rise in the number of Chinese companies with a focus on environmentally friendly methods in the food business. Plant-based meat alternatives are becoming increasingly feasible thanks to the work of companies like Hey Maet and Zhenmeat (Sun, Ortega, & Lin, 2023). Their products are geared toward the increasing number of Chinese shoppers who are worried about the effects of their meat intake on the planet.

Meanwhile new fashion companies like Neemic and Particle Fever are leading sustainable practices within the garment industry. The "closed-loop" system employed by Neemic involves taking back old garments from customers to recycle the fabric, thereby reducing waste. The company also employs a water recycling system in its dyeing process, which significantly lowers water consumption and pollution. Similarly, Particle Fever has adopted the Global Organic Textile Standard (GOTS) certification, ensuring that the organic fibers used are socially and environmentally responsible from the harvest to the final product. Both companies have integrated Radio-Frequency Identification (RFID) technology into their supply chain to track the lifecycle of each product, thereby ensuring accountability and transparency.

Moreover, these companies are active in consumer education, offering workshops and publishing reports to raise awareness about sustainable fashion. This is in line with the "Norm Activation Model" theory, which states that awareness-raising can activate social norms and result in more sustainable consumer behavior (Zreik, 2023b). Therefore, these examples provide evidence that these companies are not just reducing their environmental footprint but also promoting sustainable consumption among their customer base.

How Businesses Are Reconfiguring Their Value Chains to Foster Sustainability

Businesses typically need to make adjustments across the board in order to promote sustainability, including in procurement, production, distribution, and even customer service (Nidumolu, Prahalad, & Rangaswami, 2009). By adjusting their operations in this way, companies can lessen their negative effects on the environment, cut down on waste, and develop more eco-friendly goods and services.

In China, businesses are starting at the outset, with the procurement phase, by selecting suppliers who employ ethical and environmentally friendly procedures. This involves making sure that vendors follow fair labor policies and selecting products that are either recycled or sustainably generated. For instance, Alibaba has set up the Alibaba Sustainability Fund to encourage its suppliers to use greener production methods (Zhou, Chen, & Li, 2018).

To lessen their impact on the environment, several companies are adopting more eco-friendly production methods and equipment. More and more factories are switching to energy-efficient machinery to cut down on pollution and waste. For instance, Huawei, a global leader in telecommunications and information technology, has drastically reduced its energy use by implementing an energy management system across all of its production facilities (Huseien & Shah, 2022).

Companies are making efforts to reduce their carbon footprint by improving logistics throughout the distribution phase. For instance, JD.com is cutting down on delivery times and gas usage by making use of its extensive logistical network. The corporation is also funding the purchase of electric delivery trucks and drones to improve the environmental friendliness of their last-mile shipping options (Moshref-Javadi & Winkenbach, 2021).

In the last phase, once a product has been sold, companies are launching programs to increase product durability and recycling. Providing repair services, promoting the return of damaged products for recycling, and designing products for easier disassembly and recycling at the end of their useful lives are all examples of this. Xiaomi, a Chinese smartphone manufacturer, has launched a recycling scheme that pays customers to dispose of their old phones in an environmentally responsible manner (Vishwakarma et al., 2022).

Although difficult to adopt, these shifts are assisting Chinese companies in developing value chains that are not only effective and lucrative, but also sustainable. These companies are setting themselves up for long-term success in an increasingly environmentally sensitive market by rearranging their value chains to promote sustainability.

While China has made significant strides towards sustainability, particularly in renewable energy adoption and eco-friendly consumer products, it remains one of the largest emitters of greenhouse gases globally. Although advances in renewable energy are noteworthy, a more comprehensive analysis should also consider the country's productive aspects. For example, while China is expanding its renewable energy infrastructure, it simultaneously remains heavily reliant on coal-based industries, which contribute to greenhouse gas emissions (Robinson, Blair, & McDonough, 2021). Such a paradox raises questions about the effectiveness of the transition to cleaner energy, especially from a consumer perspective. Consumers may be using eco-friendly products, but if those products are manufactured in factories reliant on fossil fuels, the net sustainability gain is negated. This dual nature of progress in China's sustainability journey necessitates a nuanced discussion that moves beyond energy initiatives to include the manufacturing and production sectors.

THE ROLE OF CUSTOMER EXPERIENCE IN SUSTAINABLE CONSUMPTION

How Businesses Are Creating Unique and Engaging Experiences for Consumers

The importance of the customer experience in promoting sustainable consumption is especially pronounced in the Chinese market. As customers become more concerned about environmental issues, they want more than simply eco-friendly options. They're on the lookout for brands that care about the environment just as much as they do and can provide them with experiences that complement their eco-friendly way of living. As a result, companies are putting more effort into creating memorable and exciting sustainable experiences.

Sustainable practices are increasingly being incorporated into company histories as a marketing tool. Businesses are effectively incorporating the story of sustainability into their corporate identity by being open about their sustainability initiatives, environmental impact, and ethical practices. By using narratives, companies can make purchasing environmentally friendly products more than just a transaction by helping customers feel more connected to the company and its values.

Sustainable principles are also being included into the design of in-store activities. Some examples of these efforts include the use of renewable energy sources and a decrease in plastic use in retailers. These tangible marks of the company's dedication to environmental responsibility elevate the shopping experience.

In addition, companies are using the internet to have conversations with customers about environmental concerns. Businesses can use the internet as a way to spread information about environmental issues, their own sustainability efforts, and green products to consumers. Alipay's Ant Forest function, for instance, makes keeping track of your carbon footprint a game, making eco-friendly behavior more appealing (Ashfaq et al., 2021).

Businesses are considering not just the product's long-term viability, but also the customer's overall impression of the product while designing it. Eco-friendly product development entails making goods that serve their intended purposes well, look good, and are simple to operate.

Finally, sustainable customer experiences can be further enhanced by post-purchase services including recycling programs, repair services, and consumer education about product maintenance and disposal. Using these services, consumers may get the most use out of their purchases, dispose of them in an environmentally friendly manner, and cut back on their consumption.

Analysis of How These Experiences Are Driving Customer Satisfaction and Loyalty

In line with global sustainability efforts, China has increased its investment in renewable energy technologies. Between 2010 and 2020, the country's wind energy capacity grew by approximately 20%, contributing to a 15% reduction in carbon emissions during the same period (Robinson, Blair, & McDonough, 2021). This growth not only signifies China's commitment to sustainability but also serves as a benchmark for other nations in their quest for cleaner energy.

Especially in China's ever-evolving consumer market, customer happiness and loyalty have soared because to businesses' efforts to include sustainability into their offerings (Zreik, 2022). Taking a comprehensive approach to sustainability and incorporating it into all aspects of the consumer experience demonstrates this clearly.

First, building consumer trust requires being open and honest about your company's environmental initiatives. Customers value companies that are transparent about their efforts to reduce their environmental effect and increase their sustainability practices (Szabo & Webster, 2021). This kind of openness strengthens a brand's trust and brings its customers closer to the company. Customers are more satisfied and loyal as a result of this strengthened connection.

Second, consumer happiness can be increased by participation in interesting and informative sustainability-related activities. Consumers can feel like they are contributing to solutions to environmental problems by doing things like playing games that encourage sustainable behavior or reading informative content about these problems. When customers are happy with their purchases, they are more likely to repurchase from that company in the future.

Thirdly, customer happiness can be increased by the greater product experiences delivered by sustainable products. Customers are more likely to be pleased with their purchases when companies provide eco-friendly options without sacrificing quality, utility, or appearance. When consumers have a good time with a product, they are more likely to keep coming back for more.

Recycling programs and repair services are only two examples of after-sale sustainability-focused services that can improve the customer experience. Customers will see that the company is concerned about the environmental impact of their purchases throughout the product's lifetime if they offer such services. Taking a holistic approach to sustainability like this has the potential to increase customer happiness and loyalty.

Last but not least, customers tend to feel more connected to one another when companies prioritize sustainability in all aspects of their operations. Customers' loyalty might be boosted if they feel they are part of a community that shares their values and concerns for the planet.

SUSTAINABLE MARKETING IN CHINA

The Implications of the Shift Towards Sustainable Consumption for Marketing Strategies

Existing theoretical frameworks in the field of sustainable marketing highlight the transformative nature of the practice. For example, the 'Triple Bottom Line' theory postulates that companies achieve long-term success by focusing on social, environmental, and economic considerations (He et al., 2019). Research shows that marketing strategies have undergone a paradigm shift, incorporating these Triple Bottom Line elements into product development, customer engagement, and even stakeholder communication. More concretely, Porter and Kramer's concept of "Creating Shared Value" argues that companies should generate economic value in a manner that also produces value for society by addressing societal needs and challenges (Porter and Kramer, 2011). In China, companies like Alibaba and Tencent are already leveraging technology to make supply chains more transparent, thereby reducing waste and building sustainability from the ground up.

Marketers in China need to adapt their strategies as the country faces a move toward more sustainable consumption (Sun et al., 2021). Creating, conveying, and delivering value in a way that takes into account stakeholders' social, environmental, and financial interests is the crux of sustainable marketing, which is rapidly gaining ground in China's cutting-edge corporate culture.

As a first step, marketers need to think about long-term impacts while creating new products. This necessitates the creation of goods that not only fill a market niche but also reduce negative effects on the natural world. Everything that goes into making a product, from the selection of raw materials to the implementation of manufacturing techniques, should be done with sustainability in mind.

Second, as awareness of the importance of sustainable consumption grows, companies will need to adjust their methods of customer outreach. Having open communication is essential. Companies should be transparent about their sustainability initiatives so that customers can make educated purchases. Brands should avoid greenwashing at all costs since it can seriously damage their reputation by fraudulently portraying an impression of environmental commitment. Instead, organizations should be honest and open about the sustainability efforts they are undertaking.

In addition, the advertising approaches need to be long-lasting. In other words, we need to stop using intrusive, generic marketing strategies and instead focus on tailoring our messages to individual customers. With its ability to zero in on certain demographics and track customer behavior, digital marketing holds great promise as a tool for long-term marketing success.

Last but not least, the sustainable consumption trend affects marketing in the post-sale phase. A sustainable marketing plan will include eco-friendly packaging, swift shipping, and life-extension initiatives like service centers and recycling programs (Berndroth, 2013).

Marketers face both difficulties and possibilities in China as the country moves toward more sustainable consumption habits. They have to take a hard look at their tried-and-true methods of advertising and make some adjustments. However, it also provides an opportunity to strengthen bonds with customers, set the brand apart, and aid in the long-term growth of society.

Role of Sustainable Marketing in Building Positive Brand Image and Driving Market Growth

There's a growing body of evidence to suggest that sustainable marketing practices are not merely ethical decisions but also strategic ones. Theoretical frameworks like the 'Sustainability Marketing Mix' indicate that adapting traditional 4Ps (Product, Place, Price, Promotion) to include sustainability considerations can positively influence consumer behavior and brand image (Dangelico & Vocalelli, 2017). A study by Cone Communications found that 87% of consumers stated they would purchase a product because a company supported an issue they care about (Cone, 2008). Thus, by adopting sustainable marketing practices, businesses can build a strong, positive brand image.

Furthermore, empirical evidence supports these theoretical considerations. According to a paper by Katsikeas, Leonidou, & Zeriti (2016), companies that integrate sustainability in their marketing practices have a competitive advantage, demonstrating higher market share and customer loyalty. A survey conducted by Nielsen found that brands with a commitment to sustainability grew more than four times compared to non-sustainable brands over a year (Vătămănescu et al., 2021).

In today's environmentally aware consumer market, sustainable marketing is crucial for developing a favorable brand image and driving market growth. Consumers are expressing a preference for sustainable brands as they grow more conscious of environmental challenges. Thus, sustainable marketing has emerged as a critical role in molding opinions and influencing purchases.

Incorporating sustainability into marketing strategies helps organizations establish credibility as ethical, innovative leaders in their industries (Leonidou, 2017). In order to stand out in a competitive market, businesses need to effectively communicate their sustainability initiatives to their target audience. Consumers are more likely to trust and remain loyal to a brand that they perceive to be environmentally conscious.

Moreover, substantial market expansion is possible as a result of sustainable advertising. Businesses who provide and successfully promote eco-friendly goods stand to benefit from the rising demand for such goods. Green products and sustainable marketing tactics can increase a company's customer base and revenue by appealing to environmentally concerned consumers (Katsikeas, Leonidou, & Zeriti, 2016).

In addition, sustainable advertising might create fresh commercial chances. To combat environmental issues, for instance, companies might innovate by releasing cutting-edge sustainable products and services that attract new customers and fuel expansion. It's also possible for businesses to grow in regions with more severe environmental legislation or a more environmentally conscious consumer base.

A recent study indicates that firms engaging in transparent and authentic sustainable marketing saw a 20% increase in customer loyalty and a 15% increase in market share within two years (Watson et al., 2018). The data supports the argument that sustainable marketing isn't just an ethical obligation but a sound business strategy that can bolster a company's brand image and drive market growth.

Saving money through more environmentally friendly marketing practices can potentially boost profits (Cronin, 2011). Sustainable materials and energy-saving techniques, for instance, can help keep manufacturing prices down. In a similar vein, digital marketing strategies may be friendlier to the budget and the environment than more conventional approaches.

CONCLUSION

Some important insights into the fast-changing world of sustainable consumption, company innovation, and customer experience have been revealed through the research of the green route in China. What we are seeing in China is emblematic of a global movement toward sustainability, which is altering the ways in which businesses function and consumers make decisions.

The combination of China's unique socioeconomic setting, increasing middle class, and increased environmental consciousness has sparked a major shift toward sustainable consumption. As a result of this change, companies are adapting their methods to promote sustainability through measures like reorganizing their supply chains and developing fresh approaches to marketing. A growing awareness of environmental issues and the personal and societal advantages associated with addressing these concerns has pushed Chinese consumers to tilt toward greener product choices.

In response, companies of all sizes are going above and beyond to provide customers with services that will keep them coming back. They are using the story of sustainability to influence interactions with customers, which is boosting loyalty and satisfaction. This change toward greener consumer habits has far-reaching effects on advertising efforts in China and beyond. Positive brand perception and sales growth are two areas where sustainable marketing practices are making a significant impact.

After giving these results some thought, it's clear that the push for sustainability is more than a passing fad; it represents a sea change in the way our global socioeconomic systems function. Every business, every consumer, and every market will be impacted by this change. More than that, it shows how interdependent we all are. Businesses and consumers in China are making strides toward global sustainability goals, and their actions are inspiring others across the world to do the same.

This chapter has shed light on the importance of sustainability in today's business and consumer practices. The Chinese experience can be both a source of motivation and a test of ability. To witness the creativity, flexibility, and success of firms in a sustainable economy, as well as the profound impact that individual consumers can make through their purchasing decisions, is truly motivating.

However, it is also a difficult task. The need to disrupt the status quo and come up with novel, sustainable ideas that work in your industry, while also finding ways to connect with customers on a deeper, more emotional level than just making a purchase. The road to long-term viability is rocky. To succeed, one must think outside the box, keep at it, and not be afraid to question conventional wisdom. However, as evidenced by the Chinese market, the path to sustainability is not only essential, but also rich with chances for expansion, distinctiveness, and long-term success.

In light of the insights gleaned from this study, practitioners should take proactive steps to align their business models and marketing strategies with sustainable practices. Notably, organizations should implement a rigorous audit of their supply chains to identify areas where sustainable practices can be integrated, from sourcing raw materials to distribution. Corporate leadership should foster a culture that prioritizes sustainability as a key performance indicator, alongside traditional financial metrics.

This can be facilitated through employee training programs focused on sustainable practices and by providing incentives for departments that achieve notable reductions in waste or energy consumption. Moreover, businesses should publicly disclose their sustainability performance, both successes and areas needing improvement. Transparency in this regard not only satisfies regulatory requirements but also builds consumer trust, thereby enhancing brand image. In summary, the road to sustainability is fraught with challenges but is indispensable for long-term viability and success. It's high time that practitioners take heed of the consumer and market shifts toward sustainability and adapt accordingly.

Sustainability is the key to a company's success in the future. If we accept this fact now, we can make the world a better place tomorrow in terms of sustainability, equity, and prosperity. So, let's learn from China's eco-friendly example and figure out how to implement similar practices in our own lives. After all, we're all on the same path toward a better, more sustainable future.

REFERENCES

Anderson, S., & Anderson, J. (2022). Leave some for me! The role of marketing in influencing responsible consumption during times of crisis. *Journal of Strategic Marketing*, *30*(7), 703–721. doi:10.1080/0965254X.2020.1833075

Ashfaq, M., Zhang, Q., Ali, F., Waheed, A., & Nawaz, S. (2021). You plant a virtual tree, we'll plant a real tree: Understanding users' adoption of the Ant Forest mobile gaming application from a behavioral reasoning theory perspective. *Journal of Cleaner Production*, *310*, 127394. doi:10.1016/j.jclepro.2021.127394

Bascur, C., & Rusu, C. (2020). Customer experience in retail: A systematic literature review. *Applied Sciences (Basel, Switzerland)*, *10*(21), 7644. doi:10.3390/app10217644

Berndroth, J. (2013). *Theorising institutional processes and strategies: Case studies of sustainability policies on the macro and micro levels* [Doctoral dissertation, WHU-Otto Beisheim School of Management].

Cenci, M. P., Scarazzato, T., Munchen, D. D., Dartora, P. C., Veit, H. M., Bernardes, A. M., & Dias, P. R. (2022). Eco-Friendly Electronics—A Comprehensive Review. *Advanced Materials Technologies*, *7*(2), 2001263. doi:10.1002/admt.202001263

Cone. (2008). *Past. Present. Future. 25th anniversary of cause marketing*. Cone Inc. http://www.coneinc.com/content1187

Couture, V., Faber, B., Gu, Y., & Liu, L. (2021). Connecting the countryside via e-commerce: Evidence from China. *American Economic Review: Insights*, *3*(1), 35–50. doi:10.1257/aeri.20190382

Cronin, J. J. Jr, Smith, J. S., Gleim, M. R., Ramirez, E., & Martinez, J. D. (2011). Green marketing strategies: An examination of stakeholders and the opportunities they present. *Journal of the Academy of Marketing Science*, *39*(1), 158–174. doi:10.100711747-010-0227-0

Cui, G. (2014). Segmenting China's consumer market: A hybrid approach. In Consumer Behavior in Asia: Issues and Marketing Practice (pp. 55-76). Routledge.

Dangelico, R. M., & Vocalelli, D. (2017). “Green Marketing”: An analysis of definitions, strategy steps, and tools through a systematic review of the literature. *Journal of Cleaner Production*, *165*, 1263–1279. doi:10.1016/j.jclepro.2017.07.184

Dyllick, T., & Muff, K. (2016). Clarifying the meaning of sustainable business: Introducing a typology from business-as-usual to true business sustainability. *Organization & Environment*, *29*(2), 156–174. doi:10.1177/1086026615575176

Gómez-Suárez, M., & Yagüe, M. J. (2021). Making sense from experience: How a sustainable multi-sensory event spurs word-of-mouth recommendation of a destination brand. *Sustainability (Basel)*, *13*(11), 5873. doi:10.3390u13115873

Greeven, M. J., Yip, G. S., & Wei, W. (2023). *Pioneers, hidden champions, changemakers, and underdogs: Lessons from China's innovators*. MIT Press.

Gupta, S., Kumar, V., & Karam, E. (2020). New-age technologies-driven social innovation: What, how, where, and why? *Industrial Marketing Management*, *89*, 499–516. doi:10.1016/j.indmarman.2019.09.009

He, Q., Gallear, D., Ghobadian, A., & Ramanathan, R. (2019). Managing knowledge in supply chains: A catalyst to triple bottom line sustainability. *Production Planning and Control*, *30*(5-6), 448–463. doi:10.1080/09537287.2018.1501814

Huseien, G. F., & Shah, K. W. (2022). A review on 5G technology for smart energy management and smart buildings in Singapore. *Energy and AI*, *7*, 100116. doi:10.1016/j.egyai.2021.100116

Katsikeas, C. S., Leonidou, C. N., & Zeriti, A. (2016). Eco-friendly product development strategy: Antecedents, outcomes, and contingent effects. *Journal of the Academy of Marketing Science*, *44*(6), 660–684. doi:10.100711747-015-0470-5

Leonidou, L. C., Christodoulides, P., Kyrgidou, L. P., & Palihawadana, D. (2017). Internal drivers and performance consequences of small firm green business strategy: The moderating role of external forces. *Journal of Business Ethics*, *140*(3), 585–606. doi:10.100710551-015-2670-9

Li, C. (Ed.). (2010). *China's emerging middle class: beyond economic transformation*. Brookings Institution Press.

Li, Z. (2015). Eco-innovation and firm growth: Leading edge of China's electric vehicle business. *International Journal of Automotive Technology and Management*, *15*(3), 226–243. doi:10.1504/IJATM.2015.070281

Lo, K. (2020). Ecological civilization, authoritarian environmentalism, and the eco-politics of extractive governance in China. *The Extractive Industries and Society, 7*(3), 1029–1035. doi:10.1016/j.exis.2020.06.017

Moshref-Javadi, M., & Winkenbach, M. (2021). Applications and Research avenues for drone-based models in logistics: A classification and review. *Expert Systems with Applications, 177*, 114854. doi:10.1016/j.eswa.2021.114854

Neves, S. A., & Marques, A. C. (2022). Drivers and barriers in the transition from a linear economy to a circular economy. *Journal of Cleaner Production, 341*, 130865. doi:10.1016/j.jclepro.2022.130865

Nidumolu, R., Prahalad, C. K., & Rangaswami, M. R. (2009). Why sustainability is now the key driver of innovation. *Harvard Business Review, 87*(9), 56–64.

Ottman, J. A., Stafford, E. R., & Hartman, C. L. (2006). Avoiding green marketing myopia: Ways to improve consumer appeal for environmentally preferable products. *Environment, 48*(5), 22–36. doi:10.3200/ENVT.48.5.22-36

Porter, M. E., & Kramer, M. R. (2011). Creating shared value. How to Re-invent capitalism – and unleash a wave of innovation and growth. *Harvard Business Review, 89*(1), 62–77.

Reddick, C. G., Zheng, Y., & Liu, T. (2020). Roles of government in regulating the sharing economy: A case study of bike sharing in China. *Information Polity, 25*(2), 219–235. doi:10.3233/IP-190207

Robinson, S. A., Blair, C., & McDonough, M. (2021). China's climate ambition: Revisiting its First Nationally Determined Contribution and centering a just transition to clean energy. *Energy Policy, 155*, 112350. doi:10.1016/j.enpol.2021.112350

Shen, Z. M., & Sun, Y. (2023). Strengthening supply chain resilience during COVID-19: A case study of JD. com. *Journal of Operations Management, 69*(3), 359–383. doi:10.1002/joom.1161

Song, Y., Qin, Z., & Qin, Z. (2020). Green marketing to gen Z consumers in China: Examining the mediating factors of an eco-label–informed purchase. *SAGE Open, 10*(4), 2158244020963573. doi:10.1177/2158244020963573

Sperling, D. (2018). *Three revolutions: Steering automated, shared, and electric vehicles to a better future*. Island Press. doi:10.5822/978-1-61091-906-7

Su, B., Heshmati, A., Geng, Y., & Yu, X. (2013). A review of the circular economy in China: Moving from rhetoric to implementation. *Journal of Cleaner Production, 42*, 215–227. doi:10.1016/j.jclepro.2012.11.020

Sun, J., Ortega, D. L., & Lin, W. (2023). Food values drive Chinese consumers' demand for meat and milk substitutes. *Appetite*, *181*, 106392. doi:10.1016/j.appet.2022.106392 PMID:36450325

Sun, X., Su, W., Guo, X., & Tian, Z. (2021). The impact of awe induced by COVID-19 pandemic on green consumption behavior in China. *International Journal of Environmental Research and Public Health*, *18*(2), 543. doi:10.3390/ijerph18020543 PMID:33440719

Szabo, S., & Webster, J. (2021). Perceived greenwashing: The effects of green marketing on environmental and product perceptions. *Journal of Business Ethics*, *171*(4), 719–739. doi:10.100710551-020-04461-0

Vătămănescu, E. M., Dabija, D. C., Gazzola, P., Cegarro-Navarro, J. G., & Buzzi, T. (2021). Before and after the outbreak of covid-19: Linking fashion companies' corporate social responsibility approach to consumers' demand for sustainable products. *Journal of Cleaner Production*, *321*, 128945. doi:10.1016/j.jclepro.2021.128945

Vishwakarma, S., Kumar, V., Arya, S., Tembhare, M., Dutta, D., & Kumar, S. (2022). E-waste in Information and Communication Technology Sector: Existing scenario, management schemes and initiatives. *Environmental Technology & Innovation*, *27*, 102797. doi:10.1016/j.eti.2022.102797

Watson, R., Wilson, H. N., Smart, P., & Macdonald, E. K. (2018). Harnessing difference: A capability-based framework for stakeholder engagement in environmental innovation. *Journal of Product Innovation Management*, *35*(2), 254–279. doi:10.1111/jpim.12394

Wijekoon, R., & Sabri, M. F. (2021). Determinants that influence green product purchase intention and behavior: A literature review and guiding framework. *Sustainability (Basel)*, *13*(11), 6219. doi:10.3390u13116219

Zhou, Q., Chen, X., & Li, S. (2018). Innovative financial approach for agricultural sustainability: A case study of Alibaba. *Sustainability (Basel)*, *10*(3), 891. doi:10.3390u10030891

Zreik, M. (2022). The Regional Comprehensive Economic Partnership (RCEP) for the Asia–Pacific region and world. *Journal of Economic and Administrative Sciences*.

Zreik, M. (2023a). Analytical study on Foreign Direct Investment Divestment Inflows and Outflows in Developing Economies: Evidence of China. *Chinese Economy*, *56*(6), 1–16. doi:10.1080/10971475.2023.2193118

Zreik, M. (2023b). Sustainable and Smart Supply Chains in China: A Multidimensional Approach. In B. Bentalha, A. Hmioui, & L. Alla (Eds.), *Integrating Intelligence and Sustainability in Supply Chains* (pp. 179–197). IGI Global. doi:10.4018/979-8-3693-0225-5.ch010

Zreik, M., Iqbal, B. A., & Rahman, M. N. (2022). Outward FDI: Determinants and Flows in Emerging Economies: Evidence from China. *China and WTO Review*, *8*(2), 385–402. doi:10.14330/cwr.2022.8.2.07

KEY TERMS AND DEFINITIONS

Carbon Footprint: The total amount of carbon dioxide and other greenhouse gases emitted by a product, service, or organization over a specific time frame.

Circular Economy: An economic system that aims to eliminate waste and promote the continual use of resources by encouraging reuse, refurbishment, and recycling.

Consumer Ethical Responsibility: The awareness and consideration by consumers of the social and environmental impacts of their purchasing decisions.

Eco-labeling: The practice of marking products with a label to certify that they meet certain environmental standards, helping consumers make informed choices.

Greenwashing: The deceptive use of marketing to portray a company's products, services, or operations as more environmentally friendly than they actually are.

Life-Cycle Assessment: A technique to assess the environmental impact of a product or service throughout its entire life cycle, from raw material extraction to disposal.

Stakeholder Engagement: The process of interacting and communicating with stakeholders, including consumers, employees, suppliers, and communities, to address concerns and share benefits related to sustainability.

Sustainable Marketing: The process of creating, communicating, and delivering value to customers in a manner that considers and improves social, environmental, and economic aspects over the long term.

Sustainable Supply Chain Management: The management of material, information, and capital flows in a manner that minimizes environmental impacts while maximizing customer service and profitability.

Triple Bottom Line: A business approach that considers three dimensions: social, environmental, and financial, aiming to create value in all three areas.

Chapter 4
Sustainability in Fashion:
A Mandatory Approach From Museums

Julio Alexander Gonzalez Liendo
https://orcid.org/0000-0002-4074-0703
Universitat Politècnica de València, Spain

ABSTRACT

Museums have left behind their history as mere warehouses, curators, and art exhibitors. Its cultural and educational functions, intrinsically linked to heritage, have expanded. Theoretically, they have become transmedia communication spaces open to everyone and committed to society and, therefore, to sustainability. The commitment now regarding education delves into the issue of learning, a more participatory process than classic education that is unidirectional and with paternalistic nuances. After renewing their concept, where joint work with the community is emphasized, the museums are assuming their new challenge: sustainability, where governance, the environment, and human capital are the axes of work to achieve a better coexistence on the planet. Thus, the museums that have been involved in exhibitions or activities around fashion invest in transferring knowledge about sustainability in this sector.

INTRODUCTION

Fifteen years after its last update and after long debates at the international level, the General Assembly of the International Council of Museums (ICOM) announced in August 2022 the new museum concept:

A museum is a not-for-profit, permanent institution in the service of society that researches, collects, conserves, interprets, and exhibits tangible and intangible

DOI: 10.4018/978-1-6684-9277-2.ch004

heritage. Open to the public, accessible and inclusive, and museums foster diversity and sustainability. They operate and communicate ethically, professionally, and with the participation of communities, offering varied experiences for education, enjoyment, reflection, and knowledge sharing" (ICOM, 2022, s/p).

By their very original definition, museums have sustainability at their heart. Its function of conserving heritage to guarantee access for the next generations is a very broad sense of sustainability. So, with a renewed and amplified meaning, museum institutions must lead in building a better planet through joint work with the community.

In addition to their work in the preservation, conservation, exhibition, and dissemination of the tangible and intangible heritage of the planet, these organizations must become a fundamental ally to educate the population on issues currently sensitive: environment, human development, and corporate/institutional governance. In this sense, Garzón Castrillón and Ibarra Mares comment that sustainability goes far beyond generating actions to preserve the environment; it invites us to change our lifestyle, in the disproportionate consumption of resources and that significant changes are generated in the social (2014: 54). Thus, to dimension these needs, in 2015, the United Nations (UN) defined 17 Sustainable Development Goals (SDGs), whose purpose is joint work to eradicate poverty, protect the environment and guarantee peace and prosperity for all the inhabitants of the planet. For this reason, it is essential that museums understand that they are a key element, given their cultural and educational nature, for the achievement of the SDGs that are part of the goals established in the 2030 Agenda, the agreement to which most of the countries of the world (Figure 1).

Figure 1. The Sustainable Development Goals
Source: United Nations Organization

Since its appearance in the 18th century, museums have been forced to adapt to different social realities. They have faced revolutions, wars, and social and political crises in short. And as part of this deep commitment to the people, the museums were ready to generate suggestions and recommendations while formulating the SDGs to be part of this new transformation of the public work of the society. However, as highlighted by the Spanish Network for Sustainable Development (REDS), when the goals of the 2030 Agenda were established, "it did not incorporate a specific SDG that would place culture as an essential element for sustainable development" (2021, 9). This situation has made it difficult for museums to incorporate these sustainability goals in an expeditious manner because they have had to understand how to draw lines of work that address or meet the challenges of the SDGs. Garthe (2022, 14) points out: "What is bad for the planet is also bad for museums," referring to the urgent need to understand sustainability as a broader, global concept. Inaction in the face of the planet's social, institutional, and environmental problems will only generate more negative consequences for museums.

Sustainability currently plays a mere secondary role in most of the institutions of our organization. While some exhibitions, repositories, and museums have different approaches to improving their ecological or carbon footprint, there are other, more far-reaching implications related to understanding sustainability as a core value for the museum industry that is often overlooked. One of the main challenges is to take advantage of the good practices of isolated institutions to offer a coherent framework that synchronizes measures that contribute to improving sustainability in all areas of museum operations (Garthe, 2020: s/p).

In this sense, Davies (2011,142) states that museum institutions still do not see sustainability as an action to safeguard the planet's future. Still, they also recognize that coordinated actions must be taken to guarantee success in aspects such as the reduction of inequality (non discrimination, gender equality, equitable education, etc.), as well as serious lines of governance (ethics, transparency, rational use of natural resources, social responsibility, etc.).

In this way, ICOM promotes 2023 as the axis year of the commitment to "Sustainability and Well-being," an initiative welcomed by all the institutions registered in this organization worldwide. Within this group of exhibition spaces, fashion museums and those that organize exhibitions around fashion have been having exemplary actions in terms of sustainability.

Although museums, for some years now, have incorporated energy and water-saving policies, a permanent reduction in the production of printed materials, as well as creative initiatives to ensure their financial existence, it can be said that only now, museums directly linked to or indirectly with clothing, jewelry, shoes, hats and other elements of clothing, have begun to get involved in sustainability actions in front of their different audiences. In this sense, Garthe highlights that virtual and physical exhibitions are very powerful tools for positioning the theme of sustainability among museum audiences and generating commitment from those audiences to be part of the change (2023: 142).

Mosqueda (2018: s/p) reviews how in Amsterdam, The Experience Museum and the NY Local Project design studio in New York created an initiative that seeks to create artistic experiences without generating pollution, without wasting energy, and promoting decent work. The author points out that through the incorporation of information and communication technologies (ICTs), work is being done to make visitors aware of the production process of fashion. They are shown from the materials, the supply chain, and the conditions under which these garments are produced. It is about involving the user/visitor in understanding the entire fashion manufacturing process and raising awareness about the responsible consumption that must be done.

On the other hand, the Victoria & Albert Museum in London organized the exhibition "Modeled by Nature", which has focused on sustainable fashion, with special attention to the collections of designers such as Stella McCartney or Calvin Klein, who have committed to creating haute couture with respect for the environment. In this sense, as reported by the EFE Verde news agency, the curator of the exhibition, Edwina Ehrman, commented that the exhibition highlights the negative impact that the industry has had on the planet, being the most productive sector on the planet. . Having this background, it is later revealed how in the 19th century, changes in the use of animal skins began and, during the 80s, the different demonstrations that took place by activists generated a turning point in fashion.

For its part, the exhibition hall of the Faculty of Fine Arts of the Polytechnic University of Valencia built the exhibition "Sustainable fashion. The textiles of the future", an exhibition that includes the initiatives, projects, and innovations that are available for the fashion sector, to guarantee not only its sustainability but also its circularity. That circularity promotes using resources already generated to reduce the impact of the new generation of materials and supplies. Through this exhibition, which is accompanied by conferences and workshops, the UPV brings the reality of clothing and its future impact closer to the university community and the public, where a more conscious industry in production and consumption is already glimpsed.

Thus, museums, with the fashion industry's support in their different exhibition and educational formats, are developing actions to create awareness among citizens. In the 2023 edition of Mercedes Benz Fashion Week, an initiative called "Because our planet is worth it" was created, which brought together creators such as Ágatha Ruiz de la Prada, Alvarno, Andrés Sardá, Dolores Cortés, Duyos, Hannibal Laguna, Isabel Sanchís, Jorge Vázquez, Malne, Marcos Luengo, Maya Hansen, Otrura and Roberto Torretta, who incorporated pieces made with recycled fabrics into their collections. These pieces, once passed through the catwalks of Madrid Fashion

Week, are part of an exhibition open to the public, organized that also emphasizes the environmental commitment of the beauty and fashion sector.

On the other hand, there is also the experience of the Association of Fashion Creators of Spain (ACME) and The Circular Project, institutions that came together under the concept of Slow Fashion World to create the homonymous exhibition, which allowed designers and brands to convene. fashion designers who already work with sustainability and eco-design model. This is how Ecoalf came together in collaboration with Sybilla, Laura Escribano Atelier, Parallel Dimensions, SayPlease, Susana Nakatani, Sylvia Calvo BCN, Irema, Avasan, Yanapaqi, Sidikai, Monikako kids, Sepiia; or the international companies Coatally, Baraa, Qaytu, Hilar, Ek Katha, Herdentier and Common Texture, who through their different proposals showed how fashion could reduce or cancel its impact on the planet, without renouncing creativity, disruption, and innovation. fun (Rueda, 2018: s/p).

Another Haute Couture brand that has proposed to involve its museum in this sustainable movement is the Salvatore Ferragamo Museum in Florence, Italy, which has staged the exhibition "Transformazioni", which was an exercise in bringing together different Italian exponents of fashion and its methods to reduce the impact of its operations on the environment. "Fashion and materials, such as fibers and textiles, are the exhibition's core, which analyzes new business and consumption models. It combines design and science, an aesthetic based on recycling and reuse, rejecting the throwaway culture, says Sara Sozzani Maino, deputy director of special projects and director of Vogue Talents at Vogue Italia" (Spolini, 2019: s/p.).

MUSEUMS AND EDUCATIONAL STRATEGIES FOR SUSTAINABILITY

As has already been pointed out, museums must be a very powerful ally to raise public awareness regarding the urgency of taking actions that allow for more sustainable institutions. In this order of ideas, museum institutions dedicated to fashion, or those that develop fashion exhibitions as part of their programming, can channel information in three ways: on the one hand, through the narrative of the exhibition, guiding the viewer so that you understand the importance of conscious consumption of fashion, where the quality of the materials and the design affect the permanence of the garment in the closets and its long life. In addition, workshops and courses reveal the production process so that the visitor understands how the planet is affected if these processes are handled improperly. Finally, the museum shops, where textile garments are sold, highlight the traceability of these pieces so that the public is aware of the origin of the fibers, who produces them, how it is done, and how it reaches its stores. hands. In this way, the visitor's awareness is achieved, and the development of their prosumer role is promoted.

On the other hand, it is important to take advantage of museums' positive and consolidated institutional reputation since this becomes a driving force behind educational and awareness-raising activities on different topics, including sustainability. In 2019, professors Van Riel and Heijndijk from Erasmus University presented the report "Why people love art museums", highlighting that the people who participated in their study expressed a high appreciation for museums. Even most people who have not visited a museum in the last three years have a favorable impression of museums. They classify them as trustworthy, honest, and fun. Only 21 percent of non-visitors express negative associations with art museums (Van Riel and Heijndijk, 2019).

Once the study was completed, on average, people scored 79 points out of 100 for the reputation of museums. According to the Erasmus University study, this is significantly above the ratings of companies and corporations, which mostly do not exceed 64.2. This level of reputation, obtained for having guaranteed the custody and protection of art for centuries, allows us to visualize how this manifest credibility should be used to bring the narrative on sustainability closer to the public, encouraging the different museum stakeholders to assume a leading role in this change of consciousness necessary to safeguard the planet. It is about promoting sustainability in its three ESG angles: Environment, Society, and Governance, which guides the efforts of institutions in the search for the sustainability of the planet and where, as Garthe (2023, 164) point out, education and mediation is essential to obtain positive results.

On the other hand, Maloles Cebrián Sotomayor, president of the Association of Museologists and Museographers of Andalusia (AMMA), Spain, highlights that "through the departments of education and cultural mediation, museums have the possibility and the commitment to educate their community in sustainable development. Starting from the fact that education has its own Sustainable Development Goal (SDG), number 4, museums can do a great job through dialogue, debate, and critical thinking".

The expert in accessibility and education highlights that the scope of the SDGs in museums is very broad. In the case of fashion exhibitions, up to eleven of these objectives can be covered. Cebrián Sotomayor insists that museum institutions must commit to generating initiatives to reflect on the value given to clothing to raise awareness of responsible consumption and healthy habits. Then, alluding to SDG 12, she indicates that "museums must promote the rational use of natural energy, but also human resources, and value the cost not only for the environment but also for people." Cebrián Sotomayor maintains that, through the educational actions of museums, they must contemplate a significant number of activities around contents that address "the impact and action that we generate on the climate (SDG 13), underwater life (SDG 14), the life of terrestrial ecosystems (SDG 15), but also on certain populations, since the production of these objects of consumption can be very polluting, consume many natural and energy resources and also on many occasions it is not created favoring decent work and an economic growth (SDG 8) of the countries in which the industry establishes its factories".

It is important to highlight that some initiatives of Spanish museums have been oriented to achieve the incorporation of the public in these environmental practices. The Igartubeiti Farmhouse Museum carried out a series of activities under the theme "The power of museums," which focused on showing the entire production process of linen as a fabric for making clothes. It encouraged visitors to see the different options available to make the most of this textile, including recycling and reusing old garments.

On the other hand, the art center held a workshop "Weaving the fabric, go li(n) o!", through which it brought the visiting family groups of the exhibition space closer to the looms, allowing them to understand the textile process of this noble fabric, which is still used in many garments. "Upcycling: give a new life to your clothes", which was aimed at the adult public, offered, at the hands of the fashion designer Leire Santillán, a conference on the use and reuse of clothing. The participants could fix, modify, decorate, or transform the clothes they brought to the activity.

Another institution that has worked with this approach is the Cristóbal Balenciaga Museoa, in Getaria, Basque Country, which continues the legacy of the Spanish dressmaker and promotes, through its exhibitions and training activities, all the practices of the master. "The beautiful thing is that a garment spends many years with you and that it becomes something symbolic. I think we should embrace them more than get rid of them" (Vázquez, 2021: s/p), this is the conception that the fashion designer Elixabet Perdiguero has about the methods implemented by Cristóbal Balenciaga to ensure the durability of the garments, and that is part of the sustainable contribution of the teacher. Perdiguero, who was trained in the facilities of the Guetarian Museum, recognizes that, as part of his education, sustainability means guaranteeing a design that does not lose its validity and producing high-quality fabrics that remain in perfect condition over time. time.

In this order of ideas, the Cristóbal Balenciaga Museoa has proposed to generate a sustainable strategy by incorporating techniques to reduce the environmental impact during the exhibition's design, production, assembly, and disassembly. Additionally, they have designed activities that enable awareness and education in culture and responsible fashion consumption through the "Customize and recycle" workshops, which teach how to manipulate and transform a garment, allowing them to gain beauty and new value for those who own them.

IS SUSTAINABILITY IN FASHION A SOCIAL DEMAND?

With the beginning of 2023, reports about fashion and its impact on the planet appear. The industry continues to be considered second in the level of contamination. Still, it is recognized that the fashion system has launched an endless number of initiatives to change the landscape, among them the reduction of materials of petroleum origin, the increase in organic materials or of vegetable origin, the promotion of responsible consumption, and of course, the appearance of second-hand fashion, as well as the promotion of circular fashion.

In 2022, the sustainable fashion sales figure reached 6,996 million dollars globally, which seems very powerful but only represents 3.9% of the clothes sold that year. These figures, published by Statista in its report on sustainable fashion, also highlight that "according to forecasts, the positive trend will continue in the next five years until reaching around 6% in 2026" (Orus, 2022, s/p). Thus, it is expected that by 2030, the date on which the goals of the SDGs should be met, this industry will reach sales of 16,000 million dollars in recycling or circular fashion.

With this panorama, the world seems to be moving towards a greater understanding of the importance of rationally consuming fashion. However, García points out how the new generations, inspired by videos on platforms such as Tiktok, return to the industries of ow-cost pages to criminate the purchase of clothing, where the important thing is prices and not quality. "On most occasions, these hauls belong to ultra-low-cost firms such as Fashion Nova, Boohoo, and, above all, Shein, the Chinese firm that has reached a market value of over 90,000 million euros" (García 2022, s/p).

The author insists that, even though the report The State of Fashion, by the consulting firm McKinsey & Corp, has recently published that 43% of young people belonging to Generation Z, the one that has replaced millennials in the analysis of fashion consumption, the viralization of the *haute couture* continues to grow, a trend that is based on buying a lot of clothes, trying them on and returning the ones they don't like. A kind of challenge that is affordable since the orders in these are at most 20 euros.

Faced with this reality, which is increasingly palpable on social media platforms, it is imperative to bet on the formulation of communication and educational strategies that allow raising awareness about the different negative impacts that fashion has on the planet, ranging from modern slavery (long working hours, low income, and subhuman working conditions), irrational use of land and natural resources, use of harmful and polluting chemicals, among others. That, of course, contrasts the initiatives of the world of fashion because it is necessary for the public to have an overview of the problem and be able to be part of the change.

TRANSMEDIA COMMUNICATION OF SUSTAINABILITY

En Fashion as an artistic and heritage manifestation took a long time to enter museum halls. Although it has slightly surpassed that stage, it still has the commitment to continue defending the preponderance of its presence as part of the fine arts. Fashion exhibitions, in the words of the museum director of the Fashion Institute of Technology (FIT), Valerie Steele, during her conference "Deconstructing the canon", at the II Colloquium of Textile and Fashion Researchers, at the Museo del Diseño de Barcelona, pointed out that "it is crucial to understand that fashion is not isolated from culture and society, but rather is part of them. In this way, it will show the attitude of people, their behavior concerning the body, the structure of society, the economy, and politics. Any aspect important to the culture and society of an era will be emphasized in fashion. For example, in the 1960s, there was a youthquake (youth movement), and young generations worldwide became more open and sometimes even more rebellious, which translated into clothing."

This relevance of fashion as a social, political, and cultural manifestation must be transferred to museum visitors because they, in their role as prosumers of the narrative discourse of the exhibitions, will be responsible for amplifying and sharing it. Proper communication, by the museum and its store, of fashion's impact on society will undoubtedly determine how fashion will be appreciated and valued by museum visitors. This powerful and coherent communication begins during the exhibitions, where there is the possibility, through the curatorial text and the exhibition of the garments and their descriptions, of linking said garments with the different forms of expression of the human being.

In this sense, Elena López Gil of the Network of Museums and Digital Strategies (REMED), communication is an intrinsic process in exhibitions because it begins when the exhibition is being created and extends to where the visitors, whether virtual or physicists decide that the speech arrives. The expert insists that the public is the heart of the life of museums, and not communicating efficiently with them is to diminish the relevance of the most key element of the existence of museums.

However, the phenomenon of transmedia communication does not culminate in the exhibition hall since it continues social networks and, in the museum's own digital headquarters, extends to the verbal and non-verbal communication of museum staff in the catalog of the exhibition and, of course, in the stores of the institution. The museum has many and varied tools to communicate the importance of fashion. And, as part of that relevance, it cannot be ignored that fashion continues to be seen as one of the most polluting industries on the planet. So, it is imperative that the museum also become a promoter of the need for a paradigm shift in fashion. Numerous players in the sector, including representatives of Haute Couture, ready-to-wear, and even fast fashion, print initiatives to change the environmental impact of fashion, to become a much more responsible industry without sacrificing profitability. Recycling, for example, single-use bottles such as Balmain (Figure 2) or Ecoalf, are significant contributions in the sector. The production of skins based on pineapple, coconut, banana, or cactus shells are technological advances that contribute to changing the industry.

Figure 2. Dress made by Balmain with recycled PET bottle
Source: Balmain

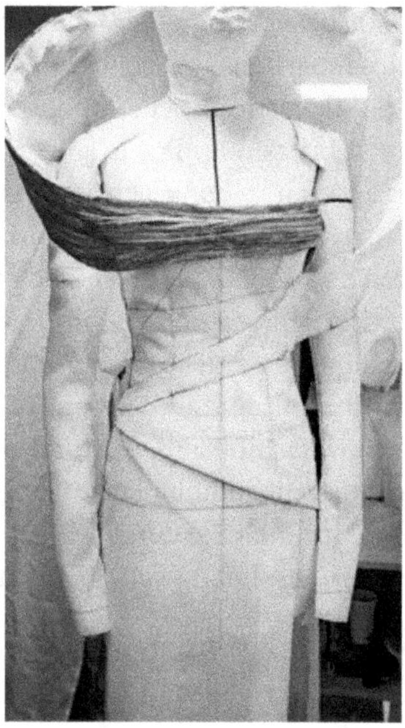

In this sense, museums must be an important part of this change in the sector since, as institutions dedicated to the culture and education of society, they must also be incorporated into the change of consciousness that is required of citizens. The design and management of global communication strategies that allow people to understand the need to modify the consumption habits of clothing, shoes, and accessories is the responsibility of museum institutions since they are part of what Roland Barthes called the "System Fashion." A composite system that is made not only up of fashion designers, producers, suppliers, distributors, and marketers but also those who are linked to it, such as the country or city where it is produced, the governments that promote their national and international commercial strategies in this industry, and, of course, the different cultural actors that take advantage of the contributions of fashion: the cinema, the theater, the museums, and many others that resort to clothing, jewelry, shoes, and other textile items to create art and culture.

Just as the negative impact of fashion is communicated, it is also necessary to disclose the actions that the fashion system implements to change this panorama. Configuring talks, workshops, and exhibitions around sustainability policies in fashion is important. Still, it is also essential to generate discussions with the community about the role of the consumer in the conscious and non-impulsive acquisition of clothing, in recycling, the use and reuse of clothing or savings in the use of detergents and other chemicals in washing garments that do not require as much washing. It is essential to start talking in depth about responsible consumption and circularity through exhibitions, training activities, and, of course, using museums' different digital communication platforms. Communication must be linked to the educational work of the museum. This framework should promote reflection on the consequences for our society and our planet of the lack of healthy habits concerning fashion, which gives the possibility of learning to through the exhibits, which facilitates the sighting of the mistakes and successes of the past, such as a more respectful production and consumption.

One element museum, especially those dedicated to fashion, continue to miss out on is the heavy investment fashion brands make to promote their sustainability initiatives. It is constant to see how firms like Balenciaga, Gucci, Ferragamo, Louis Vuitton, Armani, as well as those recognized as fast fashion such as Inditex, Mango, H&M, Uniqlo, among others, constantly appear in the media disclosing their contributions to sustainability. Although many times there are attempts at greenwashing, it is also true that the Mode System is making important changes, which should be taken advantage of. Museum institutions should take advantage of the generation of alliances with fashion houses, not to wash the face of brands but to learn from the different learning alternatives available that they can transfer to their audiences.

A great example of how museums can communicate sustainability in fashion was carried out by the Guggenheim Museum Bilbao (Figure 3). This institution joined the Ecoalf brand to create clothing for its employees. Although it seems like a simple gesture, the impact it can generate is essential. On the one hand, it allows its human capital to discover and enjoy the benefits of clothing produced under high sustainability standards since Ecoalf not only produces clothing with plastic recovered from the Mediterranean Sea but also invests significant sums of money so that fishermen of the areas are the ones who collect that plastic that damages the ecosystem. In this way, the Guggenheim becomes part of the change.

Likewise, the initiative, which is being communicated strongly in digital and analog information media, becomes an example for other museum institutions and companies of all kinds about the infinite options that exist to get involved in reversing climate change.

Figure 3. Uniform of the Guggenheim Bilbao Museum by the Ecoalf brand
Source: Interempresas

MUSEUM SHOPS AS A HUB OF COMMUNICATION

There is no visit to a museum that does not culminate in a tour and purchase in the store to take away a souvenir of the exhibitions that have been seen. In a report he did in Vogue magazine about museum shops, Blanco Medina said that they "have a special capacity to surprise us with pieces that we neither wanted nor were looking for. And yet, from the moment our eyes rest on them, we are invaded by the certainty that they will not only come home with us but that they will be much more than the memory of a trip" (2021: s/p). And it is that the museum shops have become temples for those who enjoy having cult objects at home or giving to friends.

That same preponderance of museum shops makes them a wonderful communication channel and connection with the public. There, art, and heritage institutions should focus on their strategy of transmedia communication and sustainability education, especially regarding textile objects or clothing. The possibility of implementing tools to disseminate sustainability policies is wide.

On the one hand, it is an ideal occasion to inform about the traceability of the garments: the origin of the fibers with which the textiles used are produced; the type of dye or dyes used, as well as their origin; the companies that have been linked to the production of the garments, the type of fabric that has been used and, why not, highlight whether there has been the involvement of artisans or entrepreneurs in the production of these. To make this and other information known around the textiles that are sold in the form of t-shirts, scarves, decorative silks, scarves, cloths for cleaning glasses and glasses, individual tablecloths, hats, caps, sweaters, jewelry, leather goods, and even stockings or socks, museum shops can take advantage of supports such as product labels, boxes, and other packaging, the store's own bags and even the incorporation of QR codes that allow the buyer to find out many more details about the product than has decided to buy.

Here it is also essential to involve the entire supply chain because the success of the communication and education strategy on sustainability in fashion depends on it. It is essential that those who wish to offer products in museum shops fully comply with the different sustainability policies that are being implemented. In this way, users and buyers will be aware that the museum is responsible for its impact on the environment and therefore, it will feel like an important part of the change that fashion must generate. This is highlighted by Ampuero-Canellas et al.: "Proper treatment of these products and the store can turn them into an extension of the exhibition space and transmitters of knowledge, art and culture. To achieve this, some strategies are proposed, such as personalization, choosing quality products, packaging care, and incorporating key content. All this will position the museum as an entity that disseminates culture and will move it away from the mere commercial business" (2018: 92).

On the other hand, museum store staff are also a valuable resource in this regard. Making them aware of the importance of transferring to buyers all the strategies that are institutionally implemented to ensure respectful processes for the environment and human rights is essential. A human capital that is aware of and involved with these initiatives makes it a reliable source of information and will transform it into the best institutional ambassador, which will surely result in communication benefits about said museum policies, both internally and externally.

DIGITIZATION TOWARDS SUSTAINABILITY

Podcasts, digital venues, virtual exhibitions, video games, digital newsletters, and social networks are some of the tools that museums have incorporated to connect with their audiences, share art, educate, and obtain information from their audiences. The truth is that these platforms still need to be fully exploited. The incorporation of these resources in the transmedia communication strategies of museums still needs to be made clearer. We see, for example, how museum conferences and seminars always vehemently praise the work of the Prado Museum with its profile on TikTok. Still, they don't dare to be disruptive in creating specific content for that and many other social media platforms.

Creating real digital strategies for museums where the potential they offer is fully exploited is still necessary. During 2020, in the middle of the year of the pandemic, where quarantines and confinements were daily, Nintendo carried out, through its Animal Crossing: New Horizons video game, more than 80 experiences around fashion. Dior, Chanel, Tom Ford, Gucci, Valentino, Marc Jacob, Sandy Liang, and Isabel Marant held photo sessions, fashion shows, red carpets, launching collections, and even some of them managed to sneak into the Socrates Museum, the videogame museum. And on the other hand, the Costume Museum, the MET, the Thyssen Bornemisza, and even El Prado did the same with heritage collections.

These experiences, all very successful due to the rise of the new version of Nintendo's oldest and most successful video game, which sold more than 20 million copies in just three months of existence, were not used to promote the sustainable theme nor the side of fashion brands, nor by museums. This is where the creation of alliances should be stimulated, and initiatives with a much broader vision should be undertaken. The educational power of video games is increasingly recognized, as is the impact these platforms have on audiences. It is time to take advantage of these indicators to promote a change in society's awareness of fashion consumption.

On the other hand, we also find that the social networks of fashion museums use their content little or not at all to promote sustainability. A resounding failure of sustainability communication strategies, considering the latest Global Digital Report by We Are Social and Meltwater, which indicates that 94.9% of the population of Spain uses these platforms daily. In Ireland, Norway, and Saudi Arabia, 99% of people use social networks daily; in the United States, 91.8% of its inhabitants do so, while in Latin American countries such as Mexico (78%) or Colombia (73.7%), also achieve impressive figures for the use of these platforms. With such a powerful scope, it is necessary to establish serious digital lines of action within the museums' strategic communications plan so that they do not stop at timid attempts and approximations to see how the networks work, as they have done up to now and which coincides with the vision of Isidro Moreno Sánchez and Mónica Viñarás Abad, both communication and museum scholars, who always state that it is very difficult for these institutions to change, to transform themselves.

Finally, as part of the enormous potential that digital communication has, an audience with which museums must connect are fashion influencers. These characters quickly capture the attention of followers and non-followers. On the one hand, fashion museums and those that are not - on those occasions that have fashion exhibitions - must take on the challenge of educating these content generators so that they not only share information on how to dress, how to combine, etc., but also to promote responsible clothing consumption and the need to generate a more circular fashion system. Incorporating these influencers into the museums' digital communication actions will only organically result in reaching audiences that otherwise would not find out about or approach the museum's activities.

GREENWASHING IS A PHILOSOPHY THAT SHOULD NOT REACH MUSEUMS

The communication of the different initiatives implemented by the exhibition spaces is important, not only because it reflects their commitment to building a more planet-friendly society but also because it must be part of a transparency policy within the organizational strategies. However, they should not become great flags of sustainability if they do not represent a true institutional commitment, which encompasses all instances of the museum.

Although many museum spaces in the world are very old, which makes it difficult to implement some tools for the rational use of natural and energy resources, museums can commit to designing and building new facilities or venues, as well as new museums, with deeply sustainable architecture. In Gothenburg, Sweden, the Volvo car company created a space combining natural wood and glass. This makes it a sustainable structure due to the materials used, forming part of an important natural enclave in the area. Allemansrätten is a Swedish word that refers to people's right to access nature. The architectural studio was based on that to create this new exhibition space.

Figure 4. Volvo museum
Source: KVANT

Implementing sustainability policies within museums starts from their construction and permeates all institution levels. In this sense, it is necessary to attend to these parameters from the general services or cleaning units, where it is necessary to discontinue cleaning elements that are not recyclable or biodegradable, use compostable bags, elimination of detergents and hygiene liquids that contain compounds that are harmful to the environment. or that impact on people's health. Regarding exhibitions, especially fashion shows, where you almost always want to achieve aspects of a show or spectacle, it is a sine qua non-requirement to design thinking of reusable elements with long life cycles.

Using tickets, catalogs, and other resources in digital form, avoiding paper production, is also part of being sustainable. And, just as the Guggenheim Museum did with the clothing equipment for its workers, it is necessary to look for modalities that allow the incorporation of sustainable, reusable, or recyclable textiles in all the museum's dependencies.

CONCLUSION

Museums have immense capital: a positive reputation earned, sometimes without great effort, that guarantees a significant impact on their audiences. This valuable resource must generate greater engagement from its audiences, especially in the goals the institution has established to be more sustainable. In addition, this strength of the museum must become a powerful tool to promote opportune and urgent actions regarding the achievement of the SDGs and the other challenges of the 2030 Agenda.

As has been insistently highlighted, art and heritage institutions are facing a gigantic challenge: to look at their audiences, listen to them, and connect efficiently with them. Implementing a global communication strategy, obviously transversal in the institution, is the next step to ensure that the public understands the urgent need to respect the environment and human rights and, internally, to ethical and responsible management of museum spaces.

Transmedia communication, where ICTs are of great importance, should be the driving force behind museums, allowing constant interaction and interactivity with their stakeholders and making them a leading part of the changes that the planet requires. The use of social networks, with their different formats and audiences, is part of this rich communication framework that organizations currently have. Although the urgency of incorporating social media prevails, it is vital to understand them in their deepest sense. Invite museum users/visitors to exercise their prosumer role, an essential part of the construction of transmedia narratives, whose scope is continually growing, allowing the different artistic manifestations, including fashion, to reach everyone equally, without discrimination of any kind. guy.

The scope of the SDGs is a job that deserves the entire Fashion System to articulate and work together. On the one hand, museums make audiences aware of responsible consumption and the circularity of fashion, and, on the other hand, the fashion industry invites its consumers to see much more in museums than just clothing exhibitors Nice from recognized firms. It is necessary to rescue important conclusions from the president of AMMA, Maloles Cebrián Sotomayor, who considers that "compulsive consumption habits increase inequalities and poverty, making their eradication even more difficult, since it distances people from natural resources and first-class services necessity such as water and/or sanitation".

The SDGs are an opportunity, ambitious though, for the ability to articulate actors in favor of a global awareness of the impact of fashion and the paradigm changes that the industry needs. It should not be forgotten that, in addition, fashion exhibitions allow the relevant narratives to be amplified with the need for gender equality, highlighting the roles and stereotypes that are perpetuated through clothing, which only make this problem worse. and others, such as a lack of self-esteem or eating disorders.

On the other hand, museum institutions dedicated to fashion must open their eyes and take advantage of the impact of fashion brands, especially today, when they are in full swing, and their media reach is monumental. The exhibition spaces must recognize that the fashion world is more alive than ever, not only to consume products season after season but as a manifestation of the different generations who resort to elements such as clothing, footwear, accessories, and others. to express their identities and their political and social positions, in addition to their recognition as individuals. This dialectic that has been used for fashion to reach museums as an artistic manifestation must be promoted to consolidate it in the cultural sector.

In the words of professor and researcher Isidro Molina Sánchez, museums need to understand that they must communicate strategically, analogically, and digitally. Attention to all its internal and external audiences requires planning that builds a transmedia narrative, which guarantees the permeabilization of the museums' key messages and the empowerment of prosumers. The one-way information flow model has remained in the past as museum audiences have grown and have understood the power they have to demand, discuss, contribute, and share the content generated from the museum's internal spaces. Transmedia communication, in this case as a tool for museums to disseminate the different aspects of sustainability in the fashion world, is no longer an option; it is a requirement of the planet. And, of course, it is essential that museums only approach the concept of greenwashing when they are creating fashion exhibitions that make this problem visible within the Fashion System.

It is necessary to highlight that the museum sector currently needs help to quickly incorporate itself into the development of sustainable strategies since inertia in this regard can be a serious blow to the reputation that they have managed to maintain for a long time. A strategic vision is urgently required in which transmedia communication is vital to be transparent, demonstrate commitment, and become an example for other organizations. However, museums have the ideal human capital to achieve these goals.

REFERENCES

Ampuero-Canellas, O., Tarazona-Belenguer, N., Gonzalez-del-Rio, J., & Jorda-Albiñana, B. (2018). Merchandising en museos:¿ educación, cultura o simple negocio? *EME Experimental Illustration. Art & Design*, (6), 92–101.

Blanco Mediana, E. (2021). *Las tiendas de museos españoles favoritas de Vogue.es*. Vogue. https://www.vogue.es/living/articulos/tiendas-museos-espanoles-favoritas-vogue

Davies, M. (2011). Museos y sostenibilidad. *Revista de la Subdirección General de Museos Estatales*, 7(8), 142–147.

Efe Verde. (2018). *La moda más sostenible se expone en el museo Victoria y Albert de Londres*. Efe Verde. https://efeverde.com/moda-sostenible-museo-victoria-albert-londres/

García, L. (2022). *Cómo las nuevas generaciones están volviendo a los peores hábitos del low cost más feroz*. SMODA. https://smoda.elpais.com/moda/actualidad/como-las-nuevas-generaciones-estan-volviendo-a-los-peores-habitos-del-low-cost-mas-feroz/

Garthe, C. (2020). *Gestión de la sostenibilidad en los museos: Un nuevo enfoque para implementar los Objetivos de Desarrollo Sostenible*. ICOM. https://encr.pw/dt9m1

Garthe, C. (2023). *The Sustainable Museum. How museums contribute to the great transformation*. Routledge.

Garzón Castrillón, M., & Ibarra Mares, A. (2014). Revisión sobre la sostenibilidad empresarial. *REAl Revista de Estudios Avanzados de Liderazgo*, *1*(3), 52–77.

InStyle. (2023). *La exposición que aúna belleza, moda y sostenibilidad de obligada visita*. InStyle. https://www.instyle.es/belleza/cara/exposicion-que-auna-moda-belleza-y-sostenibilidad-obligada-visita_54177

Interempresas (2023). *El Museo Guggenheim Bilbao presenta los nuevos uniformes Ecoalf de su personal confeccionados con materiales reciclados*. Interempresas. https://www.interempresas.net/Vestuario-profesional/Articulos/470695-Museo-Guggenheim-Bilbao-presenta-uniformes-Ecoalf-personal-confeccionados-materiales.html

Mosqueda, L. (2018). *Fashion for Good Experience, el primer museo dedicado la moda sostenible*. Vein. https://is.gd/K7jukq

Orús, A. (2022). *La moda sostenible en el mundo*. Statista. https://es.statista.com/temas/10262/moda-sostenible-en-el-mundo/#topicOverview

Red Española para el Desarrollo Sustentable. (2021). *Hacia una cultura sostenible. Guía práctica para integrar la Agenda 2030 en el sector cultural*. Ministerio de Cultura y Deporte. https://acortar.link/VMj5jg

Rueda, Ch. (2018). *Una exposición de moda sostenible para concienciar sobre el impacto de la industria textile*. 20 Minutos. https://blogs.20minutos.es/capeando-la-crisis/2018/01/24/una-exposicion-de-moda-sostenible-para-concienciar-sobre-el-impacto-de-la-industria-textil/

Spolini, N. (2019). *La exposición de moda de obligada visita en Florencia está en el Museo Salvatore Ferragamo*. Vogue. https://www.vogue.es/living/articulos/museo-salvatore-ferragamo-florencia-sustainable-thinking-moda-sostenible/40204 van Riel, C. B. M. (2019). *Why do people love museums so much? Empirical evidence about the stellar reputations of art museums and what companies can learn from it.* Research in Global Strategic Management., doi:10.1108/S1064-485720190000018013

Vázquez, S. (2021). *Una diseñadora revive la esencia de Cristóbal Balenciaga.* El Correo. https://bit.ly/3JpJExI

KEY TERMS AND DEFINITIONS

Circularity: Model through which fashion production seeks to take advantage of the resources already existing in the fashion system and new resources are not generated. Avoiding pollution, eliminating textile waste, taking advantage of products and supplies already available in the industry, extending the useful life of garments, recycling, and regenerating natural resources are part of the elements that promote circularity in fashion.

ESG model: This model becomes a reference standard that guides institutions that work towards sustainability within their operations. It obeys the acronym in English of Environment, Social Impact and Governance. This model seeks to measure, monitor, and control any impact that the organization has on the planet, human rights, society, and even its competition.

Fashion System: The set of people (natural and legal) that make up the entire business sector dedicated to fashion. It is considered a system because everyone contributes to the making of the industry, its advances and setbacks, and its advantages and disadvantages.

Governance: These are all actions that museums must undertake to meet their institutional objectives, where special attention is paid to the management of corporate reputation and social responsibility, to generate ethical management with a positive impact on the community, the environment, and human capital. It is defined as the institution's way of acting with attention to its different stakeholders, where the strengthening of transparency is essential, not only through the daily communication of the actions undertaken for the benefit of society but also in the issuance of periodic reports and reports that demonstrate the true impact of companies on society, the country, and the planet.

Prosumer: The combination of the words consumer and producer, which describes the new leading role assumed by the receivers of the transmedia communication process, where they become a key part of the construction and dissemination of the story or narrative. This audience reaches different elements of the narrative through different platforms, articulates it like pieces of a puzzle, translates it into its code, and shares it. The use of digital communication platforms is its main dissemination tool, but "voice to voice" is also a widely used resource.

Public: All the people (natural, legal, or institutional) with whom an organization is connected directly or indirectly. Although it has many forms of classification, the most standardized are: internal and external, which explain the type of connection that exists between the public and companies/institutions.

Sustainability: In general terms, is the process through which the requirements of citizens are met, without harming the resources that should be allocated to the care of the next generations. This fulfills the particularity of including elements such as economic development, environmental protection, and the generation of social well-being.

Transmedia Communication: The process through which a story is told through multiple platforms (analog and digital media), which leads the user to connect the fragments arranged on these supports to reconstruct the complete narrative, becoming a leading actor in this process. The receiver does not become a pure consumer of the message but rather helps in its construction and dissemination. Through communicative bricolage, you take the content, translate it into your language, and share it with your environment.

Chapter 5
Is the Oil Price Hike a New Threat to Consumers' Buying Patterns?

Sarika Faisal
BRAC University, Bangladesh

Syed Far Abid Hossain
https://orcid.org/0000-0003-0729-1456
BRAC University, Bangladesh

Rayisa Rayhana
BRAC University, Bangladesh

Shawnila Nawshin
BRAC University, Bangladesh

ABSTRACT

The purpose of this study is to examine whether oil price hikes are leading consumers to switch to alternative forms of cooking oil. This study presents the viewpoints of subject-matter specialists, as well as consumer choices. This study applied a qualitative research approach with literature review and person administered survey. The authors found that the rise of the price of soybean oil positively influences consumers to switch to alternative oils. Moreover, the authors also discovered that consumers are more conscious about health benefits while oil prices are hiked. Additionally, the availability of various kinds of oils in the market influences consumers to switch as per the study. Theoretically, the study contributes to the extant literature (buyer decision theory) by discovering the oil price hike, brand switching, and sustainable oil consumption through variety seeking tendency.

DOI: 10.4018/978-1-6684-9277-2.ch005

INTRODUCTION

Jeff Rubin quoted that "We are in a world of triple-digit oil prices for the foreseeable future.'' Whereas a politician Rodrigo Rato stated that "Oil prices have certainly become a threat for the world economy." As the prices of daily commodities are rising limitlessly, people are getting affected massively. The conventional cuisines of South Asian region like Bangladesh, India, Pakistan, Sri Lanka etc. are based on using a lot of soybean oil. Due to the massive price hike, people are facing a lot of problems to cope up with the situation (Maitra et al., 2021). One of the main reasons behind this massive price hike is the imbalance between the supply and demand of oil in the market due to the Russia and Ukraine war. Covid-19 also played a significant role here and these factors caused inflation, recession throughout the whole world (Leandro et al., 2022). Studies showed that during covid -19 people have become more health concerned. They are more focused on the nutritious diet, good substitutes and trying to minimize health issues by improving the lifestyle with a cost effective dietary plan (Dizon et al., 2021). On another side of the argument, poor and middle class people are mostly suffering because of the oil price hike, however it is affecting the whole nation. Not only it's affecting them financially but also it's affecting their conventional food habits which is now considered as a threat to their lifestyle. To overcome the problem, people need to switch to alternative oils that are convenient to them (Jetter et al., 2006).

Many academics referred to price hikes as increased prices for daily necessities in the market. Among all of them, the oil price hike gained the most attention because it caused a lot of disturbance in the whole supply chain, economic aspects and in other fields as well. That's why it's regarded as one of the biggest concerns our nation is facing and because of this many researchers are trying to find alternatives to reduce the environmental impact on mineral oil (Islam et al., 2019). There are several reasons behind the oil price hike. Some could be the internal factors like the disbalance in the supply and demand of the products, corruption etc. Other factors could be war like it generally threatens supply while increasing demand (militaries require a lot of energy) (shipping oil becomes more dangerous, and access to oil fields is limited), natural calamities, political instabilities etc. Price hike hits different groups of people. In Bangladesh, recently this issue is causing some serious damage by threatening the lifestyle of different social classes. Mostly the poor and the middle class people are suffering the most as the consumers but the entire nation is going through a tough time (Maitra et al., 2021) People are searching for alternative options which will fulfill their needs and also have biodegradable characteristics. Researchers have suggested some of the alternatives that are available in the market such as mustard oil, olive oil, sunflower oil, rice bran oil etc. These vegetable oils are environment friendly and also it is proposed for high voltage application (Islam et al., 2019) These are healthier options too but would consumers switch to these oils as a result of the current price hike? In this research we aim to find out if consumers will switch alternatives or not which is the main objective of this research.

However, the core problem that we have encountered in our research paper is whether the consumer will switch to alternatives due to the hike in soybean oil price. Oil is the most used commodity in our daily commodities. It is also highly associated with a country's economic growth and overall sustainability. But the price of oil is increasing every month. At recent time per liter oil costs 198 BDT which was 160 BDT previously i. e price has increased by 38 BDT (Bhuvandas & Gundimeda, 2020). This mere issue is affecting the whole country from wholesalers, refiners, retailers to consumers.

Therefore, oil price hike is not only affecting the consumers financially but also affecting their consumption and dietary habits. Many consumers are looking out for alternatives like mustard oil, sunflower oil, olive oil to meet their daily needs. Prof Nazma Shaheen in an interview with The Daily Star stated that the government should encourage the local farmers to boost their production in the alternative crops so that the consumers can be self-sufficient in edible oil production. She also added that even though soybean oil is a good source of unsaturated fat, vegetable oils are just fine. Because it is one of the three essential macromolecules carbohydrate, protein and fat and it's also pivotal for good health (Sujan, 2022). So, it's seen that even the nutritionists are suggesting switching to various alternatives, also considering it as an effective way for survival in such a crucial situation. Considering several alternatives, the first specific objective which will be tested is whether oil price hike is leading to consumer's switching to alternative forms of cooking oil.

Furthermore, people who are health conscious often switch their habitat and build a new one to become the best version of them. Hence, another specific objective of this study is to understand if health benefits related to cooking oils affects consumers switching to alternative forms of cooking oil. Last specific objective is to assess if availability of other alternative oils can lead consumers to switch to alternative forms of cooking oils. Keeping all the specific objectives in mind the research questions have been formulated. The questions asked to the population in this study, have been attached in the appendix section.

Since oil price hike is a very trendy issue, a lot of articles about consumers, their daily struggles and impacts on them are published but very few portions are talking about the alternatives that we can get and its effectiveness. This is the research gap that we have identified and our study aims to fill up that gap.

RESEARCH AND OBJECTIVES AND QUESTIONS

Broad objective: The main aim of the study is to find out whether the consumers will switch to alternative oil or not.

Specific objectives:

1. To test whether oil price hike is leading to consumer's switching to alternative forms of cooking oil.
2. To understand if health benefits related to cooking oils affects consumers switching to alternative forms of cooking oil.
3. Assess if availability of other alternative oils can lead to consumers to switch to alternative forms of cooking oils.

Research questions:

1. How has the price hike in the market impacted consumer's switching to alternative forms of cooking oil?

Price increases have significantly affected consumers' purchasing choices for common goods like oil, which are necessary for daily life's cooking. Usual behavior of an item's price increase results in consumers looking for an alternative which would be cheaper. As research shows significant results of price responsiveness among EU consumers (Santeramo et al., 2021). Furthermore, studies show that consumers' perception and purchase behavior can change due to price hike (Alderighi et al., 2022).

2. How does health impact consumers' intention to switch towards other available alternatives of cooking oil?

As more people take a step towards a healthy lifestyle, people's preference of food changes. Cooking oil is the main ingredient or the fat source, which has a major effect on a person's health. Research shows several alternatives like olive oil, avocado oil which are very high in nutritional value (Deng et al., 2022). Consumers' intention to switch towards other alternatives for health impacts.

3. How does availability of alternative oils impact consumers to switch to another alternative form of cooking oil?

A lot of cooking oils are currently available in the market which makes consumers choose from a lot of options. A study showed that plants like olive, soybean, sunflower, mustard, canola, and peanut, have a lower mortality rate compared to animal based oils (Wu et al., 2020). All these alternatives can easily influence consumers to switch their cooking oil.

COMPREHENSIVE SUMMARY/SYSTEMATIC REVIEW

Oil is one of the core ingredients in any cooking of food. The per capita consumption of edible oil in Bangladesh increased by 20 per cent in the last five years to reach 18.4 kilogrammes (kgs) in 2020, according to findings revealed at a webinar by The Council of Palm Oil Producing Countries (CPOPC).

Research in EU countries has found that there is a high price responsiveness of consumers when it comes to edible (vegetable) oils like palm, rapeseed, soy, and sunflower oils (Santeramo et al., 2021). People's financial condition decides a lot about how much they are able to spend on their basic necessities like food, accommodation, transport etc. A study in India came up with shocking results on how transport fuel price changes have an adverse impact on Indian households (Bhuvandas & Gundimeda, 2020). The data perceived have been alarming since results show middle income and lower middle income families have a direct relation to consumption pattern and often have to remain vulnerable while purchasing both edible and inedible oils for their daily household. Furthermore, studies have shown the negative spillover with commodities and oils (Maitra et al., 2021).

Furthermore, cooking oils are very much integrated towards health benefits and health risks in life. A study on a Chinese nationwide cohort has shown how plant based cooking oils which are extracted from plants like olive, soybean, sunflower, mustard, canola, peanut oils have a lower mortality rate compared to the animal based oils (Wu et al., 2020). No wonder why people have been promoting vegan oils, as this also helps to lower cholesterol (Ganesan et al., 2022). On the other hand, a study shows excessive use of mustard oil has shown to have some negative impact on cardiovascular health (Poddar et al., 2022). Moreover, studies have shown consumers are very drawn towards palm oil, even with some minor health hazards, most of the people are seen to be using it in the Asian region (Savarese et al., 2022).

There are several alternative oils that have been newly discovered that consumers have been very fond of. Not just the taste or smell, the alternatives of cooking oils come from various ways. Furthermore, a recent study of 2022 shows that Peony seeds oil has a potential to become the alternative oil that consumers will switch to, as it presents various health benefits including antioxidation, hypolipidemic activity, hepatoprotection, immunity regulation and so on (Deng et al., 2022). Rice bran oil has shown great potential making it another great choice for people as the extraction is way easier, cheaper than other oils (Punia et al., 2021). An Indian research of

2022 shows the potential of Sesame oil and how it can replace other oils in near future (Langyan et al., 2022).

SCRUTINIZING THE IMPACT OF PROPOSITIONS ON RESEARCH OUTCOMES

Proposition One: Correlation Between Price Hike and Availability of Alternatives

When oil price elasticity is high, customers react strongly to price changes. A price reduction will likely bring new customers. When oil prices rise, consumers use less or want to switch to another oil. Due to the increase in the price of soybean oil in our country, consumers are using other oils as alternatives to this oil such as mustard oil, sunflower oil, rapeseed oil, etc. When the price increases, it changes the buying behavior of consumers. Some oils are harmful for our health. Unhealthy oils cause many kinds of health risks for human beings. Fats and oils are not very good for us. Saturated fat raises levels of LDL, which is harmful to the human body. For this reason, choosing the right oil is important for a healthy heart. When consumers realize that the oil they are using is not good for their health, they will look for alternative oils which are healthy and good for their body. Using rice bran oil has great health benefits for the human body. It reduces oxidative stress and hypertension, anti-cancer and anti-diabetic activity. When oil prices are high, not all customers can afford to buy soybean oil . So they look for alternatives. So, when customers see available alternative oil which will meet up their needs, they will switch and purchase that oil. It will be beneficial for both customers and oil companies.

Consumers switch towards other alternatives when they are influenced by external factors like word of mouth, advertisements, promotional ads on alternative oil etc. According to research on switching to alternative products, consumers' hedonic needs and environmental needs play a significant part in consumers' intention to switch. Moreover, even though the price point of regular cooking oil has skyrocketed in Bangladesh, non-price attributes affect consumer's intention to switch. Non-price attributes such as the supply shortage of cooking oil in Bangladesh before eid made consumers search for other alternatives. Furthermore, people became more concerned about their health after the pandemic and in order to take care of one's health, one must create a healthy and balanced diet which includes fat, carbohydrates, protein etc. Hence, consumers have to switch to other alternative oils with a lower risk of cardiovascular disease and stroke.Research shows how different forms of oil consumption impacts our cardiovascular health and the ultimate results lead to consumers switching decisions.

Proposition Two: The Oil Price Hike is Positively Related to Consumers Switching to Alternative Oil Options

Oil is one of the core ingredients in any cooking process. The per capita consumption of edible oil in Bangladesh increased by 20 percent in the last five years to reach 18.4 kilograms (kg) in 2020, according to findings revealed at a webinar by the Council of Palm Oil Producing Countries (CPOPC). This study's theoretical framework is based on buyer decision theory.

Research in EU countries has found that there is a high price responsiveness among consumers when it comes to edible (vegetable) oils like palm, rapeseed, soy, and sunflower oils (Santeramo et al., 2021). People's financial condition determines a lot about how much they are able to spend on their basic necessities like food, accommodation, transport, etc. A study in India came up with shocking results on how transport fuel price changes have an adverse impact on Indian households (Bhuvandas & Gundimeda, 2020). The results suggest that middle income and lower middle income families have a direct relationship to consumption pattern and frequently have to remain vulnerable while acquiring both edible and inedible oils for their regular home needs, which has led to frightening data being interpreted. Additionally, research has demonstrated how commodities and oils have detrimental spillover effects.

Proposition Three: The Health Benefits of Oils are Positively Related to Consumers Switching to Alternative Oil Options

Cooking oils are very much integrated towards health benefits and health risks in life. A study on a Chinese nationwide cohort has shown how plant based cooking oils, which are extracted from plants like olive, soybean, sunflower, mustard, canola, and peanut, have a lower mortality rate compared to animal based oils (Wu et al., 2020). No wonder why people have been promoting vegan oils, as this also helps to lower cholesterol (Ganesan et al., 2022). On the other hand, a study shows excessive use of mustard oil has some negative impact on cardiovascular health (Poddar et al., 2022). Moreover, studies have shown consumers are very drawn towards palm oil, even with some minor health hazards; most people are seen to be using it in the Asian region (Savarese et al., 2022).

Proposition Four: Availability of Alternative Oils is Positively Related to Consumers Switching to Alternative Oil Options

There are several alternative oils that have been newly discovered that consumers have been very fond of. Cooking oil substitutes come in a variety of forms, not just for taste or smell. Furthermore, a recent study from 2022 shows that peony seed oil has the potential to become the alternative oil that consumers will switch to, as it presents various health benefits including antioxidation, hypolipidemic activity, hepatoprotection, immunity regulation, and so on (Deng et al., 2022). Rice bran oil has shown great potential, making it another great choice for people as the extraction is way easier and cheaper than other oils (Punia et al., 2021). An Indian study from 2022 shows the potential of sesame oil and how it can replace other oils in the near future (Langyan et al., 2022).

Figure 1. Graphical model
Source: Authors own creation

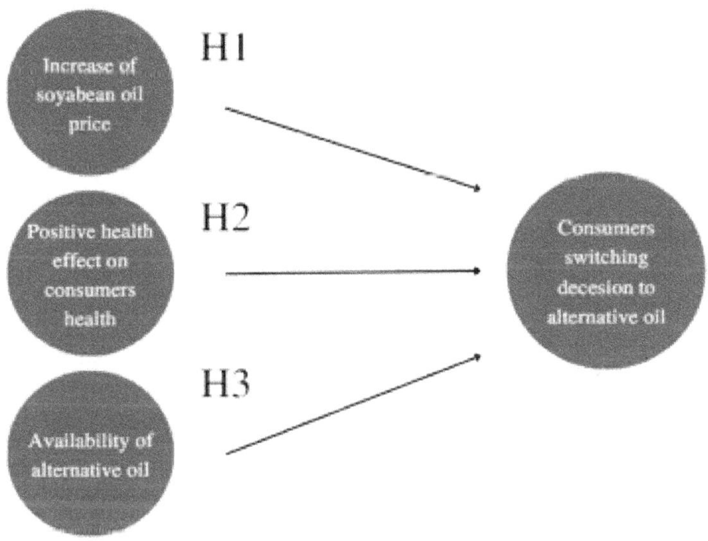

THEORY IMPLICATION

Buyer decision theory is one of the oldest theories in history. It was first introduced by John Dewey back in 1910. Generally this theory depicts the buying decision process of the consumers. The five stages of the decision making process evaluate a consumer buying decision process. In our paper we are going to use this theory to describe how each of the variables influenced each step of the framework. The following steps are cited below:

First stage (problem/need recognition): The price of soybean oil has increased to 38% which is referred to as oil price hike (Halder, 2022). Because of the price hike many consumers are looking for alternatives to meet their day to day necessities. According to research on switching to alternative products, consumers' hedonic needs and environmental needs play a significant part in consumers' intention to switch (Moshood et al., 2022b). Moreover, even though the price point of regular cooking oil has skyrocketed in Bangladesh (Correspondent, 2022), non-price attributes affect cosumer's intention to switch (Ndebele et al., 2019). Non-price attributes such as the supply shortage of cooking oil in Bangladesh before eid made consumers search for other alternatives (Halder, 2022).

Second stage (information search): The recent ' Oil Price Hike ' shifted the perspective of many consumers and researchers. People have become more concerned about their health and in order to take care of one's health, one must create a healthy and balanced diet which includes fat, carbohydrates, protein etc. which are available in the alternative oils; which will also decrease cardiovascular disease and stroke (Donat-Vargas et al., 2022). Research shows how different forms of oil consumption impacts our cardiovascular health (Poddar et al., 2022). Prof Nazma Shaheen in an interview with daily star also described many alternative oils like mustard oil, sunflower oil, olive oil and they are beneficial for our health. Hence, all the information has been searched, looked at by the consumers.

Third stage (evaluation of alternatives): In a recent article named "Soybean oil substitutes: Some healthier options for cooking" various types of oil have been discussed and their nutritious values. Like in ' Mustard Oil ' Essential fatty acids and natural antioxidants are in perfect balance. They are both very helpful in preserving a healthy heart. The oil encourages the production of healthy cholesterol while preventing the accumulation of bad cholesterol. On the other hand, research suggests that Olive oil may lower blood pressure and inflammation, shield LDL particles from oxidation, enhance the integrity of blood vessels, and aid in preventing unintended blood clotting. Moreover High-oleic sunflower oil is more widely available since it is more stable when cooking. The heart benefits from monounsaturated fats like those in high oleic sunflower oil (Tahmid, 2022) . These substitutes are not only healthy but also available in pretty much every store. Hence, in this third stage consumers are doing the evaluation among alternatives.

Fourth stage (purchase decision): After evaluating each of the alternatives, consumers will make the final decision about what to purchase as an alternative because these alternatives are healthier for our body in every possible way. Also these oils contain three essential macromolecules carbohydrate, protein and fat and it's also pivotal for good health which is why nutritionists are also suggesting switching to various alternatives (Sujan, 2022). As a result, in this fourth stage consumers are taking the decision after going through all the other steps.

Fifth stage (post purchase behavior): This stage describes the post purchase feeling of consumers. Since the above mentioned factors have influenced the consumer pattern and dietary plan of whether they will continue to this new change or go back to the old issue when oil price hike won't be an issue. A study named 'The nurses' health study and the health professionals follow-up study 'by the author Marta Guasch-Ferre, a senior research scientist at the Harvard T.H. Chan School of Public Health said that in long-term study, including more than 90,000 participants followed for up to 30 years, conducted in the American population on olive oil and mortality rate which eventually came up with a result that those who consumed 2 teaspoons (10 grams) of olive oil instead of margarine, butter, mayonnaise, or dairy fat the risk of death has decreased to 34%. He also recommended replacing saturated fat and animal fat with unsaturated plant oils to prevent health issues and to have a healthy lifestyle. Hence, evaluating these issues it's safe to say that the consumer might stick to using substitutes. Lastly, the satisfaction or dissatisfaction of the purchased good is given in this step.

LIMITATIONS, CONCLUSION, AND FUTURE RESEARCH DIRECTION

The following study had very little scope for the generalizable output because there were time constraints and the participants who wanted to take part in the survey were also small in number. Hence there was no proper data collection and data analysis in this paper. Therefore, the overall discussion delineated various aspects of the prospects which may come up with different conclusions.

This study created a model to determine whether consumers are switching to alternate types of cooking oil as a result of oil price increases and whether this poses a danger to their recent purchasing habits. The results of this study reveal that while the price increase for soybean oil encourages consumers to move to alternatives, it also threatens their regular purchasing habits.

Future study should concentrate on creating more thorough models that incorporate further elements that could potentially affect the switch to different types of cooking oil. Also, more analysis should be done to determine how rising oil prices may affect alternative cooking oils, like coconut and palm oils. The effects of rising oil prices on consumer health and the effects of greater usage of substitute cooking oils on the environment should also be evaluated.

REFERENCES

Alderighi, M., Nava, C. R., Calabrese, M., Christille, J. M., & Salvemini, C. B. (2022). Consumer perception of price fairness and dynamic pricing: Evidence from Booking.com. *Journal of Business Research, 145*, 769–783. doi:10.1016/j.jbusres.2022.03.017

Bhuvandas, D., & Gundimeda, H. (2020). Welfare impacts of transport fuel price changes on Indian households: An application of LA-AIDS model. *Energy Policy, 144*, 111583. doi:10.1016/j.enpol.2020.111583

Chakraborty, O. (2022). *Inflation and COVID-19 Supply Chain Disruption*. IGI Global eBooks. doi:10.4018/978-1-6684-5876-1.ch002

Crosby, D. G. (2018). *The Nutrition Source*. Harvard. www.hsph.harvard.edu: https://www.hsph.harvard.edu/nutritionsource/2015/04/13/ask-the-expert-concerns-about-canola-oil/?fbclid=IwAR3Ppce46Sx7tO48gFMzS-Yo_9TfCiZiTNtGhAqDax5QodnS4OWQYK9PQz

Čvirik, M., Krošláková, M., Beran, I. M., Hrosik, R. C., & Drábik, P. (2022). Influence of health-conscious consumer behaviour on consumer ethnocentrism during the COVID-19 pandemic. *Ekonomska Istrazivanja, 36*(1), 1510–1526. doi:10.1080/1331677X.2022.2090402

de Alzaa, A. F., Guillaume, C., & Ravetti, L. (2021). Cooking with Extra Virgin Olive Oil. *Olive Oil—New Perspectives and Applications*, 1-13.

Fregapane, G., & Salvador, M. (2013). Production of superior quality extra virgin olive oil modulating the content and profile of its minor components. *Food Research International, 54*(2), 1907–1914. doi:10.1016/j.foodres.2013.04.022

Ganesan, K., Sukalingam, K., & Xu, B. (2018). Impact of consumption and cooking manners of vegetable oils on cardiovascular diseases- A critical review. *Trends in Food Science & Technology, 71*, 132–154. doi:10.1016/j.tifs.2017.11.003

Gupta, T., & Saya, L. (2022). A comprehensive review on therapeutic properties of Mustard Oil and Olive Oil. *Chemical Biology Letters, 9*(1), 309–309.

Hossain, S. (2022). Despite high prices, cooking oil in Bangladesh is cheaper than most of South Asia. *Dhaka Tribune*. https://www.dhakatribune.com

Huq, Z. (2022). How safe is soybean oil? *The Financial Express*. https://thefinancialexpress.com.bd

Jetter, K. M., & Cassady, D. L. (2006). The availability and cost of healthier food alternatives. *American Journal of Preventive Medicine*, *30*(1), 38–44. doi:10.1016/j.amepre.2005.08.039 PMID:16414422

Kararrwal, K., & Kumar, K. (2022). *Traditional Method of Consuming Food Secret for Healthier Life*. WJPR. https://wjpr.s3.ap-south-1.amazonaws.com/article_issue/8f0d9d15008a8960d53d3996e8fa0502.pdf

Knothe, G., & Steidley, K. R. (2009). A comparison of used cooking oils: A very heterogeneous feedstock for biodiesel. *Bioresource Technology*, *100*(23), 5796–5801. doi:10.1016/j.biortech.2008.11.064 PMID:19592239

Leandro, G. D. S. M., & de Jesus Leandro, E. F. (2022). Impact of COVID-19 on Businesses and Consumers 2020/2022: Strategic Measures Adopted by Companies. In Handbook of Research on Global Networking Post COVID-19 (pp. 291-307). IGI Global.

Libraries, N. (2022). *Buyer decision process*. Wikipedia. https://en.wikipedia.org/wiki/Buyer_decision_process?fbclid=IwAR1B7OF1pv-lNlzvq1XK4rZ9dHcQeI-Yu5TO2Gaxqun3Vj40cmjP9eXi0_Y

Maitra, D., Guhathakurta, K., & Kang, S. H. (2021). The good, the bad and the ugly relation between oil and commodities: An analysis of asymmetric volatility connectedness and portfolio implications. *Energy Economics*, *94*, 105061. doi:10.1016/j.eneco.2020.105061

Mavis, M., & Hossain, S. (2022). No immediate impact on Bangladesh, but businesses wary of oil and food price hike. *Dhakar Tribune*. https://www.dhakatribune.com

McDermott, A. (2017). *The 4 Healthiest Substitutes for Vegetable Oil*. Healthline. https://www.healthline.com/health/food-nutrition/substitute-for-vegetable-oil?fbclid=IwAR35WvrZCoDdJeXV2wcRxA7T3-GBXB9F1pkag8T6VskdtRYVk_ZlEQg4Rvc

Meenu, M., Cai, Q., & Xu, B. (2019b). A critical review on analytical techniques to detect adulteration of extra virgin olive oil. *Trends in Food Science & Technology*, *91*, 391–408. doi:10.1016/j.tifs.2019.07.045

Mhatre, S., Rajaraman, P., Chatterjee, N., Bray, F., Goel, M., Patkar, S., & Dikshit, R. (2020). Mustard oil consumption, cooking method, diet and gallbladder cancer risk in high and low-risk regions of India. *International Journal of Cancer*, *147*(6), 1621–1628. doi:10.1002/ijc.32952 PMID:32142159

Poddar, K. H., Sikand, G., Kalra, D., Wong, N. D., & Duell, P. B. (2022). Mustard oil and cardiovascular health: Why the controversy? *Journal of Clinical Lipidology, 16*(1), 13–22. doi:10.1016/j.jacl.2021.11.002 PMID:34924350

Punia, S., Kumar, M., Sandhu, K. S., & Purewal, S. S. (2021). Rice Bran Oil: Emerging Trends in Extraction, Health Benefit, and Its Industrial Application. *Rice Science, 28*(3), 217–232. doi:10.1016/j.rsci.2021.04.002

Rudro, A. A. (2022). Price hike: Is this the new normal? *The Daily Star*. https://www.thedailystar.net

Ruixue, D., Jiayu, G., Junpeng, Y., & Liu, P. (2022). Could peony seeds oil become a high-quality edible vegetable oil? The nutritional and phytochemistry profiles, extraction, health benefits, safety and value-added-products. *Food Research International, 156*, 111200. doi:10.1016/j.foodres.2022.111200 PMID:35651052

Santeramo, F. G., Di Gioia, L., & Lamonaca, E. (2021). Price responsiveness of supply and acreage in the EU vegetable oil markets: Policy implications. *Land Use Policy, 101*, 105102. doi:10.1016/j.landusepol.2020.105102

Savarese, M., Castellini, G., Paleologo, M., & Graffigna, G. (2022). Determinants of palm oil consumption in food products: A systematic review. *Journal of Functional Foods, 96*, 105207. doi:10.1016/j.jff.2022.105207

Sifferlin, A. (2018). The 10 Best and Worst Oils For Your Health. *Time*. https://time.com/5342337/best-worst-cooking-oils-for-your-health/?fbclid=IwAR2Kcw6AXFHXHtPC5ajOv4k1dpln2hZUS7Yyl-Kt1cX2sp7_rW_wIIJ6kqI

Sujan, M. A. (2022). Edible oil crisis: Alternatives aplenty. *The Daily Star*. https://www.thedailystar.net

Suman, M. (2022). Edible oil price hike: Manipulation merry-go-round. *The Daily Star*. https://www.thedailystar.net

Van De Graaf, T., & Colgan, J. D. (2017). Russian gas games or well-oiled conflict? Energy security and the 2014 Ukraine crisis. *Energy Research & Social Science, 24*, 59–64. doi:10.1016/j.erss.2016.12.018

Wu, F., Mao, L., Zhuang, P., Chen, X., Jiao, J., & Zhang, Y. (2020). Plant-sourced cooking oil consumption is associated with lower total mortality in a longitudinal nationwide cohort study. *Clinical Nutrition (Edinburgh, Lothian), 39*(12), 3703–3710. doi:10.1016/j.clnu.2020.03.031 PMID:32359931

Yang, M., Feng, Q., Chen, C., Chen, S., Guo, Y., Su, D., & Zeng, G. (2022). Healthier diet associated with reduced risk of excessive gestational weight gain: A Chinese prospective cohort study. *Maternal and Child Nutrition*, *19*(3), e13397. doi:10.1111/mcn.13397 PMID:35821659

Yubero-Serrano, E. M., Lopez-Moreno, J., Gomez-Delgado, F., & Lopez-Miranda, J. (2018). Extra virgin olive oil: More than a healthy fat. *European Journal of Clinical Nutrition*, *72*(S1), 8–17. doi:10.103841430-018-0304-x PMID:30487558

KEY TERMS AND DEFINITIONS

Brand Switching: A situation in which a consumer decides to abandon a brand or product in favor of another brand or product.

Consumer Decision-Making Process: The process by which consumers become aware of and identify their needs; collect information on the best way to resolve these needs; evaluate available alternative options; make a purchasing decision; and evaluate their purchase.

Consumer Intention: Consumer attitude towards a specific purchasing behavior and the consumer degree of willingness to pay.

Edible (Vegetable) Oils: Fat of vegetable, animal, or microbial origin suitable for food use. The most common vegetable oils are soybean, sunflower, corn, olive, and coconut oil.

Environmental Awareness: The degree to which individuals are aware of the effect of their actions on the environment and are willing to actively minimize their impact.

Health Consciousness: The degree to which individuals are aware of the healthiness of their diet and lifestyle and care about their health. Health-conscious consumers are concerned about nutrition, fitness, stress, and the environment.

Non-Price Competition: A marketing strategy that involves attracting consumers by providing superior products, a unique selling proposition, a great location, and excellent service, rather than lower prices.

Price Hike: The unusual, abnormal, sudden, or large increase in the prices of daily fundamental commodities.

Sustainability: Society's ability to exist and develop without depleting all the natural resources necessary for the lives of future generations.

APPENDIX

Questionnaire

1. What is your gender?
2. What is your age?
3. What's your living situation?
4. What's your educational background?
5. What's the monthly income of your family?
6. Do you buy edible oils by yourself?
7. Which cooking oil do you and your family prefer?
8. Are you aware of the recent oil price hike?
9. Is the recent price hike affecting your family?
10. Where do you typically buy your cooking oil?
11. How strongly do you consider price while buying cooking oils?
12. What is the amount of edible oil you usually purchase?
13. How often do you switch an edible oil brand?
14. "(I believe that) people should use healthier cooking oil", keeping the health benefits in mind, to what extent do you agree/disagree with the statement?
15. "Soybean oil is harmful to human health"- to what extent do you agree or disagree with the statement?
16. "Soybean oil is a good source of unsaturated fat that we need daily. But for that we don't need to consume soybean oil, not necessarily. Other vegetable oils are just as fine"- to what extent do you agree or disagree with the statement?
17. "It has been an open secret that whenever there is a strain on the global supply chain of edible oils, some individuals make a lot of money by working the system"- to what extent do you agree or disagree with the statement?
18. "Rise in prices of edible oils is forcing some of the low- and middle-income households to opt for cheaper and low-quality oils"- to what extent do you agree or disagree with the statement?
19. "We will not be able to produce or refine oil if we cannot manage the raw materials from the global market,"- what's your opinion about this statement?
20. If the availability of alternative oils increases, would you consider switching to healthier oils?
21. If the price decreases, will you again switch to soybean oil?

Chapter 6
Minimalism:
A Game Changer for Industries

Amritesh
Indian Institute of technology, Ropar, India

Arjinder Kaur
https://orcid.org/0000-0003-1223-7999
Indian Institute of Technology, Ropar, India

ABSTRACT

Minimalism has become a lifestyle choice for consumers from various cultural backgrounds who are deliberately rejecting the consumerist narratives that drive market-driven lifestyles. This chapter aims to provide a comprehensive review of growing trends in minimalism, emphasizing the defining traits of minimalists, the historical origins of minimalism, and the potential risks it poses to deindustrialization. A bibliographic review method is used to address the interconnected concepts within the specified objectives. The study illuminates the global shift in consumer behaviour by examining the increasing embrace of minimalism in different consumer sectors of the economy. The authors highlight the disruptive capacity of minimalism in various industries and recommend further research to plan a systematic degrowth of unsustainable products and match it with the emerging demand for a minimalism-driven lifestyle. In summary, this chapter emphasizes the potential connections among minimalism, health and wellbeing, and environmental sustainability.

DOI: 10.4018/978-1-6684-9277-2.ch006

INTRODUCTION

Minimalism, which is said to have started as a western art movement after the Second World War, has infiltrated across many broader disciplines, such as design and architecture, literary minimalism, music, films, fashion, and now business and management (Wilsonm, 2020). It has now emerged as a way of life among consumers from culturally diverse continents ranging from east to west, who are consciously separating themselves from the lifestyles submerged in the narratives of market-driven consumerism. Minimalism, as a consumer movement, may act as an antecedent to deindustrialization in developed countries. This is because people in advanced nations are adopting minimalism as a style of consumption out of their frustration with the consequences of consumerism and seeing it as a source of future wellbeing (Lambert, 2019). The objective of this article is to present an overview of emerging practices in minimalism, the characteristics of the practicing actors (or minimalists), the historical roots of minimalism, its possible threats to deindustrialization, and to recommend further research on the disruptive potential of minimalism across industries to develop a sustainable response. Overall, this article offers insights to encourage further research on the link between minimalism and deindustrialization. Since the topic is novel and its practical implications transcend largely across disciplinary boundaries, a bibliographic method is chosen to conduct the review to address the interlinked ideas under the stated objectives. Using the bibliographic review guidelines proposed by Block & Fisch (2020), an article search is performed over the Scopus database by using the keywords "minimalism," "minimalists," and "deindustrialization." Articles published within the last five years that essentially contain the term "minimalism" in their title, abstract, and keywords were preferred. Additionally, some articles published before the last five years that were found important to address the review objectives were also incorporated. The search is further supplemented by including web articles written by practitioners to capture real-world practices. Interpretive analysis of the articles and discussions are presented further.

In the next section the concept of minimalism and minimalists is elaborated to clarify the nature of actors and practices. The third section focused on the wellbeing motivation of minimalism, i.e., how this consumption style is perceived useful in attaining the well-being outcome. The fourth and fifth sections deals with the historical development of minimalism and emerging consumption trend respectively Section sixth explains how industries are preparing for and started adopting minimalism by looking at its future potential. The sixth section discusses the disruptive potential of minimalism, i.e., drivers of deindustrialization, and recommend industries to design change management strategies to respond to this trend. The last section concludes along with detail of research contributions and Limitations.

MINIMALISM AND MINIMALISTS

Minimalism means "embracing the simple life." It is not something new but prevalent in different nations for centuries, rather, it has gained attention only when it began as an art movement in Western countries. It has transitioned from an art movement to a consumption lifestyle. As the number of minimalists are increasing worldwide, it has garnered the attention of academic researchers. The globalization has connected the nations like never before. So, even if there were a small number of minimalists in one country, they can connect to others in different countries through the Internet, and social media. Moreover, minimalists are not just limited to themselves they influence others through sharing blogpost, organizing webinars to cause awareness among the masses (Wilsonm, 2020). This lifestyle movement has the potential to become global community movement in future that may change the way industries are working today. Minimalists prefer quality over quantity. Eco-Minimalists share the concern for the planet and restrict purchases to goods not harming the planet in any way. So, the industries now need to respond to these changes. They may turn this as an opportunity by aligning their products and business models as per the values of minimalism. Otherwise, they may fail in the long run. So, we tried to explore if minimalism has the potential to become an emergent force behind deindustrialization.

Minimalism, a recent counter-consumerism trend, has been gaining traction among consumers worldwide. Minimalism has been an aesthetic notion, although its meaning has changed over time and across disciplines. This is because the maxim "less is more" is frequently used to describe minimalism and the same may be applied to lifestyle, art, fashion, architecture, literature, music, and interior design (Elangovan & Madhumathi, 2021). According to Uggla (2019), minimalism is a purposeful shift in lifestyle that runs contrary to current ideals of high speed and efficiency as well as modern consumer culture. The minimalism movement emerged as a response to the notion that material possessions could bring about contentment. It is plausible that this lifestyle has garnered a larger following as time has progressed.

Paying attention to the things, we value most is a key component of minimalism (Par. 2021). The ongoing repercussions of global warming and environmental degradation, such as extreme weather occurrences, accelerated melting of glaciers, and a deterioration in biodiversity owing to high consumerism, have recently brought attention to minimalism (Meissner, 2019). Minimalists adopt minimalism by reducing the number of possessions, use of sparse and uncluttered aesthetics and mindfully curating consumption (Wilson, & Bellezza, 2021). The objective of minimalism is to own fewer and necessary items that are useful. The control to consciously consume can be exercised through several strategies ranging from replacing already owned a greater number of items with fewer more useful ones, borrowing items that are rarely used from others, utilizing, and repairing old things, to reflecting on the usefulness of items (Dopierala, 2017). Many practitioners claim that minimalism is often mistaken to mean sacrifice, deprivation, being stingy, giving up all the modern amenities. Contrary to those misconceptions, a simple lifestyle driven by minimalism often aims to bring about inner peace and satisfaction (Par, 2021). It is a theory based on giving higher values to experiences over things. Minimalists place a high value on durability, giving preference to items that are thoughtfully crafted, versatile, and efficient with space. They steer clear of low-cost, low-quality products that are unable to withstand the passage of time (Kang et. al., 2021). A minimalist lifestyle enables a person to make purposeful judgments about what is essential to their life to make it meaningful (Hausen, 2018). Minimalism entails purposefully reducing consumption (Blonski & Witek 2019; Kang et. al. 2021).

Research on minimalism is in the nascent stage yet. In one of the most recent research, Wilson and Bellezza (2022) have proposed a three-dimension scale to measure consumer minimalism as a construct. The authors have offered a formal definition of this construct and explored the variegated subdimensions with an acceptable level of reliability and validity. The authors have conceptualized consumer minimalism as a 'value that embraces the mindful acquisition and ownership of few, curated possessions, with a preference for sparse aesthetics' (Wilson and Bellezza, 2021, pp. 801). The three dimensions proposed by the authors are, number of possessions, sparse aesthetics, and mindfully curated consumption. Before this work, researchers discussed perspectives and approaches to studying minimalism. For example, Nowak (2016), in the field of psychology, proposed a dynamic minimalism approach, which applies simplistic methods to produce complex structures and processes. Dopierala (2017) advocated minimalism, essentially a mode of anti-consumption which is having the purpose of enriching nonmaterial aspects of life. Herziger et. al. (2017) described minimalism as a mode of "voluntary simplicity" which has gained quick popularity. In a recent approach to understanding minimalism from a brand engagement perspective, Panagarkar et. al. (2021) have proposed a two-dimensional framework consisting of goal orientation (approach vs avoidance) and conditional susceptibility (normative vs economic) to position four typologies of minimalism, i.e., voluntary simplicity, reduced consumption, anti-consumption, and inconspicuous minimalism.

WELLBEING ORIENTATION

The well-being of self and others with a sense of collective existence has been a converging spirit of various notions of Minimalism. The first and obvious outcome on minimalism is financial well-being (Malik, & Ishitaq, 2023) because the very nature of minimalist principles discourages mindless spending. The findings of

Duon et al. (2023) highlighted the importance of minimalism in promoting human well-being by raising self-awareness and helping people recognize their inclusive moral identity as universal beings. While examining the connection of minimalism to well-being, Lloyd and Pennington (2020) have found five themes under well-being benefits of a low consumption lifestyle. Those were sense of autonomy, i.e., alignment with personal values with a sense of authenticity; enhanced competence due to the absence of chaos, confusion, and disorientation; larger mental space due to a decluttered external world, awareness of self and relationship to others including environment, and positive emotions such as joy and peacefulness. Jain et. al. (2023) found that a sense of fulfillment is an intermediate outcome of minimalism that further leads to well-being among millennials.

HISTORICAL ROOTS

The idea of leading a simple life or embracing simplicity has been around for millennia, although the term "minimalism" has only gained popularity in recent years (Shafqat et. al. 2023). Ohira and Masuda (2021) have highlighted the practices of voluntary simplicity in Japan are rooted in the Edo period (1603-1876). The authors observed backward consumption as one of the minimalist practices where consumers attempted to contemplate the consumption style of their ancient predecessors. Minimalism has been observed as a preferable way of living since the time of the Ancient Greeks and Romans. The idea of minimalism is observed to be readily inculcated in the ancient traditions and religious philosophies that originated in India. Buddhism, Yoga Sutras etc., are among the ancient texts from the Indian knowledge system that mention the values and practices oriented towards minimalism as self-imposed restraints to the seekers of spiritual growth (Perrett, 2002; Gould, 2022; Rathour and Mankame, 2021). In Western literature, Minimalism is known to be a movement away from materialism that said to be originated as an art movement in the United States as a reaction to abstract expressionism. It resurfaced as an art movement in the 1960s, gradually adapting to the fields of music, fashion, and design, and is now regarded as a consumption philosophy. During the outbreak of Covid-19, job loss, pay cuts, limited resources, etc., have forced everyone to rely on traditionally held minimalist values and practices to cope with the pandemic-led vulnerabilities. There has been a strong realization of the importance of a minimalist lifestyle which is gaining the share of heart and mind even in the post-pandemic world.

EMERGING TRENDS

In recent years, there has been a discernible increase in the number of individuals choosing to adopt a minimalistic way of living. Over time, minimalism evolved into a consumption style through the mediums of advertising, design, and fashion. The motivation was to live a simpler, more meaningful life based on the belief that material possessions have little social relevance. At present, there is a rising trend again across the world, including India, where people are consciously narrowing down their needs, decluttering their life, choosing 'eco-friendly' and 'organic' products, and showing concerns for health, environment, and sustainability (Rathour and Mankame, 2021). Individual consumption patterns combine to form the collective consumption patterns of the community (Jain, 2016). Over 21,000 consumers in 27 countries were surveyed for the Future Consumer Index, which found that 54% of respondents have changed their values and outlook on life. They have learned to live with less and adopted simpler and less materialistic values (Rogers, 2023). In a survey conducted by Dentsu Inc. among 1400 people in Japan and found that 54% respondents were aware about the Minimalism, 49% were sympathetic towards minimalism and 49,8% had the intention to adopt minimalism (Dentsu Inc., 2020). The reasons for gaining popularity worldwide are advances in technology, better connectivity between countries, growing environmental concerns and limited space for housing. Earlier Minimalism was practiced in different nations in the form of different movements like the "tiny house movement", "decluttering", "voluntary simplicity, "downshifters", "no plastic", "zero waste movement "etc. The objective of all these was to reduce consumption in one way or another. These small movements are now gaining momentum as their proponents are influencing others through social media platforms having a much wider outreach. As per an optimistic prediction by Ang (2021), Minimalism is not a trend that will fade away rather it is a lifestyle and a community that will keep on growing. Consumerism, overexploitation of natural resource, climate change, and change in work environment are some of the factors responsible for popularity of Minimalistic consumption.

Consumers adopt minimalism for various reasons, which find different expressions in different consumption contexts (Woodhead, 2022). For example, In the Western world, the cultural arts movement promoted minimalism mostly through fashion, design, and advertising (Chayka, 2020). Some minimalists focused on the different ways to display goods (Becker, 2018), some have stressed downsizing the quantity of buying, while others have focused on how owned goods should be disposed of (Kondo, 2014). Vladimirova (2021) reports that the motives for downsizing fashion consumption were frustration with style, frustration with excessive spending and troubling shopping habits, and dissatisfaction with the quality of life. Blonski and Witek (2019) have analyzed Polish literature discussing food wastage and fashion in the context of sustainable lifestyle consumption. For example, preferring durable goods over disposable goods and choosing things which are more functional and practical is a common approach for downsizing consumption. Thus, the literature on minimalism has primarily highlighted the exploratory studies of minimalistic practices emerging in different parts of the world.

ADAPTATION ACROSS DIVERSE INDUSTRIES

A growing number of consumers are opting not to give in to incentives from retailers to increase their volume of purchases. For businesses, this tendency may be troublesome. The 2022 Consumer Trends survey carried out by Leger USA has revealed a discernible trend that is gaining momentum across diverse market segments and industry verticals, pointing towards an increasing inclination towards minimalism. The present behavioral patterns observed in the health and wellness sector suggest that customers are no longer influenced by appealing catchphrases and packaging commitments. On the contrary, individuals are proactively pursuing food items that possess a reduced number of constituents, result in minimal packaging, and generate a lesser amount of waste. In 2023, Minimalism, comfort, connection with community and customization are proposed to be among the core themes of wellness trends in $4.4 trillion wellness industry (Golin, 2023).

In the beauty sector, multi-functional cosmetics such as 3-in-1 products that cater to the lips, eyes, and cheeks are expected to gain popularity due to the consumer preference for minimizing the overall usage of beauty products. According to Indus (2023), the popularity of minimalistic beauty regimens has led to the development of hybrid skincare-makeup products. These goods combine the advantages of skincare and cosmetics. Women's clothing in China has also been incorporating traditional culture's minimalism to meet the demands of the mass market (Cai, Chen, & Dai, 2021).

The idea of minimalism connecting to ecotourism is also getting more attention (Fennell & Weaver, 2005). Weaver's (2005) ideal of Minimalist ecotourism prioritized superficial learning opportunities centered on charismatic megafauna, with sustainability goals that were primarily site-specific and status-quo-oriented. Gradually, the clientele of the travel and tourism industry are actively seeking meaningful interactions, exceptional service provision, and experiential offerings as opposed to material possessions. For example, the preference for capsule hotels is getting more popular among both leisure and business travelers (Chen and Wei, 2022). Chen and Wei (2022), while focusing on the branding strategy of hotels, found that there are dominant value-oriented minimalistic lifestyles which are based on egoism and biospheric, that connect with different brand personalities represented by the hotels. Moreover, (Battilaniet al., 2018) have empirically demonstrated that Europeans are giving high importance to cultural values and ideologies, often associated with minimalist traditions, for sustainable tourism.

The packaging industry is also seeing a rise in the popularity of the minimalist aesthetic (Ton, et. al., 2023; Margariti, 2021). Ton et al. (2023) have found that customers are willing to pay more for simple packaging having few ingredients, and simple packaging also increases the perception of product purity. Similarly, Margariti (2021) reported the importance of white space and organic claims in food packaging, which have been successful in communicating quality as well as sustainability values. Nowadays, a lot of businesses place a focus on simple packaging. This trend makes perfect sense, in part because of the onslaught of information that modern consumers are forced to contend with Experts in marketing claim that the average consumer is now exposed to between 5,000 and 10,000 advertising messages daily, up from 3,000 to 5,000 in 2007 (Designalalytics, 2022). It is crucial to simplify packaging design to cut through the sea of information available to clients. The use of minimalist packaging has gained significant popularity, particularly in the context of organic products. The utilization of thrift stores has recently experienced an upsurge in popularity due to the trend of purchasing pre-owned goods as a means of mitigating financial and environmental strain.

DISRUPTIVE POTENTIAL TOWARDS DEINDUSTRIALIZATION

Minimalism is an antidote to consumerism, which fuels industrialization. We argue in this article that demand is the major determinant of the shift in industrial growth. The upward shift marks growth, whereas the downward shift leads to the deindustrialization of the economy (Fine, Ben & Leopold, Ellen, 1990; Flacher D., 2005; Perkins, 2005) Minimalists believe in the philosophy of "Less is more", and their lifestyle is characterized by the possession of fewer items that are required for survival. Industrialization and deindustrialization are the two stages of industrial growth. One must first understand industrialization to comprehend deindustrialization. Furthermore, it will serve as a foundation for defending our theory of "minimalization as an emergent force of deindustrialization." First, the supply side of industrialization is discussed. Then, looking from the perspective of the demand side, the study of industrialization during the last decade and a half guided our progression to discussion on industrialization, consumerism, and materialism and their ill effects on the well-being of consumers that forced them to adopt minimalism.

Industrialization

The Industrial Revolution, which started in Great Britain in the late 18th century, was the beginning of industrialization. During this time, manufacturing shifted from being performed by hand to being done by machines that were powered by steam and water. An increase in productivity, urbanization, and the expansion of the factory system were all results of the industrialization's substantial effects on society and the economy (Landes, 2003). As industrialization spread to other parts of Europe, North America, and Japan in the 19th century, it was accompanied by the rise of capitalism, which provided the financial resources needed for the expansion of industry (Hobsbawm, 2013). Novel innovations like railroads and telegraphs made trade and commerce easier, which fueled additional expansion and development. Industrialization proceeded to change the world economy throughout the 20th century, resulting in the expansion of multinational firms and the globalization of commerce. Arnold Toynbee (Wilson, 2014) further popularized the word "industrialization," which denoted a shift from an economy centered on manual labor in agriculture to one that is heavily mechanized and uses mass production techniques. From antiquity to the present, industrialization has had a tremendous impact on the world's economy, society, and environment.

The account of the industrial revolution that we are all acquainted with is largely a supply-side one, detailing how manufacturers came to be able to mass-produce new or improved commodities. The presumption seemed to be that whatever was made would be purchased, and little thought was given to the nature of the commodities themselves or why customers would desire them. According to Maxine Berg's study on "luxury" during the era of early industrialization, manufacturers were constantly looking for new ways to improve their products to meet the rising demand for consumer goods (Berg, 2005). This clearly states that the consumer revolution fueled the industrial revolution. This consumer revolution was discovered in 1982 by Neil McKendrick. "*A consumer revolution occurred in England in the eighteenth century along with the Industrial Revolution.... The consumer revolution was a turning point in the history of human experience*" (McKendrick, 1982, 9). Furthermore, historians who have emphasized industrialization as a narrative of overcoming production barriers using fossil fuels and new technologies have presumptively believed that there will always be a demand for mass-produced commodities (Gerth, K. et al., 2020; Franks, 2021). Thus, there was a parallel rise in demand and production So, the eighteenth century can be reinterpreted as a consumer revolution that raised the role of consumption or demand to that of a primary source of change that precedes and is on par with the revolution in production. The creation of the consumerist approach has been attributed to a hostility against the dominance of supply, a desire to restore the concept that the affluent make history as the cutting-edge and forward-thinking edge, and the growth of a supply and demand framework. (Fine et al., 1990).

All this historical evidence implies that consumerism is inextricably linked to industrialization. The traditional emphasis on manufacturing is likely to be shifted to consumption while studying consumerism. The relationship between industrialization and consumerism is explained in the next section.

Consumerism

The Industrial Revolution's primary driving force was consumer demand (Perkins, 2005). The 20th century saw the emergence of consumerism, a cultural and economic phenomenon that is fueled by the idea that having more possessions and material commodities improves one's quality of life (Schor, 2010). It is characterized by the constant pursuit of innovation in products and services, and the consumption of these goods is often seen as a means of achieving personal fulfillment and happiness (Eckhardt & Bardi, 2015). Consumerism has also been viewed as an organized movement by the government and public to elevate the power and rights of consumers in relation to sellers (Kumar et al., 2023). It is a socioeconomic phenomenon that has changed how societies are organized. Values, convictions, propensities, and ordinary circumstances have changed individuals and their ways of life in this manner.

The purpose of consumerism, as seen from the marketing perspective, is to encourage consumers to buy and use goods and services on a regular basis, hence increasing consumption over time (Heilbroner, 1985; Lage et. al., 2022). Philip Kotler in his study "What consumerism means for marketers", p. 53) mentioned that "Consumerism has come as a shock to many businesses because deep in their hearts they believe that they have been serving the customer extraordinary well.". Marketers' unfortunate response to consumerism was "manipulative or wild marketing," which was characterized by extensive use of promotional techniques hitting on customers' fears and anxieties, thereby encouraging them to buy more to maintain the expression of who they are as a person (Packard, 1957;Lambin, 1997). The rising concerns of market driven consumerism has invited criticism by many scholars are well (Lambert, 2019). Likewise, earlier researchers have advocated several reasons for which marketers must react to diminish the challenges of consumerism (Kanguan et. al., 1975).

Counter-Consumerism and Deindustrialization

A new philosophy of consumption known as minimalism, which encourages only purchasing what is absolutely required, has quietly emerged amid an era of unbridled materialism. This consumption strategy has received a lot of attention recently and has even inspired imitation because of the rising popularity of such minimalist lifestyle practices on social media platforms. The reasons for increased acceptance during recent times are climate change, working from home, and overconsumption (Ang, 2021). Despite having plenty of resources, these people forego the pleasures provided by commodities and adopt the opposing consumption idea, which merits further research (Zhang, 2022). Additionally, some researchers believe that minimalism can be a means for achieving liberation from anxieties, fears, and the shackles of the consumerist culture that has become our way of life (Fields Millburn & Nicodemus, n.d.).

"Minimalists," or the segment of people who subscribe to the minimalism culture, are also constituted by anti-consumerism groups. Anti-consumerism groups have emerged as a counter-culture wave of consumption to challenge the dominance of consumerism. These groups have brought about a heightened awareness of the behaviors of consumers, provided alternatives to the consumer lifestyle, and encouraged introspection regarding the positive and negative aspects of consumerism (Lage et. al., 2022). The emergence of minimalist "figureheads" over the course of the previous twelve years has contributed to a surge in the appeal of the minimalist lifestyle in developed countries such as the US, Europe, and Japan (Woodhead, 2022). The manipulative tactics used by corporations, implemented through their carefully crafted and persuasive communication strategies, have led to an increase in consumer demand, which has, in turn, contributed to the exhaustion of natural resources, and resulted in a polluted planet, which adversely affected the wellbeing entire species of life Perkins (2005). Byproducts that are readily apparent to the public include social inequality, the deterioration of human health, mental health issues, and planet health as well (Kasser, 2016). Therefore, it is the need of time to promote minimalism as a lifestyle movement against consumerism.

Meissner (2019) started a conversation about the gap between degrowth and lifestyle minimalism. He argued to show a connection across macro-economic considerations of the capitalistic development paradigm, its effects on the environment, and the micro-economic characteristics of individual consumption and wage labor. He has emphasized at the concept of accumulation, which is acting as a bridge between the expansion of the overall economy and the factors that influence it at the microeconomic level, such as individual consumption. This demonstrates that the level of consumption at the individual level has the potential to either accelerate or slow the growth of the industrial sector. Therefore, the result is likely to be deindustrialization. The transition from manufacturing goods to providing services may have been the impetus for deindustrialization, but it also had more fundamental causes, such as shifting attitudes regarding price and quality, as well as a wide range of political and cultural issues, including a modification in taste (Johnson, 2002). According to Gilbuoy (1932), who stated that the factory system, with its intricate industrial mechanism, is unable to function economically unless there is a large and expanding demand that is ready and eager to absorb its goods as quickly as they are produced, the factory system is unable to function economically. The shift from consumerism has the capacity to challenge the growth of the manufacturing sector.

CONCLUSION

Concerns about consumption and economic growth, which endanger the environment and society, have grown in recent years. This calls for reconsidering the standards of consumerism and restructuring consumption patterns as a necessity for a safe and sustainable future. The counter-consumerism movement known as minimalism is most common in countries that have recently undergone a great deal of industrialization. There is significant variation in the stages of economic development that are being experienced by the various countries that comprise the global economy. Although it is reasonable to claim that consumers in countries that have not yet experienced the effects of industrialization may not be receptive to the concept of minimalism until they reach the saturation point of consumerism, some economists feel that newly emerging economies may face premature industrialization. However, minimalism may accelerate the process of deindustrialization in developed countries, which are already experiencing this process. Industrialists do not need to worry after this scenario. Because it gives them the opportunity to redesign their products so that one item can meet a variety of needs as the minimalist segment demands. The business houses will need to work with sustainable raw materials and produce products that are durable, repairable, reusable, and recyclable.

The current article contributes to broadening the idea of minimalism and highlights its critical implications across different industries. Based on the recent studies, it won't be irrational to assume that the strong undercurrent of minimalism may be unstoppable because it is originated at the grassroot level, driven by consumer's awareness of health and environment, enacted by conscious choices, catalyzed by wellbeing motive, and most of all, advancing against high investment consumer culture narrative of materialism. This phenomenon has an obvious link to deindustrialization by directly impacting the demand patterns in the economy. Some industries have already responded to the demand of minimalistic consumers by introducing innovative products that are simple and sustainable, along with changes in packaging style. It is recommended that organizations must take it as an opportunity to build and introduce new product ranges with reduced complexity, fewer variants, and a longer shelf life. The public policy will also benefit from this. The greatest challenge facing the economies of the world is sustainability. By promoting minimalistic consumption through education and awareness, governments of nations may achieve planned degrowth of unsustainable industrial practices and products. This will help the industries to align with sustainable practices to get attention of the minimalist consumer segment, which is likely to grow in future. The level of minimalism adopted varies among consumers segments which may be a future area of research. there are consumers who may buy fewer products than before, some may prefer quality over quantity, others may prefer simplicity over complexity, some may prefer environment and animal friendly products, some are zero waste proponents, others me prefer health-oriented products, etc., depending on the kind of minimalism their lifestyles are aligned with. Moreover, it will help nations achieve the Sustainable Development Goals (SDG) chalked out by the United Nations.

Although, the coverage of literature used in this study is less, it is able to establish a rational connection between minimalism and deindustrialization. Moreover, the concept of minimalism is itself evolving. The new dimensions might be added to its definition. Various aspects of deindustrialization across different industries should also be researched well to understand the degree and direction of influence it might receive by growing minimalism. The study can be further enhanced by performing a systematic review of literature that connects these two constructs to come up with more specific premises which can be empirically validated.

ACKNOWLEDGMENT

This work is supported by the funding of the Indian Council of Social Science Research, New Delhi.

REFERENCES

Alderson, A. S. (1999). Explaining deindustrialization: Globalization, failure, or success? *American Sociological Review*, *64*(5), 701–721. doi:10.1177/000312249906400506

Ang, K. (2021, March 15). *Overconsumption Or A Move Towards Minimalism?* Social Science Space. https://www.socialsciencespace.com/2021/03/overconsumption-or-a-move-towards-minimalism/

Battilani, P., Bernini, C., & Mariotti, A. (2018). How to cope with dissonant heritage: A way towards sustainable tourism development. *Journal of Sustainable Tourism*, *26*(8), 1417–1436. doi:10.1080/09669582.2018.1458856

Becker, J. (2018). 10 Reasons why Minimalism is Growing [online]. *Becoming Minimalist.* https://www.becomingminimalist.com/10-reasons-why-minimalism-is-growinga-k-a-10-reasons-you-should-adopt-the-lifestyle/

Berg, M. (2005). *Luxury and Pleasure in Eighteenth-Century Britain.* OxfordUniversity Press.

Blazej. (n.d.). *Minimalism on Trend: When Consumers Don't Want to Consume.* CMB Info. https://www.cmbinfo.com/insights/minimalism-on-trend-when-consumers-dont-want-to-consume/

Block, J. H., & Fisch, C. (2020). Eight tips and questions for your bibliographic study in business and management research. *Management Review Quarterly, 70*(3), 307–312. doi:10.100711301-020-00188-4

Blonski K., & Witek J. (2019). Minimalism in consumption. Annales Universitatis Mariae Curie-Sklodwska, *Sectio H-Oeconomia, 53*(2).

Cai, J., Chen, N., & Dai, Q. (2021, December). The Turn of Minimalism in Chinese Women's Clothing in the New Century. In *2021 4th International Conference on Humanities Education and Social Sciences (ICHESS 2021)* (pp. 2441-2446). Atlantis Press. 10.2991/assehr.k.211220.423

Chayka, K. (2020). *The longing for less: Living with minimalism.* Bloomsbury Publishing USA.

Chen, S., & Wei, H. (2022). Minimalism in capsule hotels: Enhancing tourist responses by using minimalistic lifestyle appeals congruent with brand personality. *Tourism Management, 93*, 104579. doi:10.1016/j.tourman.2022.104579

Chen, S., Wei, H., Xiong, J., & Ran, Y. (2021). Less is more: A theoretical interpretation of minimalism in consumption. *Xinli Kexue Jinzhan, 29*(11), 2043–2061. doi:10.3724/SP.J.1042.2021.02043

Czerwiński, B., & Domański, J. (2023). Contemporary Consumer Trends. *Foundations of Management, 15*(1), 51–62. doi:10.2478/fman-2023-0004

Dentsu Inc. (2020). *Dentsu Conducts Third Consumer Survey on Sustainable Development Goals (SDGs).* Dentsu Inc.

Dopierała, R. (2017). Minimalism–a new mode of consumption? *Przegląd Socjologiczny, 66*(4), 67–83. doi:10.26485/PS/2017/66.4/4

Duong, T. T. T., Ngo, L. V., Surachartkumtonkun, J., Tran, M. D., & Northey, G. (2023). Less is more! A pathway to consumer's transcendence. *Journal of Retailing and Consumer Services*, *72*, 103294. doi:10.1016/j.jretconser.2023.103294

Eckhardt, G. M., & Bardhi, F. (2015). The Sharing Economy Is Not about Sharing at All. *Harvard Business Review*. https://hbr.org /2015/01/the-sharing-economy-isnt-about-sharing-at-all

Elangovan, S., & Madhumathi, A. (2021). Interpretation of Minimalism in Architecture According to Various Culture [IJERT]. *International Journal of Engineering Research & Technology (Ahmedabad)*, *10*(7).

Fennell, D., & Weaver, D. (2005). The ecotourium concept and tourism-conservation symbiosis. *Journal of Sustainable Tourism*, *13*(4), 373–390. doi:10.1080/09669580508668563

Fields Millburn, J., & Nicodemus, R. (n.d.). What is Minimalism? [Blog post]. *The Minimalists*. https://www.theminimalists. com/minimalism/

Fine, B. & Leopold, E. (1990). Consumerism and the Industrial Revolution. *Social History, 15*, 151-179. https://www.jstor.org/stable/4285840

Flacher, D. (2005). *Industrial Revolutions and Consumption: A Common Model to the Various Periods of Industrialization*, Working Papers halshs-00132241, HAL.

Gerth, K. (2020). Consumerism in Contemporary China. In T. Akram & S. Rashid (Eds.), *Faith, Finance, and Economy*. Palgrave Macmillan., doi:10.1007/978-3-030-38784-6_5

Gilboy Waterman, E. (1932). Demand as a Factor in the Industrial Revolution. First Published in: Cole, A.H., et al., Eds., Facts and Factors in Economic History, Harvard University Press (1932), and then in: Hartwell, R.M., ed., (2017), The Causes of the Industrial Revolution in England. Routledge, London and New York. doi:10.4159/harvard.9780674368897.c31

Golin. (2023, April). *Wellness Trends for 2023*. Golin. https://golin.com/2023/04/12/wellness-trends-for-2023/

Gould, H. (2022). Modern Minimalism and the Magical Buddhist Art of Disposal. *Buddhism and Waste: The Excess, Discard, and Afterlife of Buddhist Consumption, 53*.

Hausen, J. E. (2018). Minimalist life orientations as a dialogical tool for happiness. *British Journal of Guidance & Counselling*. doi:10.1080/03069885.2018.1523364

Heilbroner, R. L. (1985). *The Nature and Logic of Capitalism*. Norton.

Herziger, A., Berkessel, J. B., & Steinnes, K. K. (2020). Wean off green: On the (in) effectiveness of biospheric appeals for consumption curtailment. *Journal of Environmental Psychology*, *69*, 101415. doi:10.1016/j.jenvp.2020.101415

Indus. (2023, March). *Spring 2023 Beauty & Wellness Trends*. LoveIndus. https://loveindus.com/blogs/indus-ink/spring-2023-beauty-wellness-trends

Jain, D. (2016, April 1). *Changing the World by Changing Consumption*. The Acro Politian. https://theacropolitan.in/2016/04/01/changing-the-world-by-changing-consumption/

Jain, V. K., Gupta, A., & Verma, H. (2023). Goodbye materialism: Exploring antecedents of minimalism and its impact on millennials well-being. *Environment, Development and Sustainability*, 1–27. doi:10.100710668-023-03437-0 PMID:37363025

Johnson, C. (2002). De-industrialization and Globalization. *International Review of Social History*, *47*(S10), 3–33. doi:10.1017/S0020859002000767

Kang, J., Martinez, C. M. J., & Johnson, C. (2021). Minimalism as a sustainable lifestyle: Its behavioral representations and contributions to emotional well-being. *Sustainable Production and Consumption*, *27*, 802–813. doi:10.1016/j.spc.2021.02.001

Kangun, N., Cox, K. K., Higginbotham, J., & Burton, J. (1975). Consumerism and Marketing Management. *Journal of Marketing*, *39*(2), 3–10. doi:10.1177/002224297503900203

Kasser, T. (2016). Materialistic Values and Goals. *Annual Review of Psychology*, *67*(1), 489–514. doi:10.1146/annurev-psych-122414-033344 PMID:26273896

Kondo, M. (2014). *The life-changing magic of tidying up: The Japanese art of decluttering and organizing*. Ten Speed Press.

Kotler, P. (1972). What Consumerism Means to Marketers. *Harvard Business Review*, *50*, 48–57.

Kumar, R., Thapliyal, B., & Gupta, K. (2023). Consumerism: A Cultural Phenomenon. *International Journal of Research Publication and Reviews*, *4*(4), 2446–2449. doi:10.55248/gengpi.4.423.36256

Kunauskaite, G. (2023, March 10). *The Evolving Landscape of Consumerism*. Euromonitor. https://www.euromonitor.com/article/the-evolving-landscape-of-consumerism?ite=60058&ito=528&itq=fff5c656-1e85-4119-9bcf-59fcaf5a15e3&itx%5Bidio%5D=5896212

Lage, C., Lins, S., & Aquino, S. D. D. (2022). Consumerism. In *Routledge Encyclopedia of Psychology in the Real World*. Routledge. doi:10.4324/9780367198459-REPRW118-1

Lambert, C. J. (2019). Consumerism, Violence, and Dehumanization: The Vicious Dynamic Circle. In Multifaceted Explorations of Consumer Culture and Its Impact on Individuals and Society (pp. 196-209). IGI Global.

Lambin, J. J. (1997). *Strategic Marketing Management*. McGraw-Hill.

Landes, D. S. (2003). The Industrial Revolution in Britain. In The unbound Prometheus: Technological change and industrial development in Western Europe from 1750 to the present. (pp. 41–123). Cambridge Press. doi:10.1017/CBO9780511819957.004

Leger U.S.A. (2022, January 11). *Consumer Trends: Minimalism Hits the Market*. Leger USA. https://blog.legerusa.com/2022-consumer-trends-minimalism-hits-the-market

Lloyd, K., & Pennington, W. (2020). Towards a theory of Minimalism and well-being. *International Journal of Applied Positive Psychology*, *5*(3), 121–136. doi:10.100741042-020-00030-y

Malik, & Ishitaq, I. (2023, July). Impact of minimalist practices on consumer happiness and financial well-being. *Journal of Retailing and Consumer Services, 73*. doi:10.1016/j.jretconser.2023.103333

Margariti, K. (2021). "White" Space and Organic Claims on Food Packaging: Communicating Sustainability Values and Affecting Young Adults' Attitudes and Purchase Intentions. *Sustainability (Basel)*, *13*(19), 11101. doi:10.3390u131911101

Martin-Woodhead, A. (2022). Limited, considered and sustainable consumption: The (non)consumption practices of UK minimalists. *Journal of Consumer Culture*, *22*(4), 1012–1031. doi:10.1177/14695405211039608

Meissner, M. (2019). Against accumulation: Lifestyle minimalism, de-growth and the present post-ecological condition. *Journal of Cultural Economics*, *12*(3), 1–16. doi:10.1080/17530350.2019.1570962

Mokyr, J. (1977). Demand vs. Supply in the Industrial Revolution. *The Journal of Economic History*, *37*(4), 981–1008. https://www.jstor.org/stable/2119351. doi:10.1017/S0022050700094778

Nowak, A. (2016). Dynamical minimalism: Why less is more in psychology. In *Theory Construction in Social Personality Psychology* (pp. 183–192). Psychology Press.

Packard, V. (1957). *The Hidden Persuaders*. D.McKay Co.

Pangarkar, A., Shukla, P., & Charles, R. (2021). Minimalism in consumption: A typology and brand engagement strategies. *Journal of Business Research, 127*, 167–178. doi:10.1016/j.jbusres.2021.01.033

Par, T. (2021). Materialism to Minimalism. *BU Well, 6*(1), 5.

Perrett, R. W. (2002). Personal identity, minimalism, and Madhyamaka. *Philosophy East & West, 52*(3), 373–385. doi:10.1353/pew.2002.0017

Rogers. (2023). *When consumers want less but demand more, how will your business grow?* EY. https://www.ey.com/en_gl/consumer-products-retail/changing-consumption-will-reshape-business-priorities

Shafqat, T., Ishaq, M. I., & Ahmed, A. (2023). Fashion consumption using minimalism: Exploring the relationship of consumer well-being and social connectedness. *Journal of Retailing and Consumer Services, 71*, 103215. doi:10.1016/j.jretconser.2022.103215

Ton, L. A. N., Smith, R. K., & Sevilla, J. (2023). EXPRESS: Symbolically Simple: How Simple Packaging Design Influences Willingness to Pay for Consumable Products. *Journal of Marketing*, 00222429231192049. doi:10.1177/00222429231192049

Uggla, Y. (2019). Taking back control: Minimalism as a reaction to high speed and overload in contemporary society. *Sociologisk Forskning, 56*(3-4), 233–252. doi:10.37062f.56.18811

Vladimirova, K. (2021). Consumption corridors in fashion: deliberations on upper consumption limits in minimalist fashion challenges. *Sustainability: Science. Sustainability, 17*(1), 102–116. doi:10.1080/15487733.2021.1891673

Vries, D. (2008). *The Industrious Revolution: Consumer Behavior and the Household Economy,1650 to the Present*. Cambridge University Press. doi:10.1017/CBO9780511818196

Wilson, A., & Bellezza, S. (2021). Consumer Minimalism. Journal of Consumer Research Consumer Minimalism. *The Journal of Consumer Research, 48*(5), 796–816. doi:10.1093/jcr/ucab038

Wilson, A. V. (2020). *The Evolving Marketplace: Essays on How Digitization and Abundance Influence Consumption*. Harvard University.

Wilson, D. C. S. (2014). Arnold Toynbee and the Industrial Revolution: The Science of History. *Political Economy and the Machine Past. History & Memory, 26*(2), 133–161. doi:10.2979/histmemo.26.2.133

Zhang, M. (2022). Research on the Acceptability of Minimalist Consumption in China. *The Frontiers of Society. Science and Technology*, *4*(8), 64–70. doi:10.25236/FSST.2022.040811

KEY TERMS AND DEFINITIONS

Consumerism: The lifestyle guided by a growing propensity to consume, generally superfluous goods or services, due to their symbolic meaning.

Counter-Consumerism: Opposed to consumerism, it advocates the reduction of excessive and continuous purchase and consumption of material goods.

Deindustrialization: The process by which the economy of a nation or region, through the elimination or reduction of industrial capacity or activity, especially heavy industry or manufacturing, causes social and economic change.

Industrialization: The process by which the economy of a nation or region shifts from a focus primarily on agricultural production to mass-produced, technologically advanced goods and services.

Minimalism: The lifestyle that requires the possession of fewer material goods. Individuals with this lifestyle intentionally live with fewer possessions, focus only on those they need, and avoid the acquire, consume, buy mentality that more is better.

Voluntary Simplicity: The lifestyle that rejects high consumer culture, discards a materialistic lifestyle, and minimizes the pursuit of wealth for its own sake in favour of practices that promote simplicity in lifestyle. Voluntary simplicity practices include reducing the number of possessions one owns, relying less on technology and services, and spending less money.

Well-Being Orientation: Orientation that promotes the state of being healthy, happy, and comfortable, both physically and mentally.

Chapter 7
Exploring Consumer Behavior in the Context of Voluntary Simplicity

Nesenur Altinigne
Istanbul Bilgi University, Turkey

ABSTRACT

Voluntary simplicity has received growing attention during the last few years. Especially after the COVID-19 pandemic, many consumers are trying to rebuild work–life balance and reconsider their priorities. Voluntary simplicity has become one of the most popular lifestyles as a result of these efforts. Hence, this chapter aims to explore the concept of voluntary simplicity by first identifying its relationship with minimalism. Then, the concept, existing literature, and the relationship between voluntary simplicity and well-being are explained. Finally, future research directions for improving the existing literature are presented.

INTRODUCTION

Excessive consumption has been associated with the cause of many negative effects both to nature and humanity. The COVID-19 pandemic, shortage of natural resources, global warming, and even consumption-related disorders have become widespread worldwide. As a result, a need for psychological and behavioral changes to enhance environmental, social, and individual well-being has emerged. Various research in literature relates overconsumption and materialism to loss of well-being. In the existing literature, research indicated that decreased materialism is related to increased feelings of personal security and intrinsic values (Kasser, 2016; Oral and

DOI: 10.4018/978-1-6684-9277-2.ch007

Thurner, 2019). Moreover, several studies link overconsumption with the scarcity of natural resources and environmental problems. Hence, a change in consumer behavior regarding overconsumption and sustainability is required to rebuild and protect the environmental and individual balance.

Voluntary simplicity is a sustainability-rooted anti-consumption-related behavior, defined as a lifestyle that focuses on pursuing a simple life by decreasing consumption and related practices. Voluntary simplicity is a relatively new and understudied topic about the tendency of consumers who are sensitive to sustainability issues. Johnston and Burton (2003) indicated twelve dimensions that help to explain voluntary simplicity. Some are "good life, personal growth, self-determination, material simplicity, ecological awareness, and minimal consumption." In a similar vein, shared values between voluntary simplifiers and ethical consumers are established in terms of the regulation and limitation of consumption. Voluntary simplifiers attempt to transform their everyday lifestyles based on various ethical principles. Voluntary simplifiers decide "what is necessary" and keep themselves away from materialism and product ownership by limiting consumption. They intentionally only buy the products they truly want and attempt to build a meaningful life and well-being.

This chapter aims to analyze and critically discuss the concept, motivations, and consequences of voluntary simplicity. This chapter presents the categorization of voluntary simplicity and analyses: the definitions, antecedents, and impacts of the concept by investigating the existing literature. By providing existing literature on voluntary simplicity, the paper contributes to the exploration of the concept and the evaluation of the problems in the literature and opportunities for further research. The managerial implications of voluntary simplicity are discussed within the field of consumer behavior.

THE IMPORTANCE OF VOLUNTARY SIMPLICITY FOR MARKETERS

The voluntary simplicity lifestyle is crucial for marketers to understand after the pandemic. Marketers have discussed that the widespread acceptance of voluntary simplicity ideas could bring about a significantly altered landscape for researchers (Johnston, 2000). The increasing number of supporters of voluntary simplicity could have a profound impact on current marketing practices (Ensley, 1983). The voluntary simplicity approach is explained by "choosing functional products with simple packaging, responding to promotions that emphasize value and information, shopping at localized small outlets, and being open to purchasing do-it-yourself products to save money" (Shama, 1985, p:4). The behavior of voluntary simplifiers may pose challenges for marketers in terms of the frequency of their purchases and the characteristics they look for in a product or service. The findings of in-depth interviews conducted by Craig-Lees and Hill (2002) indicated that consumers embracing a voluntary simplicity perspective restrain their consumption intentionally both regarding the volume and the products they purchase. In exchange for time to do what they wish, these people reduce their consumption by looking for value for money, buying fewer items, and being mindful of the brands they choose (Johnston and Burton, 2003). Hence, marketers need to embrace the unique characteristics of this group of consumers, acknowledge their lifestyles, and treat them as a separate segment. Accordingly, effective features of the products and services such as durability, functionality, and time-saving features can be emphasized.

Voluntary Simplicity reverses the behaviors of mainstream consumers in several ways. While typical consumers usually desire more material possessions, voluntary simplifiers seek to reduce their belongings and declutter their lives. While consumers strive to earn more to consume more, simplicity advocates (voluntary simplifiers) work (earn) less and aim to minimize their consumption. Voluntary simplifiers often share the environmentalist belief in the principles of "reduce, reuse, recycle," which can often conflict with companies' aims to increase sales and profits (Hawkins et al., 2001). While mainstream consumers seek convenience and low cost, voluntary simplifiers are willing to invest extra effort and expense to get durable and eco-friendly products. It is possible to trust that mainstream consumers will buy what they desire. In contrast, voluntary simplifiers prefer to minimize their material desires and purchases and select to obtain goods by making (do-it-yourself approach), borrowing (alternative car transport), buying used (platforms for selling second-hand products), or not buying at all.

THE CONCEPT AND DEFINITION OF VOLUNTARY SIMPLICITY

The term voluntary simplicity was initially introduced by Richard Gregg in 1936, defining it as a" conscious lifestyle that limits possessions and clutter to live with purpose" (Hook et al., 2023, p: 131). Other authors further elaborated on this concept, characterizing voluntary simplicity as a "way of life that embraces frugality in consumption, a strong environmental awareness, a desire for more humane living and working conditions, and a commitment to realizing one's psychological and spiritual potential in harmony with others" (Elgin and Mitchell, 1977: p. 2). Although individual definitions of voluntary simplicity may vary, its fundamental values comprise "material simplicity, self-determination and self-sufficiency, ecological consciousness, social responsibility, as well as spirituality, and personal growth" (Boujbel and d'Astous, 2012).

Given the increasing body of research on voluntary simplicity, the concept has been employed to encompass a wide range of behaviors and motives. Voluntary simplicity includes various aspects concerning values, practices, and interactions with others and the environment. While these categories are related, they have been discussed separately in numerous research. Rebouças and Soares (2021) categorized the definitions of voluntary simplicity into six groups to gain a deeper insight into the prevalence and scope of different facets of voluntary simplicity. These categories are "(1) reduced material consumption; (2) search for intrinsic values, well-being and quality of life; (3) environmental responsibility; (4) social consciousness and focus on relationships; (5) self-sufficiency; and (1) working hours reduction" (p:308).

The six dimensions identified by Rebouças and Soares (2021) align with the values presented by Elgin and Mitchell (1977) in their paper on voluntary simplicity: material simplicity, human scale, self-determination, ecological awareness, and personal growth. The values of self-determination and self-growth are related to the pursuit of internal values, well-being, and personal development, while the facet of reducing working duration can be connected to the contemporary different movement called slow living (Botta, 2015).

The literature demonstrates that the thought of voluntary simplicity is perceived as multifaceted. The prevalence of different aspects in various studies explains that existing literature emphasizes diverse aspects when theorizing voluntary simplicity. This plurality may vary over time and across cultural contexts in research. However, a common essence of voluntary simplicity can be observed by noting the most frequently highlighted aspects, such as reducing consumption and embracing inner values, that might be considered as steppingstones to other aspects. As a result of their research covering one hundred and six articles, Rebouças and Soares (2021) conceptualize voluntary simplicity as a choice that aims to reduce consumption while focusing on intrinsic values about sustainability and social well-being.

THE RELATIONSHIP BETWEEN THE CONCEPT OF MINIMALISM AND VOLUNTARY SIMPLICITY

Voluntary simplicity and minimalism have common essential properties, such as a focus on decreasing consumption and minimizing material possessions while emphasizing self-growth and values. While some explanations of voluntary simplicity also emphasize responsibilities regarding the environment or society, the definitions of minimalism are vaguer in these fields, allowing people to express their values according to their own perspectives (Hook et al., 2023).

Global consumerism has witnessed significant growth due to internationalization, improved living standards, and exposure to diverse cultures. This perspective that indulges consumerism has developed its own cure and led to an experience-driven economy (Pine and Gilmore, 2013). The roots of minimalism date back to 1965 (Pangarkar et al., 2021) and revolve around the idea of owning fewer possessions, reducing excessive consumption, and enhancing the overall quality of life by not favoring consumerism (Lee and Ahn, 2016).

Minimalistic consumers now prioritize simplicity and consciously avoid excessive materialism as they are previously engaged, and they strive to reduce their dependence on material possessions that offer instant gratification (Iyer and Muncy, 2016; Seegebarth et al., 2016). Notably, the economic shock triggered by the COVID-19 pandemic, along with lingering financial concerns, might further amplify interest in this minimalist consumption philosophy.

Minimalism is a lifestyle that can be utilized to attain the objective of living a simple and harmonious life in pursuit of happiness, free from stress and anxieties (Black and Cherrier, 2010; Peyer et al., 2017). However, existing research reveals diverse interpretations and understandings of minimalism, which vary based on consumer interpretations. Previous studies have proposed that minimalism can manifest in different ways, such as voluntary simplicity, reduced consumption, anti-consumption, and inconspicuous minimalism (Pangarkar et al., 2021). In this context, this chapter aims to clarify and differentiate voluntary simplicity from other expressions of minimalistic consumption.

Existing literature investigated the concept of minimalism from different perspectives and several forms that minimalism may take are explained. Some of the researchers have studied the concept from the aspect of anti-consumption (Iyer and Muncy, 2009; Lee et al., 2009) which is parallel to boycotting consumption (Grigsby, 2012). Some authors embrace the view of voluntary simplicity to examine minimalism. Even though they have utilized different perspectives, they agree on a common understanding that minimalism is the embracement of a more simplistic and uncomplicated lifestyle to provide satisfaction happiness, and fulfillment by focusing on interests and activities. Consumers who prefer a minimalist lifestyle may also desire to maximize their utility of consumption. However, they reach their goal by focusing on simplicity, improvement in the quality of life, and the achievement of subjective well-being (Meissner, 2019).

There are different categorizations of minimalism in literature. For instance, Iyer and Muncy (2009) investigated anti-consumption research and they grouped anti-consumption consumers into four distinct types: general-societal consumers (concerned about societal welfare and environmental impact), general-personal consumers (inspired by spiritual or ethical beliefs, opposed to engaging in actions driven solely by personal gain), brand-societal consumers (driven by the belief that specific brands or products cause harm to society), and brand-personal consumers (avoiding a brand due to a negative event associated with it). In essence, their categorization was based on two main factors: consumers who aim to decrease their overall consumption and those focused on reducing their consumption of specific brands or products. However, Pangarkar et al. (2021) defended that a new perspective is required due to the additional changes that have occurred over the past decade (consumer lifestyles, demands, and aspirations). Particularly after the COVID-19 pandemic, consumers need to possess increased savings during times of crisis, improve their quality of life, and achieve well-being. Furthermore, as a result of demanding lifestyles and hectic work schedules, certain consumers have embraced minimalism as a way to prioritize inner peace and contentment over material possessions. Consequently, they employed two key criteria to categorize various forms of minimalistic consumption: conditional susceptibility and consumption goal orientation. Conditional susceptibility pertains to the impact of economic or normative factors that shape an individual's approach to their consumption objectives. Consumption goal orientation is a state of motivation characterized by the aspiration to achieve a goal, either by striving for success or by avoiding failure (Deci and Ryan, 1985).

EXISTING LITERATURE ON VOLUNTARY SIMPLICITY

Research into voluntary simplicity explores its relationship with sustainable consumption (Albert, 2019; Kropfeld et al., 2018) and delves into its consequences for economic growth, materialism, and social responsibility (Alexander, 2012). Furthermore, voluntary simplicity has been associated with aspects such as well-being and life satisfaction (Bayat and Sezer, 2018), along with ethical considerations (Read et al., 2018). These studies explore the association of voluntary simplicity with various significant themes, such as reducing consumption, addressing political issues, promoting well-being, fostering ethical behavior, and supporting sustainability, but they also validate the different dimensions of voluntary simplicity definitions and the fundamental values proposed previous studies (Elgin and Mitchell, 1977). Certain relevant aspects in voluntary simplicity research, like the correlation between voluntary simplifiers and conscious consumers or frugal consumers, have received less attention so far (Albert, 2019).

Pepper et al. (2009) emphasize that the study of socially conscious behavior related to voluntary simplicity is an emerging area of research. Consumer consciousness is recognized as a significant factor influencing the adoption of the voluntary simplicity lifestyle (Elgin and Mitchell, 1977) and constitutes a fundamental facet of voluntary simplicity (Huneke, 2005). Scholars also participate in discussions about the potential applications of this lifestyle on public policies, with some suggesting that individual actions can serve as antecedents to collective efforts (Haenfler et al., 2012; Kasser, 2009).

The core proposition of voluntary simplicity is to put less importance on collecting and possessing materialistic goods and instead focus on investing consumers' financial resources, attention, and energy in activities that bring greater meaning and contribute to life satisfaction. Voluntary simplicity is an approach embraced by many consumers in recent years. For consumers who embrace voluntary simplicity, the aim is to restrain consumption and develop an interest and pursuits in non-materialistic pursuits as a means of self-fulfillment (Etzioni, 1999). The economic impacts in consumers' lives guide these aspirations and suggest managing financial resources smartly.

Voluntary simplicity can be viewed as a form of awakening or enlightenment for consumers, diverging from conspicuous consumption and advocating a mindful approach characterized by responsibility, a functional lifestyle, and a balanced practice of moderation, self-discipline, and self-regulation concerning consumption habits. As explained by Turner (2010), voluntary simplicity does not encourage living in deprivation; rather, it emphasizes the importance of individuals defining their own levels of sufficiency and exercising prudence in financial matters while resisting the allure of excessive material possessions. It can be perceived as a concept linked to self-identity because its core revolves around an individual's attitudes, perceptions, and judgments about their objectives, achievements, and self-worth.

According to existing research, voluntary simplicity is a mindset that encourages people to honestly decrease or eliminate excessive elements from their lives and instead concentrate on the realization of their capabilities and fulfilling their duties (Elgin, 1981). When people embrace voluntary simplicity, they often experience a greater sense of control over their lives and engage in introspection, resulting in an overall heightened sense of ownership and positivity. This, in turn, enables them to allocate resources towards meaningful goals, such as personal growth, education, and the development of abilities (Craig-Lees and Hill, 2002).

Voluntary simplifiers intentionally choose to consume items that contribute to their happiness and satisfaction levels (Elgin, 1981). The reason for this is that self-motivation and self-regulation are essential for these types of consumers to achieve their goals to attain well-being. Voluntary simplicity assists them in achieving these goals (Cherrier and Murray, 2007; Huneke, 2005). Advocates of voluntary simplicity direct their focus toward deeper and more fulfilling life goals from their perspectives as they seek to maximize their time and financial resources in pursuing experiential and profoundly satisfying activities.

Some scholars argue that voluntary simplicity functions as a defense mechanism against the negative impacts of materialism. By adopting this lifestyle, consumers alleviate excessive concerns about acquisition and possession, choosing instead to focus on cultivating hobbies, skills, and interests that bring them genuine happiness (Craig-Lees and Hill, 2002). Voluntary simplifiers adopt this approach as a means to embrace positivity, take charge of their daily lives, and derive joy and comfort from internal sources rather than relying heavily on external factors (Leonard-Barton, 1981). Conversely, other researchers define voluntary simplicity as a revolution that empowers individuals to enhance their self-reliance and develop a discerning sense of life priorities (Zavestoski, 2002).

The conceptualizations of Pangarkar et al. (2021) and Iyer and Muncy (2016) overlap in many ways; broad-based micro-consumerist opposition, which revolves around avoiding excessive consumption to lead a simpler life. However, Pangarkar et al. (2021) extended the concept by differentiating and explaining the foundations and characteristics of voluntary simplifiers. Also, their conceptualization of voluntary simplifiers differs from a previous version focused on anti-consumption simplifiers (Iyer and Muncy, 2009). Since Iyer and Muncy (2009) argue that anti-consumption simplifiers are not influenced by economic conditions, Pangarkar et al. (2021) indicated that voluntary simplifiers tend to prioritize sensible resource allocation due to potential economic constraints. Furthermore, it is important to highlight that current research emphasizes the avoidance of specific brands known to be harmful to society and products that have negative effects or associations in the lives of voluntary simplifiers. On the other hand, other areas of research focus on delving into the motivations and underlying reasons behind why consumers adopt voluntary simplicity or engage in reduced consumption through a goal-oriented perspective.

Recently, consumers who pursue a voluntary simplicity lifestyle have chosen to declutter their homes due to the previously chaotic lifestyles characterized by continuous buying and consumption. It has been proven that reducing clutter to better utilize space and free the mind from excessive consumption is an immensely gratifying experience for such voluntary simplifiers (Pangarkar et al., 2021). Various groups and communities are advocating voluntary simplicity.

Distribution of the Articles

One hundred and eighty-seven papers about voluntary simplicity were published between 2000 and 2023. Only six papers were published before 2000 (1981-2000). Figure 1 illustrates a comparison between the years 2000 and 2023 in terms of the research advancements in the literature on voluntary simplicity. It is evident that the recent four years (2019, 2020, 2021, 2022) have seen a substantial surge in the number of published articles on voluntary simplicity. A total of 72 articles were published during the period from 2019 to 2022, with 18 articles appearing each year. These articles related to voluntary simplicity were featured in diverse journals such as the Journal of Business Ethics, Psychology & Marketing, Journal of Consumer Research, Journal of Consumer Affairs, and Journal of Macromarketing (Figure 1).

Figure 1. Progress of voluntary simplicity studies in the literature according to year
Source: Authors own creation

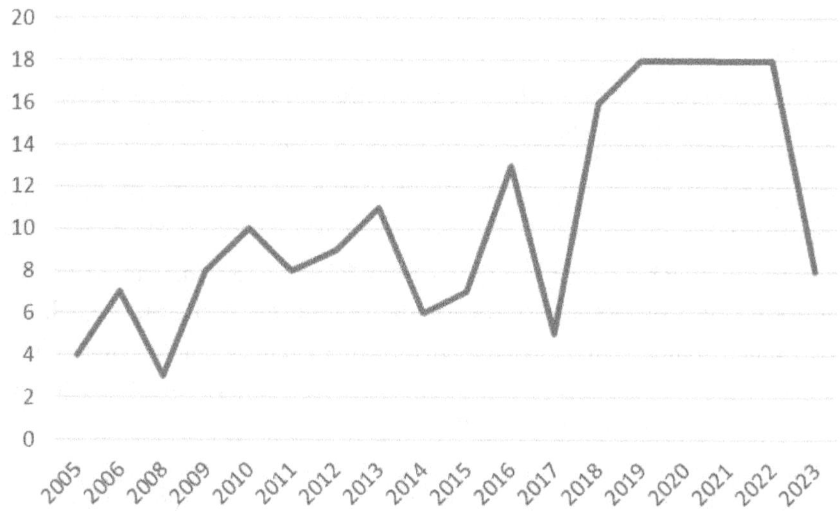

Motivations of Voluntary Simplicity

Self-determination theory delineates human motivation and personality in social contexts by differentiating between autonomous and controlled motivation (Deci and Ryan, 2002). This theory posits variations in the types of motivations (intrinsic and extrinsic) present in people. Self-determination theory is considered as the basic theory behind the voluntary simplicity act. Mainly the intrinsic motivations were emphasized in the existing literature.

The predominant intrinsic motivation found in the literature was the aspiration to live following one's values, seeking to disengage from a system that did not align with those values (Hakansson and Sengers, 2013). Following closely, another prevalent intrinsic motivation highlighted in the literature was the importance of autonomy, expressing the wish for increased independence (Vannini and Taggart, 2015). This could manifest as a need to distance oneself from a disagreeable system, leading to greater autonomy (Powers, 2010), or simply a personal desire to live more independently and enjoy the associated benefits (Rosen, 2010). The third intrinsic motivation identified was the longing for identity and a stronger sense of self (Sandlin et al., 2016).

Lang (2017) conducted a qualitative research to unveil the intrinsic and extrinsic motivations behind voluntary simplicity. According to research the main four intrinsic motivations of the voluntary simplifiers were the desire to live according to their values, the desire to feel autonomous, the desire to learn, and the interest in alternative lifestyles. Also, some extrinsic motivations such as having better physical/mental health and Less dependency, making a less negative impact on the environment, and saving money were identified.

Measures of Voluntary Simplicity

Various methods have been employed to measure voluntary simplicity in research. In some studies, participants were enlisted based on their self-identification as voluntary simplifiers or minimalists, frequently sourced from specific groups or organizations dedicated to simplicity. An alternative method includes the use of self-report measures, where assessments of values and behaviors associated with voluntary simplicity are conducted (Balderjahn et al., 2013; Iyer and Muncy, 2009).

Additionally, measurements of voluntary simplicity vary in their focal points. Some measurements primarily concentrate on consumption reduction (Balderjahn et al., 2013), while others are more comprehensive, containing items related to environmental and social responsibility (Shama and Wisenblit, 1984).

Widely Used Research Methods

Studies in literature utilize both qualitative and quantitative methods, employing diverse data collection techniques. Exploration of the methods and techniques applied in research on voluntary simplicity is valuable for gaining insights into prior research designs and comprehending the extent of exploration in this area.

A significant part of the literature consists of conceptual papers that present analyses (Etzioni, 2004; Read et al., 2018), suggest propositions, and establish connections between theories. Some qualitative studies employ semi-structured or unstructured in-depth interviews (Shaw and Moraes, 2009), while others combine interviews with focus groups or participant observations (Shaw and Newholm, 2002).

Mixed-methods studies, integrating semi-structured interviews with surveys, constitute a small part of the research (Kennedy et al., 2013). Consequently, although previous studies have employed a mix of methodologies, the limited use of focus groups, critical incident technique, netnography, or case studies suggests a need for more research utilizing these methods to gather further insight into motivations and perceptions. Table 1 presents the references, nature of work, and research design of the studies about voluntary simplicity.

Relationship Between Voluntary Simplicity and Consumer Wellbeing

Voluntary simplicity and well-being are generally explained together in the literature. Voluntary simplicity might impact well-being by providing psychological need satisfaction. According to self-determination theory, "autonomy, competence, and relatedness are psychological needs that contribute to optimal psychological development" (Ryan and Deci, 2000, p:55). This theory also emphasizes the significance of intrinsic motivation. By adopting voluntary simplicity, individuals may redirect their attention from external factors, like gathering wealth and material possessions for happiness toward internal factors that have a higher potential to fulfill their fundamental psychological needs.

Furthermore, voluntary simplicity might be linked to well-being by limiting consumption desires. The presence of consumption desires can create discomfort as individuals experience internal tension when they are unable to fulfill specific desires (Boujbel and d'Astous, 2012). Feelings of disappointment, frustration, stress, and anger may be associated with these consumption desires (Boujbel and d'Astous, 2012). Voluntary simplicity could lead to reduced levels of consumption desires resulting in higher levels of well-being. Additionally, voluntary simplicity might impact well-being by substituting materialistic values. Studies have revealed a negative correlation between materialistic goals and values and well-being (Diener and Dittmar et al., 2014). Adopting voluntary simplicity has the potential to prompt individuals to substitute materialistic values with other facets that actively contribute to well-being, such as prioritizing relations, health, and personal growth.

The literature has identified several variables that connect the voluntary simplicity lifestyle with consumer well-being. The management of consumption desires can mediate the relationship regarding voluntary simplicity and well-being. Existing research provides evidence for the positive connection between voluntary simplicity and life satisfaction through the control of consumption desires, particularly among individuals with lower incomes (Boujbel and d'Astous, 2012). Consequently, it can be inferred that voluntary simplicity is linked to a greater ability to control consumption desires, which, in turn, is related to higher levels of life fulfillment.

Furthermore, the fulfillment of psychological needs might act as a mediator between voluntary simplicity and well-being. As demonstrated by Rich et al. (2017), explored the mediating role of psychological need satisfaction in the link between voluntary simplicity and life satisfaction. Voluntary simplicity is positively related to greater psychological need satisfaction and is associated with higher levels of life satisfaction.

Income and the motivation of voluntary simplicity whether the tendency was initiated personally with inner motivations (self-initiated) or was affected by external sources (other-initiated) might be valuable to consider in this relationship. Income has the potential to moderate the voluntary simplicity and well-being relationship. The link between voluntary simplicity and well-being may be stronger among participants with lower incomes compared to those with higher incomes. Existing research suggests that for individuals with lower incomes, voluntary simplicity is positively associated with life satisfaction, whereas for those with higher incomes, voluntary simplicity and life satisfaction relationship is not significant (Boujbel and d'Astous, 2012).

Moreover, the initiation of voluntary simplicity, whether by self or other initiated, can also influence its relationship with well-being. In particular, voluntary simplicity and well-being relationship might be more favorable for individuals who self initiate their adoption of this lifestyle compared to those who are prompted by external factors. Existing studies in the literature have predominantly utilized voluntary simplifiers or evaluated participants' voluntary simplicity levels through surveys, indicating that most voluntary simplicity practices are self-initiated. Nevertheless, there are a few exceptions where researchers employed participants and encouraged them to adopt voluntary simplicity routines as part of a longitudinal study (McGouran and Prothero, 2016), in which voluntary simplicity practices were started by external influences.

Table 1. Existing literature on voluntary simplicity

References	Nature of work	Research Design
Elgin and Mitchell (1977). Van Steenbergen and Feller (1979), Olsen (1981), Williams (1984), Rudmin (1990), Little (1995), Leisinger (1998), Meier (2000), Etzioni (2004), Buell (2005), Connolly and Shaw (2006), Hellöre (2008), Librova (2008), Kasser (2009), Gambrel and Cafaro (2010), Friedman and Friedman (2010), Alexander (2011), Hall (2011), Kronenberg and Iida (2011), Alexander (2012), Romano (2012), Haenfler et al. (2012), Alexander (2013), Whitney Sanford (2013), Fraňková and Johanisová (2013), Kaynak and Eksi (2013), Garcia-Ruiz and Rodriguez-Lluesma (2014), Alexander (2014), Feola (2014), Leipämaa- Leskinen et al. (2016), Nefat (2016), Read et al. (2018), Kannisto (2018).	Conceptual papers	Content Analysis
Kuanr et al. (2020), Peifer et al. (2020), Lee (2019), Balderjahn and Hüttel (2019), Taljaard and Sonnenberg (2019), Kropfeld et al. (2018), Bayat and Sezer (2018), Chowdhury (2018), Brown and Kasser (2005), Huneke (2005), Alexander and Ussher (2012), Leonard Barton (1981), Shama (1988), Saunders (2000), Iwata (2001), Shama and Wisenblit (1984), Iwata (1997), Iwata (1999), Iwata (2006), Chhetri, et al. (2009a), Seegebarth et al. (2016), Nepomuceno and Laroche (2015), Chieh-Wen et al. (2008), Cowles and Crosby (1986), Boujbel and d'Astous (2012), Chhetri et al. (2009b), Rich et al. (2017), Peyer et al. (2017), Shama (1988), Lewandowska et al. (2018), Erdoğmuş and Karapinar (2015), Pestle et al. (1982), Boujbel and d'Astous (2012), Brown and Kasser (2005), Chowdhury (2018), Kang et al. (2021), Kuanr et al. (2020), Rich, Hanna and Wright. (2017), Seegebarth et al. (2016)	Quantitative studies	Survey
Rich et al. (2019), Kennedy et al. (2013), Boujbel and d'Astous (2015), Hagbert (2016), Balsa-Budai et al. (2019), Herziger et al. (2017), Ezell (2019), Monopolis (2010)	Mixed-method studies	In-depth interviews Focus group Surveys
Hüttel et al. (2018), Lorenzen (2018), Cherrier (2009), Craig-Lees and Hill (2002), Lorenzen (2012a), Marchand and Walker (2008), Shaw and Moraes (2009), Ballantine and Creery (2010), Vannini and Taggart (2013), Housel (2006), McGouran and Prothero (2016), Walther and Sandlin (2013), Özgen (2012), Aguilar (2015), Kraisornsuthasinee and Swierczek (2018), Carpenter (2010), Shaw and Newholm (2002), Sandlin and Walther (2009), Mourad et al. (2019), Zamwel et al. (2014), Lorenzen (2014), Kala et al. (2016), Kala et al. (2017), Oates et al. (2008), McArthur and Stratford (2020), Botta (2015), Connelly (2020), McGouran and Prothero (2016), Melhorn (2019), Murray (2005)	Qualitative studies	In-depth interviews Focus group Netnography Observations Case studies Critical Incident Technique

Source: Rebouças and Soares (2021)

DIRECTIONS FOR FUTURE RESEARCH AND LIMITATIONS

In recent years, there has been a growing interest in this area of research, as evidenced by a rising number of studies. To further enrich the knowledge in this field, future studies can play a significant role by adopting interdisciplinary perspectives, investigating voluntary simplicity in conjunction with related movements, and employing diverse research methods.

Extant literature has explored various types of research using interpretive frameworks in this domain. However, most studies have centered on the individual as the primary unit of analysis, for further studies taking an interdisciplinary, social, and collective approach to understand voluntary simplicity might be beneficial (Rebouças and Soares, 2021). While a few articles have examined voluntary simplifiers as political actors (Read et al., 2018), there is still a need for more research on political consumerism that focuses on consumption practices (Haenfler et al., 2012). Consequently, exploring voluntary simplicity and its wide-ranging impacts across different domains requires embracing interdisciplinary approaches.

Studying voluntary simplicity in various national settings may be helpful in exploring the relationship between voluntary simplicity and macro-environmental factors like economic development and cultural dimensions. Additionally, looking at voluntary simplicity from a different angle, we can view Voluntary Simplifiers as an international segment (Cannon Hugh and Yaprak, 2011).

Existing literature has various limitations. Most empirical studies adopt descriptive designs and cross-sectional methods that disable the establishment of causal relationships. Therefore, conducting experimental and longitudinal research becomes essential. Moreover, there is room for enhancing the measurement of voluntary simplicity in future studies. Many research papers interchangeably use scales for both voluntary simplicity and minimalism due to their similar definitions. However, future theories and research should consider investigating the distinctions and boundary conditions of these constructs.

MANAGERIAL CONTRIBUTIONS

Companies aiming to serve these consumers should prioritize building long-lasting brands through consistent brand experiences, establishing strong emotional connections with customers, adapting to market changes, and upholding quality standards. One key and distinctive characteristic of voluntary simplifiers is their tendency to limit consumption and material possessions to focus on fulfilling personal interests and hobbies. For instance, Uber has become a daily ritual for thousands of consumers worldwide. In several countries, many consumers who can afford to buy a car prefer using Uber because it eliminates the associated expenses of car ownership, such as financing, maintenance, repair, and servicing, aligning perfectly with their preference for a simple and minimalist lifestyle. Also, Uber is a smart choice for environmentally conscious consumers since it has a positive impact on the environment, including reduced pollution and less traffic congestion. The concept of the "sharing economy" aligns with the values of consumers seeking to reduce ownership, share resources within their budget without compromising functionality, look for renewed products with lower environmental impact, and foster a sense of community belonging.

The functionality holds significant value for voluntary simplifiers due to economic constraints and the need to maintain a balance between expenses and other activities. Consequently, companies must prioritize providing voluntary simplifiers with products that offer enhanced functional benefits. To achieve this, understanding consumer insights becomes crucial for companies in the process of developing such functionally advantageous products.

Voluntary Simplifiers adhere to a philosophy centered around simplicity, which involves decluttering their homes and surroundings by discarding unnecessary items and embracing minimalist principles for furniture and possessions. Hence, encouraging consumers to embrace minimalist approaches by offering designs that fit this philosophy might be an appealing strategy for voluntary simplifiers.

CONCLUSION

Although the previous definitions of voluntary simplicity have significantly advanced the literature and raised awareness about this type of consumption, the existing information is subject to subjective interpretations and not synthesized. There is a need for a broader perspective that identifies the founding processes guiding voluntary simplicity and its various forms. To address this, this chapter aimed to synthesize the current literature, addressing research gaps to obtain an inclusive typology that defines the components shaping the concept of voluntary simplicity.

As the literature suggests that voluntary simplifiers have different motivations there is a wide diversity of lifestyles within this group. Some groups are making modest efforts to downshift, while others are opting for more radical measures. The variety of participants and their motivations create a complex challenge for managing or comprehending the concept of 'group identity' within the movement (Sandlin and Walther, 2009). However, these participants share a common goal of minimizing or controlling their consumption and feeling a sense of connection. And, they collectively somehow form a social group with significant collective power. Hence, marketers need to understand this common ground and design their activities around these shared values.

Most marketing strategies argue that motivating consumers to make more purchases while meeting their desires and needs is crucial. However, this conflicts with what consumers embracing voluntary simplicity seek (Rebouças and Soares, 2021). Consequently, if managers lack the necessary knowledge of how to prepare and execute strategies that fulfill the expectations of these consumers and potentially exceed them, the standard concentration on increasing consumption may lead to negative returns in this significant and growing segment. Managers can neutralize this incongruity by comprehending the potential presented by voluntary simplicity-seeking consumers and devising compatible strategies to engage with this unique and globally extending consumer segment. In this chapter, the concept of voluntary simplicity in its various forms is identified, and insights and guidance to practitioners on targeting these consumers through long-term customer relationship strategies that could be part of their growth plan are explained.

REFERENCES

Albert, M. (2019). Sustainable frugal innovation—The connection between frugal innovation and sustainability. *Journal of Cleaner Production*, *237*, 117747. doi:10.1016/j.jclepro.2019.117747

Alexander, S. (2012). Planned economic contraction: The emerging case for degrowth. *Environmental Politics*, *21*(3), 349–368. doi:10.1080/09644016.2012.671569

Balderjahn, I., Buerke, A., Kirchgeorg, M., Peyer, M., Seegebarth, B., & Wiedmann, K. P. (2013). Consciousness for sustainable consumption: Scale development and new insights in the economic dimension of consumers' sustainability. *AMS Review*, *3*(4), 181–192. doi:10.100713162-013-0057-6

Bayat, M., & Sezer, A. (2018). Evaluating individuals' voluntary simplicity lifestyles and life satisfaction in terms of the tradition value: The example of Duzce University. *Turkish Journal of Business Ethics*, *11*(1), 83–87. doi:10.12711/tjbe.2018.11.1.0009

Black, I. R., & Cherrier, H. (2010). Anti-Consumption as Part of Living a Sustainable Lifestyle: Daily Practices, Contextual Motivations and Subjective Values. *Journal of Consumer Behaviour*, *9*(6), 437–453. doi:10.1002/cb.337

Botta, M. (2015). Evolution of the slow living concept within the models of sustainable communities. *Futures*, *80*, 3–16. doi:10.1016/j.futures.2015.12.004

Boujbel, L., & d'Astous, A. (2012). Voluntary simplicity and life satisfaction: Exploring the mediating role of consumption desires. *Journal of Consumer Behaviour*, *11*(6), 487–494. doi:10.1002/cb.1399

Cannon Hugh, M., & Yaprak, A. (2011). A dynamic framework for understanding cross-national segmentation. *International Marketing Review*, *28*(3), 229–243. doi:10.1108/02651331111132839

Cherrier, H. (2009). Anti-consumption discourses and consumer-resistant identities. *Journal of Business Research*, *62*(2), 181–190. doi:10.1016/j.jbusres.2008.01.025

Cherrier, H., & Murray, J. B. (2007). Reflexive Dispossession and The Self: Constructing A Processing Theory of Identity. *Consumption Markets & Culture*, *10*(1), 1–29. doi:10.1080/10253860601116452

Craig-Lees, M., & Hill, C. (2002, February). The social-psychological bases of anticonsumption attitudes. *Psychology and Marketing*, *19*(2), 187–210.

Deci, E., & Ryan, R. (1985). *Self-Determination in Human Behavior*. Plenum Press.

Diener, E., & Biswas-Diener, R. (2002). Will money increase subjective well-being? A literature review and guide to needed research. *Social Indicators Research*, *57*(2), 119–169. doi:10.1023/A:1014411319119

Dittmar, H., Bond, R., Hurst, M., & Kasser, T. (2014). The relationship between materialism and personal well-being: A metaanalysis. *Journal of Personality and Social Psychology*, *107*(5), 879–924. doi:10.1037/a0037409 PMID:25347131

Elgin, D. (1981). *Voluntary Simplicity: Toward A Way of Life That Is Outwardly Simple, Inwardly Rich*. Morrow.

Elgin, D., & Mitchell, A. (1977). Voluntary simplicity. *The Coevolution Quarterly*, (Summer), 1977.

Ensley, E. E. (1983). Voluntary simplicity: A segment of concern to marketers. In *Proceedings of the American Marketing Association*, (pp. 385-389). AMA.

Etzioni, A. (2004). The post affluent society. *Review of Social Economy*, *62*(3), 407–420. doi:10.1080/0034676042000253990

Grigsby, M. (2012). *Buying Time and Getting By: The Voluntary Simplicity Movement*. SUNY Press.

Haenfler, R., Johnson, B., & Jones, E. (2012). Lifestyle movements: Exploring the intersection of lifestyle and social movements. *Social Movement Studies*, *11*(1), 1–20. doi:10.1080/14742837.2012.640535

Håkansson, M., & Sengers, P. (2013). *Beyond Being Green: Simple Living Families and ICT*. In *Proceedings of the SIGCHI Conference on Human Factors in Computing*. ACM..10.1145/2470654.2481378

Hook, J. N., Hodge, A. S., Zhang, H., Van Tongeren, D. R., & Davis, D. E. (2023). Minimalism, voluntary simplicity, and well-being: A systematic review of the empirical literature. *The Journal of Positive Psychology*, *18*(1), 130–141. doi:10.1080/17439760.2021.1991450

Huneke, M. E. (2005). The face of the un-consumer: An empirical examination of the practice of voluntary simplicity in the United States. *Psychology and Marketing*, *22*(7), 527–550. doi:10.1002/mar.20072

Iwata, O. (1997). Attitudinal and behavioral correlates of voluntary simplicity lifestyles. *Social Behavior and Personality*, *25*(3), 233–240. doi:10.2224bp.1997.25.3.233

Iyer, R., & Muncy, J. A. (2009). Purpose and Object of Anti-Consumption. *Journal of Business Research*, *62*(2), 160–168. doi:10.1016/j.jbusres.2008.01.023

Iyer, R., & Muncy, J. A. (2016). Attitude toward consumption and subjective well-being. *The Journal of Consumer Affairs*, *62*(2), 160–168.

Johnston, T. C. (2000). Impact of voluntary simplicity movement on consumer behavior. In D. R. Deeter-Schmelz & T. P. Hartman, (Eds.) Marketing Advances in the New Millennium, Athens, OH: Society for Marketing Advances, 330.

Johnston, T. C., & Burton, J. B. (2003). Voluntary simplicity: Definitions and dimensions. *Academy of Marketing Studies Journal*, *7*(1), 19–36.

Kasser, T. (2009). Psychological need satisfaction, personal well-being, and ecological sustainability. *Ecopsychology*, *1*(4), 175–180. doi:10.1089/eco.2009.0025

Kennedy, E. H., Krahn, H., & Krogman, N. T. (2013). Downshifting: An exploration of motivations, quality of life, and environmental practices. *Sociological Forum*, *28*(4), 764–783. doi:10.1111ocf.12057

Kropfeld, M. I., Nepomuceno, M. V., & Dantas, D. C. (2018). The ecological impact of anticonsumption lifestyles and environmental concern. *Journal of Public Policy & Marketing*, *37*(2), 245–259. doi:10.1177/0743915618810448

Lang, T. (2017). *The price of anything is the life you exchange for it: A study on voluntary simplicity within the United States*. [Master Thesis, Lund University].

Lee, M. S., & Ahn, C. S. Y. (2016). Anti-consumption, materialism, and consumer well-being. *The Journal of Consumer Affairs*, *50*(1), 18–47. doi:10.1111/joca.12089

Lee, M. S., Motion, J., & Conroy, D. (2009). Anti-consumption and brand avoidance. *Journal of Business Research*, *62*(2), 169–180. doi:10.1016/j.jbusres.2008.01.024

Leonard-Barton, D. (1981). Voluntary Simplicity Lifestyles and Energy Conservation. *The Journal of Consumer Research*, *8*(3), 243–252. doi:10.1086/208861

McGouran, C., & Prothero, A. (2016). Enacted voluntary simplicity – Exploring the consequences of requesting consumers to intentionally consume less. *European Journal of Marketing*, *50*(1/2), 189–212. doi:10.1108/EJM-09-2013-0521

Meissner, M. (2019). Against Accumulation: Lifestyle minimalism, de-growth and the present post-ecological condition. *Journal of Cultural Economics*, *12*(3), 185–200. doi:10.1080/17530350.2019.1570962

Pangarkar, A., Shukla, P., & Charles, R. (2021). Minimalism in consumption: A typology and brand engagement strategies. *Journal of Business Research, 127*, 167–178. doi:10.1016/j.jbusres.2021.01.033

Pepper, M., Jackson, T., & Uzzell, D. (2009). An examination of the values that motivate socially conscious and frugal consumer behaviours. *International Journal of Consumer Studies*, *33*(2), 126–136. doi:10.1111/j.1470-6431.2009.00753.x

Peyer, M., Balderjahn, I., Seegebarth, B., & Klemm, A. (2017). The Role of Sustainability in Profiling Voluntary Simplifiers. *Journal of Business Research*, *70*, 37–43. doi:10.1016/j.jbusres.2016.07.008

Pine, B. J., & Gilmore, J. H. (2013). The experience economy: Past, present and future. In S. Jon & S. Flemming (Eds.), *Handbook on the Experience Economy* (pp. 21–44). Edward Elgar Publishing. doi:10.4337/9781781004227.00007

Powers, B. (2010). *Twelve by Twelve: A One-room Cabin Off the Grid & Beyond the American Dream*. New World Library.

Read, R., Alexander, S., & Garrett, J. (2018). Voluntary simplicity strongly backed by all three main normative-ethical traditions. *Ethical Perspectives*, *25*(1), 87–116.

Rebouças, R., & Soares, A. M. (2021). Voluntary simplicity: A literature review and research agenda. *International Journal of Consumer Studies*, *45*(3), 303–319. doi:10.1111/ijcs.12621

Rich, S. A., Hanna, S., Wright, B. J., & Bennett, P. C. (2017). Fact or fable: Increased well-being in voluntary simplicity. *International Journal of Wellbeing*, *7*(2), 64–77. doi:10.5502/ijw.v7i2.589

Rosen, N. (2010). *Off the Grid: Inside the Movement for More Space, Less Government, and True Independence in Modern America*. Penguin Books.

Ryan, R. M., & Deci, E. L. (2000). Self-determination theory and the facilitation of intrinsic motivation, social development, and well-being. *The American Psychologist*, *55*(1), 68–78. doi:10.1037/0003-066X.55.1.68 PMID:11392867

Ryan, R. M., & Deci, E. L. (2002). Overview of self-determination theory: An organismic dialectical perspective. Handbook of Self-determination Research, 2, 3-33.

Sandlin, J., & Walther, C. S. (2009). Voluntary Simplicity Movement. *Forging*, *59*(4), 298–318.

Sandlin, J. A., Walther, C. S., & Wuensch, K. (2016). Voluntary Simplifiers, Spirituality, and Happiness. *Humanity & Society*, *40*(1), 22–42. doi:10.1177/0160597614565698

Seegebarth, B., Peyer, M., Balderjahn, I., & Wiedmann, K. P. (2016). The sustainability roots of anticonsumption lifestyles and initial insights regarding their effects on consumers' well-being. *The Journal of Consumer Affairs*, *50*(1), 68–99. doi:10.1111/joca.12077

Shama, A. (1985). The voluntary simplicity consumer. *Journal of Consumer Marketing*, *2*(4), 57–63. doi:10.1108/eb008146

Shama, A., & Wisenblit, J. (1984). Values of voluntary simplicity: Lifestyle and motivation. *Psychological Reports*, *55*(1), 231–240. doi:10.2466/pr0.1984.55.1.231

Shaw, D., & Moraes, C. (2009). Voluntary simplicity: An exploration of market interactions. *International Journal of Consumer Studies*, *33*(2), 215–223. doi:10.1111/j.1470-6431.2009.00760.x

Shaw, D., & Newholm, T. (2002). Voluntary simplicity and the ethics of consumption. *Psychology and Marketing*, *19*(2), 167–185. doi:10.1002/mar.10008

Turner, J. (2010). Social Categorization and The Self-Concept: A Social Cognitive Theory of Group Behavior. In T. Postmes & N. R. Branscombe (Eds.), *Key Readings in Social Psychology. Rediscovering Social Identity*. Psychology Press.

Vannini, P., & Taggart, J. (2014). *Off the grid: Re-assembling domestic life*. Routledge. doi:10.4324/978020374406

Weinswig, D. (2016). Millennials Go Minimal: The Decluttering Lifestyle Trend That Is Taking Over. *Forbes*. https://www.forbes.com/sites/deborahweinswig/2016/09/07/millennials-go-minimal-the-decluttering-lifestyle-trend-that-is-taking-over/?sh=53f870db3755/

Zavestoski, S. (2002). The Social-Psychological Bases of Anticonsumption Attitudes. *Psychology and Marketing*, *19*(2), 149–165. doi:10.1002/mar.10007

KEY TERMS AND DEFINITIONS

Anti-Consumption: An approach in which people try to contribute to social welfare through sustainability in response to external pressures.

Inconspicuous Minimalism: An approach in which people focus on consuming minimalist brands or products that signal sophistication.

Minimalism: A lifestyle people live with fewer material possessions to gain freedom of consumption.

Other-Initiated Voluntary Simplicity: A type of voluntary simplicity behavior that is motivated by other people (externally) rather than the self (internally).

Reduced Consumption: Attempt to spend less due to uncertainties of life.

Self-Determination Theory: A theory that interests individuals' inner psychological needs and self-development tendencies. It concerns more about the self-motivation of people's choices.

Self-Initiated Voluntary Simplicity: A type of voluntary simplicity behavior that is motivated by the inner self (internally) rather than other people (externally).

Voluntary Simplicity: A lifestyle in which people try to maximize their self-enhancement and self-reliance by developing judgment regarding life priorities and limiting their consumption.

Chapter 8
The Attitude of Portuguese Consumers of Green Cosmetics:
The Influence of Environmental Concern and Health Concern

Zaila Oliveira
https://orcid.org/0000-0002-7002-7626
University of Maia, Portugal & CEOS, ISCAP, Polytechnic of Porto, Portugal

Sara Teixeira
https://orcid.org/0000-0002-3768-0420
CEOS, ISCAP, Polytechnic of Porto, Portugal

Sara Teixeira
ISCAP, Polytechnic of Porto, Portugal

Sandrina Teixeira
https://orcid.org/0000-0002-5859-0002
CEOS, ISCAP, Polytechnic of Porto, Portugal

ABSTRACT

Nowadays, environmental problems have been accentuated by the scarcity of natural resources, climate change, pollution levels, and waste. As a result, consumers have become more environmentally responsible and opt for green products. The research question arises: How do environmental and health concerns influence consumers' attitude towards green cosmetics? This chapter includes a survey of Portuguese consumers with green cosmetics purchasing habits. The methodology adopted was quantitative, using questionnaires via Google Forms. The data obtained were

DOI: 10.4018/978-1-6684-9277-2.ch008

analysed using SPSS Statistical Package (n=141). The data collected helped to highlight that environmental and health concerns influence consumer attitudes towards green cosmetics. The insights produced by this chapter represent an asset for researchers, business managers, and marketing professionals, especially those working with green cosmetics.

INTRODUCTION

Environmental awareness, regarding the preservation of the environment and ethical and sustainable manufacturing methods of products, is developing among consumers, governments, and regional regulatory authorities that create laws to reduce the impact on the environment during the manufacture and commercialization of products (Saleem et al., 2021). Thus, companies need to know the new needs of consumers, who are more aware of the impact of their actions and consumption habits on the environment (Patak et al., 2021), adapting their marketing strategies to environmentally friendly strategies (Baktash & Talib, 2019; Lin et al., 2019; Patak et al., 2021; Rajput et al., 2022). Since consumer choices determine the fate of companies, green marketing emerges as a proactive strategy for companies to meet the needs of a sustainable market by offering products and services that avoid or minimize any harmful impact on the environment (Rahman et al., 2017; Rajput et al., 2022). This includes integrating environmental concerns into all areas of operations, from strategy development and planning to interaction with consumers, making firms that have favourable attitudes towards the environment more competitive (Rajput et al., 2022).

Thus, green marketing focuses on a responsible approach to the environment, integrating into various areas of society, and incorporates a wide range of activities such as product design, sustainable manufacturing, and communication with consumers in a long-term approach that focuses mainly on environmental factors and involves the full utilization of company resources for innovation (Nadanyiova et al., 2020; Rahman et al., 2017; Saleem et al., 2021).

However, even though environmental problems affect aspects of human life, only a few academic fields have studies on green topics (Rajput et al., 2022), and although the cosmetics field has become the target of demands regarding its environmental products and processes, scientific studies are still limited. Therefore, it is essential to study it due to consumer demand for green cosmetics and sustainable manufacturing processes, reflecting an increase in green consumption in the 21st century (Pop et al., 2020). Thus, this chapter proposes to identify the perception of Portuguese consumers of green cosmetics about socially responsible brands and to understand whether the attitude of Portuguese consumers towards green cosmetics is influenced by environmental and health concerns.

To answer the research question, this chapter includes an empirical study with a quantitative method through online questionnaires. Participants were Portuguese consumers who have already purchased or intend to purchase green cosmetics.

The insights produced by this chapter are particularly interesting. The results will provide relevant data for all those with an interest in the topic: business managers and digital marketers (with a strong focus on those working with green cosmetics), the organizational and academic community, and the community at large.

THEORETICAL FRAMEWORK AND HYPOTHESES

Socially Responsible Brands

Socially responsible brands consist of brands that are aware of their environmental impact and regulate it to reduce the negative impact of their activities and contribute to the maximum benefit of society, with a notable increase in consumer interest in these brands and their environmentally friendly product offering (Abbas et al., 2019; Nadanyiova et al., 2020).

As consumers' interest in environmental problems has increased, socially responsible brands integrate these issues into their activities, shifting their business strategy towards a greener concept, including environmental protection as a key part of the company's marketing strategies and replacing traditional marketing principles with green marketing principles (Baktash & Talib, 2019; Lin et al., 2019; Nadanyiova et al., 2020; Ottman, 2017; Patak et al., 2021; Rajput et al., 2022; Schiochet, 2018). Thus, sustainability processes have become a vital opportunity for companies to connect with the consumer, who is enthusiastic about change (Chyhryn et al., 2019).

Thus, green marketing, which represents an environmentally oriented responsible marketing approach, is based on corporate social responsibility and is a communication element that influences consumer attitudes and behaviours, attracting and retaining loyalty (Grubor & Milovanov, 2017; Nadanyiova et al., 2020). Consequently, the main communication objective of these brands is to make their social, economic, and environmentally responsible activities apparent to gain a competitive advantage, increase their value, enhance their attractiveness, and improve consumer loyalty to the brand, while making a significant contribution to environmental protection (Grubor & Milovanov, 2017; Nadanyiova et al., 2020; Rajput et al., 2022; Zhang et al., 2018). It is then crucial to highlight communication with a positive environmental awareness that targets socially responsible brands, as poor communication of information is demonstrated by the fact that consumers are still unable to notice and appreciate their environmental efforts (Nadanyiova et al., 2020).

Green Cosmetics

Issues regarding environmental protection and sustainability issues have become a focus of public opinion for decades, encouraging consumers to buy green products (Amberg & Fogarassy, 2019; Fontes et al., 2021; Graciano et al., 2021; Mamun et al., 2020). Referred to in the year 1992, by the American Marketing Association, the term "green products" was used to mention products that are environmentally friendly and safe to be used by consumers, as they consist of products with ingredients that are not toxic and are produced through sustainable and environmentally friendly procedures (Sahni & Osahan, 2019; Zahid et al., 2018).

Environmental activism, however, encourages companies to develop and produce these products that are less harmful to the environment and have environmentally friendly properties (Pop et al., 2020; Wang et al., 2019). Improving them throughout their life cycle allows for future economic benefits both in the product, through recycling and substitution of hazardous materials, and in the market, reflected in better brand performance and, consequently, a competitive advantage over its competitors (Chygryn et al., 2019; Rajput et al., 2022).

The cosmetics industry responds to consumers' environmental trends and concerns with a wide range of products, namely green beauty products, for healthier lifestyles, being nowadays very competitive and global, to favour quality, science, and safety (Amberg & Fogarassy, 2019; Pop et al., 2020). Thus, global cosmetics companies have modified their strategies to respond to new challenges and incorporate aspects of sustainability into their activities, following green marketing trends and focusing on natural solutions for cosmetics, linking them to a healthy lifestyle (Amberg & Fogarassy, 2019; Sadiq et al., 2021).

Although the concept of green cosmetics is present among companies and consumers, namely on social networks, there is no global definition of them, however, in addition to the essential functions, they have as main objectives the protection and conservation of the environment, the minimization of pollution, the use of renewable resources, in a responsible way, and the preservation of fauna and species, being produced from natural resources without the use of chemicals and additives (Amberg & Fogarassy, 2019; Pop et al., 2020; Sadiq et al., 2021; Sahni & Osahan, 2019). Regarding the market for these cosmetics, according to Sequeira (2020), it "registered a value of 36.3 billion euros worldwide in 2019, and this value is expected to reach 54.5 billion euros by 2027" (p.6), which highlights the interest of consumers in them.

Green Consumer

With new generations adopting sustainable values, environmental behaviour is becoming a standard (Mamun et al., 2020; Ottman, 2017). Thus, environmental concerns are a trend of the 21st century, making environmental issues a frequent topic among consumers as they increasingly recognize the consequences of their consumption habits and consider environmental protection in their purchasing decisions (Amberg & Fogarassy, 2019; Pop et al., 2020).

Thus, global trends expose that consumers are prepared to change their behaviours and preferences, adjusting towards more sustainable purchasing habits, which gives rise to a new type of consumption - green consumption (Chygryn et al., 2019; Ghazali et al., 2017; Mamun et al., 2020). Green consumption is a movement that envisions the solution to ecological problems, i.e., green products consumption that does not have negative implications for the environment, to avoid excessive consumption of natural resources (Mamun et al., 2020; Caliskan, 2020).

Consequently, the green consumer is characterized as "the consumer who at the time of purchase associates the act of buying or consuming products with the possibility of preserving the environment, avoiding products that pose a risk to their health or that of others; harm the environment during their production, use or final disposal; are energy-intensive; have excessive packaging or are disposable; contain ingredients from endangered habitats or species; in the production process have misused or cruelly used animals; or negatively affect other peoples or countries" (Hailes, 2007 as cited in Sequeira, 2020, p. 4). In short, a green consumer is a person who includes green products in their purchasing habits for the well-being of the environment (Chygryn et al., 2020; Fontes et al., 2021).

Attitude

Attitude is a positive or negative evaluation/feelings that an individual has towards a certain behaviour (Ajzen, 1991). From an environmental perspective, attitude is one of the main drivers of behavioural intention and a determinant of green consumerism (Caliskan, 2020; Paul et al., 2016). Thus, it is also defined as the cognitive and affective evaluation of environmental protection, including judgments made by consumers that are evaluated by their perceptions (Caliskan, 2020). Eventually, if the degree of an attitude towards a specific behaviour is high, the more likely the consumer is to perform that behaviour (Arli et al., 2018; Caliskan, 2020).

Altruism reflects a humanitarian behaviour, where the consumer acts for the well-being of others without any personal benefit (Prakash et al., 2019; Yadav & Pathak, 2017), thus focusing on concern for the environment, while selfishness indicates a behaviour where the consumer acts according to their interest, reflected in their concern for their health and the health of their family (Pop et al., 2020; Prakash et al., 2019).

The literature indicates that environmental and health concerns influence consumers' attitude towards green cosmetics and are central to their purchase intention (Ahmad et al., 2021; Amberg & Fogarassy, 2019; Caliskan, 2020; Ghazali et al., 2017; Liobikienė & Bernatonienė, 2017; Mamun et al., 2020; Pop et al., 2020). Qader and Zainuddin, (2010) allude that safety and health concerns relate to consumer concerns about the quality of life, health, and environment. Moslehpour et al. (2022) consider environmental concerns to be the degree to which environmental problems are important to address.

Therefore, health concern relates to the quality of life, as consumers are increasingly interested in the composition of cosmetics from natural ingredients that are carefully selected, based on their safety and effectiveness, while synthetic materials have various impacts on health and the environment (Amberg & Fogarassy, 2019; Sadiq et al., 2021; Sahni & Osahan, 2019). Regarding environmental concern, this is also related to consumer interest in the composition of green cosmetics since, with the increase in environmental pollution, consumers have become more aware of the need for environmental protection (Liobikienė & Bernatonienė, 2017). Thus, consumers who purchase green cosmetics consider that the conservation of their health and protection of the environment are the most relevant antecedents, these being more essential than their price (Ahmad et al., 2021; Amberg & Fogarassy, 2019). Therefore, in line with the literature, the following research hypotheses were determined.

Hypothesis 1 (H1): Environmental concerns have a positive impact on the attitude of Portuguese consumers toward green cosmetics.

Hypothesis 2 (H2): Health concerns have a positive impact on the attitude of Portuguese consumers toward green cosmetics.

METHODOLOGY

To test the proposed research hypotheses that are schematically shown in Figure 1, a quantitative methodology was used. This methodology is used when it is intended to estimate the magnitude or occurrence of phenomena and test hypotheses by applying some form of measurement and statistical analysis (Malhotra et al., 2020; Sampieri, 2018).

Figure 1. Conceptual model
Source: Own elaboration

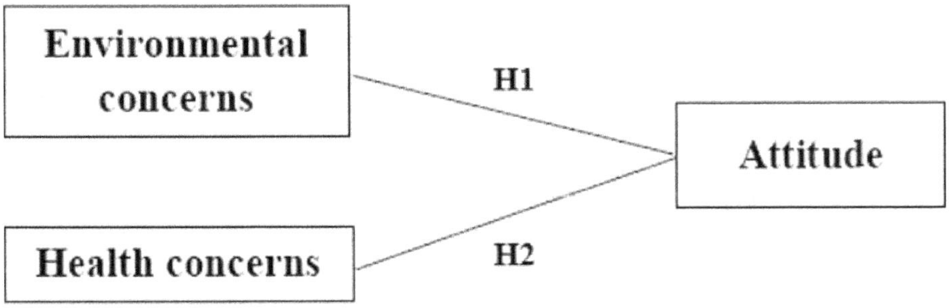

Data Collection Instrument

In the social sciences, when quantitative methodology is used to answer the research object, the most used measurement instrument is the questionnaire. Therefore, this research used a questionnaire with closed questions that included dichotomous, multiple-choice, and linear scale (Likert) questions (Sampieri, 2018). This questionnaire was answered by 243 individuals. However, given the objectives of the study, only 141 were considered for data analysis.

Measurement Scales

To understand each variable of the conceptual model, measurement scales were used (Table 1). A five-point Likert scale was used to understand the agreement degree of the respondents on each item under study (Malhotra et al., 2020).

Table 1. Items for each variable of the conceptual model

Variable	Items	Authors
Environmental Concerns	PA: I consider that my concern for the environment influences my attitude towards green cosmetics.	(Amberg & Fogarassy, 2019; Ghazali et al., 2017; Liobikienė & Bernatonienė, 2017; Pop et al., 2020; Prakash et al., 2019).
Health Concerns	PS: I consider that concern for my health influences my attitude towards green cosmetics.	(Amberg & Fogarassy, 2019; Ghazali et al., 2017; Liobikienė & Bernatonienė, 2017; Pop et al., 2020; Prakash et al., 2019).
Attitude	A1: My environmental awareness impacts my intention to purchase green cosmetics. A2: Positive beliefs regarding the well-being of the environment impact my intention to purchase green cosmetics. A3: My feelings towardss environmental well-being impact my intention to purchase green cosmetics. A4: My behavior towardss the environment influences my attitude towards green cosmetics purchase intention.	(Ajzen, 1991, como citado em Pop et al., 2020; Al Mamun et al., 2020; Caliskan, 2020; Liobikienė & Bernatonienė, 2017).

Source: Own elaboration

Statistical Procedure

The statistical software selected for the treatment and analysis of the research data collected in the questionnaire through statistical procedures was SPSS v26.

Frequency analysis was used to characterize the study sample, where the percentage of responses per response option was verified in all sociodemographic questions. In the remaining questions, a descriptive data treatment was performed, using measures of central tendency and of variability (e.g., average, median, quartiles, standard deviation) to describe and summarise the data (Malhotra et al., 2020).

To analyse the variables that influence attitude (environmental concern and health concern), we initially sought to verify the reliability and validity of the measurement instrument. Sampieri (2018) mentions that there are different procedures to calculate the reliability of a measurement instrument. Thus, in this research, Cronbach's alpha was used, which varies between 0 and 1, and unsatisfactory internal consistency reliability is when the alpha value is ≤ 0.6 (Malhotra et al., 2020). After calculating Cronbach's alpha, we sought to test the validity of the model variables and summarise the data by reducing the number of items to describe them, i.e., by factor analysis (Malhotra et al., 2020). To verify the applicability of factor analysis, the Kaiser-Meyer-Olkin (KMO) and Bartlett's test of sphericity were performed. KMO should have values between 0.5 and 1.0 to confirm that factor analysis is appropriate. Bartlett's test of sphericity seeks to understand the correlations between all variables and checks for significant intercorrelation. Therefore, this test must have a significance level lower than 0.05 to reject the hypothesis that the correlation matrix is the identity matrix (Hair et al., 2014; Malhotra et al., 2020; Marôco, 2018; Pestana & Gageiro, 2014).

In the factor analysis, the initial communalities were analysed, which must have values of 1 and the extracted common factors higher than 50% for all items. If not, the items, have a weak relationship with the extracted factors and need to be excluded (Hair et al., 2014; Marôco, 2018). To determine the number of factors, Eigenvalues were used, where only factors with eigenvalues equal to or greater than one are retained. In the total variance matrix, it is verified which component explains the most so that, based on the rotated component matrix, it is verified which components should be considered in the study (values ≥ 0.5) (Hair et al., 2014; Malhotra et al., 2020).

After analysing reliability and validity, multiple linear regression was used to verify the hypotheses under investigation. Multiple linear regression is a statistical, descriptive, and inferential technique that examines the relationship between a dependent variable and a set of independent variables (Hair et al., 2014; Malhotra et al., 2020). One criterion of linear regression is to verify the linearity between the dependent and independent variables. For this, Pearson correlation analysis was used, which allows measuring the degree of association between two quantitative variables on the assumption that their relationship is a linear relationship and the greater the association, the closer the values were to the extremes (-1 and 1) (Pestana & Gageiro, 2014). The ANOVA test was also performed to assess the effect of two or more independent variables on a dependent variable (Sampieri, 2018). Finally, the data obtained from the multiple linear regression were analysed using the R coefficient (correlation coefficient), R^2 (coefficient of determination) measures the strength of the association in the multiple regression, measured by the square of the multiple correlation coefficient, R^2 adjusted for the number of independent variables and the regression coefficient (β) to verify whether all or only some of the independent variables influence the dependent variable, as well as the level of significance of the independent variable in predicting the dependent variable (Hair et al., 2014; Malhotra et al., 2020; Marôco, 2018).

RESULTS

Characterisation of the Sample

The data referring to the sample of this investigation are expressed in Table 2.

Table 2. Sample characterization

		Frequency	%
Gender	Female	98	69,5
	Male	31	22,0
	Another one	1	,7
	I'd rather not say	11	7,8
	Sum	141	100,0
Age rank	<18	7	5,0
	18-24	65	46,1
	25-40	59	41,8
	41-54	6	4,3
	55-64	3	2,1
	65+	1	,7
	Sum	141	100,0
Academic Qualifications	Lower than 9th grade	1	,7
	9th grade	6	4,3
	12th grade	28	19,9
	Bachelor's Degree	62	44,0
	Master's Degree	23	16,3
	PhD/Doctorate	5	3,5
	Post-graduation	16	11,3
	Sum	141	100,0
Nationality	Portuguese	141	100,0
	Sum	141	100,0

Source: Adapted from SPSS

The individuals surveyed in this research are Portuguese (100%), mainly female (69.5%), aged between 18-24 years (46.1%), and 25-40 years (41.8%), with an academic degree (44%). After characterizing the sample, the data obtained will be analysed to answer the objectives of this research.

Social Responsibility of Green Cosmetics Brands

To understand the perception of Portuguese consumers regarding socially responsible brands, it is essential to understand whether they believe in their existence. Thus, most of the analysed person states, in their opinion, that there are socially responsible cosmetic brands in Portugal (85.1%; n=120), while for the rest of the sample, they do not exist (14.9%; n=21) (Table 3).

Table 3. In your opinion, are there any socially responsible cosmetics brands in Portugal?

	Frequency	%
Yes	120	85,1
No	21	14,9
Sum	141	100,0

Source: Adapted from SPSS

The results obtained in Table 4 show agreement, as most of the individuals answered: "Agree" and "Strongly Agree" (81.6%). The average was 4.13, the median 4, and the 4th quartile obtained 81.6% of the responses, which leads to the conclusion that respondents agree that when buying green cosmetics, they resort to socially responsible brands.

Table 4. Descriptive analysis: When I want to buy green cosmetics, I use socially responsible brands

When I want to buy green cosmetics, I use socially responsible brands				Frequency	%
Strongly Disagree				2	1,4
Disagree				5	3,5
Neither Disagree nor Agree				19	13,5
Agree				61	43,3
Strongly Agree				54	38,3
Sum				141	100,0
Average				4,13	
Median				4,00	
Standard Deviation				,880	
Quartiles	*Q1/4 0-1,25*	*Q2/4 1,25-2,5*	*Q3/4 2,5-3,75*	*Q4/4 3,75-5*	
	2	5	19	115	
	1,4%	3,5%	13,5%	81,6%	

Source: Adapted from SPSS

Regarding the monitoring of content posted on social media pages (Table 5), an agreement was demonstrated. Most of the respondents answered “Agree” and “Strongly Agree” (78%). The average was 3.94 and median 4, and the 4th quartile was 78% of the responses.

Table 5. Descriptive analysis: It is important to follow the content posted on the social media pages of socially responsible brands

<table>
<tr><th colspan="4">It is important to follow the content posted on the social media pages of socially responsible brands</th><th>Frequency</th><th>%</th></tr>
<tr><td colspan="4">Strongly Disagree</td><td>1</td><td>0,7</td></tr>
<tr><td colspan="4">Disagree</td><td>7</td><td>5,0</td></tr>
<tr><td colspan="4">Neither Disagree nor Agree</td><td>23</td><td>16,3</td></tr>
<tr><td colspan="4">Agree</td><td>78</td><td>55,3</td></tr>
<tr><td colspan="4">Strongly Agree</td><td>32</td><td>22,7</td></tr>
<tr><td colspan="4">Sum</td><td>141</td><td>100,0</td></tr>
<tr><td colspan="4">Average</td><td colspan="2">3,94</td></tr>
<tr><td colspan="4">Median</td><td colspan="2">4,00</td></tr>
<tr><td colspan="4">Standard Deviation</td><td colspan="2">,809</td></tr>
<tr><td rowspan="3">Quartiles</td><td>Q1/4
0-1,25</td><td>Q2/4
1,25-2,5</td><td>Q3/4
2,5-3,75</td><td colspan="2">Q4/4
3,75-5</td></tr>
<tr><td>1</td><td>7</td><td>23</td><td colspan="2">110</td></tr>
<tr><td>0,7%</td><td>5,0%</td><td>16,3%</td><td colspan="2">78%</td></tr>
</table>

Source: Adapted from SPSS

Regarding the monitoring of content posted on social media pages (Table 6), an agreement was demonstrated. Most of the respondents answered, “Agree” and “Strongly Agree” (78%). The average was 3.94 and the median was 4, and the 4th quartile was 78% of the responses.

Table 6. Descriptive analysis: Socially responsible brands are credible

<table>
<tr><th colspan="4">Socially responsible brands are credible</th><th>Frequency</th><th>%</th></tr>
<tr><td colspan="4">Strongly Disagree</td><td>0</td><td>0</td></tr>
<tr><td colspan="4">Disagree</td><td>5</td><td>3,5</td></tr>
<tr><td colspan="4">Neither Disagree nor Agree</td><td>27</td><td>19,1</td></tr>
<tr><td colspan="4">Agree</td><td>63</td><td>44,7</td></tr>
<tr><td colspan="4">Strongly Agree</td><td>46</td><td>32,6</td></tr>
<tr><td colspan="4">Sum</td><td>141</td><td>100,0</td></tr>
<tr><td colspan="4">Average</td><td colspan="2">4,06</td></tr>
<tr><td colspan="4">Median</td><td colspan="2">4,00</td></tr>
<tr><td colspan="4">Standard Deviation</td><td colspan="2">0,813</td></tr>
<tr><td rowspan="3">Quartiles</td><td>Q1/4
0-1,25</td><td>Q2/4
1,25-2,5</td><td>Q3/4
2,5-3,75</td><td colspan="2">Q4/4
3,75-5</td></tr>
<tr><td>0</td><td>5</td><td>27</td><td colspan="2">109</td></tr>
<tr><td>0%</td><td>3,5%</td><td>19,1%</td><td colspan="2">77,3%</td></tr>
</table>

Source: Adapted from SPSS

In Table 7, respondents agreed that socially responsible brands are transparent. The average of responses was 3.95, the median 4, and the 4th quartile obtained 70.9% of responses.

Table 7. Descriptive analysis: Socially responsible brands are transparent about their environmental protection policies and the quality of their products on social media

Socially responsible brands are transparent about their environmental protection policies and the quality of their products on social media				Frequency	%
Strongly Disagree				0	0
Disagree				9	6,4
Neither Disagree nor Agree				32	22,7
Agree				57	40,4
Strongly Agree				43	30,5
Sum				141	100,0
Average				3,95	
Median				4,00	
Standard Deviation				0,889	
Quartiles	*Q1/4 0-1,25*	*Q2/4 1,25-2,5*	*Q3/4 2,5-3,75*	*Q4/4 3,75-5*	
	0	9	32	61	
	0%	6,4%	22,7%	70,9%	

Source: Adapted from SPSS

Regarding consumer loyalty to brands with environmentally friendly practices (Table 8), an agreement was verified. As most individuals answered: “totally agree”. The average of responses was 4.33, the median 5, and the 4th quartile obtained 82.3% of respondents’ answers.

Table 8. Descriptive analysis: I remain loyal to brands whose practices are environmentally friendly

I remain loyal to brands whose practices are environmentally friendly				Frequency	%
Strongly Disagree				1	,7
Disagree				3	2,1
Neither Disagree nor Agree				21	14,9
Agree				40	28,4
Strongly Agree				76	53,9
Sum				141	100,0
Average				4,33	
Median				5,00	
Standard Deviation				0,858	
Quartiles	*Q1/4 0-1,25*	*Q2/4 1,25-2,5*	*Q3/4 2,5-3,75*	*Q4/4 3,75-5*	
	1	3	21	116	
	0,7%	2,1%	14,9%	82,3%	

Source: Adapted from SPSS

Attitude Towards Environmental and Health Concerns

Descriptive Analysis of Variables

Analysing Table 9, considering the variables used in the model and that these are with Likert measurement scales (between 1 and 5), the average of responses is 4 in all variables. Therefore, the concentration of responses occurred in the "Agree" value. Analysing the standard deviation, the values are between 0.7 and 0.8. So, there is a low dispersion in the responses regarding these variables.

Table 9. Descriptive analysis

	N	Minimum	Maximum	Average	Standard deviation
Environmental Concerns	141	1	5	4,25	,794
Health Concerns	141	2	5	4,36	,739
Attitude	141	2,50	5,00	4,3972	,60139

Source: Adapted from SPSS

Cronbach's Alpha

About this study and the items used to develop the variables, Cronbach's alpha values can be seen in Table 10.

Table 10. Cronbach's alpha

Variable	Cronbach's Alpha	N of itens	Cronbach's alpha if item is excluded	
Attitude	0,897	4	*A1*	0,880
			A2	0,833
			A3	0,903
			A4	0,850
Environmental Concerns	Not applicable (1 item)			
Health Concerns	Not applicable (1 item)			

Source: Adapted from SPSS

Cronbach's alpha higher than 0.6 were found for all the variables analysed, verifying the reliability of the items of the variables. The only exceptions where it was not possible to apply Cronbach's alpha were Environmental Concern and Health Concern because these variables are composed of a single item.

Factor Analysis

Analysing Table 11, the KMO value is 0.807. Thus, it was found that the recommendation regarding factor analysis is good. Observing Bartlett's sphericity test, this has an associated significance level of 0.000, which leads to the conclusion that the variables are significantly correlated. Therefore, one can proceed with factor analysis. Regarding the analysis of commonalities (Table 12), it was found that all items are greater than 0.5, therefore, none needs to be eliminated.

Table 11. Teste de KMO e Bartlett

KMO		,807
Bartlett's Sphericity Test	Approx. Chi-square	369,269
	gl	6
	Sig.	,000

Source: Adapted from SPSS

Table 12. Commonalities

	Initial	Extraction
A1	1,000	,732
A2	1,000	,863
A3	1,000	,650
A4	1,000	,824
Extraction Method: Principal Component analysis.		

Source: Adapted from SPSS

Regarding the total variance explained (Table 13), the component obtained for the Attitude variable explains 76.717% of the variance of the data. There is only one factor that has an Eigenvalue greater than or equal to 1 and that explains 76.717% of the total variance. As there is only one factor, it was not possible to perform a rotated analysis, and all the items of the construct were kept in the study (Table 14).

Table 13. Total variance explained

Component	Initial eigenvalues			Extraction sums of squared loads		
	Total	% variance	% cumulative	Total	% variance	% cumulative
1	3,069	76,717	76,717	3,069	76,717	76,717
2	,502	12,541	89,258			
3	,255	6,364	95,622			
4	,175	4,378	100,000			
Extraction method: Principal Component Analysis.						

Source: Adapted from SPSS

Table 14. Component matrix

	Component 1
A1	,855
A2	,929
A3	,806
A4	,908
Extraction method: Principal Component Analysis.	
a. 1 component was extracted.	

Source: Adapted from SPSS

Linear Regression

Multiple linear regression was used to verify the research hypotheses (H1 and H2). To use linear regression, it is necessary to check whether the dependent variable and independent variables are linear. Analysing Table 15, the linearity between the variables was verified using Pearson's correlation.

Table 15. Pearson correlation

		Attitude
Pearson Correlation	Attitude	1,000
	Environmental Concerns	,734
	Health_Concerns	,618
Sig. (1 extremity)	Attitude	.
	Environmental Concerns	,000
	Health_Concerns	,000
N	Attitude	141
	Environmental Concerns	141
	Health Concerns	141

Source: Adapted from SPSS

After performing Pearson's correlation, ANOVA analysis was performed (Table 16). Analysing the values in the table, it is possible to see that p-value (<0.05), so the independent variables (environmental concern and health concern) explain the dependent variable (attitude).

Table 16. ANOVA

ANOVA[a]						
Model		Sum of Squares	df	Mean Square	Z	Sig.
1	Regression	29,060	2	14,530	92,944	,000[b]
	Residual	21,574	138	,156		
	Total	50,634	140			

a. Dependent Variable: Attitude
b. Predictors: (Constant), Health_concern, Environmental_concern

Source: Adapted from SPSS

Table 17. Multiple linear regression

Model	R	R square	Adjusted R square	Standard error of estimate
1	,758[a]	,574	,568	,39539

Source: Adapted from SPSS

Table 17 shows that R (correlation coefficient) has a value of 0.758, confirming the linearity between the independent variables and the dependent variable. The adjusted R^2 value is 0.568, which means that the independent variables (environmental concern and health concern) explain 56.8% of the variation in the dependent variable (attitude). In Table 18, it is possible to conclude that for a significance level p-value <0.05, the environmental concern (β=0.436; p-value=0.000) and health concern (β=0.199; p-value=0.001) have an explanatory power on the attitude and are statistically significant. Therefore, H1 and H2 are confirmed.

Table 18. Regression coefficients

Model		Non-standardised coefficients		Standardised coefficients	t	Sig.
		B	Error	Beta		
1	(Constant)	1,677	,211		7,957	,000
	Environmental Concerns	,436	,055	,575	7,878	,000
	Health Concerns	,199	,059	,245	3,357	,001

Source: Adapted from SPSS

DISCUSSION

This study combines the literature on socially responsible brands, cosmetics, and green consumers and attitude, developing a theoretical model to investigate the relationships between environmental concern and health concern with attitude. Thus, this study aimed to explore the research question: How do environmental and health concerns influence consumers' attitude towards green cosmetics?, extend previous research and discuss the theoretical framework on the influence of environmental and health concerns on Portuguese consumers' attitude towards green cosmetics.

This investigation contributes multiple results and valuable insights into the existing knowledge, through empirical research with a quantitative method, with an online questionnaire application. This research involves Portuguese consumers who have already bought or intend to buy green cosmetics. The sample profile is

Portuguese consumers, mostly aged between 25 and 40 years old, with undergraduate and postgraduate studies, predominantly female.

From the analysis carried out, it was possible to perceive that the behaviour of Portuguese consumers toward green cosmetics is positive, being motivated by the perception that these cosmetics have a higher quality and are made up of ingredients that are more beneficial to health. This fact is corroborated by some authors who state that consumers have shown greater interest in the composition of cosmetics from natural ingredients, without the use of chemicals and additives, being safe for health and effective (Amberg & Fogarassy, 2019; Sadiq et al., 2021; Sahni & Osahan, 2019). Regarding the use of social media by Portuguese users, they are active and access it regularly. Their favourite content format is video. These data are in line with the study carried out in January 2022 on the digital environment, which states that 83.7% of users in Portugal are active on social networks (Hootsuite & We Are Social, 2022). This same study shows that video is the preferred content format of global social media users, and in Portugal, the trend is the same according to the results obtained in this study.

Through the analysis of the results, it was concluded that the perception of Portuguese consumers of green cosmetics about socially responsible brands is positive, and they believe that they exist in Portugal. Thus, these consumers use them to buy green cosmetics, follow the content disseminated by them on social networks, consider it important, and consider them credible and transparent about their environmental protection policies and the quality of their products. Thus, Portuguese consumers of green cosmetics remain loyal to socially responsible brands whose practices are beneficial to the environment. These results are in line with what Ottman (2011) argues, as the author states that socially responsible brands must establish their credibility, communicate their corporate commitment, and strive for full transparency. Several authors confirm these results, stating that these brands share their ecological production methods and publicize quality products and environmental properties, with the main objective of becoming environmentally credible and retaining the loyalty of their consumers, through a communication strategy focused on informative content (Grant, 2007; Grubor & Milovanov, 2017; Nadanyiova et al., 2020; Ottman, 2017).

Regarding the study on whether the attitude of Portuguese consumers towards green cosmetics is influenced by environmental concerns and health concerns, it was concluded that it is positively impacted by their environmental concerns and health concerns. However, environmental concerns have a greater effect on attitude than health concerns, demonstrating the more altruistic behaviour of these consumers. These results are corroborated by some authors who claim that environmental concern and health concerns positively influence consumer attitudes towards green cosmetics (Amberg & Fogarassy, 2019; Ghazali et al., 2017; Liobikienė & Bernatonienė,

2017; Pop et al., 2020; Prakash et al., 2019). The altruistic behaviour of consumers is also confirmed by authors who indicate that consumers act without any personal benefit, focusing mostly on the well-being of others and the environment (Prakash et al., 2019; Yadav & Pathak, 2016).

REFERENCES

Abbas, J., Mahmood, S., Ali, H., Ali Raza, M., Ali, G., Aman, J., Bano, S., & Nurunnabi, M. (2019). The Effects of Corporate Social Responsibility Practices and Environmental Factors through a Moderating Role of Social Media Marketing on Sustainable Performance of Business Firms. *Sustainability, 11*(12). *Artigo, 12*. doi:10.3390u11123434

Ahmad, F., Rosli, N. T., & Quoquab, F. (2021). Environmental quality awareness, green trust, green self-efficacy and environmental attitude in influencing green purchase behaviour. *International Journal of Ethics and Systems, 38*(1), 68–90. doi:10.1108/IJOES-05-2020-0072

Ajzen, I. (1991). The theory of planned behavior. *Organizational Behavior and Human Decision Processes, 50*(2), 179–211. doi:10.1016/0749-5978(91)90020-T

Amberg, N., & Fogarassy, C. (2019). Green Consumer Behavior in the Cosmetics Market. *Resources, 8*(3). *Resources, 3*(3), 137. doi:10.3390/resources8030137

Arli, D., Tan, L. P., Tjiptono, F., & Yang, L. (2018). Exploring consumers' purchase intention towards green products in an emerging market: The role of consumers' perceived readiness. *International Journal of Consumer Studies, 42*(4), 389–401. doi:10.1111/ijcs.12432

Baktash, L., & Talib, M. A. (2019). Green marketing strategies: Exploring intrinsic and extrinsic factors towards green customers' loyalty. *Quality - Access to Success, 20*, 127–134.

Caliskan, A. (2020). *Antecedents of Green Consumerism*., doi:10.4018/978-1-5225-9558-8.ch001

Chygryn, O. Y., Pimonenko, T. V., Bilan, Y. V., & Starchenko, L. V. (2019). *Digital marketing for green goods promotion: Modern trends in entrepreneurship*. Essuir. https://essuir.sumdu.edu.ua/handle/123456789/83845

Chyhryn, O. Y., Pimonenko, T. V., Bilan, Y. V., & Starchenko, L. V. (2019). *Digital marketing for green goods promotion: Modern trends in entrepreneurship*. Essuir. https://essuir.sumdu.edu.ua/handle/123456789/83845

Fontes, E., Moreira, A., & Carlos, V. (2021). The influence of ecological concern on green purchase behavior. *Management & Marketing. Challenges for the Knowledge Society, 16*(3), 246–267. doi:10.2478/mmcks-2021-0015

Ghazali, E., Soon, P. C., Mutum, D. S., & Nguyen, B. (2017). Health and cosmetics: Investigating consumers' values for buying organic personal care products. *Journal of Retailing and Consumer Services, 39*, 154–163. doi:10.1016/j.jretconser.2017.08.002

Graciano, P., Gularte, A. C., Lermen, F. H., & de Barcellos, M. D. (2021). Consumer values in the Brazilian market for ethical cosmetics. *International Journal of Retail & Distribution Management, 50*(4), 458–478. doi:10.1108/IJRDM-01-2021-0040

Grant, J. (2007). *The Green Marketing Manifesto* (1st ed.). Wiley.

Grubor, A., & Milovanov, O. (2017). Brand strategies in the era of sustainability. *Interdisciplinary Description of Complex Systems - Scientific Journal, 15*(1), 78–88.

Hailes, J. (2007). *The New Green Consumer Guide*. Simon and Schuster. https://www.simonandschuster.com.au/books/The-New-Green-Consumer-Guide/Julia-Hailes/9780743295307

Hair, J. F., Black, W. C., Babin, B. J., & Anderson, R. E. (2014). Multivariate Data Analysis: Pearson New International Edition (17.a ed.). Pearson Education Limited.

Hootsuite & We Are Social. (2022). *Digital 2022: Global Overview Report—DataReportal – Global Digital Insights*. Hootsuite. https://datareportal.com/reports/digital-2022-global-overview-report

Lin, J., Lobo, A., & Leckie, C. (2019). The influence of green brand innovativeness and value perception on brand loyalty: The moderating role of green knowledge. *Journal of Strategic Marketing, 27*(1), 81–95. doi:10.1080/0965254X.2017.1384044

Liobikienė, G., & Bernatonienė, J. (2017). Why determinants of green purchase cannot be treated equally? The case of green cosmetics: Literature review. *Journal of Cleaner Production, 162*, 109–120. doi:10.1016/j.jclepro.2017.05.204

Malhotra, N. K., Nunan, D., & Birks, D. F. (2020). *Marketing Research.*

Mamun, A. (2020). Predicting the Purchase Intention and Behaviour towards Green Skincare Products among Malaysian Consumers. *Sustainability (Basel), 12*(24), 1–18. doi:10.3390u122410663

Marôco, J. (2018). *Análise Estatística com o SPSS Statistics* (7ª). ReportNumber, Lda.

Moslehpour, M., Chau, K. Y., Du, L., Qiu, R., Lin, C.-Y., & Batbayar, B. (2022). Predictors of green purchase intention toward eco-innovation and green products: Evidence from Taiwan. *Economic Research-Ekonomska Istraživanja*, *0*(0), 1–22. doi:10.1080/1331677X.2022.2121934

Nadanyiova, M., Gajanova, L., Majerova, J., & Lizbetinova, L. (2020). Influencer marketing and its impact on consumer lifestyles. *Forum Scientiae Oeconomia, 8*(2). *Artigo*, *2*. doi:10.23762/FSO_VOL8_NO2_7

Ottman, J. (2017). *The New Rules of Green Marketing: Strategies, Tools, and Inspiration for Sustainable Branding*. Routledge. doi:10.4324/9781351278683

Patak, M., Branska, L., & Pecinova, Z. (2021). Consumer Intention to Purchase Green Consumer Chemicals. *Sustainability, 13*(14). *Sustainability (Basel)*, *14*(14), 7992. doi:10.3390u13147992

Paul, J., Modi, A., & Patel, J. (2016). Predicting green product consumption using theory of planned behavior and reasoned action. *Journal of Retailing and Consumer Services*, *29*, 123–134. doi:10.1016/j.jretconser.2015.11.006

Pestana, M. H., & Gageiro, J. N. (2014). *Análise de Dados para Ciências Sociais A Complementaridade do SPSS (6.*[a] (E. Silabo, Ed.).

Pop, R.-A., Saplacan, Z., & Alt, M. (2020). Social Media Goes Green—The Impact of Social Media on Green Cosmetics Purchase Motivation and Intention. *Information (Basel)*, *11*(9), 447. doi:10.3390/info11090447

Prakash, G., Choudhary, S., Kumar, A., Garza-Reyes, J. A., Khan, S. A. R., & Panda, T. K. (2019). Do altruistic and egoistic values influence consumersâ€™ attitudes and purchase intentions towards eco-friendly packaged products? An empirical investigation. *Journal of Retailing and Consumer Services*, *50*(C), 163–169. doi:10.1016/j.jretconser.2019.05.011

Qader, I. K. A., & Zainuddin, Y. (2010). Intention to Purchase Green Electronic Products: The Consequences of Perceived Government Legislation, Media Exposure and Safety & Health Concern and the Role of Attitude as Mediator. *International Journal of Innovation and Technology Management*, *1*, 9.

Rahman, A. S. M. S., Barua, A., Hoque, R., & Zahir, R. (2017). Influence of Green Marketing on Consumer Behavior: A Realistic Study on Bangladesh. *Global Journal of Management and Business Research*, *17*, 9–16.

Rajput, N., Sharma, U., Kaur, B., Rani, P., Tongkachok, K., & Dornadula, V. H. R. (2022). Current global green marketing standard: Changing market and company branding. *International Journal of System Assurance Engineering and Management*, *13*(1), 727–735. doi:10.100713198-021-01604-y

Sadiq, M., Adil, M., & Paul, J. (2021). An innovation resistance theory perspective on purchase of eco-friendly cosmetics. *Journal of Retailing and Consumer Services*, *59*, 102369. doi:10.1016/j.jretconser.2020.102369

Sahni, S. K., & Osahan, M. K. (2019). Green Lifestyle Dimensions and Cultural Orientation of the Users of Green Products: A Conceptual Analysis. *IUP Journal of Business Strategy*, *16*(2), 43–52.

Saleem, F., Khattak, A. U. R., Rehman, S., & Ashiq, M. (2021). Bibliometric Analysis of Green Marketing Research from 1977 to 2020. *Publications / MDPI*, *9*(1), 1. doi:10.3390/publications9010001

Sampieri, R. H. (2018). *Metodología de la investigación: las rutas cuantitativa, cualitativa y mixta*. McGraw-Hill Interamericana.

Schiochet, R. O. (2018). A Evolução do Conceito de Marketing "Verde". *Revista Meio Ambiente e Sustentabilidade, 15*(7). *Artigo*, *7*(7). doi:10.22292/mas.v15i7.834

Sequeira, S. I. de M. (2020). *Fatores influenciadores da intenção de compra de produtos de cosmética Cruelty-Free em Portugal* [MasterThesis, Instituto Superior de Economia e Gestão]. https://www.repository.utl.pt/handle/10400.5/21615

Wang, H., Ma, B., & Bai, R. (2019). How Does Green Product Knowledge Effectively Promote Green Purchase Intention? *Sustainability, 11*(4). *Sustainability (Basel)*, *4*(4), 1193. doi:10.3390u11041193

Yadav, R., & Pathak, G. (2017). Determinants of Consumers' Green Purchase Behavior in a Developing Nation: Applying and Extending the Theory of Planned Behavior. *Ecological Economics*, *134*, 114–122. doi:10.1016/j.ecolecon.2016.12.019

Zahid, M. M., Ali, B., Ahmad, M. S., Thurasamy, R., & Amin, N. (2018). Factors Affecting Purchase Intention and Social Media Publicity of Green Products: The Mediating Role of Concern for Consequences. *Corporate Social Responsibility and Environmental Management*, *25*(3), 225–236. doi:10.1002/csr.1450

Zhang, L., Li, D., Cao, C., & Huang, S. (2018). The influence of greenwashing perception on green purchasing intentions: The mediating role of green word-of-mouth and moderating role of green concern. *Journal of Cleaner Production*, *187*, 740–750. doi:10.1016/j.jclepro.2018.03.201

ADDITIONAL READING

Boztepe, A. (2012). Green marketing and its impact on consumer buying behavior. *European Journal of Economic & Political Studies*, *5*(1).

Hazaea, S. A., Al-Matari, E. M., Zedan, K., Khatib, S. F., Zhu, J., & Al Amosh, H. (2022). Green purchasing: Past, present and future. *Sustainability (Basel)*, *14*(9), 5008. doi:10.3390u14095008

Shimul, A. S., Cheah, I., & Khan, B. B. (2022). Investigating female shoppers' attitude and purchase intention toward green cosmetics in South Africa. *Journal of Global Marketing*, *35*(1), 37–56. doi:10.1080/08911762.2021.1934770

Suphasomboon, T., & Vassanadumrongdee, S. (2022). Toward sustainable consumption of green cosmetics and personal care products: The role of perceived value and ethical concern. *Sustainable Production and Consumption*, *33*, 230–243. doi:10.1016/j.spc.2022.07.004

Wijekoon, R., & Sabri, M. F. (2021). Determinants that influence green product purchase intention and behavior: A literature review and guiding framework. *Sustainability (Basel)*, *13*(11), 6219. doi:10.3390u13116219

Witek, L., & Kuźniar, W. (2020). Green purchase behavior: The effectiveness of sociodemographic variables for explaining green purchases in emerging market. *Sustainability (Basel)*, *13*(1), 209. doi:10.3390u13010209

KEY TERMS AND DEFINITIONS

Attitude: Range of beliefs and behaviours in relation to a given situation.

Environmental Concerns: Preoccupation with e.g., climate change, pollution, environmental degradation, and resource scarcity, i.e., harmful effects of human activity on the environment.

Green consumer: Consumer who associates the act of buying or consuming products with the possibility of preserving the environment.

Green Cosmetics: Cosmetics developed from natural raw materials and produced considering sustainability.

Health Concerns: Consumer concern regarding quality of life and health issues for humans.

Socially Responsible Brands: Corresponds to the responsibility assumed by an organization for the impacts of its decisions and activities on society and the environment, through ethical and transparent behaviour.

Sustainability: Ability to use natural resources conscientiously.

Compilation of References

Abbas, J., Mahmood, S., Ali, H., Ali Raza, M., Ali, G., Aman, J., Bano, S., & Nurunnabi, M. (2019). The Effects of Corporate Social Responsibility Practices and Environmental Factors through a Moderating Role of Social Media Marketing on Sustainable Performance of Business Firms. *Sustainability, 11*(12). *Artigo*, *12*. doi:10.3390u11123434

Abrego, M. L., Amado, M. A., Gursoy, T., Nicholls, G. P., & Perez-Saiz, H. (2019). *The African Continental Free Trade Agreement: welfare gains estimates from a general equilibrium model.* International Monetary Fund. doi:10.5089/9781498314398.001

Abrego, M. L., de Zamaroczy, M. M., Gursoy, T., Nicholls, G. P., Perez-Saiz, H., & Rosas, J. N. (2020). *The African Continental Free Trade Area: Potential Economic Impact and Challenges.* International Monetary Fund. doi:10.5089/9781513542379.006

AfDB - African Development Bank. (2018). African Economic Outlook. AfDB. https://www.AfDB.org/fileadmin/uploads/AfDB/Documents/Publications/African_Economic_Outlook_2018_-_EN.pdf

AfDB - African Development Bank. (2019). *Integration for Africa's Economic Prosperity*. AfDB. https://www.afdb.org/fileadmin/uploads/afdb/Documents/Publications/2019AEO/AEO_2019-EN-CHAP3.pdf

Ahmad, F., Rosli, N. T., & Quoquab, F. (2021). Environmental quality awareness, green trust, green self-efficacy and environmental attitude in influencing green purchase behaviour. *International Journal of Ethics and Systems*, *38*(1), 68–90. doi:10.1108/IJOES-05-2020-0072

Ajzen, I. (1991). The theory of planned behavior. *Organizational Behavior and Human Decision Processes*, *50*(2), 179–211. doi:10.1016/0749-5978(91)90020-T

Aksoy, L., Buoye, A. J., Fors, M., Keiningham, T. L., & Rosengren, S. (2022). Environmental, Social and Governance (ESG) metrics do not serve services customers: A missing link between sustainability metrics and customer perceptions of social innovation. *Journal of Service Management*, *33*(4/5), 565–577. doi:10.1108/JOSM-11-2021-0428

Albert, M. (2019). Sustainable frugal innovation—The connection between frugal innovation and sustainability. *Journal of Cleaner Production*, *237*, 117747. doi:10.1016/j.jclepro.2019.117747

Albert, T. (2019). *The African Continental Free Trade Agreement: Opportunities and Challenges*. CUTS International, Geneva.

Albitar, K., Abdoush, T., & Hussainey, K. (n.d.). Do corporate governance mechanisms and ESG disclosure drive CSR narrative tones? *International Journal of Finance & Economics*. doi:10.1002/ijfe.2625

Alderighi, M., Nava, C. R., Calabrese, M., Christille, J. M., & Salvemini, C. B. (2022). Consumer perception of price fairness and dynamic pricing: Evidence from Booking.com. *Journal of Business Research*, *145*, 769–783. doi:10.1016/j.jbusres.2022.03.017

Alderson, A. S. (1999). Explaining deindustrialization: Globalization, failure, or success? *American Sociological Review*, *64*(5), 701–721. doi:10.1177/000312249906400506

Alexander, S. (2012). Planned economic contraction: The emerging case for degrowth. *Environmental Politics*, *21*(3), 349–368. doi:10.1080/09644016.2012.671569

Al-Haddad, S., Sharabati, A.-A. A., Al-Khasawneh, M., Maraqa, R., & Hashem, R. (2022). The Influence of Corporate Social Responsibility on Consumer Purchase Intention: The Mediating Role of Consumer Engagement via Social Media. *Sustainability (Basel)*, *14*(11), 11. doi:10.3390u14116771

Alvarez-Milan, A., Felix, R., Rauschnabel, P., & Hinsch, C. (2018). Strategic customer engagement marketing: A decision making framework. *Journal of Business Research*, *92*, 61–70. doi:10.1016/j.jbusres.2018.07.017

Al-Yazidi, S., Berri, J., Al-Qurishi, M., & Al-Alrubaian, M. (2020). Measuring Reputation and Influence in Online Social Networks: A Systematic Literature Review. *IEEE Access : Practical Innovations, Open Solutions*, *8*, 105824–105851. doi:10.1109/ACCESS.2020.2999033

Amberg, N., & Fogarassy, C. (2019). Green Consumer Behavior in the Cosmetics Market. *Resources, 8*(3). *Resources*, *3*(3), 137. doi:10.3390/resources8030137

Amel-Zadeh, A., & Serafeim, G. (2017). *Why and How Investors Use ESG Information: Evidence from a Global Survey* (SSRN Scholarly Paper 2925310). doi:10.2139/ssrn.2925310

Ampuero-Canellas, O., Tarazona-Belenguer, N., Gonzalez-del-Rio, J., & Jorda-Albiñana, B. (2018). Merchandising en museos:¿ educación, cultura o simple negocio? *EME Experimental Illustration. Art & Design*, (6), 92–101.

Anderson, S., & Anderson, J. (2022). Leave some for me! The role of marketing in influencing responsible consumption during times of crisis. *Journal of Strategic Marketing*, *30*(7), 703–721. doi:10.1080/0965254X.2020.1833075

Ang, K. (2021, March 15). *Overconsumption Or A Move Towards Minimalism?* Social Science Space. https://www.socialsciencespace.com/2021/03/overconsumption-or-a-move-towards-minimalism/

Arli, D., Tan, L. P., Tjiptono, F., & Yang, L. (2018). Exploring consumers' purchase intention towards green products in an emerging market: The role of consumers' perceived readiness. *International Journal of Consumer Studies, 42*(4), 389–401. doi:10.1111/ijcs.12432

Asante Boadi, E., He, Z., Bosompem, J., Opata, C. N., & Boadi, E. K. (2020). Employees' perception of corporate social responsibility (CSR) and its effects on internal outcomes. *Service Industries Journal, 40*(9–10), 611–632. doi:10.1080/02642069.2019.1606906

Ashfaq, M., Zhang, Q., Ali, F., Waheed, A., & Nawaz, S. (2021). You plant a virtual tree, we'll plant a real tree: Understanding users' adoption of the Ant Forest mobile gaming application from a behavioral reasoning theory perspective. *Journal of Cleaner Production, 310*, 127394. doi:10.1016/j.jclepro.2021.127394

AU - African Union. (2018). Template for Goods and Services. *7th African Union Ministers of Trade Meeting*. AU.

AU - African Union. (2019). Agreement Establishing the African Continental Free Trade Area. *African Union Trade Meeting*. AU.

Baah, C., Opoku-Agyeman, D., Acquah, I. S. K., Agyabeng-Mensah, Y., Afum, E., Faibil, D., & Abdoulaye, F. A. M. (2021). Examining the correlations between stakeholder pressures, green production practices, firm reputation, environmental and financial performance: Evidence from manufacturing SMEs. *Sustainable Production and Consumption, 27*, 100–114. doi:10.1016/j.spc.2020.10.015

Baktash, L., & Talib, M. A. (2019). Green marketing strategies: Exploring intrinsic and extrinsic factors towards green customers' loyalty. *Quality - Access to Success, 20*, 127–134.

Balderjahn, I., Buerke, A., Kirchgeorg, M., Peyer, M., Seegebarth, B., & Wiedmann, K. P. (2013). Consciousness for sustainable consumption: Scale development and new insights in the economic dimension of consumers' sustainability. *AMS Review, 3*(4), 181–192. doi:10.100713162-013-0057-6

Bansal, P. (2002). The corporate challenges of sustainable development. *The Academy of Management Perspectives, 16*(2), 122–131. doi:10.5465/ame.2002.7173572

Bascur, C., & Rusu, C. (2020). Customer experience in retail: A systematic literature review. *Applied Sciences (Basel, Switzerland), 10*(21), 7644. doi:10.3390/app10217644

Battilani, P., Bernini, C., & Mariotti, A. (2018). How to cope with dissonant heritage: A way towards sustainable tourism development. *Journal of Sustainable Tourism, 26*(8), 1417–1436. doi:10.1080/09669582.2018.1458856

Bayat, M., & Sezer, A. (2018). Evaluating individuals' voluntary simplicity lifestyles and life satisfaction in terms of the tradition value: The example of Duzce University. *Turkish Journal of Business Ethics, 11*(1), 83–87. doi:10.12711/tjbe.2018.11.1.0009

Becker, J. (2018). 10 Reasons why Minimalism is Growing [online]. *Becoming Minimalist.* https://www.becomingminimalist.com/10-reasons-why-minimalism-is-growinga-k-a-10-reasons-you-should-adopt-the-lifestyle/

Becker-Olsen, K. L., Cudmore, B. A., & Hill, R. P. (2006). The impact of perceived corporate social responsibility on consumer behavior. *Journal of Business Research, 59*(1), 46–53. doi:10.1016/j.jbusres.2005.01.001

Berg, F., Kölbel, J. F., & Rigobon, R. (2022). Aggregate Confusion: The Divergence of ESG Ratings*. *Review of Finance, 26*(6), 1315–1344. doi:10.1093/rof/rfac033

Berg, M. (2005). *Luxury and Pleasure in Eighteenth-Century Britain.* OxfordUniversity Press.

Berndroth, J. (2013). *Theorising institutional processes and strategies: Case studies of sustainability policies on the macro and micro levels* [Doctoral dissertation, WHU-Otto Beisheim School of Management].

Bettencourt, L. A., Brown, S. W., & Sirianni, N. J. (2013). The secret to true service innovation. *Business Horizons, 56*(1), 13–22. doi:10.1016/j.bushor.2012.09.001

Bhuvandas, D., & Gundimeda, H. (2020). Welfare impacts of transport fuel price changes on Indian households: An application of LA-AIDS model. *Energy Policy, 144*, 111583. doi:10.1016/j.enpol.2020.111583

Bititci, U., Garengo, P., Dörfler, V., & Nudurupati, S. (2012). Performance Measurement: Challenges for Tomorrow. *International Journal of Management Reviews, 14*(3), 305–327. doi:10.1111/j.1468-2370.2011.00318.x

Black, I. R., & Cherrier, H. (2010). Anti-Consumption as Part of Living a Sustainable Lifestyle: Daily Practices, Contextual Motivations and Subjective Values. *Journal of Consumer Behaviour, 9*(6), 437–453. doi:10.1002/cb.337

Blanco Mediana, E. (2021). *Las tiendas de museos españoles favoritas de Vogue.es.* Vogue. https://www.vogue.es/living/articulos/tiendas-museos-espanoles-favoritas-vogue

Blazej. (n.d.). *Minimalism on Trend: When Consumers Don't Want to Consume.* CMB Info. https://www.cmbinfo.com/insights/minimalism-on-trend-when-consumers-dont-want-to-consume/

Block, J. H., & Fisch, C. (2020). Eight tips and questions for your bibliographic study in business and management research. *Management Review Quarterly, 70*(3), 307–312. doi:10.100711301-020-00188-4

Blonski K., & Witek J. (2019). Minimalism in consumption. Annales Universitatis Mariae Curie-Sklodwska, *Sectio H-Oeconomia, 53*(2).

Bögel, P. M. (2019). Company reputation and its influence on consumer trust in response to ongoing CSR communication. *Journal of Marketing Communications, 25*(2), 115–136. doi:10.1080/13527266.2016.1166146

Botta, M. (2015). Evolution of the slow living concept within the models of sustainable communities. *Futures*, *80*, 3–16. doi:10.1016/j.futures.2015.12.004

Boujbel, L., & d'Astous, A. (2012). Voluntary simplicity and life satisfaction: Exploring the mediating role of consumption desires. *Journal of Consumer Behaviour*, *11*(6), 487–494. doi:10.1002/cb.1399

Cai, J., Chen, N., & Dai, Q. (2021, December). The Turn of Minimalism in Chinese Women's Clothing in the New Century. In *2021 4th International Conference on Humanities Education and Social Sciences (ICHESS 2021)* (pp. 2441-2446). Atlantis Press. 10.2991/assehr.k.211220.423

Caliskan, A. (2020). *Antecedents of Green Consumerism.*, doi:10.4018/978-1-5225-9558-8.ch001

Cannon Hugh, M., & Yaprak, A. (2011). A dynamic framework for understanding cross-national segmentation. *International Marketing Review*, *28*(3), 229–243. doi:10.1108/02651331111132839

Cardillo, G., Bendinelli, E., & Torluccio, G. (2023). COVID-19, ESG investing, and the resilience of more sustainable stocks: Evidence from European firms. *Business Strategy and the Environment*, *32*(1), 602–623. doi:10.1002/bse.3163 PMID:35942337

Carmine, S., & De Marchi, V. (2022). Reviewing Paradox Theory in Corporate Sustainability Toward a Systems Perspective. *Journal of Business Ethics*, *184*(1), 139–158. doi:10.100710551-022-05112-2

Cenci, M. P., Scarazzato, T., Munchen, D. D., Dartora, P. C., Veit, H. M., Bernardes, A. M., & Dias, P. R. (2022). Eco-Friendly Electronics—A Comprehensive Review. *Advanced Materials Technologies*, *7*(2), 2001263. doi:10.1002/admt.202001263

CFR - Council on Foreign Relations. (2019). *African Continental Free Trade Area: A New Horizon for Trade in Africa*. CFR. https://www.cfr.org/blog/african-continental-free-trade-area-new-horizon-trade-africa

Chakraborty, O. (2022). *Inflation and COVID-19 Supply Chain Disruption*. IGI Global eBooks. doi:10.4018/978-1-6684-5876-1.ch002

Chayka, K. (2020). *The longing for less: Living with minimalism*. Bloomsbury Publishing USA.

Chen, S., & Wei, H. (2022). Minimalism in capsule hotels: Enhancing tourist responses by using minimalistic lifestyle appeals congruent with brand personality. *Tourism Management*, *93*, 104579. doi:10.1016/j.tourman.2022.104579

Chen, S., Wei, H., Xiong, J., & Ran, Y. (2021). Less is more: A theoretical interpretation of minimalism in consumption. *Xinli Kexue Jinzhan*, *29*(11), 2043–2061. doi:10.3724/SP.J.1042.2021.02043

Cherrier, H. (2009). Anti-consumption discourses and consumer-resistant identities. *Journal of Business Research*, *62*(2), 181–190. doi:10.1016/j.jbusres.2008.01.025

Cherrier, H., & Murray, J. B. (2007). Reflexive Dispossession and The Self: Constructing A Processing Theory of Identity. *Consumption Markets & Culture, 10*(1), 1–29. doi:10.1080/10253860601116452

Cho, M., Furey, L. D., & Mohr, T. (2017). Communicating Corporate Social Responsibility on Social Media: Strategies, Stakeholders, and Public Engagement on Corporate Facebook. *Business and Professional Communication Quarterly, 80*(1), 52–69. doi:10.1177/2329490616663708

Cho, S. Y., Lee, C., & Pfeiffer, R. J. Jr. (2013). Corporate social responsibility performance and information asymmetry. *Journal of Accounting and Public Policy, 32*(1), 71–83. doi:10.1016/j.jaccpubpol.2012.10.005

Chu, S.-C., Chen, H.-T., & Gan, C. (2020a). Consumers' engagement with corporate social responsibility (CSR) communication in social media: Evidence from China and the United States. *Journal of Business Research, 110*, 260–271. doi:10.1016/j.jbusres.2020.01.036

Chygryn, O. Y., Pimonenko, T. V., Bilan, Y. V., & Starchenko, L. V. (2019). *Digital marketing for green goods promotion: Modern trends in entrepreneurship*. Essuir. https://essuir.sumdu.edu.ua/handle/123456789/83845

Chyhryn, O. Y., Pimonenko, T. V., Bilan, Y. V., & Starchenko, L. V. (2019). *Digital marketing for green goods promotion: Modern trends in entrepreneurship*. Essuir. https://essuir.sumdu.edu.ua/handle/123456789/83845

Clarkson, M. E. (1995). A Stakeholder Framework for Analyzing and Evaluating Corporate Social Performance. *Academy of Management Review, 20*(1), 92–117. doi:10.2307/258888

Cohen, R., & Serafeim, G. (2020, September 3). How to Measure a Company's Real Impact. *Harvard Business Review*. https://hbr.org/2020/09/how-to-measure-a-companys-real-impact

Colicev, A., Malshe, A., Pauwels, K., & O'Connor, P. (2018). Improving Consumer Mindset Metrics and Shareholder Value through Social Media: The Different Roles of Owned and Earned Media. *Journal of Marketing, 82*(1), 37–56. doi:10.1509/jm.16.0055

Cone. (2008). *Past. Present. Future. 25th anniversary of cause marketing*. Cone Inc. http://www.coneinc.com/content1187

Connelly, B., Certo, T., Ireland, R., & Reutzel, C. (2011). Signaling Theory: A Review and Assessment. *Journal of Management -. Journal of Management, 37*(1), 39–67. doi:10.1177/0149206310388419

Costa, R., & Menichini, T. (2013). A multidimensional approach for CSR assessment: The importance of the stakeholder perception. *Expert Systems with Applications, 40*(1), 150–161. doi:10.1016/j.eswa.2012.07.028

Couture, V., Faber, B., Gu, Y., & Liu, L. (2021). Connecting the countryside via e-commerce: Evidence from China. *American Economic Review: Insights, 3*(1), 35–50. doi:10.1257/aeri.20190382

Cowan, K., & Guzman, F. (2020). How CSR reputation, sustainability signals, and country-of-origin sustainability reputation contribute to corporate brand performance: An exploratory study. *Journal of Business Research, 117*, 683–693. doi:10.1016/j.jbusres.2018.11.017

Craig-Lees, M., & Hill, C. (2002, February). The social-psychological bases of anticonsumption attitudes. *Psychology and Marketing, 19*(2), 187–210.

Cronin, J. J. Jr, Smith, J. S., Gleim, M. R., Ramirez, E., & Martinez, J. D. (2011). Green marketing strategies: An examination of stakeholders and the opportunities they present. *Journal of the Academy of Marketing Science, 39*(1), 158–174. doi:10.100711747-010-0227-0

Crosby, D. G. (2018). *The Nutrition Source*. Harvard. www.hsph.harvard.edu: https://www.hsph.harvard.edu/nutritionsource/2015/04/13/ask-the-expert-concerns-about-canola-oil/?fbclid=IwAR3Ppce46Sx7tO48gFMzS-Yo_9TfCiZiTNtGhAqDax5QodnS4OWQYK9PQz

Cui, G. (2014). Segmenting China's consumer market: A hybrid approach. In Consumer Behavior in Asia: Issues and Marketing Practice (pp. 55-76). Routledge.

Cui, J., Jo, H., & Na, H. (2018). Does Corporate Social Responsibility Affect Information Asymmetry? *Journal of Business Ethics, 148*(3), 549–572. doi:10.100710551-015-3003-8

Čvirik, M., Krošláková, M., Beran, I. M., Hrosik, R. C., & Drábik, P. (2022). Influence of health-conscious consumer behaviour on consumer ethnocentrism during the COVID-19 pandemic. *Ekonomska Istrazivanja, 36*(1), 1510–1526. doi:10.1080/1331677X.2022.2090402

Czerwiński, B., & Domański, J. (2023). Contemporary Consumer Trends. *Foundations of Management, 15*(1), 51–62. doi:10.2478/fman-2023-0004

Dangelico, R. M., & Vocalelli, D. (2017). "Green Marketing": An analysis of definitions, strategy steps, and tools through a systematic review of the literature. *Journal of Cleaner Production, 165*, 1263–1279. doi:10.1016/j.jclepro.2017.07.184

Davies, M. (2011). Museos y sostenibilidad. *Revista de la Subdirección General de Museos Estatales, 7*(8), 142–147.

de Alzaa, A. F., Guillaume, C., & Ravetti, L. (2021). Cooking with Extra Virgin Olive Oil. *Olive Oil—New Perspectives and Applications*, 1-13.

de Jong, M. D. T., Huluba, G., & Beldad, A. D. (2020). Different Shades of Greenwashing: Consumers' Reactions to Environmental Lies, Half-Lies, and Organizations Taking Credit for Following Legal Obligations. *Journal of Business and Technical Communication, 34*(1), 38–76. doi:10.1177/1050651919874105

De Melo, J., & Tsikata, Y. (2015). Regional Integration in Africa: Challenges and Prospects. In C. Monga & J. Y. Lin (Eds.), *The Oxford Handbook of Africa and Economics* (Vol. 2). Oxford University Press.

Deci, E., & Ryan, R. (1985). *Self-Determination in Human Behavior*. Plenum Press.

Deng, D., Wu, Y., & Qin, L. (2023). CSR preference, market competition, and corporate financial performance. *MDE. Managerial and Decision Economics, 44*(3), 1396–1409. doi:10.1002/mde.3754

Dentsu Inc. (2020). *Dentsu Conducts Third Consumer Survey on Sustainable Development Goals (SDGs).* Dentsu Inc.

Diener, E., & Biswas-Diener, R. (2002). Will money increase subjective well-being? A literature review and guide to needed research. *Social Indicators Research, 57*(2), 119–169. doi:10.1023/A:1014411319119

Dittmar, H., Bond, R., Hurst, M., & Kasser, T. (2014). The relationship between materialism and personal well-being: A metaanalysis. *Journal of Personality and Social Psychology, 107*(5), 879–924. doi:10.1037/a0037409 PMID:25347131

Dix-Carneiro, R., & Kovak, B. K. (2017). Trade Liberalization and Regional Dynamics. *The American Economic Review, 107*(10), 29–46. doi:10.1257/aer.20161214

Dopierała, R. (2017). Minimalism–a new mode of consumption? *Przegląd Socjologiczny, 66*(4), 67–83. doi:10.26485/PS/2017/66.4/4

Drempetic, S., Klein, C., & Zwergel, B. (2020). The Influence of Firm Size on the ESG Score: Corporate Sustainability Ratings Under Review. *Journal of Business Ethics, 167*(2), 333–360. doi:10.100710551-019-04164-1

Drucker, P. F. (1974). *Management: Tasks, Responsibilities, Practices.* Harper & Row.

Duong, T. T. T., Ngo, L. V., Surachartkumtonkun, J., Tran, M. D., & Northey, G. (2023). Less is more! A pathway to consumer's transcendence. *Journal of Retailing and Consumer Services, 72*, 103294. doi:10.1016/j.jretconser.2023.103294

Dyllick, T., & Hockerts, K. (2002). Beyond the business case for corporate sustainability. *Business Strategy and the Environment, 11*(2), 130–141. doi:10.1002/bse.323

Dyllick, T., & Muff, K. (2016). Clarifying the meaning of sustainable business: Introducing a typology from business-as-usual to true business sustainability. *Organization & Environment, 29*(2), 156–174. doi:10.1177/1086026615575176

Eckhardt, G. M., & Bardhi, F. (2015). The Sharing Economy Is Not about Sharing at All. *Harvard Business Review.* https://hbr.org /2015/01/the-sharing-economy-isnt-about-sharing-at-all

Efe Verde. (2018). *La moda más sostenible se expone en el museo Victoria y Albert de Londres.* Efe Verde. https://efeverde.com/moda-sostenible-museo-victoria-albert-londres/

Elalfy, A., Darwish, K., & Weber, O. (2020). Corporations and sustainable development goals communication on social media: Corporate social responsibility or just another buzzword? *Sustainable Development (Bradford), 28*(5), 1418–1430. doi:10.1002d.2095

Elangovan, S., & Madhumathi, A. (2021). Interpretation of Minimalism in Architecture According to Various Culture [IJERT]. *International Journal of Engineering Research & Technology (Ahmedabad)*, *10*(7).

Elgin, D. (1981). *Voluntary Simplicity: Toward A Way of Life That Is Outwardly Simple, Inwardly Rich*. Morrow.

Elgin, D., & Mitchell, A. (1977). Voluntary simplicity. *The Coevolution Quarterly*, (Summer), 1977.

Elkington, J. (1997). *Cannibals with forks – Triple bottom line of 21st century business*. New Society Publishers.

Ensley, E. E. (1983). Voluntary simplicity: A segment of concern to marketers. In *Proceedings of the American Marketing Association*, (pp. 385-389). AMA.

Erasmus, G. (2019). *The AfCFTA Institutions: Could the Secretariat Hold the Key to Implementation?* Working Paper No. U S19WP01/2019.

ESG Ratings Methodology. (2023). MSCI. https://www.msci.com/esg-and-climate-methodologies

Etzioni, A. (2004). The post affluent society. *Review of Social Economy*, *62*(3), 407–420. doi:10.1080/0034676042000253990

Farmaki, A., Hadjielias, E., Olya, H., Taheri, B., & Hadjielia Drotarova, M. (2022). CSR communication and international marketing: Insights from the COVID-19 pandemic. *International Marketing Review*. doi:10.1108/IMR-12-2021-0375

Fatima, T., & Elbanna, S. (2023). Corporate Social Responsibility (CSR) Implementation: A Review and a Research Agenda Towards an Integrative Framework. *Journal of Business Ethics*, *183*(1), 105–121. doi:10.100710551-022-05047-8 PMID:35125567

Fennell, D., & Weaver, D. (2005). The ecotourium concept and tourism-conservation symbiosis. *Journal of Sustainable Tourism*, *13*(4), 373–390. doi:10.1080/09669580508668563

Fields Millburn, J., & Nicodemus, R. (n.d.). What is Minimalism? [Blog post]. *The Minimalists.* https://www.theminimalists. com/minimalism/

Figge, F., Hahn, T., Schaltegger, S., & Wagner, M. (2002). The Sustainability Balanced Scorecard – linking sustainability management to business strategy. *Business Strategy and the Environment*, *11*(5), 269–284. doi:10.1002/bse.339

Fine, B. & Leopold, E. (1990). Consumerism and the Industrial Revolution. *Social History, 15*, 151-179. https://www.jstor.org/stable/4285840

Flacher, D. (2005). *Industrial Revolutions and Consumption: A Common Model to the Various Periods of Industrialization*, Working Papers halshs-00132241, HAL.

Fontes, E., Moreira, A., & Carlos, V. (2021). The influence of ecological concern on green purchase behavior. *Management & Marketing. Challenges for the Knowledge Society*, *16*(3), 246–267. doi:10.2478/mmcks-2021-0015

France 24. (2019). *Leaders launch landmark trade deal at African Union Summit*. France24. https://www.france24.com/en/20190707-africa-au-leaders-sign-landmark-afcfta-trade-deal-african- union-summit-Niamey

Freeman, R. E. (1984). *Strategic management: A stakeholder approach*. Pitman.

Fregapane, G., & Salvador, M. (2013). Production of superior quality extra virgin olive oil modulating the content and profile of its minor components. *Food Research International*, *54*(2), 1907–1914. doi:10.1016/j.foodres.2013.04.022

Freudenreich, B., Lüdeke-Freund, F., & Schaltegger, S. (2020). A Stakeholder Theory Perspective on Business Models: Value Creation for Sustainability. *Journal of Business Ethics*, *166*(1), 3–18. doi:10.100710551-019-04112-z

Frooman, J. (1999). Stakeholder Influence Strategies. *Academy of Management Review*, *24*(2), 191–205. doi:10.2307/259074

Gaganis, C., Pasiouras, F., Tasiou, M., & Zopounidis, C. (2021). CISEF: A composite index of social, environmental and financial performance. *European Journal of Operational Research*, *291*(1), 394–409. doi:10.1016/j.ejor.2020.09.035

Ganesan, K., Sukalingam, K., & Xu, B. (2018). Impact of consumption and cooking manners of vegetable oils on cardiovascular diseases- A critical review. *Trends in Food Science & Technology*, *71*, 132–154. doi:10.1016/j.tifs.2017.11.003

García, L. (2022). *Cómo las nuevas generaciones están volviendo a los peores hábitos del low cost más feroz*. SMODA. https://smoda.elpais.com/moda/actualidad/como-las-nuevas-generaciones-estan-volviendo-a-los-peores-habitos-del-low-cost-mas-feroz/

García-Sánchez, I.-M., Rodríguez-Ariza, L., Aibar-Guzmán, B., & Aibar-Guzmán, C. (2020). Do institutional investors drive corporate transparency regarding business contribution to the sustainable development goals? *Business Strategy and the Environment*, *29*(5), 2019–2036. doi:10.1002/bse.2485

Garthe, C. (2020). *Gestión de la sostenibilidad en los museos: Un nuevo enfoque para implementar los Objetivos de Desarrollo Sostenible*. ICOM. https://encr.pw/dt9m1

Garthe, C. (2023). *The Sustainable Museum. How museums contribute to the great transformation*. Routledge.

Garzón Castrillón, M., & Ibarra Marcs, A. (2014). Revisión sobre la sostenibilidad empresarial. *REAl Revista de Estudios Avanzados de Liderazgo*, *1*(3), 52–77.

Gensler, S., Völckner, F., Liu-Thompkins, Y., & Wiertz, C. (2013). Managing brands in the social media environment. *Journal of Interactive Marketing*, *27*(4), 4. doi:10.1016/j.intmar.2013.09.004

Gerth, K. (2020). Consumerism in Contemporary China. In T. Akram & S. Rashid (Eds.), *Faith, Finance, and Economy*. Palgrave Macmillan., doi:10.1007/978-3-030-38784-6_5

Ghazali, E., Soon, P. C., Mutum, D. S., & Nguyen, B. (2017). Health and cosmetics: Investigating consumers' values for buying organic personal care products. *Journal of Retailing and Consumer Services*, *39*, 154–163. doi:10.1016/j.jretconser.2017.08.002

Gilboy Waterman, E. (1932). Demand as a Factor in the Industrial Revolution. First Published in: Cole, A.H., et al., Eds., Facts and Factors in Economic History, Harvard University Press (1932), and then in: Hartwell, R.M., ed., (2017), The Causes of the Industrial Revolution in England. Routledge, London and New York. doi:10.4159/harvard.9780674368897.c31

Global Industry Classification Sector (GICS ®). (2023). MSCI. https://www.msci.com/our-solutions/indexes/gics

Golin. (2023, April). *Wellness Trends for 2023*. Golin. https://golin.com/2023/04/12/wellness-trends-for-2023/

Gómez-Suárez, M., & Yagüe, M. J. (2021). Making sense from experience: How a sustainable multi-sensory event spurs word-of-mouth recommendation of a destination brand. *Sustainability (Basel)*, *13*(11), 5873. doi:10.3390u13115873

Goodpaster, K. E. (1991). Business Ethics and Stakeholder Analysis. *Business Ethics Quarterly*, *1*(1), 53–73. doi:10.2307/3857592

Gould, H. (2022). Modern Minimalism and the Magical Buddhist Art of Disposal. *Buddhism and Waste: The Excess, Discard, and Afterlife of Buddhist Consumption, 53*.

Graciano, P., Gularte, A. C., Lermen, F. H., & de Barcellos, M. D. (2021). Consumer values in the Brazilian market for ethical cosmetics. *International Journal of Retail & Distribution Management*, *50*(4), 458–478. doi:10.1108/IJRDM-01-2021-0040

Grant, J. (2007). *The Green Marketing Manifesto* (1st ed.). Wiley.

Greeven, M. J., Yip, G. S., & Wei, W. (2023). *Pioneers, hidden champions, changemakers, and underdogs: Lessons from China's innovators*. MIT Press.

Grigsby, M. (2012). *Buying Time and Getting By: The Voluntary Simplicity Movement*. SUNY Press.

Grubor, A., & Milovanov, O. (2017). Brand strategies in the era of sustainability. *Interdisciplinary Description of Complex Systems - Scientific Journal, 15*(1), 78–88.

Gupta, S., Kumar, V., & Karam, E. (2020). New-age technologies-driven social innovation: What, how, where, and why? *Industrial Marketing Management*, *89*, 499–516. doi:10.1016/j.indmarman.2019.09.009

Gupta, T., & Saya, L. (2022). A comprehensive review on therapeutic properties of Mustard Oil and Olive Oil. *Chemical Biology Letters*, *9*(1), 309–309.

Haenfler, R., Johnson, B., & Jones, E. (2012). Lifestyle movements: Exploring the intersection of lifestyle and social movements. *Social Movement Studies*, *11*(1), 1–20. doi:10.1080/14742837.2012.640535

Hahn, T., & Figge, F. (2018). Why architecture does not matter: On the fallacy of sustainability balanced scorecards. *Journal of Business Ethics, 150*(4), 919–935. doi:10.100710551-016-3135-5

Hahn, T., Pinkse, J., Preuss, L., & Figge, F. (2015). Tensions in Corporate Sustainability: Towards an Integrative Framework. *Journal of Business Ethics, 127*(2), 297–316. doi:10.100710551-014-2047-5

Hailes, J. (2007). *The New Green Consumer Guide*. Simon and Schuster. https://www.simonandschuster.com.au/books/The-New-Green-Consumer-Guide/Julia-Hailes/9780743295307

Hailu, M. B. (2014). Regional Economic Integration in Africa: Challenges and Prospects. *Mizan Law Review, 8*(2), 299–332. doi:10.4314/mlr.v8i2.2

Hair, J. F., Black, W. C., Babin, B. J., & Anderson, R. E. (2014). Multivariate Data Analysis: Pearson New International Edition (17.a ed.). Pearson Education Limited.

Håkansson, M., & Sengers, P. (2013). *Beyond Being Green: Simple Living Families and ICT.* In *Proceedings of the SIGCHI Conference on Human Factors in Computing*. ACM..10.1145/2470654.2481378

Hansen, E. G., & Schaltegger, S. (2016). The Sustainability Balanced Scorecard: A Systematic Review of Architectures. *Journal of Business Ethics, 133*(2), 193–221. doi:10.100710551-014-2340-3

Harik, R. E. L., Hachem, W., Medini, K., & Bernard, A. (2015). Towards a holistic sustainability index for measuring sustainability of manufacturing companies. *International Journal of Production Research, 53*(13), 4117–4139. doi:10.1080/00207543.2014.993773

Hausen, J. E. (2018). Minimalist life orientations as a dialogical tool for happiness. *British Journal of Guidance & Counselling*. doi:10.1080/03069885.2018.1523364

Heilbroner, R. L. (1985). *The Nature and Logic of Capitalism*. Norton.

He, Q., Gallear, D., Ghobadian, A., & Ramanathan, R. (2019). Managing knowledge in supply chains: A catalyst to triple bottom line sustainability. *Production Planning and Control, 30*(5-6), 448–463. doi:10.1080/09537287.2018.1501814

Herziger, A., Berkessel, J. B., & Steinnes, K. K. (2020). Wean off green: On the (in) effectiveness of biospheric appeals for consumption curtailment. *Journal of Environmental Psychology, 69*, 101415. doi:10.1016/j.jenvp.2020.101415

Hook, J. N., Hodge, A. S., Zhang, H., Van Tongeren, D. R., & Davis, D. E. (2023). Minimalism, voluntary simplicity, and well-being: A systematic review of the empirical literature. *The Journal of Positive Psychology, 18*(1), 130–141. doi:10.1080/17439760.2021.1991450

Hootsuite & We Are Social. (2022). *Digital 2022: Global Overview Report—DataReportal – Global Digital Insights*. Hootsuite. https://datareportal.com/reports/digital-2022-global-overview-report

Hossain, S. (2022). Despite high prices, cooking oil in Bangladesh is cheaper than most of South Asia. *Dhaka Tribune*. https://www.dhakatribune.com

Hristov, I., & Chirico, A. (2019). The Role of Sustainability Key Performance Indicators (KPIs) in Implementing Sustainable Strategies. *Sustainability (Basel)*, *11*(20), 20. doi:10.3390u11205742

Huang, Y.-F., Do, M.-H., & Kumar, V. (2019). Consumers' perception on corporate social responsibility: Evidence from Vietnam. *Corporate Social Responsibility and Environmental Management*, *26*(6), 1272–1284. doi:10.1002/csr.1746

Huneke, M. E. (2005). The face of the un-consumer: An empirical examination of the practice of voluntary simplicity in the United States. *Psychology and Marketing*, *22*(7), 527–550. doi:10.1002/mar.20072

Huq, Z. (2022). How safe is soybean oil? *The Financial Express*. https://thefinancialexpress.com.bd

Huseien, G. F., & Shah, K. W. (2022). A review on 5G technology for smart energy management and smart buildings in Singapore. *Energy and AI*, *7*, 100116. doi:10.1016/j.egyai.2021.100116

ICTSD - International Center for Trade and Sustainable Development. (2019). *Towards Africa's own mega-regional: The CFTA*. ICTSD. https://etradeforall.org/fr/ictsd-african-leaders-launch-continental-free-trade-area/ICTSD

IMF - International Monetary Fund. (2018). *Sub-Saharan Africa Regional Economic Outlook: Recovery Amid Elevated Uncertainty*. IMF.

IMF - International Monetary Fund. (2019). *The African Continental Free Trade Agreement: Welfare Gains Estimates from a General Equilibrium Model*. IMF. https://www.imf.org/en/Publications/WP/Issues/2019/06/07/The-African-Continental-Free-Trade- Agreement-Welfare-Gains-Estimates-from-a-General-46881

Indus. (2023, March). *Spring 2023 Beauty & Wellness Trends*. LoveIndus. https://loveindus.com/blogs/indus-ink/spring-2023-beauty-wellness-trends

InStyle. (2023). *La exposición que aúna belleza, moda y sostenibilidad de obligada visita*. InStyle. https://www.instyle.es/belleza/cara/exposicion-que-auna-moda-belleza-y-sostenibilidad-obligada-visita_54177

Interempresas (2023). *El Museo Guggenheim Bilbao presenta los nuevos uniformes Ecoalf de su personal confeccionados con materiales reciclados*. Interempresas. https://www.interempresas.net/Vestuario-profesional/Articulos/470695-Museo-Guggenheim-Bilbao-presenta-uniformes-Ecoalf-personal-confeccionados-materiales.html

ITC - International Trade Center. (2018). *A business Guide to the African Free Trade Agreement*. ITC. https://www.intracen.org/uploadedFiles/intracenorg/Content/Publications/AfCFTA%20Business%20Guide_final_Low-res.pdf

Iwata, O. (1997). Attitudinal and behavioral correlates of voluntary simplicity lifestyles. *Social Behavior and Personality*, *25*(3), 233–240. doi:10.2224bp.1997.25.3.233

Iyer, R., & Muncy, J. A. (2009). Purpose and Object of Anti-Consumption. *Journal of Business Research, 62*(2), 160–168. doi:10.1016/j.jbusres.2008.01.023

Iyer, R., & Muncy, J. A. (2016). Attitude toward consumption and subjective well-being. *The Journal of Consumer Affairs, 62*(2), 160–168.

Jain, D. (2016, April 1). *Changing the World by Changing Consumption.* The Acro Politian. https://theacropolitan.in/2016/04/01/changing-the-world-by-changing-consumption/

Jain, V. K., Gupta, A., & Verma, H. (2023). Goodbye materialism: Exploring antecedents of minimalism and its impact on millennials well-being. *Environment, Development and Sustainability*, 1–27. doi:10.100710668-023-03437-0 PMID:37363025

Jetter, K. M., & Cassady, D. L. (2006). The availability and cost of healthier food alternatives. *American Journal of Preventive Medicine, 30*(1), 38–44. doi:10.1016/j.amepre.2005.08.039 PMID:16414422

Johnson, C. (2002). De-industrialization and Globalization. *International Review of Social History, 47*(S10), 3–33. doi:10.1017/S0020859002000767

Johnston, T. C. (2000). Impact of voluntary simplicity movement on consumer behavior. In D. R. Deeter-Schmelz & T. P. Hartman, (Eds.) Marketing Advances in the New Millennium, Athens, OH: Society for Marketing Advances, 330.

Johnston, T. C., & Burton, J. B. (2003). Voluntary simplicity: Definitions and dimensions. *Academy of Marketing Studies Journal, 7*(1), 19–36.

Joo, S., Miller, E. G., & Fink, J. S. (2019). Consumer evaluations of CSR authenticity: Development and validation of a multidimensional CSR authenticity scale. *Journal of Business Research, 98*, 236–249. doi:10.1016/j.jbusres.2019.01.060

Joseph, J., Borland, H., Orlitzky, M., & Lindgreen, A. (2020). Seeing Versus Doing: How Businesses Manage Tensions in Pursuit of Sustainability. *Journal of Business Ethics, 164*(2), 349–370. doi:10.100710551-018-4065-1

Kang, J., Martinez, C. M. J., & Johnson, C. (2021). Minimalism as a sustainable lifestyle: Its behavioral representations and contributions to emotional well-being. *Sustainable Production and Consumption, 27*, 802–813. doi:10.1016/j.spc.2021.02.001

Kangun, N., Cox, K. K., Higginbotham, J., & Burton, J. (1975). Consumerism and Marketing Management. *Journal of Marketing, 39*(2), 3–10. doi:10.1177/002224297503900203

Kararrwal, K., & Kumar, K. (2022). *Traditional Method of Consuming Food Secret for Healthier Life.* WJPR. https://wjpr.s3.ap-south-1.amazonaws.com/article_issue/8f0d9d15008a8960d53d3996e8fa0502.pdf

Kasser, T. (2009). Psychological need satisfaction, personal well-being, and ecological sustainability. *Ecopsychology, 1*(4), 175–180. doi:10.1089/eco.2009.0025

Kasser, T. (2016). Materialistic Values and Goals. *Annual Review of Psychology*, *67*(1), 489–514. doi:10.1146/annurev-psych-122414-033344 PMID:26273896

Katsikeas, C. S., Leonidou, C. N., & Zeriti, A. (2016). Eco-friendly product development strategy: Antecedents, outcomes, and contingent effects. *Journal of the Academy of Marketing Science*, *44*(6), 660–684. doi:10.100711747-015-0470-5

Keiningham, T., Aksoy, L., Bruce, H. L., Cadet, F., Clennell, N., Hodgkinson, I. R., & Kearney, T. (2020). Customer experience driven business model innovation. *Journal of Business Research*, *116*, 431–440. doi:10.1016/j.jbusres.2019.08.003

Keller, K. L., & Lehmann, D. R. (2006). Brands and Branding: Research Findings and Future Priorities. *Marketing Science*, *25*(6), 740–759. doi:10.1287/mksc.1050.0153

Kennedy, E. H., Krahn, H., & Krogman, N. T. (2013). Downshifting: An exploration of motivations, quality of life, and environmental practices. *Sociological Forum*, *28*(4), 764–783. doi:10.1111ocf.12057

Kesavan, R., Bernacchi, M. D., & Mascarenhas, O. A. J. (2013). *Word of Mouse: CSR Communication and the Social Media, 9*(1).

Kim, J., Taylor, C., Kim, K. H., & Lee, K. (2015a). Measures of perceived sustainability. *Journal of Global Scholars of Marketing Science*, *25*(2), 182–193. doi:10.1080/21639159.2015.1015473

Kim, M., & Stepchenkova, S. (2020). Corporate social responsibility authenticity from the perspective of restaurant consumers. *Service Industries Journal*, *40*(15–16), 1140–1166. doi:10.1080/02642069.2020.1760249

Kim, S. (2019). The Process Model of Corporate Social Responsibility (CSR) Communication: CSR Communication and its Relationship with Consumers' CSR Knowledge, Trust, and Corporate Reputation Perception. *Journal of Business Ethics*, *154*(4), 1143–1159. doi:10.100710551-017-3433-6

Knothe, G., & Steidley, K. R. (2009). A comparison of used cooking oils: A very heterogeneous feedstock for biodiesel. *Bioresource Technology*, *100*(23), 5796–5801. doi:10.1016/j.biortech.2008.11.064 PMID:19592239

Koh, H.-K., Burnasheva, R., & Suh, Y. G. (2022). Perceived ESG (Environmental, Social, Governance) and Consumers' Responses: The Mediating Role of Brand Credibility, Brand Image, and Perceived Quality. *Sustainability (Basel)*, *14*(8), 8. doi:10.3390u14084515

Kondo, M. (2014). *The life-changing magic of tidying up: The Japanese art of decluttering and organizing*. Ten Speed Press.

Kotler, P. (1972). What Consumerism Means to Marketers. *Harvard Business Review*, *50*, 48–57.

Kropfeld, M. I., Nepomuceno, M. V., & Dantas, D. C. (2018). The ecological impact of anticonsumption lifestyles and environmental concern. *Journal of Public Policy & Marketing*, *37*(2), 245–259. doi:10.1177/0743915618810448

Kumar, R., Thapliyal, B., & Gupta, K. (2023). Consumerism: A Cultural Phenomenon. *International Journal of Research Publication and Reviews*, *4*(4), 2446–2449. doi:10.55248/gengpi.4.423.36256

Kumar, V., Bhaskaran, V., Mirchandani, R., & Shah, M. (2013). Creating a Measurable Social Media Marketing Strategy: Increasing the Value and ROI of Intangibles and Tangibles for Hokey Pokey. *Marketing Science*, *32*(2), 194–212. doi:10.1287/mksc.1120.0768

Kunauskaite, G. (2023, March 10). *The Evolving Landscape of Consumerism*. Euromonitor. https://www.euromonitor.com/article/the-evolving-landscape-of-consumerism?ite=60058&ito=528&itq=fff5c656-1e85-4119-9bcf-59fcaf5a15e3&itx%5Bidio%5D=5896212

Kuriakose, F. (2022). Measuring Corporate Social Responsibility in India: A Composite Indicator Model. *Indian Journal of Corporate Governance*, *15*(2), 295–320. doi:10.1177/09746862221129334

Lage, C., Lins, S., & Aquino, S. D. D. (2022). Consumerism. In *Routledge Encyclopedia of Psychology in the Real World*. Routledge. doi:10.4324/9780367198459-REPRW118-1

Lambert, C. J. (2019). Consumerism, Violence, and Dehumanization: The Vicious Dynamic Circle. In Multifaceted Explorations of Consumer Culture and Its Impact on Individuals and Society (pp. 196-209). IGI Global.

Lambin, J. J. (1997). *Strategic Marketing Management*. McGraw-Hill.

Landes, D. S. (2003). The Industrial Revolution in Britain. In The unbound Prometheus: Technological change and industrial development in Western Europe from 1750 to the present. (pp. 41–123). Cambridge Press. doi:10.1017/CBO9780511819957.004

Lang, T. (2017). *The price of anything is the life you exchange for it: A study on voluntary simplicity within the United States*. [Master Thesis, Lund University].

Leandro, G. D. S. M., & de Jesus Leandro, E. F. (2022). Impact of COVID-19 on Businesses and Consumers 2020/2022: Strategic Measures Adopted by Companies. In Handbook of Research on Global Networking Post COVID-19 (pp. 291-307). IGI Global.

Lee, H.-H. M., van Dolen, W., & Kolk, A. (2013). *On the Role of Social Media in the 'Responsible' Food Business: Blogger Buzz on Health and Obesity Issues* (*SSRN* Scholarly Paper 2355697). https://papers.ssrn.com/abstract=2355697 doi:10.1007/s10551-013-1955-0

Lee, E. M., Park, S.-Y., Rapert, M. I., & Newman, C. L. (2012). Does perceived consumer fit matter in corporate social responsibility issues? *Journal of Business Research*, *65*(11), 1558–1564. doi:10.1016/j.jbusres.2011.02.040

Lee, M. S., & Ahn, C. S. Y. (2016). Anti-consumption, materialism, and consumer well-being. *The Journal of Consumer Affairs*, *50*(1), 18–47. doi:10.1111/joca.12089

Lee, M. S., Motion, J., & Conroy, D. (2009). Anti consumption and brand avoidance. *Journal of Business Research*, *62*(2), 169–180. doi:10.1016/j.jbusres.2008.01.024

Lee, Y., & Lin, C. A. (2021). The effects of a sustainable vs conventional apparel advertisement on consumer perception of CSR image and attitude toward the brand. *Corporate Communications*, *27*(2), 388–403. doi:10.1108/CCIJ-05-2021-0051

Leger U.S.A. (2022, January 11). *Consumer Trends: Minimalism Hits the Market*. Leger USA. https://blog.legerusa.com/2022-consumer-trends-minimalism-hits-the-market

Leonard-Barton, D. (1981). Voluntary Simplicity Lifestyles and Energy Conservation. *The Journal of Consumer Research*, *8*(3), 243–252. doi:10.1086/208861

Leonidou, L. C., Christodoulides, P., Kyrgidou, L. P., & Palihawadana, D. (2017). Internal drivers and performance consequences of small firm green business strategy: The moderating role of external forces. *Journal of Business Ethics*, *140*(3), 585–606. doi:10.100710551-015-2670-9

Libraries, N. (2022). *Buyer decision process*. Wikipedia. https://en.wikipedia.org/wiki/Buyer_decision_process?fbclid=IwAR1B7OF1pv-lNlzvq1XK4rZ9dHcQeI-Yu5TO2Gaxqun3Vj40cmjP9eXi0_Y

Li, C. (Ed.). (2010). *China's emerging middle class: beyond economic transformation*. Brookings Institution Press.

Limao, N. (2016). Preferential Trade Arrangements. In Handbook of Commercial Policy (vol. 1B, pp. 279–367), edited by K. Bagwell and Robert W. Staiger. Amsterdam: Elsevier.

Lin, J., Lobo, A., & Leckie, C. (2019). The influence of green brand innovativeness and value perception on brand loyalty: The moderating role of green knowledge. *Journal of Strategic Marketing*, *27*(1), 81–95. doi:10.1080/0965254X.2017.1384044

Liobikienė, G., & Bernatonienė, J. (2017). Why determinants of green purchase cannot be treated equally? The case of green cosmetics: Literature review. *Journal of Cleaner Production*, *162*, 109–120. doi:10.1016/j.jclepro.2017.05.204

Li, Z. (2015). Eco-innovation and firm growth: Leading edge of China's electric vehicle business. *International Journal of Automotive Technology and Management*, *15*(3), 226–243. doi:10.1504/IJATM.2015.070281

Lloyd, K., & Pennington, W. (2020). Towards a theory of Minimalism and well-being. *International Journal of Applied Positive Psychology*, *5*(3), 121–136. doi:10.100741042-020-00030-y

Lo, K. (2020). Ecological civilization, authoritarian environmentalism, and the eco-politics of extractive governance in China. *The Extractive Industries and Society*, *7*(3), 1029–1035. doi:10.1016/j.exis.2020.06.017

Lund-Thomsen, P. (2020). Corporate social responsibility: A supplier-centered perspective. *Environment and Planning A. Environment & Planning A*, *52*(8), 1700–1709. doi:10.1177/0308518X20948070

Maas, K., Schaltegger, S., & Crutzen, N. (2016). Reprint of Advancing the integration of corporate sustainability measurement, management and reporting. *Journal of Cleaner Production, 136*, 1–4. doi:10.1016/j.jclepro.2016.08.055

Maitra, D., Guhathakurta, K., & Kang, S. H. (2021). The good, the bad and the ugly relation between oil and commodities: An analysis of asymmetric volatility connectedness and portfolio implications. *Energy Economics, 94*, 105061. doi:10.1016/j.eneco.2020.105061

Malhotra, N. K., Nunan, D., & Birks, D. F. (2020). *Marketing Research.*

Malik, & Ishitaq, I. (2023, July). Impact of minimalist practices on consumer happiness and financial well-being. *Journal of Retailing and Consumer Services, 73*. doi:10.1016/j.jretconser.2023.103333

Mamun, A. (2020). Predicting the Purchase Intention and Behaviour towards Green Skincare Products among Malaysian Consumers. *Sustainability (Basel), 12*(24), 1–18. doi:10.3390u122410663

Margariti, K. (2021). "White" Space and Organic Claims on Food Packaging: Communicating Sustainability Values and Affecting Young Adults' Attitudes and Purchase Intentions. *Sustainability (Basel), 13*(19), 11101. doi:10.3390u131911101

Marôco, J. (2018). *Análise Estatística com o SPSS Statistics* (7ª). ReportNumber, Lda.

Martin-Woodhead, A. (2022). Limited, considered and sustainable consumption: The (non) consumption practices of UK minimalists. *Journal of Consumer Culture, 22*(4), 1012–1031. doi:10.1177/14695405211039608

Matters, D. (2017, September 25). *Ever heard of SDG washing? The urgency of SDG Due Diligence*. Development Matters. https://oecd-development-matters.org/2017/09/25/ever-heard-of-sdg-washing-the-urgency-of-sdg-due-diligence/

Mavis, M., & Hossain, S. (2022). No immediate impact on Bangladesh, but businesses wary of oil and food price hike. *Dhakar Tribune*. https://www.dhakatribune.com

McDermott, A. (2017). *The 4 Healthiest Substitutes for Vegetable Oil*. Healthline. https://www.healthline.com/health/food-nutrition/substitute-for-vegetable-oil?fbclid=IwAR35WvrZCoDdJeXV2wcRxA7T3-GBXB9F1pkag8T6VskdtRYVk_ZlEQg4Rvc

McGouran, C., & Prothero, A. (2016). Enacted voluntary simplicity – Exploring the consequences of requesting consumers to intentionally consume less. *European Journal of Marketing, 50*(1/2), 189–212. doi:10.1108/EJM-09-2013-0521

Meenu, M., Cai, Q., & Xu, B. (2019b). A critical review on analytical techniques to detect adulteration of extra virgin olive oil. *Trends in Food Science & Technology, 91*, 391–408. doi:10.1016/j.tifs.2019.07.045

Meira, E., Cunha, F. A. F. de S., Orsato, R. J., Miralles-Quirós, M. M., & Miralles-Quirós, J. L. (2023). The added value and differentiation among ESG investment strategies in stock markets. *Business Strategy and the Environment, 32*(4), 1816–1834. doi:10.1002/bse.3221

Meissner, M. (2019). Against accumulation: Lifestyle minimalism, de-growth and the present post-ecological condition. *Journal of Cultural Economics*, *12*(3), 1–16. doi:10.1080/17530350.2019.1570962

Mhatre, S., Rajaraman, P., Chatterjee, N., Bray, F., Goel, M., Patkar, S., & Dikshit, R. (2020). Mustard oil consumption, cooking method, diet and gallbladder cancer risk in high-and low-risk regions of India. *International Journal of Cancer*, *147*(6), 1621–1628. doi:10.1002/ijc.32952 PMID:32142159

Mio, C., Panfilo, S., & Blundo, B. (2020). Sustainable development goals and the strategic role of business: A systematic literature review. *Business Strategy and the Environment*, *29*(8), 3220–3245. doi:10.1002/bse.2568

Mokyr, J. (1977). Demand vs. Supply in the Industrial Revolution. *The Journal of Economic History*, *37*(4), 981–1008. https://www.jstor.org/stable/2119351. doi:10.1017/S0022050700094778

Moldavska, A., & Welo, T. (2019). A Holistic approach to corporate sustainability assessment: Incorporating sustainable development goals into sustainable manufacturing performance evaluation. *Journal of Manufacturing Systems*, *50*, 53–68. doi:10.1016/j.jmsy.2018.11.004

Montiel, I., & Delgado-Ceballos, J. (2014). Defining and Measuring Corporate Sustainability: Are We There Yet? *Organization & Environment*, *27*(2), 113–139. doi:10.1177/1086026614526413

Morsing, M., & Schultz, M. (2006). Corporate social responsibility communication: Stakeholder information, response and involvement strategies. *Business Ethics (Oxford, England)*, *15*(4), 323–338. doi:10.1111/j.1467-8608.2006.00460.x

Moser, C., & Rose, A. K. (2012). Why Do Trade Negotiations Take So Long? *Journal of Economic Integration*, *2*, 80–90.

Moshref-Javadi, M., & Winkenbach, M. (2021). Applications and Research avenues for drone-based models in logistics: A classification and review. *Expert Systems with Applications*, *177*, 114854. doi:10.1016/j.eswa.2021.114854

Moslehpour, M., Chau, K. Y., Du, L., Qiu, R., Lin, C.-Y., & Batbayar, B. (2022). Predictors of green purchase intention toward eco-innovation and green products: Evidence from Taiwan. *Economic Research-Ekonomska Istraživanja*, *0*(0), 1–22. doi:10.1080/1331677X.2022.2121934

Mosqueda, L. (2018). *Fashion for Good Experience, el primer museo dedicado la moda sostenible*. Vein. https://is.gd/K7jukq

Muñoz, M. M., Rojas-de-Gracia, M.-M., & Navas-Sarasola, C. (2022). Measuring engagement on twitter using a composite index: An application to social media influencers. *Journal of Informetrics*, *16*(4), 101323. doi:10.1016/j.joi.2022.101323

Mura, M., Longo, M., Micheli, P., & Bolzani, D. (2018a). The Evolution of Sustainability Measurement Research. *International Journal of Management Reviews*, *20*(3), 661–695. doi:10.1111/ijmr.12179

Nadanyiova, M., Gajanova, L., Majerova, J., & Lizbetinova, L. (2020). Influencer marketing and its impact on consumer lifestyles. *Forum Scientiae Oeconomia, 8*(2). *Artigo, 2.* doi:10.23762/FSO_VOL8_NO2_7

Neves, S. A., & Marques, A. C. (2022). Drivers and barriers in the transition from a linear economy to a circular economy. *Journal of Cleaner Production, 341*, 130865. doi:10.1016/j.jclepro.2022.130865

Nidumolu, R., Prahalad, C. K., & Rangaswami, M. R. (2009). Why sustainability is now the key driver of innovation. *Harvard Business Review, 87*(9), 56–64.

Nikolaou, I., Tsalis, T., & Evangelinos, K. (2018). A framework to measure corporate sustainability performance: A strong sustainability-based view of firm. *Sustainable Production and Consumption, 18*, 1–18. Advance online publication. doi:10.1016/j.spc.2018.10.004

Nowak, A. (2016). Dynamical minimalism: Why less is more in psychology. In *Theory Construction in Social Personality Psychology* (pp. 183–192). Psychology Press.

Öberseder, M., Schlegelmilch, B. B., & Murphy, P. E. (2013). CSR practices and consumer perceptions. *Journal of Business Research, 66*(10), 1839–1851. doi:10.1016/j.jbusres.2013.02.005

OECD - Organisation for Economic Co-operation and Development. (2010). *Seizing the Benefits of Trade for Employment and Growth.* OECD, International Labour Organization, World Bank, and World Trade Organization final report. Presented at the G20 Summit meeting, Seoul.

Onuwa, G. C., Mailumo, S. S., Okeke-Agulu, K. I., & Chizea, C. I. (2020). Globalization and Economic Growth in Nigeria: An Econometric Approach. *International Research Journal of Modernization in Engineering Technology and Science (IRJMETS), 2*(9), 1685-1694. https://irjmets.com/rootaccess/forms/uploads/IRJMETS999913.pdf

Onuwa, G. C., Yitnoe, G., & Wuyep, G. (2021). Meta-Analysis of Illicit Financial Flows from Nigeria. *Proceedings of the 1st International Economic Conference, Department of Economics, Gombe State University..*

Ortas, E., Gallego-Alvarez, I., & Etxeberria, I. Á. (2015). Financial Factors Influencing the Quality of Corporate Social Responsibility and Environmental Management Disclosure: A Quantile Regression Approach. *Corporate Social Responsibility and Environmental Management, 22*(6), 362–380. doi:10.1002/csr.1351

Orús, A. (2022). *La moda sostenible en el mundo.* Statista. https://es.statista.com/temas/10262/moda-sostenible-en-el-mundo/#topicOverview

Ottman, J. (2017). *The New Rules of Green Marketing: Strategies, Tools, and Inspiration for Sustainable Branding.* Routledge. doi:10.4324/9781351278683

Ottman, J. A., Stafford, E. R., & Hartman, C. L. (2006). Avoiding green marketing myopia: Ways to improve consumer appeal for environmentally preferable products. *Environment, 48*(5), 22–36. doi:10.3200/ENVT.48.5.22-36

Packard, V. (1957). *The Hidden Persuaders*. D.McKay Co.

Pangarkar, A., Shukla, P., & Charles, R. (2021). Minimalism in consumption: A typology and brand engagement strategies. *Journal of Business Research*, *127*, 167–178. doi:10.1016/j.jbusres.2021.01.033

Paredes-Gazquez, J. D., Rodriguez-Fernandez, J. M., & de la Cuesta-Gonzalez, M. (2016). Measuring corporate social responsibility using composite indices: Mission impossible? The case of the electricity utility industry. *Revista de Contabilidad*, *19*(1), 142–153. doi:10.1016/j.rcsar.2015.10.001

Par, T. (2021). Materialism to Minimalism. *BU Well*, *6*(1), 5.

Patak, M., Branska, L., & Pecinova, Z. (2021). Consumer Intention to Purchase Green Consumer Chemicals. *Sustainability, 13*(14). *Sustainability (Basel)*, *14*(14), 7992. doi:10.3390u13147992

Paul, J., Modi, A., & Patel, J. (2016). Predicting green product consumption using theory of planned behavior and reasoned action. *Journal of Retailing and Consumer Services*, *29*, 123–134. doi:10.1016/j.jretconser.2015.11.006

Pepper, M., Jackson, T., & Uzzell, D. (2009). An examination of the values that motivate socially conscious and frugal consumer behaviours. *International Journal of Consumer Studies*, *33*(2), 126–136. doi:10.1111/j.1470-6431.2009.00753.x

Perrett, R. W. (2002). Personal identity, minimalism, and Madhyamaka. *Philosophy East & West*, *52*(3), 373–385. doi:10.1353/pew.2002.0017

Pestana, M. H., & Gageiro, J. N. (2014). *Análise de Dados para Ciências Sociais A Complementaridade do SPSS (6.ª* (E. Silabo, Ed.).

Peyer, M., Balderjahn, I., Seegebarth, B., & Klemm, A. (2017). The Role of Sustainability in Profiling Voluntary Simplifiers. *Journal of Business Research*, *70*, 37–43. doi:10.1016/j.jbusres.2016.07.008

Pfeffer, J., & Salancik, G. R. (1978). *The External Control of Organizations: A Resource Dependence Perspective* (SSRN Scholarly Paper 1496213). https://papers.ssrn.com/abstract=1496213

Pine, B. J., & Gilmore, J. H. (2013). The experience economy: Past, present and future. In S. Jon & S. Flemming (Eds.), *Handbook on the Experience Economy* (pp. 21–44). Edward Elgar Publishing. doi:10.4337/9781781004227.00007

Poddar, K. H., Sikand, G., Kalra, D., Wong, N. D., & Duell, P. B. (2022). Mustard oil and cardiovascular health: Why the controversy? *Journal of Clinical Lipidology*, *16*(1), 13–22. doi:10.1016/j.jacl.2021.11.002 PMID:34924350

Pop, R.-A., Saplacan, Z., & Alt, M. (2020). Social Media Goes Green—The Impact of Social Media on Green Cosmetics Purchase Motivation and Intention. *Information (Basel)*, *11*(9), 447. doi:10.3390/info11090447

Porter, M. E., & Kramer, M. R. (2011). Creating shared value. How to Re-invent capitalism – and unleash a wave of innovation and growth. *Harvard Business Review*, *89*(1), 62–77.

Powers, B. (2010). *Twelve by Twelve: A One-room Cabin Off the Grid & Beyond the American Dream*. New World Library.

Prakash, G., Choudhary, S., Kumar, A., Garza-Reyes, J. A., Khan, S. A. R., & Panda, T. K. (2019). Do altruistic and egoistic values influence consumersâ€™ attitudes and purchase intentions towards eco-friendly packaged products? An empirical investigation. *Journal of Retailing and Consumer Services*, *50*(C), 163–169. doi:10.1016/j.jretconser.2019.05.011

PricewaterhouseCoopers. (2021). *How much does the public care about ESG?* PwC. https://www.pwc.com/gx/en/services/sustainability/publications/cop26/how-much-does-the-public-care-about-esg-pwc-cop26.html

Puggioni, D., & Stefanou, S. E. (2019). The value of being socially responsible: A primal-dual approach. *European Journal of Operational Research*, *276*(3), 1090–1103. doi:10.1016/j.ejor.2019.01.065

Punia, S., Kumar, M., Sandhu, K. S., & Purewal, S. S. (2021). Rice Bran Oil: Emerging Trends in Extraction, Health Benefit, and Its Industrial Application. *Rice Science*, *28*(3), 217–232. doi:10.1016/j.rsci.2021.04.002

PWC. (2023). *The African Continental Free Trade Agreement: The much-needed shapeshifter for the African trade community*. PWC. www.pwc.co.za/tax-alert

Qader, I. K. A., & Zainuddin, Y. (2010). Intention to Purchase Green Electronic Products: The Consequences of Perceived Government Legislation, Media Exposure and Safety & Health Concern and the Role of Attitude as Mediator. *International Journal of Innovation and Technology Management*, *1*, 9.

Rahman, A. S. M. S., Barua, A., Hoque, R., & Zahir, R. (2017). Influence of Green Marketing on Consumer Behavior: A Realistic Study on Bangladesh. *Global Journal of Management and Business Research*, *17*, 9–16.

Rajput, N., Sharma, U., Kaur, B., Rani, P., Tongkachok, K., & Dornadula, V. H. R. (2022). Current global green marketing standard: Changing market and company branding. *International Journal of System Assurance Engineering and Management*, *13*(1), 727–735. doi:10.100713198-021-01604-y

Read, R., Alexander, S., & Garrett, J. (2018). Voluntary simplicity strongly backed by all three main normative-ethical traditions. *Ethical Perspectives*, *25*(1), 87–116.

Rebouças, R., & Soares, A. M. (2021). Voluntary simplicity: A literature review and research agenda. *International Journal of Consumer Studies*, *45*(3), 303–319. doi:10.1111/ijcs.12621

Red Española para el Desarrollo Sustentable. (2021). *Hacia una cultura sostenible. Guía práctica para integrar la Agenda 2030 en el sector cultural*. Ministerio de Cultura y Deporte. https://acortar.link/VMj5jg

Reddick, C. G., Zheng, Y., & Liu, T. (2020). Roles of government in regulating the sharing economy: A case study of bike sharing in China. *Information Polity*, *25*(2), 219–235. doi:10.3233/IP-190207

Reuters (2019). *Economic 'game changer'? African leaders launch free-trade zone.* Reuters. https://www.reuters.com/article/us-africa-trade/economic-game-changer-african-leaders-launch-free-trade- zone-idUSKCN1U20BX

Rich, S. A., Hanna, S., Wright, B. J., & Bennett, P. C. (2017). Fact or fable: Increased well-being in voluntary simplicity. *International Journal of Wellbeing*, *7*(2), 64–77. doi:10.5502/ijw.v7i2.589

Robinson, S. A., Blair, C., & McDonough, M. (2021). China's climate ambition: Revisiting its First Nationally Determined Contribution and centering a just transition to clean energy. *Energy Policy*, *155*, 112350. doi:10.1016/j.enpol.2021.112350

Rogers. (2023). *When consumers want less but demand more, how will your business grow?* EY. https://www.ey.com/en_gl/consumer-products-retail/changing-consumption-will-reshape-business-priorities

Rosen, N. (2010). *Off the Grid: Inside the Movement for More Space, Less Government, and True Independence in Modern America*. Penguin Books.

Rudro, A. A. (2022). Price hike: Is this the new normal? *The Daily Star*. https://www.thedailystar.net

Rueda, Ch. (2018). *Una exposición de moda sostenible para concienciar sobre el impacto de la industria textile.* 20 Minutos. https://blogs.20minutos.es/capeando-la-crisis/2018/01/24/una-exposicion-de-moda-sostenible-para-concienciar-sobre-el-impacto-de-la-industria-textil/

Ruixue, D., Jiayu, G., Junpeng, Y., & Liu, P. (2022). Could peony seeds oil become a high-quality edible vegetable oil? The nutritional and phytochemistry profiles, extraction, health benefits, safety and value-added-products. *Food Research International*, *156*, 111200. doi:10.1016/j.foodres.2022.111200 PMID:35651052

Rust, R. T., Rand, W., Huang, M.-H., Stephen, A. T., Brooks, G., & Chabuk, T. (2021). Real-Time Brand Reputation Tracking Using Social Media. *Journal of Marketing*, *85*(4), 21–43. doi:10.1177/0022242921995173

Ryan, R. M., & Deci, E. L. (2002). Overview of self-determination theory: An organismic dialectical perspective. Handbook of Self-determination Research, 2, 3-33.

Ryan, R. M., & Deci, E. L. (2000). Self-determination theory and the facilitation of intrinsic motivation, social development, and well-being. *The American Psychologist*, *55*(1), 68–78. doi:10.1037/0003-066X.55.1.68 PMID:11392867

Sadiq, M., Adil, M., & Paul, J. (2021). An innovation resistance theory perspective on purchase of eco-friendly cosmetics. *Journal of Retailing and Consumer Services*, *59*, 102369. doi:10.1016/j.jretconser.2020.102369

Sahni, S. K., & Osahan, M. K. (2019). Green Lifestyle Dimensions and Cultural Orientation of the Users of Green Products: A Conceptual Analysis. *IUP Journal of Business Strategy*, *16*(2), 43–52.

Saleem, F., Khattak, A. U. R., Rehman, S., & Ashiq, M. (2021). Bibliometric Analysis of Green Marketing Research from 1977 to 2020. *Publications / MDPI*, *9*(1), 1. doi:10.3390/publications9010001

Sampieri, R. H. (2018). *Metodología de la investigación: las rutas cuantitativa, cualitativa y mixta*. McGraw-Hill Interamericana.

Sandlin, J. A., Walther, C. S., & Wuensch, K. (2016). Voluntary Simplifiers, Spirituality, and Happiness. *Humanity & Society*, *40*(1), 22–42. doi:10.1177/0160597614565698

Sandlin, J., & Walther, C. S. (2009). Voluntary Simplicity Movement. *Forging*, *59*(4), 298–318.

Santeramo, F. G., Di Gioia, L., & Lamonaca, E. (2021). Price responsiveness of supply and acreage in the EU vegetable oil markets: Policy implications. *Land Use Policy*, *101*, 105102. doi:10.1016/j.landusepol.2020.105102

Savarese, M., Castellini, G., Paleologo, M., & Graffigna, G. (2022). Determinants of palm oil consumption in food products: A systematic review. *Journal of Functional Foods*, *96*, 105207. doi:10.1016/j.jff.2022.105207

Saxton, G. D., Gomez, L. M., Ngoh, Z., Lin, Y., & Dietrich, S. (2017). *Do CSR Messages Resonate? Examining Public Reactions to Firms' CSR Efforts on Social Media*. (SSRN Scholarly Paper 3673584). https://papers.ssrn.com/abstract=3673584

Saygili, M., Peters, R., & Knebel, C. (2018). *African continental free trade area: challenges and opportunities of tariff reductions*. (UNCTAD Blue Series Papers, 82). TRALAC. https://www.tralac.org/resources/by- region/cfta.html

Schaefers, T., Falk, T., Kumar, A., & Schamari, J. (2021). More of the same? Effects of volume and variety of social media brand engagement behavior. *Journal of Business Research*, *135*, 282–294. doi:10.1016/j.jbusres.2021.06.033

Scheyvens, R., Banks, G., & Hughes, E. (2016). The Private Sector and the SDGs: The Need to Move Beyond 'Business as Usual.'. *Sustainable Development (Bradford)*, *24*(6), 371–382. doi:10.1002d.1623

Schiochet, R. O. (2018). A Evolução do Conceito de Marketing "Verde". *Revista Meio Ambiente e Sustentabilidade, 15*(7). *Artigo*, *7*(7). doi:10.22292/mas.v15i7.834

Searcy, C. (2016). Measuring Enterprise Sustainability. *Business Strategy & the Environment (John Wiley & Sons, Inc)*, *25*(2), 120–133. doi:10.1002/bse.1861

Searcy, C. (2012). Corporate Sustainability Performance Measurement Systems: A Review and Research Agenda. *Journal of Business Ethics*, *107*(3), 239–253. doi:10.100710551-011-1038-z

Seegebarth, B., Peyer, M., Balderjahn, I., & Wiedmann, K. P. (2016). The sustainability roots of anticonsumption lifestyles and initial insights regarding their effects on consumers' well-being. *The Journal of Consumer Affairs*, *50*(1), 68–99. doi:10.1111/joca.12077

Sequeira, S. I. de M. (2020). *Fatores influenciadores da intenção de compra de produtos de cosmética Cruelty-Free em Portugal* [MasterThesis, Instituto Superior de Economia e Gestão]. https://www.repository.utl.pt/handle/10400.5/21615

Shafqat, T., Ishaq, M. I., & Ahmed, A. (2023). Fashion consumption using minimalism: Exploring the relationship of consumer well-being and social connectedness. *Journal of Retailing and Consumer Services*, *71*, 103215. doi:10.1016/j.jretconser.2022.103215

Shama, A. (1985). The voluntary simplicity consumer. *Journal of Consumer Marketing*, *2*(4), 57–63. doi:10.1108/eb008146

Shama, A., & Wisenblit, J. (1984). Values of voluntary simplicity: Lifestyle and motivation. *Psychological Reports*, *55*(1), 231–240. doi:10.2466/pr0.1984.55.1.231

Shaw, D., & Moraes, C. (2009). Voluntary simplicity: An exploration of market interactions. *International Journal of Consumer Studies*, *33*(2), 215–223. doi:10.1111/j.1470-6431.2009.00760.x

Shaw, D., & Newholm, T. (2002). Voluntary simplicity and the ethics of consumption. *Psychology and Marketing*, *19*(2), 167–185. doi:10.1002/mar.10008

Shen, Z. M., & Sun, Y. (2023). Strengthening supply chain resilience during COVID-19: A case study of JD. com. *Journal of Operations Management*, *69*(3), 359–383. doi:10.1002/joom.1161

Shin, J., Moon, J. J., & Kang, J. (2023). Where does ESG pay? The role of national culture in moderating the relationship between ESG performance and financial performance. *International Business Review*, *32*(3), 102071. doi:10.1016/j.ibusrev.2022.102071

Shukla, A., Goel, G., & Tiwari, N. (2019). Consumer perception of corporate social responsibility and purchase behaviour. *International Journal of Business Excellence*, *18*(1), 22–41. doi:10.1504/IJBEX.2019.099448

Siano, A., Vollero, A., Conte, F., & Amabile, S. (2017). "More than words": Expanding the taxonomy of greenwashing after the Volkswagen scandal. *Journal of Business Research*, *71*, 27–37. doi:10.1016/j.jbusres.2016.11.002

Sifferlin, A. (2018). The 10 Best and Worst Oils For Your Health. *Time*. https://time.com/5342337/best-worst-cooking-oils-for-your-health/?fbclid=IwAR2Kcw6AXFHXHtPC5ajOv4k1dpln2hZUS7Yyl-Kt1cX2sp7_rW_wIIJ6kqI

Singh, R. K., Murty, H. R., Gupta, S. K., & Dikshit, A. K. (2007). Development of composite sustainability performance index for steel industry. *Ecological Indicators*, *7*(3), 565–588. doi:10.1016/j.ecolind.2006.06.004

Song, Y., Qin, Z., & Qin, Z. (2020). Green marketing to gen Z consumers in China: Examining the mediating factors of an eco-label–informed purchase. *SAGE Open*, *10*(4), 2158244020963573. doi:10.1177/2158244020963573

Sperling, D. (2018). *Three revolutions: Steering automated, shared, and electric vehicles to a better future*. Island Press. doi:10.5822/978-1-61091-906-7

Spolini, N. (2019). *La exposición de moda de obligada visita en Florencia está en el Museo Salvatore Ferragamo*. Vogue. https://www.vogue.es/living/articulos/museo-salvatore-ferragamo-florencia-sustainable-thinking-moda-sostenible/40204

Steinhoff, L., Arli, D., Weaven, S., & Kozlenkova, I. (2019). Online relationship marketing. *Journal of the Academy of Marketing Science*, *47*(3), 369–393. doi:10.100711747-018-0621-6

Steurer, R., Langer, M. E., Konrad, A., & Martinuzzi, A. (2005). Corporations, Stakeholders and Sustainable Development I: A Theoretical Exploration of Business-Society Relations. *Journal of Business Ethics*, *61*(3), 263–281. doi:10.100710551-005-7054-0

Su, B., Heshmati, A., Geng, Y., & Yu, X. (2013). A review of the circular economy in China: Moving from rhetoric to implementation. *Journal of Cleaner Production*, *42*, 215–227. doi:10.1016/j.jclepro.2012.11.020

Sujan, M. A. (2022). Edible oil crisis: Alternatives aplenty. *The Daily Star*. https://www.thedailystar.net

Sullivan, K., Thomas, S., & Rosano, M. (2018). Using industrial ecology and strategic management concepts to pursue the Sustainable Development Goals. *Journal of Cleaner Production*, *174*, 237–246. doi:10.1016/j.jclepro.2017.10.201

Suman, M. (2022). Edible oil price hike: Manipulation merry-go-round. *The Daily Star*. https://www.thedailystar.net

Sun, J., Ortega, D. L., & Lin, W. (2023). Food values drive Chinese consumers' demand for meat and milk substitutes. *Appetite*, *181*, 106392. doi:10.1016/j.appet.2022.106392 PMID:36450325

Sun, X., Su, W., Guo, X., & Tian, Z. (2021). The impact of awe induced by COVID-19 pandemic on green consumption behavior in China. *International Journal of Environmental Research and Public Health*, *18*(2), 543. doi:10.3390/ijerph18020543 PMID:33440719

Swaen, V., Demoulin, N., & Pauwels-Delassus, V. (2021). Impact of customers' perceptions regarding corporate social responsibility and irresponsibility in the grocery retailing industry: The role of corporate reputation. *Journal of Business Research*, *131*, 709–721. doi:10.1016/j.jbusres.2020.12.016

Szabo, S., & Webster, J. (2021). Perceived greenwashing: The effects of green marketing on environmental and product perceptions. *Journal of Business Ethics*, *171*(4), 719–739. doi:10.100710551-020-04461-0

TIPS - Trade and Industrial Policy Strategies. (2018, December). Advancing the Continental Free Trade Area in the Context of Changing Architecture of Global Trade. *Agenda (Durban, South Africa)*, 2063.

Ton, L. A. N., Smith, R. K., & Sevilla, J. (2023). EXPRESS: Symbolically Simple: How Simple Packaging Design Influences Willingness to Pay for Consumable Products. *Journal of Marketing*, 00222429231192049. doi:10.1177/00222429231192049

TRALAC - Trade Law Centre. (2018). *Where does the AfCFTA fit in Africa's development Agenda?* E-Newsletter.

TRALAC - Trade Law Centre. (2019). *The African Continental Free Trade Area (AfCFTA).* TRALAC - Trade Law Centre. https://www.tralac.org/resources/by- region/cfta.html

TRALAC - Trade Law Centre. (2021). *Regional Integration as a building block for the Multilateral Trading System.* TRALAC. https://www.tralac.org/blog/article/13683-regional-integration-as-a-building-block-for-the-multilateral- trading-system.html

Turner, J. (2010). Social Categorization and The Self-Concept: A Social Cognitive Theory of Group Behavior. In T. Postmes & N. R. Branscombe (Eds.), *Key Readings in Social Psychology. Rediscovering Social Identity*. Psychology Press.

Uggla, Y. (2019). Taking back control: Minimalism as a reaction to high speed and overload in contemporary society. *Sociologisk Forskning*, *56*(3-4), 233–252. doi:10.37062f.56.18811

UNCTAD - United Nations Conference on Trade and Development. (2018). *African Continental Free Trade Area, Policy and Negotiation Options for Trade in Goods.* New York and Geneva. https://unctad.org/en/PublicationsLibrary/webditc2018d7_en.pdf

UNCTAD - United Nations Conference on Trade and Development. (2019). *African Continental Free Trade Area: Developing and strengthening Regional Value Chains in Agricultural Commodities and Processed Food Products.* New York and Geneva. https://unctad.org/en/PublicationsLibrary/webditc2019d4_en.pdf

UNCTAD - United Nations Conference on Trade and Development. (2020). *AfCFTA: Challenges and opportunities of Tariff Reductions.* UNCTAD. https://unctad.org/en/PublicationsLibrary/ser-rp-2020d15_en.pdf

UNCTAD - United Nations Conference on Trade and Development. (2021). *Rules of Origin Key to Success of African Continental Free Trade Area.* UNCTAD. https://unctad.org/en/pages/newsdetails.aspx?OriginalVersionID=2128

UNECA - United Nations Economic Commission for Africa. (2019). *Assessing Regional Integration in Africa IX.* UNECA. https://www.uneca.org/sites/default/files/PublicationFiles/aria9_en_fin_web.pdf

United Nations Department of Economic and Social Affairs. (2023). *The Sustainable Development Goals Report 2023* (Special Edition). United Nations. doi:10.18356/9789210024914

United Nations. (2015). Transforming our world: the 2030 Agenda for Sustainable Development, Resolution adopted by the General Assembly on 25 September 2015, A/RES/70/1, General Distribution, 21 Oct 2015.

Van De Graaf, T., & Colgan, J. D. (2017). Russian gas games or well-oiled conflict? Energy security and the 2014 Ukraine crisis. *Energy Research & Social Science*, *24*, 59–64. doi:10.1016/j.erss.2016.12.018

van Marrewijk, M. (2003). Concepts and Definitions of CSR and Corporate Sustainability: Between Agency and Communion. *Journal of Business Ethics, 44*(2/3), 95–105. doi:10.1023/A:1023331212247

van Riel, C. B. M. (2019). *Why do people love museums so much? Empirical evidence about the stellar reputations of art museums and what companies can learn from it.* Research in Global Strategic Management., doi:10.1108/S1064-485720190000018013

van Zanten, J. A., & van Tulder, R. (2021). Analyzing companies' interactions with the Sustainable Development Goals through network analysis: Four corporate sustainability imperatives. *Business Strategy and the Environment, 30*(5), 2396–2420. doi:10.1002/bse.2753

Vannini, P., & Taggart, J. (2014). *Off the grid: Re-assembling domestic life.* Routledge. doi:10.4324/978020374406

Vanzetti, D., Peters, R., & Knebel, C. (2017). *Non-Tariff Measures: Lifting CFTA and ACP trade to the next level* (No. 78). *United Nations Conference on Trade and Development.*

Vătămănescu, E. M., Dabija, D. C., Gazzola, P., Cegarro-Navarro, J. G., & Buzzi, T. (2021). Before and after the outbreak of covid-19: Linking fashion companies' corporate social responsibility approach to consumers' demand for sustainable products. *Journal of Cleaner Production, 321*, 128945. doi:10.1016/j.jclepro.2021.128945

Vázquez, S. (2021). *Una diseñadora revive la esencia de Cristóbal Balenciaga.* El Correo. https://bit.ly/3JpJExI

Vishwakarma, S., Kumar, V., Arya, S., Tembhare, M., Dutta, D., & Kumar, S. (2022). E-waste in Information and Communication Technology Sector: Existing scenario, management schemes and initiatives. *Environmental Technology & Innovation, 27*, 102797. doi:10.1016/j.eti.2022.102797

Vladimirova, K. (2021). Consumption corridors in fashion: deliberations on upper consumption limits in minimalist fashion challenges. *Sustainability: Science. Sustainability, 17*(1), 102–116. doi:10.1080/15487733.2021.1891673

Vries, D. (2008). *The Industrious Revolution: Consumer Behavior and the Household Economy,1650 to the Present.* Cambridge University Press. doi:10.1017/CBO9780511818196

Wang, H., Ma, B., & Bai, R. (2019). How Does Green Product Knowledge Effectively Promote Green Purchase Intention? *Sustainability, 11*(4). *Sustainability (Basel), 4*(4), 1193. doi:10.3390u11041193

Wang, Y., Xu, S., & Wang, Y. (2020). The consequences of employees' perceived corporate social responsibility: A meta-analysis. *Business Ethics (Oxford, England), 29*(3), 471–496. doi:10.1111/beer.12273

Watson, R., Wilson, H. N., Smart, P., & Macdonald, E. K. (2018). Harnessing difference: A capability-based framework for stakeholder engagement in environmental innovation. *Journal of Product Innovation Management, 35*(2), 254–279. doi:10.1111/jpim.12394

WEF - World Economic Forum. (2018). Who are the winners and the losers Africa's Continental Free Trade area? WEF.

Weinswig, D. (2016). Millennials Go Minimal: The Decluttering Lifestyle Trend That Is Taking Over. *Forbes*. https://www.forbes.com/sites/deborahweinswig/2016/09/07/millennials-go-minimal-the-decluttering-lifestyle-trend-that-is-taking-over/?sh=53f870db3755/

White, C. L., Nielsen, A. E., & Valentini, C. (2017). CSR research in the apparel industry: A quantitative and qualitative review of existing literature. *Corporate Social Responsibility and Environmental Management*, *24*(5), 382–394. doi:10.1002/csr.1413

Wijekoon, R., & Sabri, M. F. (2021). Determinants that influence green product purchase intention and behavior: A literature review and guiding framework. *Sustainability (Basel)*, *13*(11), 6219. doi:10.3390u13116219

Wilson, A. V. (2020). *The Evolving Marketplace: Essays on How Digitization and Abundance Influence Consumption*. Harvard University.

Wilson, A., & Bellezza, S. (2021). Consumer Minimalism. Journal of Consumer Research Consumer Minimalism. *The Journal of Consumer Research*, *48*(5), 796–816. doi:10.1093/jcr/ucab038

Wilson, D. C. S. (2014). Arnold Toynbee and the Industrial Revolution: The Science of History. *Political Economy and the Machine Past. History & Memory*, *26*(2), 133–161. doi:10.2979/histmemo.26.2.133

WTO - World Trade Organization. (2020). *African nations to seize opportunities for trade facilitation assistance*. WTO. https://www.wto.org/english/news_e/news17_e/ddgra_08may20_e.html

Wu, F., Mao, L., Zhuang, P., Chen, X., Jiao, J., & Zhang, Y. (2020). Plant-sourced cooking oil consumption is associated with lower total mortality in a longitudinal nationwide cohort study. *Clinical Nutrition (Edinburgh, Lothian)*, *39*(12), 3703–3710. doi:10.1016/j.clnu.2020.03.031 PMID:32359931

Yadav, R., & Pathak, G. (2017). Determinants of Consumers' Green Purchase Behavior in a Developing Nation: Applying and Extending the Theory of Planned Behavior. *Ecological Economics*, *134*, 114–122. doi:10.1016/j.ecolecon.2016.12.019

Yang, M., Feng, Q., Chen, C., Chen, S., Guo, Y., Su, D., & Zeng, G. (2022). Healthier diet associated with reduced risk of excessive gestational weight gain: A Chinese prospective cohort study. *Maternal and Child Nutrition*, *19*(3), e13397. doi:10.1111/mcn.13397 PMID:35821659

Yang, Y., & Jiang, Y. (2023). Buyer-supplier CSR alignment and firm performance: A contingency theory perspective. *Journal of Business Research*, *154*, 113340. doi:10.1016/j.jbusres.2022.113340

Yang, Z., Nguyen, T., Nguyen, N., Nguyen, T., & Cao, T. (2020). Greenwashing behaviours: Causes, taxonomy and consequences based on a systematic literature review. *Journal of Business Economics and Management*, *21*(5), 1486–1507. doi:10.3846/jbem.2020.13225

Yubero-Serrano, E. M., Lopez-Moreno, J., Gomez-Delgado, F., & Lopez-Miranda, J. (2018). Extra virgin olive oil: More than a healthy fat. *European Journal of Clinical Nutrition*, *72*(S1), 8–17. doi:10.103841430-018-0304-x PMID:30487558

Zahid, M. M., Ali, B., Ahmad, M. S., Thurasamy, R., & Amin, N. (2018). Factors Affecting Purchase Intention and Social Media Publicity of Green Products: The Mediating Role of Concern for Consequences. *Corporate Social Responsibility and Environmental Management*, *25*(3), 225–236. doi:10.1002/csr.1450

Zavestoski, S. (2002). The Social-Psychological Bases of Anticonsumption Attitudes. *Psychology and Marketing*, *19*(2), 149–165. doi:10.1002/mar.10007

Zhang, L., Li, D., Cao, C., & Huang, S. (2018). The influence of greenwashing perception on green purchasing intentions: The mediating role of green word-of-mouth and moderating role of green concern. *Journal of Cleaner Production*, *187*, 740–750. doi:10.1016/j.jclepro.2018.03.201

Zhang, M. (2022). Research on the Acceptability of Minimalist Consumption in China. *The Frontiers of Society. Science and Technology*, *4*(8), 64–70. doi:10.25236/FSST.2022.040811

Zhou, Q., Chen, X., & Li, S. (2018). Innovative financial approach for agricultural sustainability: A case study of Alibaba. *Sustainability (Basel)*, *10*(3), 891. doi:10.3390u10030891

Zreik, M. (2022). The Regional Comprehensive Economic Partnership (RCEP) for the Asia–Pacific region and world. *Journal of Economic and Administrative Sciences*.

Zreik, M. (2023a). Analytical study on Foreign Direct Investment Divestment Inflows and Outflows in Developing Economies: Evidence of China. *Chinese Economy*, *56*(6), 1–16. doi:10.1080/10971475.2023.2193118

Zreik, M. (2023b). Sustainable and Smart Supply Chains in China: A Multidimensional Approach. In B. Bentalha, A. Hmioui, & L. Alla (Eds.), *Integrating Intelligence and Sustainability in Supply Chains* (pp. 179–197). IGI Global. doi:10.4018/979-8-3693-0225-5.ch010

Zreik, M., Iqbal, B. A., & Rahman, M. N. (2022). Outward FDI: Determinants and Flows in Emerging Economies: Evidence from China. *China and WTO Review*, *8*(2), 385–402. doi:10.14330/cwr.2022.8.2.07

Related References

To continue our tradition of advancing information science and technology research, we have compiled a list of recommended IGI Global readings. These references will provide additional information and guidance to further enrich your knowledge and assist you with your own research and future publications.

Abdul Razak, R., & Mansor, N. A. (2021). Instagram Influencers in Social Media-Induced Tourism: Rethinking Tourist Trust Towards Tourism Destination. In M. Dinis, L. Bonixe, S. Lamy, & Z. Breda (Eds.), *Impact of New Media in Tourism* (pp. 135-144). IGI Global. https://doi.org/10.4018/978-1-7998-7095-1.ch009

Abir, T., & Khan, M. Y. (2022). Importance of ICT Advancement and Culture of Adaptation in the Tourism and Hospitality Industry for Developing Countries. In C. Ramos, S. Quinteiro, & A. Gonçalves (Eds.), *ICT as Innovator Between Tourism and Culture* (pp. 30–41). IGI Global. https://doi.org/10.4018/978-1-7998-8165-0.ch003

Abtahi, M. S., Behboudi, L., & Hasanabad, H. M. (2017). Factors Affecting Internet Advertising Adoption in Ad Agencies. *International Journal of Innovation in the Digital Economy*, *8*(4), 18–29. doi:10.4018/IJIDE.2017100102

Afenyo-Agbe, E., & Mensah, I. (2022). Principles, Benefits, and Barriers to Community-Based Tourism: Implications for Management. In I. Mensah & E. Afenyo-Agbe (Eds.), *Prospects and Challenges of Community-Based Tourism and Changing Demographics* (pp. 1–29). IGI Global. doi:10.4018/978-1-7998-7335-8.ch001

Agbo, V. M. (2022). Distributive Justice Issues in Community-Based Tourism. In I. Mensah & E. Afenyo-Agbe (Eds.), *Prospects and Challenges of Community-Based Tourism and Changing Demographics* (pp. 107–129). IGI Global. https://doi.org/10.4018/978-1-7998-7335-8.ch005

Agrawal, S. (2017). The Impact of Emerging Technologies and Social Media on Different Business(es): Marketing and Management. In O. Rishi & A. Sharma (Eds.), *Maximizing Business Performance and Efficiency Through Intelligent Systems* (pp. 37–49). Hershey, PA: IGI Global. doi:10.4018/978-1-5225-2234-8.ch002

Ahmad, A., & Johari, S. (2022). Georgetown as a Gastronomy Tourism Destination: Visitor Awareness Towards Revisit Intention of Nasi Kandar Restaurant. In M. Valeri (Ed.), *New Governance and Management in Touristic Destinations* (pp. 71–83). IGI Global. https://doi.org/10.4018/978-1-6684-3889-3.ch005

Alkhatib, G., & Bayouq, S. T. (2021). A TAM-Based Model of Technological Factors Affecting Use of E-Tourism. *International Journal of Tourism and Hospitality Management in the Digital Age*, *5*(2), 50–67. https://doi.org/10.4018/IJTHMDA.20210701.oa1

Altinay Ozdemir, M. (2021). Virtual Reality (VR) and Augmented Reality (AR) Technologies for Accessibility and Marketing in the Tourism Industry. In C. Eusébio, L. Teixeira, & M. Carneiro (Eds.), *ICT Tools and Applications for Accessible Tourism* (pp. 277-301). IGI Global. https://doi.org/10.4018/978-1-7998-6428-8.ch013

Anantharaman, R. N., Rajeswari, K. S., Angusamy, A., & Kuppusamy, J. (2017). Role of Self-Efficacy and Collective Efficacy as Moderators of Occupational Stress Among Software Development Professionals. *International Journal of Human Capital and Information Technology Professionals*, *8*(2), 45–58. doi:10.4018/IJHCITP.2017040103

Aninze, F., El-Gohary, H., & Hussain, J. (2018). The Role of Microfinance to Empower Women: The Case of Developing Countries. *International Journal of Customer Relationship Marketing and Management*, *9*(1), 54–78. doi:10.4018/IJCRMM.2018010104

Antosova, G., Sabogal-Salamanca, M., & Krizova, E. (2021). Human Capital in Tourism: A Practical Model of Endogenous and Exogenous Territorial Tourism Planning in Bahía Solano, Colombia. In V. Costa, A. Moura, & M. Mira (Eds.), *Handbook of Research on Human Capital and People Management in the Tourism Industry* (pp. 282–302). IGI Global. https://doi.org/10.4018/978-1-7998-4318-4.ch014

Arsenijević, O. M., Orčić, D., & Kastratović, E. (2017). Development of an Optimization Tool for Intangibles in SMEs: A Case Study from Serbia with a Pilot Research in the Prestige by Milka Company. In M. Vemić (Ed.), *Optimal Management Strategies in Small and Medium Enterprises* (pp. 320–347). Hershey, PA: IGI Global. doi:10.4018/978-1-5225-1949-2.ch015

Aryanto, V. D., Wismantoro, Y., & Widyatmoko, K. (2018). Implementing Eco-Innovation by Utilizing the Internet to Enhance Firm's Marketing Performance: Study of Green Batik Small and Medium Enterprises in Indonesia. *International Journal of E-Business Research, 14*(1), 21–36. doi:10.4018/IJEBR.2018010102

Asero, V., & Billi, S. (2022). New Perspective of Networking in the DMO Model. In M. Valeri (Ed.), *New Governance and Management in Touristic Destinations* (pp. 105–118). IGI Global. https://doi.org/10.4018/978-1-6684-3889-3.ch007

Atiku, S. O., & Fields, Z. (2017). Multicultural Orientations for 21st Century Global Leadership. In N. Baporikar (Ed.), *Management Education for Global Leadership* (pp. 28–51). Hershey, PA: IGI Global. doi:10.4018/978-1-5225-1013-0.ch002

Atiku, S. O., & Fields, Z. (2018). Organisational Learning Dimensions and Talent Retention Strategies for the Service Industries. In N. Baporikar (Ed.), *Global Practices in Knowledge Management for Societal and Organizational Development* (pp. 358–381). Hershey, PA: IGI Global. doi:10.4018/978-1-5225-3009-1.ch017

Atsa'am, D. D., & Kuset Bodur, E. (2021). Pattern Mining on How Organizational Tenure Affects the Psychological Capital of Employees Within the Hospitality and Tourism Industry: Linking Employees' Organizational Tenure With PsyCap. *International Journal of Tourism and Hospitality Management in the Digital Age, 5*(2), 17–28. https://doi.org/10.4018/IJTHMDA.2021070102

Ávila, L., & Teixeira, L. (2018). The Main Concepts Behind the Dematerialization of Business Processes. In M. Khosrow-Pour, D.B.A. (Ed.), Encyclopedia of Information Science and Technology, Fourth Edition (pp. 888-898). Hershey, PA: IGI Global. https://doi.org/ doi:10.4018/978-1-5225-2255-3.ch076

Ayorekire, J., Mugizi, F., Obua, J., & Ampaire, G. (2022). Community-Based Tourism and Local People's Perceptions Towards Conservation: The Case of Queen Elizabeth Conservation Area, Uganda. In I. Mensah & E. Afenyo-Agbe (Eds.), *Prospects and Challenges of Community-Based Tourism and Changing Demographics* (pp. 56–82). IGI Global. https://doi.org/10.4018/978-1-7998-7335-8.ch003

Baleiro, R. (2022). Tourist Literature and the Architecture of Travel in Olga Tokarczuk and Patti Smith. In R. Baleiro & R. Pereira (Eds.), *Global Perspectives on Literary Tourism and Film-Induced Tourism* (pp. 202-216). IGI Global. https://doi.org/10.4018/978-1-7998-8262-6.ch011

Barat, S. (2021). Looking at the Future of Medical Tourism in Asia. *International Journal of Tourism and Hospitality Management in the Digital Age, 5*(1), 19–33. https://doi.org/10.4018/IJTHMDA.2021010102

Barbosa, C. A., Magalhães, M., & Nunes, M. R. (2021). Travel Instagramability: A Way of Choosing a Destination? In M. Dinis, L. Bonixe, S. Lamy, & Z. Breda (Eds.), *Impact of New Media in Tourism* (pp. 173-190). IGI Global. https://doi.org/10.4018/978-1-7998-7095-1.ch011

Bari, M. W., & Khan, Q. (2021). Pakistan as a Destination of Religious Tourism. In E. Alaverdov & M. Bari (Eds.), *Global Development of Religious Tourism* (pp. 1-10). IGI Global. https://doi.org/10.4018/978-1-7998-5792-1.ch001

Bartens, Y., Chunpir, H. I., Schulte, F., & Voß, S. (2017). Business/IT Alignment in Two-Sided Markets: A COBIT 5 Analysis for Media Streaming Business Models. In S. De Haes & W. Van Grembergen (Eds.), *Strategic IT Governance and Alignment in Business Settings* (pp. 82–111). Hershey, PA: IGI Global. doi:10.4018/978-1-5225-0861-8.ch004

Bashayreh, A. M. (2018). Organizational Culture and Organizational Performance. In W. Lee & F. Sabetzadeh (Eds.), *Contemporary Knowledge and Systems Science* (pp. 50–69). Hershey, PA: IGI Global. doi:10.4018/978-1-5225-5655-8.ch003

Bechthold, L., Lude, M., & Prügl, R. (2021). Crisis Favors the Prepared Firm: How Organizational Ambidexterity Relates to Perceptions of Organizational Resilience. In A. Zehrer, G. Glowka, K. Schwaiger, & V. Ranacher-Lackner (Eds.), *Resiliency Models and Addressing Future Risks for Family Firms in the Tourism Industry* (pp. 178–205). IGI Global. https://doi.org/10.4018/978-1-7998-7352-5.ch008

Bedford, D. A. (2018). Sustainable Knowledge Management Strategies: Aligning Business Capabilities and Knowledge Management Goals. In N. Baporikar (Ed.), *Global Practices in Knowledge Management for Societal and Organizational Development* (pp. 46–73). Hershey, PA: IGI Global. doi:10.4018/978-1-5225-3009-1.ch003

Bekjanov, D., & Matyusupov, B. (2021). Influence of Innovative Processes in the Competitiveness of Tourist Destination. In J. Soares (Ed.), *Innovation and Entrepreneurial Opportunities in Community Tourism* (pp. 243–263). IGI Global. https://doi.org/10.4018/978-1-7998-4855-4.ch014

Bharwani, S., & Musunuri, D. (2018). Reflection as a Process From Theory to Practice. In M. Khosrow-Pour, D.B.A. (Ed.), Encyclopedia of Information Science and Technology, Fourth Edition (pp. 1529-1539). Hershey, PA: IGI Global. doi:10.4018/978-1-5225-2255-3.ch132

Bhatt, G. D., Wang, Z., & Rodger, J. A. (2017). Information Systems Capabilities and Their Effects on Competitive Advantages: A Study of Chinese Companies. *Information Resources Management Journal, 30*(3), 41–57. doi:10.4018/IRMJ.2017070103

Bhushan, M., & Yadav, A. (2017). Concept of Cloud Computing in ESB. In R. Bhadoria, N. Chaudhari, G. Tomar, & S. Singh (Eds.), *Exploring Enterprise Service Bus in the Service-Oriented Architecture Paradigm* (pp. 116–127). Hershey, PA: IGI Global. doi:10.4018/978-1-5225-2157-0.ch008

Bhushan, S. (2017). System Dynamics Base-Model of Humanitarian Supply Chain (HSCM) in Disaster Prone Eco-Communities of India: A Discussion on Simulation and Scenario Results. *International Journal of System Dynamics Applications*, *6*(3), 20–37. doi:10.4018/IJSDA.2017070102

Binder, D., & Miller, J. W. (2021). A Generations' Perspective on Employer Branding in Tourism. In V. Costa, A. Moura, & M. Mira (Eds.), *Handbook of Research on Human Capital and People Management in the Tourism Industry* (pp. 152–174). IGI Global. https://doi.org/10.4018/978-1-7998-4318-4.ch008

Birch Freeman, A. A., Mensah, I., & Antwi, K. B. (2022). Smiling vs. Frowning Faces: Community Participation for Sustainable Tourism in Ghanaian Communities. In I. Mensah & E. Afenyo-Agbe (Eds.), *Prospects and Challenges of Community-Based Tourism and Changing Demographics* (pp. 83–106). IGI Global. https://doi.org/10.4018/978-1-7998-7335-8.ch004

Biswas, A., & De, A. K. (2017). On Development of a Fuzzy Stochastic Programming Model with Its Application to Business Management. In S. Trivedi, S. Dey, A. Kumar, & T. Panda (Eds.), *Handbook of Research on Advanced Data Mining Techniques and Applications for Business Intelligence* (pp. 353–378). Hershey, PA: IGI Global. doi:10.4018/978-1-5225-2031-3.ch021

Boragnio, A., & Faracce Macia, C. (2021). "Taking Care of Yourself at Home": Use of E-Commerce About Food and Care During the COVID-19 Pandemic in the City of Buenos Aires. In M. Korstanje (Ed.), *Socio-Economic Effects and Recovery Efforts for the Rental Industry: Post-COVID-19 Strategies* (pp. 45–71). IGI Global. https://doi.org/10.4018/978-1-7998-7287-0.ch003

Borges, V. D. (2021). Happiness: The Basis for Public Policy in Tourism. In A. Perinotto, V. Mayer, & J. Soares (Eds.), *Rebuilding and Restructuring the Tourism Industry: Infusion of Happiness and Quality of Life* (pp. 1–25). IGI Global. https://doi.org/10.4018/978-1-7998-7239-9.ch001

Bücker, J., & Ernste, K. (2018). Use of Brand Heroes in Strategic Reputation Management: The Case of Bacardi, Adidas, and Daimler. In A. Erdemir (Ed.), *Reputation Management Techniques in Public Relations* (pp. 126–150). Hershey, PA: IGI Global. doi:10.4018/978-1-5225-3619-2.ch007

Buluk Eşitti, B. (2021). COVID-19 and Alternative Tourism: New Destinations and New Tourism Products. In M. Demir, A. Dalgıç, & F. Ergen (Eds.), *Handbook of Research on the Impacts and Implications of COVID-19 on the Tourism Industry* (pp. 786–805). IGI Global. https://doi.org/10.4018/978-1-7998-8231-2.ch038

Bureš, V. (2018). Industry 4.0 From the Systems Engineering Perspective: Alternative Holistic Framework Development. In R. Brunet-Thornton & F. Martinez (Eds.), *Analyzing the Impacts of Industry 4.0 in Modern Business Environments* (pp. 199–223). Hershey, PA: IGI Global. doi:10.4018/978-1-5225-3468-6.ch011

Buzady, Z. (2017). Resolving the Magic Cube of Effective Case Teaching: Benchmarking Case Teaching Practices in Emerging Markets – Insights from the Central European University Business School, Hungary. In D. Latusek (Ed.), *Case Studies as a Teaching Tool in Management Education* (pp. 79–103). Hershey, PA: IGI Global. doi:10.4018/978-1-5225-0770-3.ch005

Camillo, A. (2021). *Legal Matters, Risk Management, and Risk Prevention: From Forming a Business to Legal Representation*. IGI Global. doi:10.4018/978-1-7998-4342-9.ch004

Căpusneanu, S., & Topor, D. I. (2018). Business Ethics and Cost Management in SMEs: Theories of Business Ethics and Cost Management Ethos. In I. Oncioiu (Ed.), *Ethics and Decision-Making for Sustainable Business Practices* (pp. 109–127). Hershey, PA: IGI Global. doi:10.4018/978-1-5225-3773-1.ch007

Chan, R. L., Mo, P. L., & Moon, K. K. (2018). Strategic and Tactical Measures in Managing Enterprise Risks: A Study of the Textile and Apparel Industry. In K. Strang, M. Korstanje, & N. Vajjhala (Eds.), *Research, Practices, and Innovations in Global Risk and Contingency Management* (pp. 1–19). Hershey, PA: IGI Global. doi:10.4018/978-1-5225-4754-9.ch001

Charlier, S. D., Burke-Smalley, L. A., & Fisher, S. L. (2018). Undergraduate Programs in the U.S: A Contextual and Content-Based Analysis. In J. Mendy (Ed.), *Teaching Human Resources and Organizational Behavior at the College Level* (pp. 26–57). Hershey, PA: IGI Global. doi:10.4018/978-1-5225-2820-3.ch002

Chumillas, J., Güell, M., & Quer, P. (2022). The Use of ICT in Tourist and Educational Literary Routes: The Role of the Guide. In C. Ramos, S. Quinteiro, & A. Gonçalves (Eds.), *ICT as Innovator Between Tourism and Culture* (pp. 15–29). IGI Global. https://doi.org/10.4018/978-1-7998-8165-0.ch002

Dahlberg, T., Kivijärvi, H., & Saarinen, T. (2017). IT Investment Consistency and Other Factors Influencing the Success of IT Performance. In S. De Haes & W. Van Grembergen (Eds.), *Strategic IT Governance and Alignment in Business Settings* (pp. 176–208). Hershey, PA: IGI Global. doi:10.4018/978-1-5225-0861-8.ch007

Damnjanović, A. M. (2017). Knowledge Management Optimization through IT and E-Business Utilization: A Qualitative Study on Serbian SMEs. In M. Vemić (Ed.), *Optimal Management Strategies in Small and Medium Enterprises* (pp. 249–267). Hershey, PA: IGI Global. doi:10.4018/978-1-5225-1949-2.ch012

Daneshpour, H. (2017). Integrating Sustainable Development into Project Portfolio Management through Application of Open Innovation. In M. Vemić (Ed.), *Optimal Management Strategies in Small and Medium Enterprises* (pp. 370–387). Hershey, PA: IGI Global. doi:10.4018/978-1-5225-1949-2.ch017

Daniel, A. D., & Reis de Castro, V. (2018). Entrepreneurship Education: How to Measure the Impact on Nascent Entrepreneurs. In A. Carrizo Moreira, J. Guilherme Leitão Dantas, & F. Manuel Valente (Eds.), *Nascent Entrepreneurship and Successful New Venture Creation* (pp. 85–110). Hershey, PA: IGI Global. doi:10.4018/978-1-5225-2936-1.ch004

David, R., Swami, B. N., & Tangirala, S. (2018). Ethics Impact on Knowledge Management in Organizational Development: A Case Study. In N. Baporikar (Ed.), *Global Practices in Knowledge Management for Societal and Organizational Development* (pp. 19–45). Hershey, PA: IGI Global. doi:10.4018/978-1-5225-3009-1.ch002

De Uña-Álvarez, E., & Villarino-Pérez, M. (2022). Fostering Ecocultural Resources, Identity, and Tourism in Inland Territories (Galicia, NW Spain). In G. Fernandes (Ed.), *Challenges and New Opportunities for Tourism in Inland Territories: Ecocultural Resources and Sustainable Initiatives* (pp. 1-16). IGI Global. https://doi.org/10.4018/978-1-7998-7339-6.ch001

Delias, P., & Lakiotaki, K. (2018). Discovering Process Horizontal Boundaries to Facilitate Process Comprehension. *International Journal of Operations Research and Information Systems, 9*(2), 1–31. doi:10.4018/IJORIS.2018040101

Denholm, J., & Lee-Davies, L. (2018). Success Factors for Games in Business and Project Management. In *Enhancing Education and Training Initiatives Through Serious Games* (pp. 34–68). Hershey, PA: IGI Global. doi:10.4018/978-1-5225-3689-5.ch002

Deshpande, M. (2017). Best Practices in Management Institutions for Global Leadership: Policy Aspects. In N. Baporikar (Ed.), *Management Education for Global Leadership* (pp. 1–27). Hershey, PA: IGI Global. doi:10.4018/978-1-5225-1013-0.ch001

Deshpande, M. (2018). Policy Perspectives for SMEs Knowledge Management. In N. Baporikar (Ed.), *Knowledge Integration Strategies for Entrepreneurship and Sustainability* (pp. 23–46). Hershey, PA: IGI Global. doi:10.4018/978-1-5225-5115-7.ch002

Dezdar, S. (2017). ERP Implementation Projects in Asian Countries: A Comparative Study on Iran and China. *International Journal of Information Technology Project Management*, *8*(3), 52–68. doi:10.4018/IJITPM.2017070104

Domingos, D., Respício, A., & Martinho, R. (2017). Reliability of IoT-Aware BPMN Healthcare Processes. In C. Reis & M. Maximiano (Eds.), *Internet of Things and Advanced Application in Healthcare* (pp. 214–248). Hershey, PA: IGI Global. doi:10.4018/978-1-5225-1820-4.ch008

Dosumu, O., Hussain, J., & El-Gohary, H. (2017). An Exploratory Study of the Impact of Government Policies on the Development of Small and Medium Enterprises in Developing Countries: The Case of Nigeria. *International Journal of Customer Relationship Marketing and Management*, *8*(4), 51–62. doi:10.4018/IJCRMM.2017100104

Durst, S., Bruns, G., & Edvardsson, I. R. (2017). Retaining Knowledge in Smaller Building and Construction Firms. *International Journal of Knowledge and Systems Science*, *8*(3), 1–12. doi:10.4018/IJKSS.2017070101

Edvardsson, I. R., & Durst, S. (2017). Outsourcing, Knowledge, and Learning: A Critical Review. *International Journal of Knowledge-Based Organizations*, *7*(2), 13–26. doi:10.4018/IJKBO.2017040102

Edwards, J. S. (2018). Integrating Knowledge Management and Business Processes. In M. Khosrow-Pour, D.B.A. (Ed.), Encyclopedia of Information Science and Technology, Fourth Edition (pp. 5046-5055). Hershey, PA: IGI Global. doi:10.4018/978-1-5225-2255-3.ch437

Eichelberger, S., & Peters, M. (2021). Family Firm Management in Turbulent Times: Opportunities for Responsible Tourism. In A. Zehrer, G. Glowka, K. Schwaiger, & V. Ranacher-Lackner (Eds.), *Resiliency Models and Addressing Future Risks for Family Firms in the Tourism Industry* (pp. 103–124). IGI Global. https://doi.org/10.4018/978-1-7998-7352-5.ch005

Eide, D., Hjalager, A., & Hansen, M. (2022). Innovative Certifications in Adventure Tourism: Attributes and Diffusion. In R. Augusto Costa, F. Brandão, Z. Breda, & C. Costa (Eds.), *Planning and Managing the Experience Economy in Tourism* (pp. 161-175). IGI Global. https://doi.org/10.4018/978-1-7998-8775-1.ch009

Ejiogu, A. O. (2018). Economics of Farm Management. In *Agricultural Finance and Opportunities for Investment and Expansion* (pp. 56–72). Hershey, PA: IGI Global. doi:10.4018/978-1-5225-3059-6.ch003

Ekanem, I., & Abiade, G. E. (2018). Factors Influencing the Use of E-Commerce by Small Enterprises in Nigeria. *International Journal of ICT Research in Africa and the Middle East*, *7*(1), 37–53. doi:10.4018/IJICTRAME.2018010103

Ekanem, I., & Alrossais, L. A. (2017). Succession Challenges Facing Family Businesses in Saudi Arabia. In P. Zgheib (Ed.), *Entrepreneurship and Business Innovation in the Middle East* (pp. 122–146). Hershey, PA: IGI Global. doi:10.4018/978-1-5225-2066-5.ch007

El Faquih, L., & Fredj, M. (2017). Ontology-Based Framework for Quality in Configurable Process Models. *Journal of Electronic Commerce in Organizations*, *15*(2), 48–60. doi:10.4018/JECO.2017040104

Faisal, M. N., & Talib, F. (2017). Building Ambidextrous Supply Chains in SMEs: How to Tackle the Barriers? *International Journal of Information Systems and Supply Chain Management*, *10*(4), 80–100. doi:10.4018/IJISSCM.2017100105

Fernandes, T. M., Gomes, J., & Romão, M. (2017). Investments in E-Government: A Benefit Management Case Study. *International Journal of Electronic Government Research*, *13*(3), 1–17. doi:10.4018/IJEGR.2017070101

Figueira, L. M., Honrado, G. R., & Dionísio, M. S. (2021). Human Capital Management in the Tourism Industry in Portugal. In V. Costa, A. Moura, & M. Mira (Eds.), *Handbook of Research on Human Capital and People Management in the Tourism Industry* (pp. 1–19). IGI Global. doi:10.4018/978-1-7998-4318-4.ch001

Gao, S. S., Oreal, S., & Zhang, J. (2018). Contemporary Financial Risk Management Perceptions and Practices of Small-Sized Chinese Businesses. In I. Management Association (Ed.), Global Business Expansion: Concepts, Methodologies, Tools, and Applications (pp. 917-931). Hershey, PA: IGI Global. doi:10.4018/978-1-5225-5481-3.ch041

Garg, R., & Berning, S. C. (2017). Indigenous Chinese Management Philosophies: Key Concepts and Relevance for Modern Chinese Firms. In B. Christiansen & G. Koc (Eds.), *Transcontinental Strategies for Industrial Development and Economic Growth* (pp. 43–57). Hershey, PA: IGI Global. doi:10.4018/978-1-5225-2160-0.ch003

Gencer, Y. G. (2017). Supply Chain Management in Retailing Business. In U. Akkucuk (Ed.), *Ethics and Sustainability in Global Supply Chain Management* (pp. 197–210). Hershey, PA: IGI Global. doi:10.4018/978-1-5225-2036-8.ch011

Gera, R., Arora, S., & Malik, S. (2021). Emotional Labor in the Tourism Industry: Strategies, Antecedents, and Outcomes. In V. Costa, A. Moura, & M. Mira (Eds.), *Handbook of Research on Human Capital and People Management in the Tourism Industry* (pp. 73–91). IGI Global. https://doi.org/10.4018/978-1-7998-4318-4.ch004

Giacosa, E. (2018). The Increasing of the Regional Development Thanks to the Luxury Business Innovation. In L. Carvalho (Ed.), *Handbook of Research on Entrepreneurial Ecosystems and Social Dynamics in a Globalized World* (pp. 260–273). Hershey, PA: IGI Global. doi:10.4018/978-1-5225-3525-6.ch011

Glowka, G., Tusch, M., & Zehrer, A. (2021). The Risk Perception of Family Business Owner-Manager in the Tourism Industry: A Qualitative Comparison of the Intra-Firm Senior and Junior Generation. In A. Zehrer, G. Glowka, K. Schwaiger, & V. Ranacher-Lackner (Eds.), *Resiliency Models and Addressing Future Risks for Family Firms in the Tourism Industry* (pp. 126–153). IGI Global. https://doi.org/10.4018/978-1-7998-7352-5.ch006

Glykas, M., & George, J. (2017). Quality and Process Management Systems in the UAE Maritime Industry. *International Journal of Productivity Management and Assessment Technologies*, *5*(1), 20–39. doi:10.4018/IJPMAT.2017010102

Glykas, M., Valiris, G., Kokkinaki, A., & Koutsoukou, Z. (2018). Banking Business Process Management Implementation. *International Journal of Productivity Management and Assessment Technologies*, *6*(1), 50–69. doi:10.4018/IJPMAT.2018010104

Gomes, J., & Romão, M. (2017). The Balanced Scorecard: Keeping Updated and Aligned with Today's Business Trends. *International Journal of Productivity Management and Assessment Technologies*, *5*(2), 1–15. doi:10.4018/IJPMAT.2017070101

Gomes, J., & Romão, M. (2017). Aligning Information Systems and Technology with Benefit Management and Balanced Scorecard. In S. De Haes & W. Van Grembergen (Eds.), *Strategic IT Governance and Alignment in Business Settings* (pp. 112–131). Hershey, PA: IGI Global. doi:10.4018/978-1-5225-0861-8.ch005

Goyal, A. (2021). Communicating and Building Destination Brands With New Media. In M. Dinis, L. Bonixe, S. Lamy, & Z. Breda (Eds.), *Impact of New Media in Tourism* (pp. 1-20). IGI Global. https://doi.org/10.4018/978-1-7998-7095-1.ch001

Grefen, P., & Turetken, O. (2017). Advanced Business Process Management in Networked E-Business Scenarios. *International Journal of E-Business Research, 13*(4), 70–104. doi:10.4018/IJEBR.2017100105

Guasca, M., Van Broeck, A. M., & Vanneste, D. (2021). Tourism and the Social Reintegration of Colombian Ex-Combatants. In J. da Silva, Z. Breda, & F. Carbone (Eds.), *Role and Impact of Tourism in Peacebuilding and Conflict Transformation* (pp. 66-86). IGI Global. https://doi.org/10.4018/978-1-7998-5053-3.ch005

Haider, A., & Saetang, S. (2017). Strategic IT Alignment in Service Sector. In S. Rozenes & Y. Cohen (Eds.), *Handbook of Research on Strategic Alliances and Value Co-Creation in the Service Industry* (pp. 231–258). Hershey, PA: IGI Global. doi:10.4018/978-1-5225-2084-9.ch012

Hajilari, A. B., Ghadaksaz, M., & Fasghandis, G. S. (2017). Assessing Organizational Readiness for Implementing ERP System Using Fuzzy Expert System Approach. *International Journal of Enterprise Information Systems, 13*(1), 67–85. doi:10.4018/IJEIS.2017010105

Haldorai, A., Ramu, A., & Murugan, S. (2018). Social Aware Cognitive Radio Networks: Effectiveness of Social Networks as a Strategic Tool for Organizational Business Management. In H. Bansal, G. Shrivastava, G. Nguyen, & L. Stanciu (Eds.), *Social Network Analytics for Contemporary Business Organizations* (pp. 188–202). Hershey, PA: IGI Global. doi:10.4018/978-1-5225-5097-6.ch010

Hall, O. P. Jr. (2017). Social Media Driven Management Education. *International Journal of Knowledge-Based Organizations, 7*(2), 43–59. doi:10.4018/IJKBO.2017040104

Hanifah, H., Halim, H. A., Ahmad, N. H., & Vafaei-Zadeh, A. (2017). Innovation Culture as a Mediator Between Specific Human Capital and Innovation Performance Among Bumiputera SMEs in Malaysia. In N. Ahmad, T. Ramayah, H. Halim, & S. Rahman (Eds.), *Handbook of Research on Small and Medium Enterprises in Developing Countries* (pp. 261–279). Hershey, PA: IGI Global. doi:10.4018/978-1-5225-2165-5.ch012

Hartlieb, S., & Silvius, G. (2017). Handling Uncertainty in Project Management and Business Development: Similarities and Differences. In Y. Raydugin (Ed.), *Handbook of Research on Leveraging Risk and Uncertainties for Effective Project Management* (pp. 337–362). Hershey, PA: IGI Global. doi:10.4018/978-1-5225-1790-0.ch016

Hass, K. B. (2017). Living on the Edge: Managing Project Complexity. In Y. Raydugin (Ed.), *Handbook of Research on Leveraging Risk and Uncertainties for Effective Project Management* (pp. 177–201). Hershey, PA: IGI Global. doi:10.4018/978-1-5225-1790-0.ch009

Hawking, P., & Carmine Sellitto, C. (2017). Developing an Effective Strategy for Organizational Business Intelligence. In M. Tavana (Ed.), *Enterprise Information Systems and the Digitalization of Business Functions* (pp. 222–237). Hershey, PA: IGI Global. doi:10.4018/978-1-5225-2382-6.ch010

Hawking, P., & Sellitto, C. (2017). A Fast-Moving Consumer Goods Company and Business Intelligence Strategy Development. *International Journal of Enterprise Information Systems, 13*(2), 22–33. doi:10.4018/IJEIS.2017040102

Hawking, P., & Sellitto, C. (2017). Business Intelligence Strategy: Two Case Studies. *International Journal of Business Intelligence Research, 8*(2), 17–30. doi:10.4018/IJBIR.2017070102

Hee, W. J., Jalleh, G., Lai, H., & Lin, C. (2017). E-Commerce and IT Projects: Evaluation and Management Issues in Australian and Taiwanese Hospitals. *International Journal of Public Health Management and Ethics, 2*(1), 69–90. doi:10.4018/IJPHME.2017010104

Hernandez, A. A. (2018). Exploring the Factors to Green IT Adoption of SMEs in the Philippines. *Journal of Cases on Information Technology, 20*(2), 49–66. doi:10.4018/JCIT.2018040104

Hollman, A., Bickford, S., & Hollman, T. (2017). Cyber InSecurity: A Post-Mortem Attempt to Assess Cyber Problems from IT and Business Management Perspectives. *Journal of Cases on Information Technology, 19*(3), 42–70. doi:10.4018/JCIT.2017070104

Ibrahim, F., & Zainin, N. M. (2021). Exploring the Technological Impacts: The Case of Museums in Brunei Darussalam. *International Journal of Tourism and Hospitality Management in the Digital Age, 5*(1), 1–18. https://doi.org/10.4018/IJTHMDA.2021010101

Igbinakhase, I. (2017). Responsible and Sustainable Management Practices in Developing and Developed Business Environments. In Z. Fields (Ed.), *Collective Creativity for Responsible and Sustainable Business Practice* (pp. 180–207). Hershey, PA: IGI Global. doi:10.4018/978-1-5225-1823-5.ch010

Iwata, J. J., & Hoskins, R. G. (2017). Managing Indigenous Knowledge in Tanzania: A Business Perspective. In P. Jain & N. Mnjama (Eds.), *Managing Knowledge Resources and Records in Modern Organizations* (pp. 198–214). Hershey, PA: IGI Global. doi:10.4018/978-1-5225-1965-2.ch012

Jain, P. (2017). Ethical and Legal Issues in Knowledge Management Life-Cycle in Business. In P. Jain & N. Mnjama (Eds.), *Managing Knowledge Resources and Records in Modern Organizations* (pp. 82–101). Hershey, PA: IGI Global. doi:10.4018/978-1-5225-1965-2.ch006

James, S., & Hauli, E. (2017). Holistic Management Education at Tanzanian Rural Development Planning Institute. In N. Baporikar (Ed.), *Management Education for Global Leadership* (pp. 112–136). Hershey, PA: IGI Global. doi:10.4018/978-1-5225-1013-0.ch006

Janošková, M., Csikósová, A., & Čulková, K. (2018). Measurement of Company Performance as Part of Its Strategic Management. In R. Leon (Ed.), *Managerial Strategies for Business Sustainability During Turbulent Times* (pp. 309–335). Hershey, PA: IGI Global. doi:10.4018/978-1-5225-2716-9.ch017

Jean-Vasile, A., & Alecu, A. (2017). Theoretical and Practical Approaches in Understanding the Influences of Cost-Productivity-Profit Trinomial in Contemporary Enterprises. In A. Jean Vasile & D. Nicolò (Eds.), *Sustainable Entrepreneurship and Investments in the Green Economy* (pp. 28–62). Hershey, PA: IGI Global. doi:10.4018/978-1-5225-2075-7.ch002

Joia, L. A., & Correia, J. C. (2018). CIO Competencies From the IT Professional Perspective: Insights From Brazil. *Journal of Global Information Management, 26*(2), 74–103. doi:10.4018/JGIM.2018040104

Juma, A., & Mzera, N. (2017). Knowledge Management and Records Management and Competitive Advantage in Business. In P. Jain & N. Mnjama (Eds.), *Managing Knowledge Resources and Records in Modern Organizations* (pp. 15–28). Hershey, PA: IGI Global. doi:10.4018/978-1-5225-1965-2.ch002

K., I., & A, V. (2018). Monitoring and Auditing in the Cloud. In K. Munir (Ed.), *Cloud Computing Technologies for Green Enterprises* (pp. 318-350). Hershey, PA: IGI Global. https://doi.org/ doi:10.4018/978-1-5225-3038-1.ch013

Kabra, G., Ghosh, V., & Ramesh, A. (2018). Enterprise Integrated Business Process Management and Business Intelligence Framework for Business Process Sustainability. In A. Paul, D. Bhattacharyya, & S. Anand (Eds.), *Green Initiatives for Business Sustainability and Value Creation* (pp. 228–238). Hershey, PA: IGI Global. doi:10.4018/978-1-5225-2662-9.ch010

Kaoud, M. (2017). Investigation of Customer Knowledge Management: A Case Study Research. *International Journal of Service Science, Management, Engineering, and Technology*, *8*(2), 12–22. doi:10.4018/IJSSMET.2017040102

Katuu, S. (2018). A Comparative Assessment of Enterprise Content Management Maturity Models. In N. Gwangwava & M. Mutingi (Eds.), *E-Manufacturing and E-Service Strategies in Contemporary Organizations* (pp. 93–118). Hershey, PA: IGI Global. doi:10.4018/978-1-5225-3628-4.ch005

Khan, M. Y., & Abir, T. (2022). The Role of Social Media Marketing in the Tourism and Hospitality Industry: A Conceptual Study on Bangladesh. In C. Ramos, S. Quinteiro, & A. Gonçalves (Eds.), *ICT as Innovator Between Tourism and Culture* (pp. 213–229). IGI Global. https://doi.org/10.4018/978-1-7998-8165-0.ch013

Kinnunen, S., Ylä-Kujala, A., Marttonen-Arola, S., Kärri, T., & Baglee, D. (2018). Internet of Things in Asset Management: Insights from Industrial Professionals and Academia. *International Journal of Service Science, Management, Engineering, and Technology*, *9*(2), 104–119. doi:10.4018/IJSSMET.2018040105

Klein, A. Z., Sabino de Freitas, A., Machado, L., Freitas, J. C. Jr, Graziola, P. G. Jr, & Schlemmer, E. (2017). Virtual Worlds Applications for Management Education. In L. Tomei (Ed.), *Exploring the New Era of Technology-Infused Education* (pp. 279–299). Hershey, PA: IGI Global. doi:10.4018/978-1-5225-1709-2.ch017

Kővári, E., Saleh, M., & Steinbachné Hajmásy, G. (2022). The Impact of Corporate Digital Responsibility (CDR) on Internal Stakeholders' Satisfaction in Hungarian Upscale Hotels. In M. Valeri (Ed.), *New Governance and Management in Touristic Destinations* (pp. 35–51). IGI Global. https://doi.org/10.4018/978-1-6684-3889-3.ch003

Kożuch, B., & Jabłoński, A. (2017). Adopting the Concept of Business Models in Public Management. In M. Lewandowski & B. Kożuch (Eds.), *Public Sector Entrepreneurship and the Integration of Innovative Business Models* (pp. 10–46). Hershey, PA: IGI Global. doi:10.4018/978-1-5225-2215-7.ch002

Kumar, J., Adhikary, A., & Jha, A. (2017). Small Active Investors' Perceptions and Preferences Towards Tax Saving Mutual Fund Schemes in Eastern India: An Empirical Note. *International Journal of Asian Business and Information Management*, *8*(2), 35–45. doi:10.4018/IJABIM.2017040103

Latusi, S., & Fissore, M. (2021). Pilgrimage Routes to Happiness: Comparing the Camino de Santiago and Via Francigena. In A. Perinotto, V. Mayer, & J. Soares (Eds.), *Rebuilding and Restructuring the Tourism Industry: Infusion of Happiness and Quality of Life* (pp. 157–182). IGI Global. https://doi.org/10.4018/978-1-7998-7239-9.ch008

Lavassani, K. M., & Movahedi, B. (2017). Applications Driven Information Systems: Beyond Networks toward Business Ecosystems. *International Journal of Innovation in the Digital Economy*, *8*(1), 61–75. doi:10.4018/IJIDE.2017010104

Lazzareschi, V. H., & Brito, M. S. (2017). Strategic Information Management: Proposal of Business Project Model. In G. Jamil, A. Soares, & C. Pessoa (Eds.), *Handbook of Research on Information Management for Effective Logistics and Supply Chains* (pp. 59–88). Hershey, PA: IGI Global. doi:10.4018/978-1-5225-0973-8.ch004

Lechuga Sancho, M. P., & Martín Navarro, A. (2022). Evolution of the Literature on Social Responsibility in the Tourism Sector: A Systematic Literature Review. In G. Fernandes (Ed.), *Challenges and New Opportunities for Tourism in Inland Territories: Ecocultural Resources and Sustainable Initiatives* (pp. 169–186). IGI Global. https://doi.org/10.4018/978-1-7998-7339-6.ch010

Lederer, M., Kurz, M., & Lazarov, P. (2017). Usage and Suitability of Methods for Strategic Business Process Initiatives: A Multi Case Study Research. *International Journal of Productivity Management and Assessment Technologies*, *5*(1), 40–51. doi:10.4018/IJPMAT.2017010103

Lee, I. (2017). A Social Enterprise Business Model and a Case Study of Pacific Community Ventures (PCV). In V. Potocan, M. Üngan, & Z. Nedelko (Eds.), *Handbook of Research on Managerial Solutions in Non-Profit Organizations* (pp. 182–204). Hershey, PA: IGI Global. doi:10.4018/978-1-5225-0731-4.ch009

Leon, L. A., Seal, K. C., Przasnyski, Z. H., & Wiedenman, I. (2017). Skills and Competencies Required for Jobs in Business Analytics: A Content Analysis of Job Advertisements Using Text Mining. *International Journal of Business Intelligence Research*, *8*(1), 1–25. doi:10.4018/IJBIR.2017010101

Levy, C. L., & Elias, N. I. (2017). SOHO Users' Perceptions of Reliability and Continuity of Cloud-Based Services. In M. Moore (Ed.), *Cybersecurity Breaches and Issues Surrounding Online Threat Protection* (pp. 248–287). Hershey, PA: IGI Global. doi:10.4018/978-1-5225-1941-6.ch011

Levy, M. (2018). Change Management Serving Knowledge Management and Organizational Development: Reflections and Review. In N. Baporikar (Ed.), *Global Practices in Knowledge Management for Societal and Organizational Development* (pp. 256–270). Hershey, PA: IGI Global. doi:10.4018/978-1-5225-3009-1.ch012

Lewandowski, M. (2017). Public Organizations and Business Model Innovation: The Role of Public Service Design. In M. Lewandowski & B. Kożuch (Eds.), *Public Sector Entrepreneurship and the Integration of Innovative Business Models* (pp. 47–72). Hershey, PA: IGI Global. doi:10.4018/978-1-5225-2215-7.ch003

Lhannaoui, H., Kabbaj, M. I., & Bakkoury, Z. (2017). A Survey of Risk-Aware Business Process Modelling. *International Journal of Risk and Contingency Management*, *6*(3), 14–26. doi:10.4018/IJRCM.2017070102

Li, J., Sun, W., Jiang, W., Yang, H., & Zhang, L. (2017). How the Nature of Exogenous Shocks and Crises Impact Company Performance?: The Effects of Industry Characteristics. *International Journal of Risk and Contingency Management*, *6*(4), 40–55. doi:10.4018/IJRCM.2017100103

Lopez-Fernandez, M., Perez-Perez, M., Serrano-Bedia, A., & Cobo-Gonzalez, A. (2021). Small and Medium Tourism Enterprise Survival in Times of Crisis: "El Capricho de Gaudí. In D. Toubes & N. Araújo-Vila (Eds.), *Risk, Crisis, and Disaster Management in Small and Medium-Sized Tourism Enterprises* (pp. 103–129). IGI Global. doi:10.4018/978-1-7998-6996-2.ch005

Mahajan, A., Maidullah, S., & Hossain, M. R. (2022). Experience Toward Smart Tour Guide Apps in Travelling: An Analysis of Users' Reviews on Audio Odigos and Trip My Way. In R. Augusto Costa, F. Brandão, Z. Breda, & C. Costa (Eds.), *Planning and Managing the Experience Economy in Tourism* (pp. 255-273). IGI Global. https://doi.org/10.4018/978-1-7998-8775-1.ch014

Malega, P. (2017). Small and Medium Enterprises in the Slovak Republic: Status and Competitiveness of SMEs in the Global Markets and Possibilities of Optimization. In M. Vemić (Ed.), *Optimal Management Strategies in Small and Medium Enterprises* (pp. 102–124). Hershey, PA: IGI Global. doi:10.4018/978-1-5225-1949-2.ch006

Malewska, K. M. (2017). Intuition in Decision-Making on the Example of a Non-Profit Organization. In V. Potocan, M. Ünğan, & Z. Nedelko (Eds.), *Handbook of Research on Managerial Solutions in Non-Profit Organizations* (pp. 378–399). Hershey, PA: IGI Global. doi:10.4018/978-1-5225-0731-4.ch018

Maroofi, F. (2017). Entrepreneurial Orientation and Organizational Learning Ability Analysis for Innovation and Firm Performance. In N. Baporikar (Ed.), *Innovation and Shifting Perspectives in Management Education* (pp. 144–165). Hershey, PA: IGI Global. doi:10.4018/978-1-5225-1019-2.ch007

Marques, M., Moleiro, D., Brito, T. M., & Marques, T. (2021). Customer Relationship Management as an Important Relationship Marketing Tool: The Case of the Hospitality Industry in Estoril Coast. In M. Dinis, L. Bonixe, S. Lamy, & Z. Breda (Eds.), Impact of New Media in Tourism (pp. 39-56). IGI Global. https://doi.org/doi:10.4018/978-1-7998-7095-1.ch003

Martins, P. V., & Zacarias, M. (2017). A Web-based Tool for Business Process Improvement. *International Journal of Web Portals, 9*(2), 68–84. doi:10.4018/IJWP.2017070104

Matthies, B., & Coners, A. (2017). Exploring the Conceptual Nature of e-Business Projects. *Journal of Electronic Commerce in Organizations, 15*(3), 33–63. doi:10.4018/JECO.2017070103

Mayer, V. F., Fraga, C. C., & Silva, L. C. (2021). Contributions of Neurosciences to Studies of Well-Being in Tourism. In A. Perinotto, V. Mayer, & J. Soares (Eds.), *Rebuilding and Restructuring the Tourism Industry: Infusion of Happiness and Quality of Life* (pp. 108–128). IGI Global. https://doi.org/10.4018/978-1-7998-7239-9.ch006

McKee, J. (2018). Architecture as a Tool to Solve Business Planning Problems. In M. Khosrow-Pour, D.B.A. (Ed.), Encyclopedia of Information Science and Technology, Fourth Edition (pp. 573-586). Hershey, PA: IGI Global. doi:10.4018/978-1-5225-2255-3.ch050

McMurray, A. J., Cross, J., & Caponecchia, C. (2018). The Risk Management Profession in Australia: Business Continuity Plan Practices. In N. Bajgoric (Ed.), *Always-On Enterprise Information Systems for Modern Organizations* (pp. 112–129). Hershey, PA: IGI Global. doi:10.4018/978-1-5225-3704-5.ch006

Meddah, I. H., & Belkadi, K. (2018). Mining Patterns Using Business Process Management. In R. Hamou (Ed.), *Handbook of Research on Biomimicry in Information Retrieval and Knowledge Management* (pp. 78–89). Hershey, PA: IGI Global. doi:10.4018/978-1-5225-3004-6.ch005

Melian, A. G., & Camprubí, R. (2021). The Accessibility of Museum Websites: The Case of Barcelona. In C. Eusébio, L. Teixeira, & M. Carneiro (Eds.), *ICT Tools and Applications for Accessible Tourism* (pp. 234–255). IGI Global. https://doi.org/10.4018/978-1-7998-6428-8.ch011

Mendes, L. (2017). TQM and Knowledge Management: An Integrated Approach Towards Tacit Knowledge Management. In D. Jaziri-Bouagina & G. Jamil (Eds.), *Handbook of Research on Tacit Knowledge Management for Organizational Success* (pp. 236–263). Hershey, PA: IGI Global. doi:10.4018/978-1-5225-2394-9.ch009

Menezes, V. D., & Cavagnaro, E. (2021). Communicating Sustainable Initiatives in the Hotel Industry: The Case of the Hotel Jakarta Amsterdam. In F. Brandão, Z. Breda, R. Costa, & C. Costa (Eds.), *Handbook of Research on the Role of Tourism in Achieving Sustainable Development Goals* (pp. 224-234). IGI Global. https://doi.org/10.4018/978-1-7998-5691-7.ch013

Menezes, V. D., & Cavagnaro, E. (2021). Communicating Sustainable Initiatives in the Hotel Industry: The Case of the Hotel Jakarta Amsterdam. In F. Brandão, Z. Breda, R. Costa, & C. Costa (Eds.), *Handbook of Research on the Role of Tourism in Achieving Sustainable Development Goals* (pp. 224-234). IGI Global. https://doi.org/10.4018/978-1-7998-5691-7.ch013

Mitas, O., Bastiaansen, M., & Boode, W. (2022). If You're Happy, I'm Happy: Emotion Contagion at a Tourist Information Center. In R. Augusto Costa, F. Brandão, Z. Breda, & C. Costa (Eds.), *Planning and Managing the Experience Economy in Tourism* (pp. 122-140). IGI Global. https://doi.org/10.4018/978-1-7998-8775-1.ch007

Mnjama, N. M. (2017). Preservation of Recorded Information in Public and Private Sector Organizations. In P. Jain & N. Mnjama (Eds.), *Managing Knowledge Resources and Records in Modern Organizations* (pp. 149–167). Hershey, PA: IGI Global. doi:10.4018/978-1-5225-1965-2.ch009

Mokoqama, M., & Fields, Z. (2017). Principles of Responsible Management Education (PRME): Call for Responsible Management Education. In Z. Fields (Ed.), *Collective Creativity for Responsible and Sustainable Business Practice* (pp. 229–241). Hershey, PA: IGI Global. doi:10.4018/978-1-5225-1823-5.ch012

Monteiro, A., Lopes, S., & Carbone, F. (2021). Academic Mobility: Bridging Tourism and Peace Education. In J. da Silva, Z. Breda, & F. Carbone (Eds.), *Role and Impact of Tourism in Peacebuilding and Conflict Transformation* (pp. 275-301). IGI Global. https://doi.org/10.4018/978-1-7998-5053-3.ch016

Muniapan, B. (2017). Philosophy and Management: The Relevance of Vedanta in Management. In P. Ordóñez de Pablos (Ed.), *Managerial Strategies and Solutions for Business Success in Asia* (pp. 124–139). Hershey, PA: IGI Global. doi:10.4018/978-1-5225-1886-0.ch007

Murad, S. E., & Dowaji, S. (2017). Using Value-Based Approach for Managing Cloud-Based Services. In A. Turuk, B. Sahoo, & S. Addya (Eds.), *Resource Management and Efficiency in Cloud Computing Environments* (pp. 33–60). Hershey, PA: IGI Global. doi:10.4018/978-1-5225-1721-4.ch002

Mutahar, A. M., Daud, N. M., Thurasamy, R., Isaac, O., & Abdulsalam, R. (2018). The Mediating of Perceived Usefulness and Perceived Ease of Use: The Case of Mobile Banking in Yemen. *International Journal of Technology Diffusion*, *9*(2), 21–40. doi:10.4018/IJTD.2018040102

Naidoo, V. (2017). E-Learning and Management Education at African Universities. In N. Baporikar (Ed.), *Management Education for Global Leadership* (pp. 181–201). Hershey, PA: IGI Global. doi:10.4018/978-1-5225-1013-0.ch009

Naidoo, V., & Igbinakhase, I. (2018). Opportunities and Challenges of Knowledge Retention in SMEs. In N. Baporikar (Ed.), *Knowledge Integration Strategies for Entrepreneurship and Sustainability* (pp. 70–94). Hershey, PA: IGI Global. doi:10.4018/978-1-5225-5115-7.ch004

Naumov, N., & Costandachi, G. (2021). Creativity and Entrepreneurship: Gastronomic Tourism in Mexico. In J. Soares (Ed.), *Innovation and Entrepreneurial Opportunities in Community Tourism* (pp. 90–108). IGI Global. https://doi.org/10.4018/978-1-7998-4855-4.ch006

Nayak, S., & Prabhu, N. (2017). Paradigm Shift in Management Education: Need for a Cross Functional Perspective. In N. Baporikar (Ed.), *Management Education for Global Leadership* (pp. 241–255). Hershey, PA: IGI Global. doi:10.4018/978-1-5225-1013-0.ch012

Nedelko, Z., & Potocan, V. (2017). Management Solutions in Non-Profit Organizations: Case of Slovenia. In V. Potocan, M. Üngan, & Z. Nedelko (Eds.), *Handbook of Research on Managerial Solutions in Non-Profit Organizations* (pp. 1–22). Hershey, PA: IGI Global. doi:10.4018/978-1-5225-0731-4.ch001

Nedelko, Z., & Potocan, V. (2017). Priority of Management Tools Utilization among Managers: International Comparison. In V. Wang (Ed.), *Encyclopedia of Strategic Leadership and Management* (pp. 1083–1094). Hershey, PA: IGI Global. doi:10.4018/978-1-5225-1049-9.ch075

Nedelko, Z., Raudeliūnienė, J., & Črešnar, R. (2018). Knowledge Dynamics in Supply Chain Management. In N. Baporikar (Ed.), *Knowledge Integration Strategies for Entrepreneurship and Sustainability* (pp. 150–166). Hershey, PA: IGI Global. doi:10.4018/978-1-5225-5115-7.ch008

Nguyen, H. T., & Hipsher, S. A. (2018). Innovation and Creativity Used by Private Sector Firms in a Resources-Constrained Environment. In S. Hipsher (Ed.), *Examining the Private Sector's Role in Wealth Creation and Poverty Reduction* (pp. 219–238). Hershey, PA: IGI Global. doi:10.4018/978-1-5225-3117-3.ch010

Obicci, P. A. (2017). Risk Sharing in a Partnership. In *Risk Management Strategies in Public-Private Partnerships* (pp. 115–152). Hershey, PA: IGI Global. doi:10.4018/978-1-5225-2503-5.ch004

Obidallah, W. J., & Raahemi, B. (2017). Managing Changes in Service Oriented Virtual Organizations: A Structural and Procedural Framework to Facilitate the Process of Change. *Journal of Electronic Commerce in Organizations*, *15*(1), 59–83. doi:10.4018/JECO.2017010104

Ojo, O. (2017). Impact of Innovation on the Entrepreneurial Success in Selected Business Enterprises in South-West Nigeria. *International Journal of Innovation in the Digital Economy*, *8*(2), 29–38. doi:10.4018/IJIDE.2017040103

Okdinawati, L., Simatupang, T. M., & Sunitiyoso, Y. (2017). Multi-Agent Reinforcement Learning for Value Co-Creation of Collaborative Transportation Management (CTM). *International Journal of Information Systems and Supply Chain Management*, *10*(3), 84–95. doi:10.4018/IJISSCM.2017070105

Olivera, V. A., & Carrillo, I. M. (2021). Organizational Culture: A Key Element for the Development of Mexican Micro and Small Tourist Companies. In J. Soares (Ed.), *Innovation and Entrepreneurial Opportunities in Community Tourism* (pp. 227–242). IGI Global. doi:10.4018/978-1-7998-4855-4.ch013

Ossorio, M. (2022). Corporate Museum Experiences in Enogastronomic Tourism. In R. Augusto Costa, F. Brandão, Z. Breda, & C. Costa (Eds.), Planning and Managing the Experience Economy in Tourism (pp. 107-121). IGI Global. https://doi.org/doi:10.4018/978-1-7998-8775-1.ch006

Ossorio, M. (2022). Enogastronomic Tourism in Times of Pandemic. In G. Fernandes (Ed.), *Challenges and New Opportunities for Tourism in Inland Territories: Ecocultural Resources and Sustainable Initiatives* (pp. 241–255). IGI Global. https://doi.org/10.4018/978-1-7998-7339-6.ch014

Özekici, Y. K. (2022). ICT as an Acculturative Agent and Its Role in the Tourism Context: Introduction, Acculturation Theory, Progress of the Acculturation Theory in Extant Literature. In C. Ramos, S. Quinteiro, & A. Gonçalves (Eds.), *ICT as Innovator Between Tourism and Culture* (pp. 42–66). IGI Global. https://doi.org/10.4018/978-1-7998-8165-0.ch004

Pal, K. (2018). Building High Quality Big Data-Based Applications in Supply Chains. In A. Kumar & S. Saurav (Eds.), *Supply Chain Management Strategies and Risk Assessment in Retail Environments* (pp. 1–24). Hershey, PA: IGI Global. doi:10.4018/978-1-5225-3056-5.ch001

Palos-Sanchez, P. R., & Correia, M. B. (2018). Perspectives of the Adoption of Cloud Computing in the Tourism Sector. In J. Rodrigues, C. Ramos, P. Cardoso, & C. Henriques (Eds.), *Handbook of Research on Technological Developments for Cultural Heritage and eTourism Applications* (pp. 377–400). Hershey, PA: IGI Global. doi:10.4018/978-1-5225-2927-9.ch018

Papadopoulou, G. (2021). Promoting Gender Equality and Women Empowerment in the Tourism Sector. In F. Brandão, Z. Breda, R. Costa, & C. Costa (Eds.), Handbook of Research on the Role of Tourism in Achieving Sustainable Development Goals (pp. 152-174). IGI Global. https://doi.org/ doi:10.4018/978-1-7998-5691-7.ch009

Papp-Váry, Á. F., & Tóth, T. Z. (2022). Analysis of Budapest as a Film Tourism Destination. In R. Baleiro & R. Pereira (Eds.), *Global Perspectives on Literary Tourism and Film-Induced Tourism* (pp. 257-279). IGI Global. https://doi.org/10.4018/978-1-7998-8262-6.ch014

Patiño, B. E. (2017). New Generation Management by Convergence and Individual Identity: A Systemic and Human-Oriented Approach. In N. Baporikar (Ed.), *Innovation and Shifting Perspectives in Management Education* (pp. 119–143). Hershey, PA: IGI Global. doi:10.4018/978-1-5225-1019-2.ch006

Patro, C. S. (2021). Digital Tourism: Influence of E-Marketing Technology. In M. Dinis, L. Bonixe, S. Lamy, & Z. Breda (Eds.), *Impact of New Media in Tourism* (pp. 234-254). IGI Global. https://doi.org/10.4018/978-1-7998-7095-1.ch014

Pawliczek, A., & Rössler, M. (2017). Knowledge of Management Tools and Systems in SMEs: Knowledge Transfer in Management. In A. Bencsik (Ed.), *Knowledge Management Initiatives and Strategies in Small and Medium Enterprises* (pp. 180–203). Hershey, PA: IGI Global. doi:10.4018/978-1-5225-1642-2.ch009

Pejic-Bach, M., Omazic, M. A., Aleksic, A., & Zoroja, J. (2018). Knowledge-Based Decision Making: A Multi-Case Analysis. In R. Leon (Ed.), *Managerial Strategies for Business Sustainability During Turbulent Times* (pp. 160–184). Hershey, PA: IGI Global. doi:10.4018/978-1-5225-2716-9.ch009

Perano, M., Hysa, X., & Calabrese, M. (2018). Strategic Planning, Cultural Context, and Business Continuity Management: Business Cases in the City of Shkoder. In A. Presenza & L. Sheehan (Eds.), *Geopolitics and Strategic Management in the Global Economy* (pp. 57–77). Hershey, PA: IGI Global. doi:10.4018/978-1-5225-2673-5.ch004

Pereira, R., Mira da Silva, M., & Lapão, L. V. (2017). IT Governance Maturity Patterns in Portuguese Healthcare. In S. De Haes & W. Van Grembergen (Eds.), *Strategic IT Governance and Alignment in Business Settings* (pp. 24–52). Hershey, PA: IGI Global. doi:10.4018/978-1-5225-0861-8.ch002

Pérez-Uribe, R. I., Torres, D. A., Jurado, S. P., & Prada, D. M. (2018). Cloud Tools for the Development of Project Management in SMEs. In R. Perez-Uribe, C. Salcedo-Perez, & D. Ocampo-Guzman (Eds.), *Handbook of Research on Intrapreneurship and Organizational Sustainability in SMEs* (pp. 95–120). Hershey, PA: IGI Global. doi:10.4018/978-1-5225-3543-0.ch005

Petrisor, I., & Cozmiuc, D. (2017). Global Supply Chain Management Organization at Siemens in the Advent of Industry 4.0. In L. Saglietto & C. Cezanne (Eds.), *Global Intermediation and Logistics Service Providers* (pp. 123–142). Hershey, PA: IGI Global. doi:10.4018/978-1-5225-2133-4.ch007

Pierce, J. M., Velliaris, D. M., & Edwards, J. (2017). A Living Case Study: A Journey Not a Destination. In N. Silton (Ed.), *Exploring the Benefits of Creativity in Education, Media, and the Arts* (pp. 158–178). Hershey, PA: IGI Global. doi:10.4018/978-1-5225-0504-4.ch008

Pipia, S., & Pipia, S. (2021). Challenges of Religious Tourism in the Conflict Region: An Example of Jerusalem. In E. Alaverdov & M. Bari (Eds.), *Global Development of Religious Tourism* (pp. 135-148). IGI Global. https://doi.org/10.4018/978-1-7998-5792-1.ch009

Poulaki, P., Kritikos, A., Vasilakis, N., & Valeri, M. (2022). The Contribution of Female Creativity to the Development of Gastronomic Tourism in Greece: The Case of the Island of Naxos in the South Aegean Region. In M. Valeri (Ed.), *New Governance and Management in Touristic Destinations* (pp. 246–258). IGI Global. https://doi.org/10.4018/978-1-6684-3889-3.ch015

Radosavljevic, M., & Andjelkovic, A. (2017). Multi-Criteria Decision Making Approach for Choosing Business Process for the Improvement: Upgrading of the Six Sigma Methodology. In J. Stanković, P. Delias, S. Marinković, & S. Rochhia (Eds.), *Tools and Techniques for Economic Decision Analysis* (pp. 225–247). Hershey, PA: IGI Global. doi:10.4018/978-1-5225-0959-2.ch011

Radovic, V. M. (2017). Corporate Sustainability and Responsibility and Disaster Risk Reduction: A Serbian Overview. In M. Camilleri (Ed.), *CSR 2.0 and the New Era of Corporate Citizenship* (pp. 147–164). Hershey, PA: IGI Global. doi:10.4018/978-1-5225-1842-6.ch008

Raghunath, K. M., Devi, S. L., & Patro, C. S. (2018). Impact of Risk Assessment Models on Risk Factors: A Holistic Outlook. In K. Strang, M. Korstanje, & N. Vajjhala (Eds.), *Research, Practices, and Innovations in Global Risk and Contingency Management* (pp. 134–153). Hershey, PA: IGI Global. doi:10.4018/978-1-5225-4754-9.ch008

Raman, A., & Goyal, D. P. (2017). Extending IMPLEMENT Framework for Enterprise Information Systems Implementation to Information System Innovation. In M. Tavana (Ed.), *Enterprise Information Systems and the Digitalization of Business Functions* (pp. 137–177). Hershey, PA: IGI Global. doi:10.4018/978-1-5225-2382-6.ch007

Rao, Y., & Zhang, Y. (2017). The Construction and Development of Academic Library Digital Special Subject Databases. In L. Ruan, Q. Zhu, & Y. Ye (Eds.), *Academic Library Development and Administration in China* (pp. 163–183). Hershey, PA: IGI Global. doi:10.4018/978-1-5225-0550-1.ch010

Ravasan, A. Z., Mohammadi, M. M., & Hamidi, H. (2018). An Investigation Into the Critical Success Factors of Implementing Information Technology Service Management Frameworks. In K. Jakobs (Ed.), *Corporate and Global Standardization Initiatives in Contemporary Society* (pp. 200–218). Hershey, PA: IGI Global. doi:10.4018/978-1-5225-5320-5.ch009

Rezaie, S., Mirabedini, S. J., & Abtahi, A. (2018). Designing a Model for Implementation of Business Intelligence in the Banking Industry. *International Journal of Enterprise Information Systems*, *14*(1), 77–103. doi:10.4018/IJEIS.2018010105

Richards, V., Matthews, N., Williams, O. J., & Khan, Z. (2021). The Challenges of Accessible Tourism Information Systems for Tourists With Vision Impairment: Sensory Communications Beyond the Screen. In C. Eusébio, L. Teixeira, & M. Carneiro (Eds.), *ICT Tools and Applications for Accessible Tourism* (pp. 26–54). IGI Global. https://doi.org/10.4018/978-1-7998-6428-8.ch002

Rodrigues de Souza Neto, V., & Marques, O. (2021). Rural Tourism Fostering Welfare Through Sustainable Development: A Conceptual Approach. In A. Perinotto, V. Mayer, & J. Soares (Eds.), *Rebuilding and Restructuring the Tourism Industry: Infusion of Happiness and Quality of Life* (pp. 38–57). IGI Global. https://doi.org/10.4018/978-1-7998-7239-9.ch003

Romano, L., Grimaldi, R., & Colasuonno, F. S. (2017). Demand Management as a Success Factor in Project Portfolio Management. In L. Romano (Ed.), *Project Portfolio Management Strategies for Effective Organizational Operations* (pp. 202–219). Hershey, PA: IGI Global. doi:10.4018/978-1-5225-2151-8.ch008

Rubio-Escuderos, L., & García-Andreu, H. (2021). Competitiveness Factors of Accessible Tourism E-Travel Agencies. In C. Eusébio, L. Teixeira, & M. Carneiro (Eds.), *ICT Tools and Applications for Accessible Tourism* (pp. 196–217). IGI Global. https://doi.org/10.4018/978-1-7998-6428-8.ch009

Rucci, A. C., Porto, N., Darcy, S., & Becka, L. (2021). Smart and Accessible Cities?: Not Always – The Case for Accessible Tourism Initiatives in Buenos Aries and Sydney. In C. Eusébio, L. Teixeira, & M. Carneiro (Eds.), *ICT Tools and Applications for Accessible Tourism* (pp. 115–145). IGI Global. https://doi.org/10.4018/978-1-7998-6428-8.ch006

Ruhi, U. (2018). Towards an Interdisciplinary Socio-Technical Definition of Virtual Communities. In M. Khosrow-Pour, D.B.A. (Ed.), Encyclopedia of Information Science and Technology, Fourth Edition (pp. 4278-4295). Hershey, PA: IGI Global. doi:10.4018/978-1-5225-2255-3.ch371

Ryan, L., Catena, M., Ros, P., & Stephens, S. (2021). Designing Entrepreneurial Ecosystems to Support Resource Management in the Tourism Industry. In V. Costa, A. Moura, & M. Mira (Eds.), *Handbook of Research on Human Capital and People Management in the Tourism Industry* (pp. 265–281). IGI Global. https://doi.org/10.4018/978-1-7998-4318-4.ch013

Sabuncu, I. (2021). Understanding Tourist Perceptions and Expectations During Pandemic Through Social Media Big Data. In M. Demir, A. Dalgıç, & F. Ergen (Eds.), *Handbook of Research on the Impacts and Implications of COVID-19 on the Tourism Industry* (pp. 330–350). IGI Global. https://doi.org/10.4018/978-1-7998-8231-2.ch016

Safari, M. R., & Jiang, Q. (2018). The Theory and Practice of IT Governance Maturity and Strategies Alignment: Evidence From Banking Industry. *Journal of Global Information Management, 26*(2), 127–146. doi:10.4018/JGIM.2018040106

Sahoo, J., Pati, B., & Mohanty, B. (2017). Knowledge Management as an Academic Discipline: An Assessment. In B. Gunjal (Ed.), *Managing Knowledge and Scholarly Assets in Academic Libraries* (pp. 99–126). Hershey, PA: IGI Global. doi:10.4018/978-1-5225-1741-2.ch005

Saini, D. (2017). Relevance of Teaching Values and Ethics in Management Education. In N. Baporikar (Ed.), *Management Education for Global Leadership* (pp. 90–111). Hershey, PA: IGI Global. doi:10.4018/978-1-5225-1013-0.ch005

Sambhanthan, A. (2017). Assessing and Benchmarking Sustainability in Organisations: An Integrated Conceptual Model. *International Journal of Systems and Service-Oriented Engineering*, *7*(4), 22–43. doi:10.4018/IJSSOE.2017100102

Sambhanthan, A., & Potdar, V. (2017). A Study of the Parameters Impacting Sustainability in Information Technology Organizations. *International Journal of Knowledge-Based Organizations*, *7*(3), 27–39. doi:10.4018/IJKBO.2017070103

Sánchez-Fernández, M. D., & Manríquez, M. R. (2018). The Entrepreneurial Spirit Based on Social Values: The Digital Generation. In P. Isaias & L. Carvalho (Eds.), *User Innovation and the Entrepreneurship Phenomenon in the Digital Economy* (pp. 173–193). Hershey, PA: IGI Global. doi:10.4018/978-1-5225-2826-5.ch009

Sanchez-Ruiz, L., & Blanco, B. (2017). Process Management for SMEs: Barriers, Enablers, and Benefits. In M. Vemić (Ed.), *Optimal Management Strategies in Small and Medium Enterprises* (pp. 293–319). Hershey, PA: IGI Global. doi:10.4018/978-1-5225-1949-2.ch014

Sanz, L. F., Gómez-Pérez, J., & Castillo-Martinez, A. (2018). Analysis of the European ICT Competence Frameworks. In V. Ahuja & S. Rathore (Eds.), *Multidisciplinary Perspectives on Human Capital and Information Technology Professionals* (pp. 225–245). Hershey, PA: IGI Global. doi:10.4018/978-1-5225-5297-0.ch012

Sarvepalli, A., & Godin, J. (2017). Business Process Management in the Classroom. *Journal of Cases on Information Technology*, *19*(2), 17–28. doi:10.4018/JCIT.2017040102

Saxena, G. G., & Saxena, A. (2021). Host Community Role in Medical Tourism Development. In M. Singh & S. Kumaran (Eds.), *Growth of the Medical Tourism Industry and Its Impact on Society: Emerging Research and Opportunities* (pp. 105–127). IGI Global. https://doi.org/10.4018/978-1-7998-3427-4.ch006

Saygili, E. E., Ozturkoglu, Y., & Kocakulah, M. C. (2017). End Users' Perceptions of Critical Success Factors in ERP Applications. *International Journal of Enterprise Information Systems*, *13*(4), 58–75. doi:10.4018/IJEIS.2017100104

Saygili, E. E., & Saygili, A. T. (2017). Contemporary Issues in Enterprise Information Systems: A Critical Review of CSFs in ERP Implementations. In M. Tavana (Ed.), *Enterprise Information Systems and the Digitalization of Business Functions* (pp. 120–136). Hershey, PA: IGI Global. doi:10.4018/978-1-5225-2382-6.ch006

Schwaiger, K. M., & Zehrer, A. (2021). The COVID-19 Pandemic and Organizational Resiliencc in Hospitality Family Firms: A Qualitative Approach. In A. Zehrer, G. Glowka, K. Schwaiger, & V. Ranacher-Lackner (Eds.), *Resiliency Models and Addressing Future Risks for Family Firms in the Tourism Industry* (pp. 32–49). IGI Global. https://doi.org/10.4018/978-1-7998-7352-5.ch002

Scott, N., & Campos, A. C. (2022). Cognitive Science of Tourism Experiences. In R. Augusto Costa, F. Brandão, Z. Breda, & C. Costa (Eds.), Planning and Managing the Experience Economy in Tourism (pp. 1-21). IGI Global. https://doi.org/ doi:10.4018/978-1-7998-8775-1.ch001

Seidenstricker, S., & Antonino, A. (2018). Business Model Innovation-Oriented Technology Management for Emergent Technologies. In M. Khosrow-Pour, D.B.A. (Ed.), Encyclopedia of Information Science and Technology, Fourth Edition (pp. 4560-4569). Hershey, PA: IGI Global. doi:10.4018/978-1-5225-2255-3.ch396

Selvi, M. S. (2021). Changes in Tourism Sales and Marketing Post COVID-19. In M. Demir, A. Dalgıç, & F. Ergen (Eds.), *Handbook of Research on the Impacts and Implications of COVID-19 on the Tourism Industry* (pp. 437–460). IGI Global. doi:10.4018/978-1-7998-8231-2.ch021

Senaratne, S., & Gunarathne, A. D. (2017). Excellence Perspective for Management Education from a Global Accountants' Hub in Asia. In N. Baporikar (Ed.), *Management Education for Global Leadership* (pp. 158–180). Hershey, PA: IGI Global. doi:10.4018/978-1-5225-1013-0.ch008

Sensuse, D. I., & Cahyaningsih, E. (2018). Knowledge Management Models: A Summative Review. *International Journal of Information Systems in the Service Sector, 10*(1), 71–100. doi:10.4018/IJISSS.2018010105

Seth, M., Goyal, D., & Kiran, R. (2017). Diminution of Impediments in Implementation of Supply Chain Management Information System for Enhancing its Effectiveness in Indian Automobile Industry. *Journal of Global Information Management, 25*(3), 1–20. doi:10.4018/JGIM.2017070101

Seyal, A. H., & Rahman, M. N. (2017). Investigating Impact of Inter-Organizational Factors in Measuring ERP Systems Success: Bruneian Perspectives. In M. Tavana (Ed.), *Enterprise Information Systems and the Digitalization of Business Functions* (pp. 178–204). Hershey, PA: IGI Global. doi:10.4018/978-1-5225-2382-6.ch008

Shaqrah, A. A. (2018). Analyzing Business Intelligence Systems Based on 7s Model of McKinsey. *International Journal of Business Intelligence Research, 9*(1), 53–63. doi:10.4018/IJBIR.2018010104

Sharma, A. J. (2017). Enhancing Sustainability through Experiential Learning in Management Education. In N. Baporikar (Ed.), *Management Education for Global Leadership* (pp. 256–274). Hershey, PA: IGI Global. doi:10.4018/978-1-5225-1013-0.ch013

Shetty, K. P. (2017). Responsible Global Leadership: Ethical Challenges in Management Education. In N. Baporikar (Ed.), *Innovation and Shifting Perspectives in Management Education* (pp. 194–223). Hershey, PA: IGI Global. doi:10.4018/978-1-5225-1019-2.ch009

Sinthupundaja, J., & Kohda, Y. (2017). Effects of Corporate Social Responsibility and Creating Shared Value on Sustainability. *International Journal of Sustainable Entrepreneurship and Corporate Social Responsibility*, *2*(1), 27–38. doi:10.4018/IJSECSR.2017010103

Škarica, I., & Hrgović, A. V. (2018). Implementation of Total Quality Management Principles in Public Health Institutes in the Republic of Croatia. *International Journal of Productivity Management and Assessment Technologies*, *6*(1), 1–16. doi:10.4018/IJPMAT.2018010101

Skokic, V. (2021). How Small Hotel Owners Practice Resilience: Longitudinal Study Among Small Family Hotels in Croatia. In A. Zehrer, G. Glowka, K. Schwaiger, & V. Ranacher-Lackner (Eds.), *Resiliency Models and Addressing Future Risks for Family Firms in the Tourism Industry* (pp. 50–73). IGI Global. doi:10.4018/978-1-7998-7352-5.ch003

Smuts, H., Kotzé, P., Van der Merwe, A., & Loock, M. (2017). Framework for Managing Shared Knowledge in an Information Systems Outsourcing Context. *International Journal of Knowledge Management*, *13*(4), 1–30. doi:10.4018/IJKM.2017100101

Sousa, M. J., Cruz, R., Dias, I., & Caracol, C. (2017). Information Management Systems in the Supply Chain. In G. Jamil, A. Soares, & C. Pessoa (Eds.), *Handbook of Research on Information Management for Effective Logistics and Supply Chains* (pp. 469–485). Hershey, PA: IGI Global. doi:10.4018/978-1-5225-0973-8.ch025

Spremic, M., Turulja, L., & Bajgoric, N. (2018). Two Approaches in Assessing Business Continuity Management Attitudes in the Organizational Context. In N. Bajgoric (Ed.), *Always-On Enterprise Information Systems for Modern Organizations* (pp. 159–183). Hershey, PA: IGI Global. doi:10.4018/978-1-5225-3704-5.ch008

Steenkamp, A. L. (2018). Some Insights in Computer Science and Information Technology. In *Examining the Changing Role of Supervision in Doctoral Research Projects: Emerging Research and Opportunities* (pp. 113–133). Hershey, PA: IGI Global. doi:10.4018/978-1-5225-2610-0.ch005

Stipanović, C., Rudan, E., & Zubović, V. (2022). Reaching the New Tourist Through Creativity: Sustainable Development Challenges in Croatian Coastal Towns. In M. Valeri (Ed.), *New Governance and Management in Touristic Destinations* (pp. 231–245). IGI Global. https://doi.org/10.4018/978-1-6684-3889-3.ch014

Tabach, A., & Croteau, A. (2017). Configurations of Information Technology Governance Practices and Business Unit Performance. *International Journal of IT/Business Alignment and Governance*, *8*(2), 1–27. doi:10.4018/IJITBAG.2017070101

Talaue, G. M., & Iqbal, T. (2017). Assessment of e-Business Mode of Selected Private Universities in the Philippines and Pakistan. *International Journal of Online Marketing*, *7*(4), 63–77. doi:10.4018/IJOM.2017100105

Tam, G. C. (2017). Project Manager Sustainability Competence. In *Managerial Strategies and Green Solutions for Project Sustainability* (pp. 178–207). Hershey, PA: IGI Global. doi:10.4018/978-1-5225-2371-0.ch008

Tambo, T. (2018). Fashion Retail Innovation: About Context, Antecedents, and Outcome in Technological Change Projects. In I. Management Association (Ed.), Fashion and Textiles: Breakthroughs in Research and Practice (pp. 233-260). Hershey, PA: IGI Global. https://doi.org/ doi:10.4018/978-1-5225-3432-7.ch010

Tantau, A. D., & Frăţilă, L. C. (2018). Information and Management System for Renewable Energy Business. In *Entrepreneurship and Business Development in the Renewable Energy Sector* (pp. 200–244). Hershey, PA: IGI Global. doi:10.4018/978-1-5225-3625-3.ch006

Teixeira, N., Pardal, P. N., & Rafael, B. G. (2018). Internationalization, Financial Performance, and Organizational Challenges: A Success Case in Portugal. In L. Carvalho (Ed.), *Handbook of Research on Entrepreneurial Ecosystems and Social Dynamics in a Globalized World* (pp. 379–423). Hershey, PA: IGI Global. doi:10.4018/978-1-5225-3525-6.ch017

Teixeira, P., Teixeira, L., Eusébio, C., Silva, S., & Teixeira, A. (2021). The Impact of ICTs on Accessible Tourism: Evidence Based on a Systematic Literature Review. In C. Eusébio, L. Teixeira, & M. Carneiro (Eds.), *ICT Tools and Applications for Accessible Tourism* (pp. 1–25). IGI Global. doi:10.4018/978-1-7998-6428-8.ch001

Trad, A., & Kalpić, D. (2018). The Business Transformation Framework, Agile Project and Change Management. In M. Khosrow-Pour, D.B.A. (Ed.), Encyclopedia of Information Science and Technology, Fourth Edition (pp. 620-635). Hershey, PA: IGI Global. https://doi.org/ doi:10.4018/978-1-5225-2255-3.ch054

Trad, A., & Kalpić, D. (2018). The Business Transformation and Enterprise Architecture Framework: The Financial Engineering E-Risk Management and E-Law Integration. In B. Sergi, F. Fidanoski, M. Ziolo, & V. Naumovski (Eds.), *Regaining Global Stability After the Financial Crisis* (pp. 46–65). Hershey, PA: IGI Global. doi:10.4018/978-1-5225-4026-7.ch003

Trengereid, V. (2022). Conditions of Network Engagement: The Quest for a Common Good. In R. Augusto Costa, F. Brandão, Z. Breda, & C. Costa (Eds.), *Planning and Managing the Experience Economy in Tourism* (pp. 69-84). IGI Global. https://doi.org/10.4018/978-1-7998-8775-1.ch004

Turulja, L., & Bajgoric, N. (2018). Business Continuity and Information Systems: A Systematic Literature Review. In N. Bajgoric (Ed.), *Always-On Enterprise Information Systems for Modern Organizations* (pp. 60–87). Hershey, PA: IGI Global. doi:10.4018/978-1-5225-3704-5.ch004

Vargas-Hernández, J. G. (2017). Professional Integrity in Business Management Education. In N. Baporikar (Ed.), *Management Education for Global Leadership* (pp. 70–89). Hershey, PA: IGI Global. doi:10.4018/978-1-5225-1013-0.ch004

Varnacı Uzun, F. (2021). The Destination Preferences of Foreign Tourists During the COVID-19 Pandemic and Attitudes Towards: Marmaris, Turkey. In M. Demir, A. Dalgıç, & F. Ergen (Eds.), *Handbook of Research on the Impacts and Implications of COVID-19 on the Tourism Industry* (pp. 285–306). IGI Global. https://doi.org/10.4018/978-1-7998-8231-2.ch014

Vasista, T. G., & AlAbdullatif, A. M. (2017). Role of Electronic Customer Relationship Management in Demand Chain Management: A Predictive Analytic Approach. *International Journal of Information Systems and Supply Chain Management, 10*(1), 53–67. doi:10.4018/IJISSCM.2017010104

Vieru, D., & Bourdeau, S. (2017). Survival in the Digital Era: A Digital Competence-Based Multi-Case Study in the Canadian SME Clothing Industry. *International Journal of Social and Organizational Dynamics in IT, 6*(1), 17–34. doi:10.4018/IJSODIT.2017010102

Vijayan, G., & Kamarulzaman, N. H. (2017). An Introduction to Sustainable Supply Chain Management and Business Implications. In M. Khan, M. Hussain, & M. Ajmal (Eds.), *Green Supply Chain Management for Sustainable Business Practice* (pp. 27–50). Hershey, PA: IGI Global. doi:10.4018/978-1-5225-0635-5.ch002

Vlachvei, A., & Notta, O. (2017). Firm Competitiveness: Theories, Evidence, and Measurement. In A. Vlachvei, O. Notta, K. Karantininis, & N. Tsounis (Eds.), *Factors Affecting Firm Competitiveness and Performance in the Modern Business World* (pp. 1–42). Hershey, PA: IGI Global. doi:10.4018/978-1-5225-0843-4.ch001

Wang, C., Schofield, M., Li, X., & Ou, X. (2017). Do Chinese Students in Public and Private Higher Education Institutes Perform at Different Level in One of the Leadership Skills: Critical Thinking?: An Exploratory Comparison. In V. Wang (Ed.), *Encyclopedia of Strategic Leadership and Management* (pp. 160–181). Hershey, PA: IGI Global. doi:10.4018/978-1-5225-1049-9.ch013

Wang, J. (2017). Multi-Agent based Production Management Decision System Modelling for the Textile Enterprise. *Journal of Global Information Management, 25*(4), 1–15. doi:10.4018/JGIM.2017100101

Wiedemann, A., & Gewald, H. (2017). Examining Cross-Domain Alignment: The Correlation of Business Strategy, IT Management, and IT Business Value. *International Journal of IT/Business Alignment and Governance, 8*(1), 17–31. doi:10.4018/IJITBAG.2017010102

Wolf, R., & Thiel, M. (2018). Advancing Global Business Ethics in China: Reducing Poverty Through Human and Social Welfare. In S. Hipsher (Ed.), *Examining the Private Sector's Role in Wealth Creation and Poverty Reduction* (pp. 67–84). Hershey, PA: IGI Global. doi:10.4018/978-1-5225-3117-3.ch004

Yablonsky, S. (2018). Innovation Platforms: Data and Analytics Platforms. In *Multi-Sided Platforms (MSPs) and Sharing Strategies in the Digital Economy: Emerging Research and Opportunities* (pp. 72–95). Hershey, PA: IGI Global. doi:10.4018/978-1-5225-5457-8.ch003

Yaşar, B. (2021). The Impact of COVID-19 on Volatility of Tourism Stocks: Evidence From BIST Tourism Index. In M. Demir, A. Dalgıç, & F. Ergen (Eds.), *Handbook of Research on the Impacts and Implications of COVID-19 on the Tourism Industry* (pp. 23–44). IGI Global. https://doi.org/10.4018/978-1-7998-8231-2.ch002

Yusoff, A., Ahmad, N. H., & Halim, H. A. (2017). Agropreneurship among Gen Y in Malaysia: The Role of Academic Institutions. In N. Ahmad, T. Ramayah, H. Halim, & S. Rahman (Eds.), *Handbook of Research on Small and Medium Enterprises in Developing Countries* (pp. 23–47). Hershey, PA: IGI Global. doi:10.4018/978-1-5225-2165-5.ch002

Zacher, D., & Pechlaner, H. (2021). Resilience as an Opportunity Approach: Challenges and Perspectives for Private Sector Participation on a Community Level. In A. Zehrer, G. Glowka, K. Schwaiger, & V. Ranacher-Lackner (Eds.), *Resiliency Models and Addressing Future Risks for Family Firms in the Tourism Industry* (pp. 75–102). IGI Global. https://doi.org/10.4018/978-1-7998-7352-5.ch004

Zanin, F., Comuzzi, E., & Costantini, A. (2018). The Effect of Business Strategy and Stock Market Listing on the Use of Risk Assessment Tools. In *Management Control Systems in Complex Settings: Emerging Research and Opportunities* (pp. 145–168). Hershey, PA: IGI Global. doi:10.4018/978-1-5225-3987-2.ch007

Zgheib, P. W. (2017). Corporate Innovation and Intrapreneurship in the Middle East. In P. Zgheib (Ed.), *Entrepreneurship and Business Innovation in the Middle East* (pp. 37–56). Hershey, PA: IGI Global. doi:10.4018/978-1-5225-2066-5.ch003

About the Contributors

Maria Amélia Carvalho (Ph.D.) is an invited adjunct professor at the Business School of Polytechnic of Porto. She has published papers in the Journal of Marketing Theory and Practice, the International Journal of Tourism Cities, and the Tourism Recreation Research Journal.

Maria Antónia G. Rodrigues (Ph.D.) is a senior lecturer at the business school of Polytecnic of Porto. She is a director of Bachelor in Marketing, researcher at CEOS P.Porto and SIIS. She has published several papers. Maria Antónia Rodrigues has also a professional experience in business, banking, telecomunications and cars trade.

* * *

Amritesh is presently working as Assistant Professor (Services Marketing Area) at IIT Ropar. Prior to that, he has held positions as Assistant Professor (Marketing Management) at BITS Pilani Dubai Campus and Senior Researcher in a European research project OPAALS. He has completed his Ph.D. from IIT Kanpur, India. His research articles have appeared in reputed international journals and his top three areas of research interest include Transformative Services, Consumer Research, and Online Marketing.

Oludare Adedire is a Senior Research Fellow, Federal College of Forestry, Jos (Forestry Research Institute of Nigeria)

Nesenur Altinigne is an Assistant Professor at the Marketing Department of Istanbul Bilgi University. She is a Ph.D. graduate of Istanbul Technical University. She has visited SKEMA Business School (France) as a visiting scholar supported by the French Embassy Research Fellowship. Her research interests mainly focus on consumer-technology interactions, consumer ethics, brand relationships, and consumers' reactions to product harm/firm crises. Her work has been published in the Journal of Business Research, Journal of Retailing and Consumer Services,

Journal of Product & Brand Management and Journal of Vacation Marketing, and presented at several leading international conferences.

Amandine Bavent is a Ph.D. student at ICN Business School. In parallel, she is also a brand valuation practitioner and the global head of brand valuation at Kantar. Her research focuses on the relationship between consumer perception, ESG credentials, and corporate financial performance.

Sarika Faisal is a research assistant at BBS, BRAC University

Julio Alexander Gonzalez Liendo is a researcher at the Polytechnic University of Valencia in sustainability, museums and transmedia communication, and sustainability models in mass media education in the European Group SUMED. Visiting researcher at Erasmus University of Rotterdam, Netherlands. Lecturer at the Universidad Anáhuac México, Next Education Madrid, the Fashion Design Center, Guadalajara México, and Director of TFM at the International University of La Rioja. Founder and president of the communications agency Avant-Garde RP 2003-2022. Communications Director of the Bogotá Fashion Film Festival in its 2019 and 2020 editions. He has consulted national and international companies in communications, corporate image, events, and corporate social responsibility. He was also the editor of fashion and variety magazines and culture and society sections. He has a degree in Social Communication from the Central University of Venezuela, a Master's in Communications Management from the University of Barcelona, Spain, and a Master's in Communication and Corporate Identity from the International University of La Rioja, Spain—Ph.D. candidate in Communication and Cultural Industries at the UPV.

Syed Far Abid Hossain is an Asst. Professor at the BRAC Business School, BRAC University. He has obtained PhD in Management Science from the School of Management, Xi'an Jiaotong University, PRC. He holds an MBA degree from the University of Sunderland, UK and a BBA (Marketing) degree from Dhaka University. Dr. Abid authored more than 50 academic journal articles, conference papers and book chapters in internationally recognized, peer reviewed and well-indexed Journals from Elsevier, Springer, SAGE, Taylor and Francis, Frontiers, Science Direct, Emerald, MDPI and IGI global. His research interests include academic performance, education psychology, education management, technology in education, women entrepreneurship, innovation and media entrepreneurship. Apart from his current roles at BRAC Business School, Mr. Abid serves as a regular reviewer of famous journals from reputed publishers including Elsevier, Wiley, Springer, SAGE, Taylor and Francis, Frontiers, Emerald, IGI Global.

Arjinder Kaur is a Part-time Ph.D. Student in the Department of Humanities and Social Sciences at IIT, Ropar, and also working as an Associate Professor in the Department of Management Studies, Amritsar Group of Colleges, Amritsar. She has presented papers at various national-level conferences. Her research area is consumer behavior.

Shawnila Nawshin is a research assistant at BBS, BRAC University

Zaila Oliveira is Professor of Marketing at the University of Maia-ISMAI. PhD in Management from the University of Porto. His main areas of research are digital marketing, consumer behavior, tourism and sustainability. Co-author of several indexed scientific publications. Member of CEOS.PP - Center for Organizational and Social Studies of the Polytechnic of Porto, a research center accredited by the FCT.

Godfrey Onuwa is a Senior Research Fellow, Federal College of Forestry, Jos (Forestry Research Institute of Nigeria)

Elisabeth Paulet is a professor of Finance at ICN Business School in Nancy. She holds a Ph.D. at the European University Institute of Florence and a Jean Monnet Chair. In charge of doctoral programs, her main interests are in banking structures and financial policy of firms on historical and contemporary levels. She has published several books in this field in editorial houses like Pickering Chatto, Chandos Elsevier and Cambridge. She has published several scientific articles in Corporate Governance, Journal of Business Strategy, Journal of Business Ethics, Journal of European Economic History, Strategic Change, Asia Pacific Business Review, and Applied Economics.

Rayisa Rayhana is a student at BBS, BRAC University

Sandrina Teixeira is a Professor of Marketing at the School of Accounting and Administration of Porto, Polytechnic Institute of Porto. She got a Ph.D. in Marketing and Advertising from Vigo University. Her main areas of investigation are digital marketing, digital communication, e-commerce, and consumer behavior. She is the author and co-author of several scientific publications indexed. She was the Head of CEOS.PP - Centre for Organisational and Social Studies of Polytechnic of Porto and coordinates a research line of Marketing and Digital Communication Strategies. She organizes the annual Digital Marketing and Branding Workshop at the International Conference on Marketing and Technologies - ICMarkTech and other international events. She is a member of the Scientific Council of indexed international journals.

She is a member of the Scientific Committee of several events. She participates in funded projects and is a member of international partnerships.

Sara Teixeira has a PhD in Communication from the University of Vigo - Spain. Sara performs teaching functions in higher education at ISCAP. She worked in the area of digital marketing and e-learning in Portugal. She is a researcher at CEOS. PP - Center for Organizational and Social Studies at the Polytechnic of Porto.

Mohamad Zreik, a Postdoctoral Fellow at Sun Yat-sen University, is a recognized scholar in International Relations, specializing in China's Arab-region foreign policy. His recent work in soft power diplomacy compares China's methods in the Middle East and East Asia. His extensive knowledge spans Middle Eastern Studies, China-Arab relations, East Asian and Asian Affairs, Eurasian geopolitics, and Political Economy, providing him a unique viewpoint in his field. Dr. Zreik is a proud recipient of a PhD from Central China Normal University (Wuhan). He's written numerous acclaimed papers, many focusing on China's Belt and Road Initiative and its Arab-region impact. His groundbreaking research has established him as a leading expert in his field. Presently, he furthers his research on China's soft power diplomacy tactics at Sun Yat-sen University. His significant contributions make him a crucial figure in understanding contemporary international relations.

Index

F

G

H

I

L

M

N

O

P

R

S

T

V

W

Ensure Quality Research is Introduced to the Academic Community

Become an Evaluator for IGI Global Authored Book Projects

The overall success of an authored book project is dependent on quality and timely manuscript evaluations.

Applications and Inquiries may be sent to:
development@igi-global.com

Applicants must have a doctorate (or equivalent degree) as well as publishing, research, and reviewing experience. Authored Book Evaluators are appointed for one-year terms and are expected to complete at least three evaluations per term. Upon successful completion of this term, evaluators can be considered for an additional term.

If you have a colleague that may be interested in this opportunity, we encourage you to share this information with them.

www.ingramcontent.com/pod-product-compliance
Lightning Source LLC
LaVergne TN
LVHW061536290926
849162LV00004B/818
* 9 7 8 1 6 6 8 4 9 2 7 7 2 *